THE BRAZILIAN TRUTH COMMISSION

Studies in Latin American and Spanish History

This series bridges the divide between studies of Latin America and peninsular Spain by employing transnational and comparative approaches that shed light on the complex societies, cultures and economies of the modern age. Focusing on the cross-pollination that was the legacy of colonialism on both sides of the Atlantic, these monographs and collections explore a variety of issues such as race, class, gender and politics in the Spanish-speaking world.

Volume 4
The Brazilian Truth Commission: Local, National and Global Perspectives
Edited by Nina Schneider

Volume 3
José Antonio Primo De Rivera: The Reality and Myth of a Spanish Fascist Leader
Joan Maria Thomàs

Volume 2
Conflict, Domination, and Violence: Episodes in Mexican Social History
Carlos Illades

Volume 1
Metaphors of Spain: Representations of Spanish National Identity in the Twentieth Century
Edited by Javier Moreno Luzón and Xosé M. Núñez Seixas

The Brazilian Truth Commission

Local, National and Global Perspectives

Edited by

Nina Schneider

berghahn
NEW YORK • OXFORD
www.berghahnbooks.com

First published in 2019 by
Berghahn Books
www.berghahnbooks.com

Library of Congress Cataloging-in-Publication Data

Names: Schneider, Nina, 1980- editor.
Title: The Brazilian Truth Commission : local, national and global perspectives / edited by Nina Schneider.
Description: New York : Berghahn Books, 2019. | Series: Studies in Latin American and Spanish history ; Volume 4 | Includes bibliographical references and index.
Identifiers: LCCN 2019005550 (print) | LCCN 2019006791 (ebook) | ISBN 9781789200041 (ebook) | ISBN 9781789200034 (hardback : alk. paper)
Subjects: LCSH: Brazil. Comissão Nacional da Verdade. | Truth commissions--Brazil. | Crimes against humanity--Brazil. | Reparations for historical injustices--Brazil.
Classification: LCC KHD5649 (ebook) | LCC KHD5649 .B73 2019 (print) | DDC 323.4/90981--dc23
LC record available at https://lccn.loc.gov/2019005550

British Library Cataloguing in Publication Data

A catalogue record for this book is available from the British Library

ISBN 978-1-78920-003-4 hardback
ISBN 978-1-78920-004-1 ebook

Dedicated to
Marielle Franco (1979–2018)

Rio City Councillor,
critic of police and military action in Rio state,

…

and much more.

The question we have in common, the never-ending challenge, is how to better resist the backlashes that may curtail democracy and repeat the cycle of violence and unnecessary suffering.

—Vera Paiva, in this volume

Contents

List of Illustrations xii

Acknowledgements xiv

Introduction The Brazilian Truth Commission in Local, National and Global Perspective 1
Nina Schneider

Part I The Brazilian National Truth Commission

Section 1 Emergence and Context

Chapter 1 Dear Madame President: A Never-Delivered Speech and a Never-Ending Story 37
Vera Paiva

Chapter 2 The Public Prosecutor's Office of São Paulo and the Legacy of the Dictatorship: A Brief Report on Activities Prior to the Truth Commission 58
Eugenia Augusta Gonzaga

Chapter 3 The Censorship of History and Fact-Finding in Brazil (1964–2018) 68
Antoon De Baets

Chapter 4 Democratic Transition and Conciliation: Human Rights and the Legacy of the Brazilian Dictatorship 86
Janaína de Almeida Teles

Section 2 Novelties of the Brazilian Model: The National Commission, Local Committees and Corporate Complicity

Chapter 5 The National Truth Commission (NTC): Truth and Responsibility 111
Carolina de Campos Melo and André Saboia Martins

Chapter 6 Repression, Resistance and the Intergenerational Dialogue: Establishing a Truth Commission at the University of Brasília 126
Cristiano Paixão and José Otávio Guimarães

Chapter 7 Truth Commissions in the Digital Age: An Analysis of the Brazilian Case 138
Ana Lúcia Migowski

Chapter 8 Corporate Complicity in the Brazilian Dictatorship 157
Leigh A. Payne

Chapter 9 Volkswagen do Brasil during the Military Dictatorship: An Economic and Political Assessment 182
Christopher Kopper

Section 3 First Assessments of Brazil's National Truth Commission

Chapter 10 The Outcomes of the Brazilian Truth Commission: Successes and Failures in a Lengthy Transitional Justice Process 203
Marlon Alberto Weichert

Chapter 11 The Struggle for the Voice of the Victims in the National Truth Commission (Brazil): Memories and Truth, Yesterday and Today 227
San Romanelli Assumpção

Chapter 12 *'Nunca Mais'*: Lessons from Brazil's Dictatorial Past 243
Gisele Iecker de Almeida

Part II Truth Commissions in Context: Comparing Latin America

Section 1 Comparing Specific Truth Commissions

Chapter 13 Truth Commissions and Their Archives in El Salvador, Peru and Brazil 265
Ann M. Schneider

Chapter 14 Memory, Truth and Auto-Fiction in the Recent Latin American Novel 286
Jobst Welge

Part III Truth Commissions between the Global and the Local

Section 1 Truth Commissions' Worldwide Dispersion and Function

Chapter 15 Reconfigurations of Transitional Justice in the Wake of the Arab Uprisings: Global, Regional and Local Developments 305
Fatima Kastner

Chapter 16 Truth Commissions: A Bottom-Up Approach to Institution-Building 323
Anja Mihr

Afterword 339
Nina Schneider

Appendix 1 List of Selected Local Truth Commissions in Brazil by Region and State 345

Appendix 2 Selected List of Brazilian Online Resources (in alphabetical order) 349

Appendix 3 Photos from the Brazilian Truth Commission 350

Index 353

Illustrations

Figures

Figure 1.1 Military officials during the official signing of the law to instate the Brazilian Truth Commission. Palácio do Planalto, Brasília. 39
Figure 1.2 Declassified archival material first page. National Archives and Records Administration, United States. 51
Figure 1.3 Declassified archival material second page. National Archives and Records Administration, United States. 52
Figure A 3.1 President Dilma gives a speech on the occasion of the presentation of the Brazilian National Truth Commission's final report on 10 December 2014. Palácio do Planalto, Brasília. 350
Figure A 3.2 President Dilma Rousseff receives the Brazilian National Truth Commission's final report from Coordinator Pedro Dallari. 10 December 2014, Palácio do Planalto, Brasília. 351
Figure A 3.3 Press meeting with truth commissioners after the handover of the final report. From the left: Commissioner Rosa Cardoso and Coordinator Pedro Dallari. 10 December 2014, Palácio do Planalto, Brasília. 351
Figure A 3.4 A protest banner of the organization Levante Popular (Popular Uprising) demanding the punishment of perpetrators of the military regime. The banner was shown at the end of the official ceremony handing over the final report to the president on 10 December 2014 in the Palácio do Planalto, Brasília. 352
Figure A 3.5 Public hearing on violence against women. When Amelinha Teles recounts her experience of sexual violence in prison, Eleonore Menicucci shows her solidarity. For decades, Amelinha Teles has been engaged in the

struggle for clarification of the political disappeared. She is also a leading protagonist of the Brazilian feminist movement and has published on Brazilian women's history. In the local truth commission of the state of São Paulo (Rubens Paiva Commission), she was one of the key coordinators. 352

Table

Table 10.1 Difficulties faced by truth commissions. 214

Acknowledgements

Above all, I wish to thank the contributors to this volume for their work and engagement. I would also like to thank the anonymous reviewers for their constructive comments, which were highly appreciated, and Britta Weiffen and Martin Vorspel, who kindly commented on an early chapter draft.

I wish to express my special thanks to the Berghahn team for their much-appreciated help, guidance and patience, in particular the Series Editor, Vincent Sanz, the Editorial Assistants, Soyolmaa Lkhagvadorj and Amanda Horn, and our acquiring editor Chris Chappell, whose comments were highly appreciated.

This book project is the result of five years' work and was completed with the help of a number of supporters. Thanks to Stefanie Preuss (University of Konstanz) and Boris Barth (Charles University, Prague), and also to Joana Zanotto for providing initial research on local truth commissions.

For supporting the project at an earlier stage, my deepest gratitude goes to Wilhelm Krull, Secretary General of the Volkswagen Foundation in Hannover, and Claudia Soetbeer, Director of the Symposia Program. My kind thanks also go to Silke Aumann and Margot Jäckel.

Special thanks go to my colleagues from the Global South Studies Center (GSSC) at the University of Cologne, in particular Barbara Potthast, Clemens Greiner and Martina Gockel for their continuing support in the latter phase of the book project. I furthermore express my thanks to Tara Dadhkhah (University of Cologne) for her manuscript support, to Lisa McKee (University of Essex) for her wonderful proofreading work, and Lu Vorspel for her much-appreciated advice. I would also like to thank Marcia Esparza, Director of the Historical Memory Project, for her expertise and inspiration.

I wish to thank the research team at the Käte Hamburger Kolleg/Centre for Global Cooperation Research (KHK/GCR21) at the

University of Duisburg-Essen, for the instrumental support in the final phase of the book project.

Furthermore, I thank the German Research Foundation (DFG, Grant No. SCHN 1438/1-1 and 1-3) for providing the resources to conduct the research for this project.

Lastly, my warmest thanks go to my partner, Martin.

Nina Schneider

Introduction

The Brazilian Truth Commission in Local, National and Global Perspective

Nina Schneider

After Brazilian President Dilma Rousseff was ousted from office in 2016, human rights violations in Brazil increased substantially.[1] On 16 February 2018, her successor, the unelected President Michel Temer (2016–18), issued a decree that legitimized the intervention of the armed forces in the state of Rio de Janeiro, targeting especially the slums (favelas) of the city of Rio de Janeiro. The decree was not intended as a short-term measure: it allowed military intervention until the end of 2018, with the next Brazilian presidential election scheduled for October of that year. While the decree in itself worried legal, security and human rights activists because it blurred the military-civilian divide and increased military interference in politics, the situation worsened when General Eduardo Villas Bôas of the Brazilian army made a stunning demand.

On 19 February 2018, following Temer's military decree, Villas Bôas asked President Temer to provide his assurance that there would be no 'new truth commission'.[2] In effect, this was a request for a 'licence to kill' that was sanctioned by the president with subsequent impunity guaranteed. Human rights critics reacted promptly. The Special Commission of the Political Dead and Disappeared (CEMDP), established in 2005 and currently presided over by the state attorney, Eugenia Augusta Gonzaga, declared that truth commissions were necessary precisely in those moments when state agents who violated the law were granted impunity.[3] (In the second chapter of this book, Eugenia Gonzaga provides details of the CEMDP's work, which has in a sense both preceded and succeeded the Brazilian Truth Commission.)

One of the fiercest public critics of military and police violence in the *favelas* in Rio was Marielle Franco, a young and popular Rio city councillor who was also a resident of the Maré slum, a lesbian feminist and an activist against racism. In the 2016 Rio city council election, she received the second most votes of any female candidate. On 14 March 2018, she was assassinated at the age of thirty-eight.[4] While being driven home from a public event devoted to black women's political action, a car pulled alongside hers and Franco was shot four times in the head. Her driver was also killed.[5] The intended message of the crime was clear: human rights activists were in danger in Brazil, perhaps increasingly so. Marielle's death caused widespread shock, grief, anger and despair, both nationally and internationally.

There was one person, however, who kept conspicuously silent and did not publicly mourn Marielle: the former army captain, Roman Catholic with close ties to the evangelical Protestant church and member of parliament Jair Messias Bolsonaro, one of the candidates preparing for the 2018 presidential election. Meanwhile Bolsonaro has won the election and been vowed in as Brazil's next President. Jair Bolsonaro has publicly justified rape and repeatedly praised human rights violators.[6] On 9 December 2014, he attacked the former human rights minister and legislator Maria do Rosário of the Workers' Party (PT), saying that he would not rape her because 'she was not worth raping' and 'very ugly'.[7] On 17 April 2016, when the members of the Brazilian lower house (*Câmara*) cast their votes on whether to proceed with the 'impeachment' process and remove President Dilma Rousseff from office, Bolsonaro dedicated his vote in favour to Colonel Carlos A. Brilhante Ustra, who had been a notorious and unrepentant mass torturer under the military regime.[8] As a nineteen-year-old guerrilla fighter opposing the regime, President Rousseff had been imprisoned and tortured with electrical shocks on various parts of her body.[9]

Bolsonaro's dedication to Ustra was brought before the so-called Ethics Council of the Brazilian lower house in June 2016, on the charge of endorsing the crime of torture. The formal procedure did not go very far. On 9 November 2016, the Ethics Council cleared him of charges by a vote of eleven to one and closed the case. They argued that the member of parliament 'only expressed his free opinion' and invoked the immunity granted to members of parliament.[10] (As we will learn in the first chapter of this volume, Bolsonaro also humiliated victims' families, including that of parliamentarian Rubens Paiva, who had been disappeared under the military dictatorship.) In April 2018, President Luiz Inácio Lula da Silva, while still leading presidential polls at 37 per cent (nearly twenty points ahead of Bolsonaro), was sentenced to twelve years in jail for corruption in a much-criticized legal trial, clearing one of the main obstacles to electoral victory for Bolsonaro.[11] Recent evidence suggests that Bolsonaro's son Flávio, recently elected senator, employed family members of the retired military police officer suspected of having masterminded the assassination of Marielle Franco – showing a direct link between Bolsonaro's family and the assassination of Marielle.

To understand the current attacks on the Brazilian Truth Commission, the assassination of Marielle and the ongoing aggression and militarization in Brazilian public life, we need to study the legacy of past violence. This collection of chapters provides the world's first systematic analysis of the Brazilian Truth Commission from a local, national and global perspective. The historically unique structure of the Brazilian National Truth Commission makes it an ideal case for closer examination: besides establishing a conventional official inquiry commission operating on a nation-state level, the Comissão Nacional da Verdade or National Truth Commission of Brazil (2012–14; hereafter NTC), the Brazilian model pioneered a network of approximately one hundred local truth and justice committees (hereafter local truth commissions).[12] These local truth commissions emerged all over the country and were often run or supported by civilians.

This volume approaches the Brazilian Truth Commission from three analytical angles: a local, national and global perspective. The local perspective refers to the work carried out by these local truth commissions, and the meaning and impact that they had. It transcends both an exclusively national and an exclusively state-focused reading. This is a new perspective, because most commonly truth commissions are understood as national institutions instated by the government for a limited period of time in post-conflict scenarios. Some authors in this volume adopt a primarily national point of view, which privileges the emergence, functioning, meaning and value of the NTC rather than local commissions, and analyses and interprets truth commissions as an instrument of nation-building. Lastly, the global view refers to the meaning that the Brazilian Truth Commission has beyond its own domestic framework. It analyses the similarities and differences with other Latin American commissions and the role and merits of truth commissions more generally. From a global perspective, the volume asks the question: what can an analysis specifically of the Brazilian Truth Commission model add to broader discussions of the role of truth commissions and the ways we produce knowledge about them in post-violence settings? While most authors privilege one of these perspectives, the key task is to explore how truth commissions (and other human rights institutions) can be studied as a complex negotiation process that may involve local, national and global protagonists.[13]

This introductory chapter aims to contextualize the themes and debates addressed in this volume. It serves four functions. It offers a short overview of the Brazilian truth commissions for those readers less familiar with the Brazilian case. It also provides a brief introduction to the development of truth commissions worldwide, identifies relevant ongoing research debates about truth commissions, and explains how the book implicitly and explicitly seeks to advance these discussions. Individual chapters in the first two parts provide a thick description of a specific aspect of the Brazilian National Truth Commission or the local commissions, respectively, while the chapters in the last part adopt a comparative or entangled perspective on truth commissions more generally. When read as a whole, however, they yield important insights into the way we conceptualize, assess and produce knowledge about truth commissions in general. Thus, this study seeks to contribute to current debates on truth commissions in two main ways. First, it aims to problematize and expand our methodological and theoretical horizons, by systematically testing and evaluating local, national and global perspectives. This methodological reflection addresses the very production of knowledge about truth commissions, including the silencing of specific kinds of knowledge. It also deals with the relative absence of some disciplines from discussions about the truth commission (historians, for example, have written comparatively little about truth commissions), and the way they may expand and deepen scholarship on the topic. Second, it aims to advance our empirical knowledge of truth commissions by providing an in-depth analysis of one of the most recent examples, the National Truth Commission of Brazil (2012–14), along with its accompanying local commissions.

Least Studied: The Brazilian National Truth Commission and Local Commissions

Between 1964 and 1985, Brazil was ruled by a military regime that systematically tortured several thousand citizens, while hundreds were killed or disappeared.[14] For decades Brazil was the only post-military country in South America that had neither instated a truth commission nor tried state criminals for their actions during the authoritarian period (1964–85). Rebecca Atencio has described this lack of official reckoning with the dictatorship as 'institutionalized forgetting'.[15] Only in May 2012 did Brazil finally inaugurate the Comissão Nacional da Verdade (National Truth Commission, NTC; Law Decree no. 12.528/11). The commission was instated by the Brazilian president, Dilma Rousseff (2011–16), who had herself opposed the regime and suffered torture. The seven commissioners (two women and five men, most of them lawyers) were tasked with investigating gross violations of human rights committed between 1946 and 1988. This longer time frame, ranging from the start of the Second Brazilian Republic (1946) to the establishment of the Constitution in 1988, was a concession to revisionists who were keen to downplay the brutality of the dictatorship. The commission officially presented its 3,383-page final report on 10 December 2014 and was dissolved soon afterwards.

From its inception, the Brazilian Truth Commission was attacked by families of victims, survivors, lawyers and human rights activists who – twenty-seven years after the formal return to democracy – regarded it as 'too little too late'.[16] Yet the commission also raised high hopes among survivors and families of victims, as some of this book's chapters will show. At the same time, it faced massive criticism from conservatives and the military.[17] Large sectors of the Brazilian public have remained indifferent to it or shown outright refusal to accept a reworking of the military regime.[18] The commission's work was further hampered by serious conflicts between the commissioners. They disagreed, for example, about which would be the most appropriate public relations strategy to pursue: while some commissioners advocated publicly discussing their work as it proceeded, others preferred to work behind closed doors and only present the findings after the investigations had been completed.[19]

As this volume seeks to show, a truth commission and its final report is the outcome of a process involving many actors with different kinds of manoeuvring spaces (as occurs in every major hierarchized institution). In the Brazilian case, internal conflicts between individual commissioners often made the daily work of subordinate staff difficult, and it was not by chance that many of the early personnel were exchanged over the course of the commission's two-year mandate (2012–14). Little research has been done into these dynamics. Three chapters in this volume offer exclusive insights into the daily work and constraints of truth commission personnel. Former key executives of the National Truth Commission, André Saboia Martins (Executive Secretary) and Carolina de Campos Melo (Final Report Executive Team), debate the challenges and limitations faced by the NTC, but also the commission's achievements (establishing the chain of command; drafting final recommendations), which were steps intended to consolidate democracy in Brazil. They provide first-time insights into how they developed the report, including the final recommendations, and elucidate the resistance faced in that process, especially concerning the armed forces.

The chapter by San Romanelli Assumpção likewise offers an insider's perspective by illuminating the *modus operandi* of one of the Brazilian Truth Commission's subgroups, which was charged with the delicate task of recording the testimonies of victims of gross human rights violations. It analyses the working group's ethical code, methodology and achievements, but perhaps most importantly sheds light on the psychological strain placed on the often unpaid volunteers and researchers who conducted the interviews with victims of brutal sexual violence. One chapter reveals the workings of a local truth commission, the Anísio Teixeira Commission, instated by the National University of Brasília (UNB). Cristiano Paixão and José Otávio Guimarães, two of its former commissioners, show how the University of Brasília, a vanguard educational project, became a prime target of repression after the 1964 coup. They argue that only an intergenerational perspective can enable us to understand the specific kind of oppression experienced at universities. While criticizing the lack of truth commissions from an outside perspective is always easy, these chapters illuminate how the manoeuvring power of those actors working for the truth commissions was limited, and, importantly, help explain why certain policies may have failed to advance. Three chapters furthermore offer first assessments of the NTC. One chapter, for example, is authored by Federal Prosecutor Marlon Alberto Weichert, who pioneered many legal actions relating to human rights crimes committed under the post-1964 dictatorship. Weichert analyses the National Truth Commission's final report, key findings and recommendations, and also elucidates the challenges that the commission faced, if from an outsider perspective.

Ultimately, the Brazilian National Truth Commission is historically unique for two reasons. First, the time lapse between the formal transition to democracy (1985) and the inauguration of the truth commission (2012) is unprecedented. Second, and most importantly for this volume, it pioneered a new model comprised of a National Truth Commission and a nationwide network of approximately eighty local commissions (see a preliminary list of sixty-seven local truth commissions in Appendix 1). The dynamics between the local and the national commission changed over time and were case-specific. Many local commissions supported the NTC by providing information and exchanging evidence, while others questioned or rejected its findings. Local commissions were organized by numerous institutions including universities, municipal and regional government bodies, and trade unions. They all tried to investigate the role that their institutions played in human rights crimes committed during the military dictatorship. It is important to acknowledge that the work of the NTC – most importantly the final report – was shaped at various times by both friendly and hostile dialogue with local truth commissions, most of which were run by civilians. The National Truth Commission was thus complemented, and to a certain extent challenged, by local commissions.[20]

The Brazilian National Truth Commission did not emerge from nowhere. It has to be understood in both national and international contexts, and with reference to previous human rights initiatives, as described in the chapters by Eugenia Gonzaga and Janaína de Almeida Teles. Gonzaga offers a brief report on the work of state attorneys from São Paulo and the CEMDP. Janaína de Almeida Teles, survivor, activist and historian, revisits the democratic transition and traces the struggles waged by the families of the dead and disappeared from the 1970s until the end of the transition process. Their quest for truth and justice arguably led to the Brazilian truth commissions in the first place. Teles also shows how those who sympathized with the dictatorship systematically tried to block the families' demands.

While the NTC resulted in part from national struggles, it also developed in response to rising pressure from the international human rights community. In December 2011, the Inter-American Court of Human Rights of the Organization of American States (OAS) condemned the Brazilian state for not systematically examining the circumstances surrounding the murder and disappearance of guerrilla fighters in the Araguaia region and for granting amnesty to the human rights transgressors who had been involved (by refusing to revoke the 1979 Amnesty Law), charges that Brazil has yet to respond to.[21] Lastly, there is another international link: the Brazilian National Truth Commission was but the latest in a line of truth commissions in Latin America and elsewhere.

Latin American Truth Commissions in Global Perspective

The development of modern truth commissions is closely linked to the history of political repression in Cold War Latin America. During the 1960s and 1970s, authoritarian regimes seized power throughout most of Latin America, leading to hundreds of thousands of citizens being tortured, killed or disappeared.[22] While these regimes differed according to the nature of the conflict, the actors involved and the level of brutality, they shared a new form of state violence justified under the umbrella term 'national security', directed against the idea of a constant threat from so-called internal enemies. Political opponents were systematically supressed by domestic organs of repression, and even transregionally through the secret programme known as Operation Condor.[23]

Most Latin American countries continue to struggle with their authoritarian legacy today. A pressing unresolved problem is that the whereabouts of hundreds of thousands of disappeared persons remains unknown, denying family members the basic right to bury their loved ones. Victims' families and human rights activists have fought a long and ongoing campaign for the clarification of these crimes, as states have tended to obstruct rather than support effective clarification and accountability mechanisms. Complete or partial impunity for the perpetrators continues to fuel mass protests among survivors and victims' families, human rights activists and artists all over the continent.

In post-authoritarian and post-war scenarios, one of the oldest and most significant policy instruments that are used to investigate and publicly acknowledge systematic human rights crimes committed in the past are truth commissions.[24] Different definitions abound, yet one of the earliest and most frequently cited was coined by Priscilla Hayner: truth commissions are 'temporary' institutions 'officially sanctioned' through legislation, with a legal mandate to clarify the repressive *systems* (rather than *single acts* of violence), tasked with producing an official report including recommendations.[25] In the case of the Brazilian Truth Commission, which comprised an officially sanctioned National Truth Commission as well as an unprecedented number of private, public and mixed local commissions, Hayner's definition of a truth commission may need to be broadened. Local commissions were neither necessarily official nor based on official law.

A key difference between Hayner's definition and the many alternatives revolves around the issue of whether truth commissions must be officially established or whether privately initiated short-term investigative commissions also qualify as truth commissions. In the Brazilian case, for example, the Brasil Nunca Mais Report (BNM; Brazil Never Again), instituted by the Catholic Church, is sometimes regarded as the first Brazilian truth commission.[26] Although not officially instated, it nonetheless produced a privately organized report on the basis of documents relating to military trials that were secretly copied during the regime.[27] Most definitions concur, however, that truth commissions are tasked with: collecting testimonies from victims, witnesses and occasionally even perpetrators, with the goal of illuminating the structures of systematic state violence (sometimes also non-state violence); requesting and analysing archival documents (classified material is often unavailable to ordinary citizens or historians); and producing a final report. The final report includes a set of non-binding recommendations, which, therefore, cannot be enforced. In the Brazilian case, many local commissions produced a final report, yet some lacked the financial and staff resources to do so.

Although truth commissions have spread all over the world, their origins lie in Latin America and most chapters in this volume refer to this region. In quantitative terms, 38 per cent of the world's truth commissions were set up in Latin America, while Africa was not far behind, accounting for 36 per cent.[28] While Bolivia was the first country to instate a national commission to investigate state-sponsored murders (1982–84), Argentina hosted the first truth commission to produce a final report – the Comisión Nacional sobre la Desaparición de Personas, CONADEP (1983–84). Therefore, the Argentinean commission qualifies as the world's first truth commission according to Hayner's definition. Many scholars argue that the CONADEP had an influence on most of the other commissions that followed it throughout the world, as it set a model for its institutional design and reporting structure.[29]

Over time, truth commissions have adopted different names and approaches, investigated different kinds of violence and pursued various goals. The first Chilean truth commission, for example, the Rettig Commission (1990–91), was the world's first to include the term 'reconciliation' in its title. Reconciliation was made a priority as opposed to other goals like 'justice'. Many subsequent commissions have followed suit, most famously the South African Truth and Reconciliation Commission, but also those in other countries such as Sierra Leone (2002–04), East Timor (2002–05), Peru (2001–03) and Honduras (2010–11).[30] The truth commissions in Guatemala (1997–99) and Peru (2001–03) were the first to pay specific attention to indigenous populations and to pioneer gender-specific investigations.[31] In Guatemala, the Comisión para el Esclarecimiento Histórico (CEH; Commission for Historical Clarification) uncovered the fact that 83 per cent of the citizens who had been killed were Mayan, and that the state had committed genocide.[32] The Peruvian commission set up a special unit to investigate gender-related violence – most importantly sexual violence – and two chapters of its final report focus specifically on the gender aspect. In sum, truth commissions have varied significantly in scope and quality.[33]

Importantly, the spread of truth commissions was not accidental or unplanned, unlike some rather triumphalist and depoliticized accounts may suggest. From the 1990s onwards, truth commissions have been actively promoted by former commissioners, non-governmental organizations (NGOs) like the International Center for Transitional Justice

(ICTJ), and the United Nations.[34] A succession of official truth commissions have been founded all over Latin America: in Chile (Rettig Commission, 1990–91; Valech Commission, 2003–05), El Salvador (1992–93), Haiti (Comisión Nationale de Vérité et de Justice, 1995–96), Ecuador (Comisión de Verdad y Justicia, 1996–97; Comisión de la Verdad para impedir la impunidad, 2007–09), Guatemala (Comisión para el Esclarecimiento Histórico, 1997–99), Uruguay (Comisión Para la Paz, 2000–02), Peru (Comisión de la Verdad y Reconciliación, 2001–03), Panama (Comisión de la Verdad, 2001–04), Paraguay (Comisión Verdad y Justicia, 2004–08) and Honduras (Comisión de la Verdad y la Reconciliación, 2010–11).[35] One of the most recent Latin American truth commissions was the Brazilian Comissão Nacional da Verdade (2012–14), the Brazilian National Truth Commission, which presented its final report on 10 December 2014.[36]

The mandate and function of truth commissions has evolved over time, as has the scholarship. The first generation of commissions tended to focus exclusively on disappeared persons and the search for truth rather than punishment of the perpetrators.[37] In these cases, 'truth' meant two things: first, families of the disappeared wanted to know the circumstances of their family members' death and the locations of their remains, and the state was often the only resource available to them through which they could trace the victims and obtain access to relevant archives; second, the right to truth was increasingly invoked to pressure states into accepting accountability for their citizens, and truth was linked to an official acknowledgement of state violence that had long been withheld. It is vital to remember that authoritarian regimes in Cold War Latin America operated secretly, and organized systems of repression designed to spread fear and terror. Often the new formal democracies failed to shed light on these crimes. Early scholarly discussions on truth commissions mirrored the balancing act performed by the politicians to secure peace (*peace versus justice* debate), and tended to discuss truth commissions and prosecutions as though they were alternatives rather than complementary initiatives (*truth versus justice* debate).[38] Later, truth commissions expanded their mandates to investigate larger victim groups and broadened their goals. They increasingly claimed to pursue reconciliation and public education, and sometimes collected evidence for criminal trials. Again, this evolution was reflected in the accompanying scholarly debates; instead of a political compromise, truth commissions were now seen as independent bodies with various functions and as constituting one means of transitional justice among several others.[39]

Meanwhile, studies on truth commissions have become associated with the field of so-called transitional justice. Since the term was first coined in the 1990s, transitional justice has evolved into a worldwide, institutionalized, heterogeneous field involving both human rights practitioners and scholars with a focus on transition processes and the instruments that were used to facilitate countries' transitions from periods of violence to peaceful democracies.[40] Truth commissions constitute one among a number of other transitional justice mechanisms, including trials, amnesties, reparations and memory initiatives. Both broad and narrow definitions of transitional justice coexist. For instance, the non-governmental organization ICTJ, which is based in New York, defines 'transitional justice' as 'the set of *judicial* and *non-judicial* measures that have been implemented ... to redress the legacies of massive human rights abuses'.[41] Despite the rise of transitional justice, the concept itself, along with its uncritical promotion, has become increasingly problematic.[42] Various empirical, conceptual and increasingly political-epistemological points of criticism that have been levelled against transitional justice are paralleled in the critical scholarship on truth commissions. An important point of critique involves the opaque and scientifically questionable way in which the role and impact of truth commissions has been assessed.

Sketching the State of Art: Irreconcilable Analytical Approaches

Scholars have applied a panoply of analytical approaches to examine, explain and assess truth commissions. Many studies on Latin American truth commissions examine individual cases with a focus on the context in which they were created, their outcomes and their medium- and long-term socio-political legacies.[43] These studies have analysed truth commissions from a predominantly national perspective. Increasingly, scholars have also tried to draw comparisons between cases. A recent international cooperative project, for example, compares the recommendations made by various Latin American truth commissions.[44] Scholars disagree about the scale of analysis to be applied and the goals that truth commissions have tried to achieve. For the purpose of this volume, the truth commission literature may be heuristically divided into two broad groups: scholars who regard truth commissions predominantly as an instrument for nation-building and national democratization (national approach); and those who frame their analysis around a global trend towards human rights standards and democratization (global approach).[45]

Scholars have found diverse ways of adopting a national approach towards truth commissions. The Argentinean sociologist Elizabeth Jelin emphasized the commissions' role in the process of redefining a national identity.[46] Jelin traces back the process – albeit a slow and non-linear one – of how the Argentinean government became increasingly involved in human rights concerns. Human rights, she argues, became the ethical foundation of the new democracy (and, I add, in marked contrast to post-authoritarian Brazil).[47]

The historian Greg Grandin has called truth commissions 'modern-day instruments' that are used to build and rebuild a nation.[48] Grandin invokes Benedict Anderson's paradigm of the nation as being founded on a paradox: '[they] need to forget acts of violence central to state formation that can never be forgotten'.[49] Yet Grandin also situates the upsurge in truth commissions in the wider international context, which is also associated with the abandonment of social democratic principles, the rise of neoliberalism, and a specific moment in history when the concept of democracy became pared down to mean just political and legal rights.[50] Grandin and Klubock both regard truth commissions as a form of 'national catharsis', yet one that harmonizes with neoliberalism's free-market economics.[51] Overall, Grandin and Klubock seem to find the exclusively national approach to truth commissions too limited and therefore espouse complementing it with international contextualization.

Studies that adopt a global approach share the view that a national framework is inadequate. However, most global studies prefer to focus on truth commissions' role in diffusing (Western) international human rights norms. Importantly, and similarly to the polarization of views that has occurred regarding the globalization process, many authors welcome this diffusion of global norms, while a sizeable minority of others regard it with suspicion or even connect it to a new form of Western dominance, and complicity with a number of drawbacks to globalization (like Grandin's intervention against neoliberalism).[52]

The sociologist Fatima Kastner, for example, adopts Luhmann's system-theoretical approach and regards truth commissions primarily as a tool for initiating and framing a new field of communication that transcends national boundaries.[53] Her chapter in this volume identifies international and translocal agents who contribute to the global diffusion of post-conflict norms, standards and institutions, drawing on North Africa and the Middle East. By contrast, the German sociologist Anne Krüger analyses how truth commissions have become 'globally diffused' by drawing on a neo-institutional approach.[54] She compares the mandates of different truth commissions in search of similar proclaimed goals and underlying norms. The German sociologist Anika Oettler, on the other hand, has rightly cautioned that despite this global proliferation of truth commissions (involving professionalization and standardization), each one can only be understood within its specific power constellation.[55] Oettler highlights the tension that exists between what she calls the 'transnationalization' of truth commissions, on the one hand, and the local experience and shaping of truth commissions, on the other hand. This conflict between a context-sensitive in-depth analysis of a historically and locally specific truth commission, and broader conclusions that integrate individual commissions into a larger explanatory framework without overdetermining the research results, remains to be resolved. Furthermore, both the national and the global approach fail to account for the type of local truth commissions that existed in the Brazilian case. It seems that Brazil requires yet another analytical perspective – a local reading of truth commissions. In what way these different perspectives may be fruitfully combined remains unresolved.

Most of the scholarship on truth commissions has been written by non-historians. This might seem surprising given the notable expansion of historical writing on human rights in general since the late 1990s. Historical accounts of truth commissions and similar truth-seeking initiatives may profit from that work. In contrast to traditional histories and conceptualizations of human rights as transhistorical, universal, decontextualized, and following a linear evolution (and ultimately constituting a success story), a more sophisticated historical account treats human rights as the outcome of particular contexts and specific struggles, not an *a priori* moral certainty destined to triumph.[56]

Some historians have investigated particular commissions in a national rather than a global context.[57] A few have tried to connect the rise of truth commissions (and similar responses to past atrocities) to a larger historical framework. One example is Elazar Barkan, who both described and sought to explain the new global trend to redress the past – a practice that he terms 'restitution'.[58] Barkan stresses two developments: first, the increasing human rights mobilization that began with a first wave of minority rights movements between the 1950s and 1970s in the United States, along with subsequent efforts by indigenous groups; and second, a changed view of history and historical identity as 'constructed' or 'negotiated'.[59] In Barkan's view, both of these tendencies contributed to a new, more central role for history to play, because it now was both 'a formative political force' and 'malleable'. Initiatives to redress the violent past demonstrated that the process of renegotiating history was underway.[60] According to Barkan, a new kind of moral order has emerged that increasingly has shaped foreign policies as well as national state–citizen relations.

As mentioned previously, the historian Greg Grandin has also related the rise of truth commissions to the wider international historical context, especially with reference to social democracy and neoliberalism. Truth commissions, he remarks, appeared at a specific moment in history, when socialist movements in Latin America were defeated, and when the meaning of democracy was narrowing. Truth commissions, in his reading, thus relate to a larger history of neoliberal free-market economics.[61] Currently, historians are working to connect specific truth commissions to the larger history of colonialism, as in the case of Canada.[62] Overall, this kind of historical research seems to be in its early stages.

Diverse Assessments

Global and national approaches also diverge in their assessment of truth commissions' achievements. The contributions to this volume show how scholars, who each privilege a particular local, national or global perspective, attribute diverse meanings to truth commissions. Although most authors do not explicitly address the debates surrounding truth commissions, they provide the empirical substance with which to advance such discussions. Currently, the impact of truth commissions – broadly understood as how commissions transform the field of policy-making and moral values – remains contested.[63]

It is useful to first briefly sketch the main benefits and shortcomings identified in the vast literature on truth commissions.[64] Some key positive traits mentioned include: the capacity to 'give victims a voice' (a term that requires definition) and a platform for their stories; to help clarify cases of human rights crimes, most pertinently those relating to disappeared persons; to underline the importance of human rights and prevent future violence; to build archives for future generations; to facilitate peace and reconciliation; to officially acknowledge state violence; and to issue recommendations designed to enhance social cohesion and the government's commitment to human rights and democracy.[65] The main points of criticism of truth commissions include: the neglect of victims' and their families' needs at the expense of those of wider society; the use of truth commissions as alternatives to prosecutions, which leads them to support impunity;

and their failure to enforce recommendations (which has resulted in them gaining a reputation as toothless instruments).[66] Lastly and very importantly, the name 'truth commission' in itself is unavoidably misleading. Whether or not they are state-sanctioned, truth commissions are ultimately political organizations, and they face specific political and financial constraints. Historical accounts produced by truth commissions should not be mistaken for those written by trained historians, although there are certainly similarities, as will be discussed further in the afterword. Historically, few professional historians have been appointed to truth commissions. In the case of the Brazilian National Truth Commission, for instance, most of the commissioners were legal experts, but historians were noticeably absent.[67] Truth commissions involve a complex interplay between opposing agents who each favour a different kind of truth. In addition, the declared goal of reconciliation may actually obstruct the process of gaining historical knowledge about a violent past.[68] However, despite these numerous points of criticism, most scholars and practitioners seem to regard truth commissions in a generally positive light.

Another important key question asked of both truth commissions and transitional justice initiatives revolves around their legitimacy and impact.[69] Although addressed implicitly rather than explicitly in this volume, it is a vital concern and thus merits a brief discussion. As Hirsch, MacKenzie, Sesay and others have pointed out, much of the truth commission (and transitional justice) literature is based upon unproven assumptions, while the proclaimed positive effects of truth commissions are often grounded on methodologically dubious measurements.[70] The authors identify three methodological biases: sociological, methodological and epistemological.[71] The first relates to the fact that scholarly standards are often sacrificed in favour of human rights advocacy goals. Due to pressure from donors, the same protagonists that promote and operationalize truth commissions also tend to evaluate them. This blurring of professional roles can lead to dependent and interest-driven assessments.[72] Additionally, the main methods used rarely account for local specificities or for marginal views (methodological bias), and third, surveys use vague key terms like justice and reconciliation that are defined in very different ways (epistemological bias). The authors conclude that these methodological biases 'reinforce and deepen the gap between how TRCs [truth and reconciliation committees] are evaluated internationally and how local communities perceive them'.[73]

Two leading truth commission researchers, Eric Wiebelhaus-Brahm and Onur Bakiner, likewise acknowledge that the precise effects of truth commissions remain unknown, that antagonistic consequences persist, and that the method used to measure the impact of truth commissions is complex and allows for variation, leading to results that are not comparable.[74] While some scholars argue that the success of a truth commission must be judged according to its specific mandate, others highlight that even a respectable report may fail to generate public repercussions. Hence, privileging specific evaluation criteria leads to very different results. Wiebelhaus-Brahm also highlights what may be called a bibliographical bias: most studies relate to only three truth commissions (Argentina, Chile and South Africa), resulting in a misrepresentation of what is regarded as the standard model of a truth commission.[75] Examining the timely and understudied Brazilian case may help to rectify this bias. In addition, more recent quantitative attempts to measure the effects of truth commissions have used criteria and sources that are not comparable, and have often only been able to draw on databases with a high level of aggregate information that have themselves been accused of containing statistical biases.[76]

It is also conceivable that something is lost in translation. Several truth commissions have been praised by international scholars, while domestically they have provoked controversy or even outright rejection, one of the most prominent examples being the South African Truth and Reconciliation Commission (SA TRC).[77] Likewise, the Peruvian truth commission was viewed as an international success, while nationally it remains fiercely contested.[78] Similar points of critique have been raised by numerous 'transitional justice' sceptics. Drawing on the case of East Timor, Lia Kent, for instance, has called for more scholarly attention to be paid to a possible mismatch between international assumptions and local meanings.[79] Focusing on the 'experiences, priorities and perceptions' of local victim groups, her work offers a 'corrective' to assumptions that are widely promoted nationally and internationally (e.g. by the United Nations).[80] A similar claim has been made by Marcia Esparza and by me: we have argued that transitional justice is a Janus-faced paradigm that in contrast to much of its rhetoric may not always be experienced as supporting human rights at the local level.[81] These insights into how local actors' pursuit of justice disrupts international transitional justice discourses may be of particular relevance here. This study interrogates to what extent a global (and often hypothetical rather than empirical) view of the Brazilian Truth Commission may diverge from local experiences and empirical evidence. Critical interrogation of human rights rhetoric is key here.

This volume, similarly, aims to test 'facts' that are assumed to be true and critically revisit methods and forms of knowledge production about truth commissions: it asks which analytical approach or perspective is most suited to studying, analysing and judging the role of truth commissions – a local, national or global perspective, or all three? If the latter, how are these three perspectives interrelated (entangled histories of truth commissions)? How does the choice of a particular method or perspective influence (or manipulate) the findings? While the chapters in this volume may only succeed in providing partial or incomplete answers to some of these pending questions, they may at least highlight the urgency with which they require addressing.

The Brazilian Truth Commission seems to provide an ideal case study with which to investigate local, national and global approaches to truth commissions, and thus advance the scholarly literature both empirically and methodologically. A comprehensive analysis of the Brazilian National Truth Commission and local truth commissions involves reading it not as exclusively local, national or global, but as the product of local, national and global interest groups engaged in a complex process of political negotiation.[82] Disentangling the various actors, each chapter in this volume offers an in-depth understanding of one specific aspect of the Brazilian Truth Commission.

Scope and Structure of the Book

The book is divided into three parts, ranging from the local and historically specific perspective (Brazil) to a broader global and general view (truth commissions in the twenty-first century).

The chapters that comprise the most extensive part (Part I: The Brazilian National Truth Commission) thoroughly contextualize the Brazilian commission in its local and national historical setting. Section 1 (Emergence and Context) offers a thick description of the context in which truth commissions emerged. It starts with a special contribution by Vera Paiva, Professor of Social Psychology and human rights activist, and daughter of the disappeared Brazilian deputy, Rubens Paiva (1929–71), whose disappearance represents one of the dictatorship's most emblematic cases. It is a translated version of what she calls a 'non-speech' that was prepared for the inauguration ceremony of the Brazilian Truth Commission in May 2012, but was never actually delivered, as she was barred from speaking at the eleventh hour due to protests from military generals. It is the first time her suppressed historical speech has been published in the English language (except for an online blog, see the chapter of Vera Paiva). Vera Paiva, who saw the recent political and human rights backlashes coming, reminds us: 'democracy is built and rebuilt day by day, every day'; human rights can never be taken for granted. As mentioned previously, the chapters by Eugenia Gonzaga and Janaína de Almeida Teles elucidate memory and justice initiatives that both preceded and survived the Brazilian Truth Commission, though from different angles. While Gonzaga privileges state-led actions including the crucial role of state attorneys, Teles focuses on the vital role of the families of the dead and disappeared and their opponents. The section is complemented by a piece that maps the manifold attempts to silence information on human rights violations – precisely the opposite of what truth commissions ought to do. Antoon De Baets, expert in history, ethics and human rights, traces the history of censorship in military Brazil and outlines how the work of truth commissions in other Latin American countries has been impeded in this way. His contribution thus helps to elucidate both the history of censorship related to human rights crimes prior to the Brazilian Truth Commission and to set the Brazilian case in a broader Latin American context.

Section 2 (Novelties of the Brazilian Model) is divided into two parts. The first part provides insights into the work of national and local commissions and their staff, as mentioned previously, and includes an innovative chapter on the relation between truth commissions and social media. The chapter by communication scholar Ana Lúcia Migowski analyses social networking sites as new arenas for public debate about both the military regime and the Truth Commission, in particular. Taking the Brazilian National Truth Commission's Facebook page as a case study, she reveals that social media reflect a highly polarized view of the past. While it has offered a public platform to human rights defenders, it has also been used by those who celebrate past crimes (similar to the case of Bolsonaro's online supporters). This double-edged impact merits reflection for all public discussion platforms beyond social media. The next two chapters focus on Corporate Complicity. A chapter by Oxford professor Leigh A. Payne shows that Brazil is a particularly interesting case for corporate complicity research for two reasons. First, there were civilian groups that mobilized specifically to draw attention to corporate complicity. Second, the business community remains deeply fragmented over its relationship to the dictatorship. Christopher Kopper, Professor of Economic and Social History at Bielefeld, addresses corporate complicity in Brazil from a transnational rather than domestic perspective. Kopper elucidates the challenges and findings of a special report he was commissioned to produce on Volkswagen do Brasil's support for the military dictatorship. In response to his report, the Volkswagen Company offered reparation payments to former staff who were tortured during the military regime. Kopper's chapter thus gives further substance to a key claim of this volume: that it takes an entangled and holistic perspective to fully unravel the local, national and global actors involved in human rights crimes. Corporate complicity research remains an understudied and promising research field.

Meanwhile, Section 3 (First Assessments of Brazil's National Truth Commission) includes contributions from Federal Prosecutor Marlon Alberto Weichert and San Romanelli Assumpção mentioned previously, and is complemented by a chapter by Gisele Iecker de Almeida, who combines a philosophical approach to history with empirical evidence from Brazil.[83] She focuses in particular on the slogan 'Never Again', frequently invoked by the Brazilian National Truth Commission, and asks what kind of reading of the past can help to prevent the reoccurrence of violence.

While the first part of the volume is dedicated to the Brazilian case, the second part (Truth Commissions in Context: Comparing Latin America) compares the Brazilian model with other Latin American truth commissions. This comparative approach serves as an antidote to an overemphasis on national particularities and reveals that truth commissions share difficulties, advantages and even scandals. Ann Schneider's chapter, for example, compares the truth commissions of Brazil, El Salvador and Peru. Focusing on archival evidence collected by commissions in contexts where offenders have been granted immunity, her contribution analyses the plans that truth commissions have had for their archives, and the importance of these archives for possible future prosecutions of egregious human rights violations. Jobst Welge's chapter also adopts a comparative perspective, by examining recent Latin American fiction. Welge analyses how literary narratives address the problem of historical truth and justice, and the tendency among recent works of fiction to be transgenerational or marked by generational discontinuity.

The goal of identifying similarities and differences among truth commissions across the world is also addressed by the third and final part of this volume (Truth Commissions between the Global and the Local). This part explores the dispersal of truth commissions worldwide, their general function and meaning, and the tension between global and locally specific interpretations of these commissions' work. In addition to the already mentioned chapter by Fatima Kastner, the chapter by Anja Mihr analyses the role played by truth commissions in the creation of democratic institutions. Public and democratic institutions, she argues, cannot exist or function effectively without the support and trust of citizens. The third part, in sum, explores truth commissions from a global perspective.

Altogether, this interdisciplinary collection of essays seeks to offer a unique blend of contrasting and thought-provoking views that provide the necessary ingredients for a truly critical and controversial debate. Presenting a range of opinions, it aims to contribute to ongoing debates, 'give voice' to silenced perspectives (with Vera Paiva's censored speech as a central example) and allow readers to form their own opinions on the basis of clear evidence. Many of the contributors to this volume have directly participated in truth commissions in Brazil, and their texts are rarely available to an English-speaking audience. They include some of the world's leading scholars, key practitioners, human rights activists and survivors of the Brazilian military dictatorship. Overall, this volume seeks to advance critical research on truth commissions, as a means of strengthening – not just rhetorically but substantially – a local, national and global human rights culture.

Nina Schneider is Senior Research Fellow at the Käte Hamburger Kolleg/Centre for Global Cooperation Research (KHK/GCR21) at the University of Duisburg-Essen, Germany. She was Visiting Scholar at Columbia University's Institute for the Study of Human Rights (ISHR, 2012), Marie-Curie Fellow at the Zukunftskolleg, at the University of Konstanz (2013–15), Visiting Scholar at the National University of Brasília (UNB, 2015), and Senior Fellow of the Global South Studies Center (GSSC) at the University of Cologne (2015–18). She is the author of *Brazilian Propaganda: Legitimizing an Authoritarian Regime* (University Press of Florida, 2014); 'Between Promise and Skepticism: The "Global South" and Our Role as Engaged Intellectuals', *The Global South* 11(2) (2017), 18–38; and (with R. Atencio) 'Reckoning with Dictatorship in Brazil: The Double-Edged Role of Cultural-Artistic Production', *Latin American Perspectives* 43(5) (2016), 12–28 (Honorary Mention for the Best Article of 2016, Latin American Studies Association's Brazil Section).

Notes

1. Technically it is termed 'impeachment', but critics have called it a political 'coup' because it brought to power a group of centre-right politicians who would never have won by public vote, as opinion polls at the time clearly confirm. The naming remains a controversial issue; opponents of

the Workers' Party (PT) use the word 'impeachment', while supporters and several critical intellectuals use the word 'coup'.

2. A. Benites, 'Intervenção federal no Rio desperta fantasmas sobre o papel do Exército', *El País (Brasil)*, retrieved 21 February 2018 from https://brasil.elpais.com/brasil/2018/02/20/politica/1519155351_378130.html.
3. Ibid.
4. Fernanda Chaves, 'Tribuna: Marielle Franco e o futuro do Brasil', *El País (Brasil)*, retrieved 21 June 2018 from https://brasil.elpais.com/brasil/2018/06/13/opinion/1528925943_158923.html.
5. J. Carneiro, 'Marielle Franco: Vivacious Fighter Shaped by the Favela', BBC, retrieved 25 March 2018 from https://www.bbc.com/news/world-latin-america-43484449.
6. G. Bezerra and F.R. Pozzebom, 'Bolsonaro é inocente no caso da apologia ao estupro', *Veja*, retrieved 1 March 2018 from https://veja.abril.com.br/blog/o-leitor/bolsonaro-e-inocente-no-caso-da-apologia-ao-estupro.
7. A. de Souza, 'Bolsonaro cogitou acordo com PGR para suspender processo sobre incitação ao estupro, mas desistiu', *O Globo*, retrieved 21 June 2018 from https://oglobo.globo.com/brasil/bolsonaro-cogitou-acordo-com-pgr-para-suspender-processo-sobre-incitacao-ao-estupro-mas-desistiu-22549281#ixzz5MACU7CCg.
8. For Bolsonaro's entire dedication, see R. Bragon, 'Conselho de Ética livra Bolsonaro de processo por homenagem a Ustra', *Folha de S. Paulo*, retrieved 15 May 2018 from https://www1.folha.uol.com.br/poder/2016/11/1830828-conselho-de-etica-livra-bolsonaro-de-processo-por-homenagem-a-ustra.shtml.
9. P. Wilcken, 'The Reckoning: Investigating Torture in Brazil', *New Left Review* 78 (2012), 73–90.
10. Maria de Rosario issued a criminal procedure against Bolsonaro which is still pending at the time of writing and may be decided by the Brazilian Supreme Court. According to a recent law called *Ficha Limpa* [Clean Record], parliamentarians may be barred from presidential elections if they have been involved in a crime or have a criminal case pending. Bragon, 'Conselho de Ética'.
11. 'Brazil's Election after the Jailing of Lula', *The Economist* 427(9087) (2018), 44. Bolsonaro is often called the 'Brazilian Trump'. As these examples have shown, this is a clear understatement. BBC, 'Brazil Far-Right Politician Enters Presidential Race', retrieved 25 July 2018 from https://www.bbc.co.uk/news/world-latin-america-44919769. According to critics, it was a political trial that violated rule of law standards and served to ban Lula from running for the 2018 presidential elections (according to the April 2018 polls possibly even winning them).
12. Officially, the NTC signed cooperation agreements with twenty-nine local commissions. See Comissão Nacional da Verdade (CNV), 'The Final Report of the Brazilian Truth Commission', retrieved 20 December 2014 from http://www.cnv.gov.br/index.php/outros-destaques/574-conheca-e-acesse-o-relatorio-final-da-cnv, 10.

13. For truth commissions as a dynamic process, see N. Schneider, '"Too Little Too Late" or "Premature"? The Brazilian Truth Commission and the Question of "Best Timing"', *Journal of Iberian & Latin-American Research* 19(1) (2013), 159. A similar conception of truth commissions as a dynamic interplay was suggested by Vera Paiva, keynote speaker at an international symposium on the Brazilian Truth Commission in Hannover in October 2015.
14. For a timely, balanced and concise introduction to the history of the Brazilian military regime and its controversies, see M. Napolitano, *1964: História do regime militar brasileiro* (São Paulo: Contexto, 2014). For a recent bibliographical overview, see M.C.D. Araújo, 'Taking Stock (with Discomfort) of the Military Dictatorship Fifty Years after the 1964 Coup: A Bibliographical Essay', *Brazilian Political Science Review* 9(3) (2015), 143–63; and C. Fico, 'Brazilian Military Dictatorship: Theoretical and Historiographical Approximations', *Tempo e Argumento* 9(20) (2017), 400–67. Some scholars refer to the regime as a civil-military regime to stress its extensive complicity with civilians. For more on that discussion, see Napolitano, *1964*, 37.
15. R. Atencio, *Memory's Turn: Culture and Transitional Justice in Brazil* (Madison: University of Wisconsin Press, 2014), 12.
16. Schneider, '"Too Little Too Late"'.
17. N. Schneider, 'Truth No More? The Struggle over the National Truth Commission in Brazil', *Iberoamericana* 42 (2011), 164–70.
18. P. Abrão and M. Torelly, 'As dimensões da Justiça de Transição no Brasil', in L.A. Payne, P. Abrão and M.D. Torelly (eds), *A anista na era da responsibilização: o Brasil em perspectiva internacional* (Oxford: Oxford University Press, 2011), 212–49.
19. Schneider, '"Too Little Too Late"'.
20. For more details on the relationship between the local commissions and the Brazilian National Truth Commission, see N. Schneider and G.I.D. Almeida, 'The Brazilian Truth Commission (2012–2014) as a State-Commissioned History Project', in B. Bevernage and N. Wouters (eds), *The Palgrave Handbook of State-Commissioned History after 1945* (London: Palgrave MacMillan, 2018), 641–42, 648. The final report explicitly relates to the findings of local commissions. See CNV, 'Final Report'.
21. For more details, see N. Schneider, 'The Supreme Court's Recent Verdict on the Amnesty Law: Impunity in Post-Authoritarian Brazil', *European Review of Latin American and Caribbean Studies* 90 (2011), 39–54.
22. The overall number of disappearances in Cold War Latin America remains unknown. Even national estimates remain contested. In Argentina, for example, the official report of the Comisión Nacional sobre la Desaparición de Personas (CONADEP, 1983–84) estimates a total number of 8,961 disappeared persons from 1976 to 1983. Human rights organizations, by contrast, speak of approximately thirty thousand. In 1980, the United Nations Working Group on Enforced or Involuntary Disappearances (UNWGEID) began collecting figures on the number of forced disappearances. As of September 2017, they had been notified of 45,120 cases of

disappearance involving ninety-one states. This likely underrepresents the number. For details, see the official webpage of the UNWGEID, retrieved 20 July 2018 from https://www.ohchr.org/EN/Issues/Disappearances/Pages/DisappearancesIndex.aspx.

23. J. Dinges, *The Condor Years: How Pinochet and His Allies brought Terrorism to Three Continents* (New York: New Press, 2004) and P. McSherry, *Predatory States: The Operation Condor and Covert War in Latin America* (Boulder, CO: Rowman & Littlefield, 2005).
24. While literature on truth commissions is abundant, key books include P. Hayner, *Unspeakable Truths: Facing the Challenge of Truth Commissions* (New York: Routledge, 2002); M. Freeman, *Truth Commissions and Procedural Fairness* (Cambridge: Cambridge University Press, 2006); E. Wiebelhaus-Brahm, *Truth Commissions and Transitional Societies: The Impact on Human Rights and Democracy* (New York: Routledge, 2009); O. Bakiner, *Truth Commissions: Memory, Power, and Legitimacy* (Pennsylvania: University of Pennsylvania Press, 2016); and R.I. Rothberg and D. Thompson (eds), *Truth v. Justice: The Morality of Truth Commissions* (Princeton, NJ: Princeton University Press, 2000). For a concise overview, see N. Mnewabe, 'Truth Commissions', in L. Stan and N. Nedelsky (eds), *Encyclopedia of Transitional Justice*, Vol. 1 (Cambridge: Cambridge University Press, 2013), 98–106.
25. Hayner, *Unspeakable Truths*, 14.
26. See T.D. Olsen, L.A. Payne, and A.G. Reiter, *Transitional Justice in Balance: Comparing Processes, Weighing Efficacy* (Washington, DC: United States Institute of Peace, 2010). This also explains the diverging total numbers of truth commissions in the literature.
27. The Portuguese version is available online, retrieved 5 May 2016 from http://bnmdigital.mpf.mp.br/. For an English version, see Archdiocese of Sao Paulo, *Torture in Brazil* (Austin: University of Texas, 1998).
28. K. Sikkink and C.B. Walling, 'Argentina's Contribution to Global Trends in Transitional Justice', in N. Roht-Arriaza and J. Mariezcurrena (eds), *Transitional Justice in the Twenty-First Century: Beyond Truth versus Justice* (Cambridge: Cambridge University Press, 2006), 309.
29. Hayner, *Unspeakable Truths*, 33; Sikkink and Walling, 'Argentina's Contribution', 305–6, 308. For a classic history of the production, public circulation and reinterpretations of the CONADEP's Nunca Mas report, see E. Crenzel, *Memory of the Argentina Disappearances: The Political History of Nunca Más* (New York/London: Routledge, 2017).
30. Mnewabe, 'Truth Commissions', 101.
31. Sikkink and Walling, 'Argentina's Contribution', 305–6, 308.
32. A summarized English translation of the report was published as Historical Clarification Commission (CEH), *Guatemala: Memory of Silence* (Guatemala City: CEH, 1999).
33. For a recent, concise overview of truth commissions' diversity and trajectory, see E. Wiebelhaus-Brahm, 'Truth Commissions and the Construction of History', in Bevernage and Wouters, *The Palgrave Handbook*, 599–621.

34. Ibid., 600.
35. See United States Institute for Peace (USIP), 'Truth Commission Digital Collection', retrieved 20 December 2014 from http://www.usip.org/publications/truth-commission-digital-collection.
36. See CNV, 'Final Report'.
37. Mnewabe, 'Truth Commissions', 101.
38. For the *peace versus justice* debate, see C.L. Sriram and S. Pillay (eds), *Peace versus Justice? The Dilemma of Transitional Justice in Africa* (Cape Town: University of KwaZulu-Natal Press, 2009); for the *truth versus justice* debate, see Rothberg and Thomson, *Truth v. Justice*.
39. Mnewabe, 'Truth Commissions', 99, 102.
40. The language of transitional justice relates to two key events: the 1992 Salzburg Conference 'Justice in Times of Transition' and a three-volume publication edited by Neil Kritz, *Transitional Justice: How Emerging Democracies Reckon with Former Regimes* (Washington, DC: Institute of Peace Press, 1995). Both projects were funded by US-based foundations: the Charter 77 Foundation and the United States Institute of Peace (USIP), a neutral institution founded in 1984 and financed by the US federal government. G. Mouralis, 'The Invention of "Transitional Justice" in the 1990s', in L. Israel (ed.), *Dealing with Wars and Dictatorships* (The Hague: Asser Press, 2014), 83–100. The definition, scope and goals of transitional justice are contested and have developed over time. See J. Elster, *Closing the Books: Transitional Justice in Historical Perspective* (Cambridge: Cambridge University Press, 2004); R. Teitel, 'Transitional Justice Genealogy', *Harvard Human Rights Journal* 16 (2003), 69–94; C. Bell, 'Transitional Justice, Interdisciplinarity and the State of the "Field" or "Non-Field"', *The International Journal of Transitional Justice* 3 (2009), 5–27; and P. Arthur, 'How Transitions Reshaped Human Rights: A Conceptual History of Transitional Justice', *Human Rights Quarterly* 31(2) (2009), 321–67.
41. International Center for Transitional Justice (ICTJ), 'What Is Transitional Justice?', retrieved 5 March 2015 from https://www.ictj.org/about/transitional-justice.
42. See K. McEvoy and L. McGregor, *Transitional Justice from Below: Grassroots Activism and the Struggle for Change* (Portland, OR: Hart, 2008); N. Palmer, P. Clark, and D. Granville (eds), *Critical Perspectives in Transitional Justice* (Cambridge, Antwerp, Portland: Intersentia, 2012); R.E. Brooks, 'The New Imperialism: Violence, Norms, Rule of Law', *Michigan Law Review* 101(7) (2003), 2275–340; R. Nagy, 'Transitional Justice as Global Project: Critical Reflections', *Third World Quarterly* 29(2) (2008), 275–89; N. Schneider and M. Esparza, 'Introduction', in Schneider and Esparza (eds), *Legacies of State Violence and Transitional Justice in Latin America: A Janus-Faced Paradigm?* (Lanham, MD: Lexington Books, 2015), xi–xxviii.
43. On Latin America, see A. Ferrara, *Assessing the Long-Term Impact of Truth Commissions: The Chilean Truth and Reconciliation Commission in Historical*

Perspective (London and New York: Routledge, 2015); G. Grandin, 'The Instruction of Great Catastrophe: Truth Commissions, National History, and State Formation in Argentina, Chile, and Guatemala', *American Historical Review* 110(1) (2005), 46–67; A. Oettler, 'Der Stachel der Wahrheit: Zur Geschichte und Zukunft der Wahrheitskommission in Lateinamerika', *Lateinamerika Analysen* 9 (2004), 93–126; and A. Oettler, *Erinnerungsarbeit und Vergangenheitspolitik in Guatemala* (Frankfurt/M: Vervuert, 2004); L. Laplante and K. Theidon, 'Truth with Consequences: Justice and Reparations in Post-Truth Commission Peru', *Human Rights Quarterly* 29 (2007), 228–50; D. Gairdner, *Truth in Transition: The Role of Truth Commissions in Political Transition in Chile and El Salvador* (Bergen: CMI, 1999); E. Allier-Montano, 'Exploration – the Peace Commission: A Consensus on the Recent Past in Uruguay?', *European Review of Latin American and Caribbean Studies* 81 (2006): 87; Schneider, '"Too Little Too Late"'.

44. See E. Wiebelhaus-Brahm, J. García-Godos, and E. Skaar (eds), *Beyond Words: Latin American Truth Commissions' Recommendations* (forthcoming).
45. Arguably, a third group comprises scholars (mainly theological, psychological, and peace and conflict scholars) who focus on the commissions' role in rehabilitating victim groups with a view to what is known as 'reconciliation' (itself a problematic term), irrespective of the victim's nationality. This approach, less relevant for this volume, acknowledges a universal human dignity often related to Christian beliefs (I call this the human dignity approach).
46. E. Jelin, *State Repression and the Labors of Memory* (Minnesota: University of Minnesota Press, 2003); and E. Jelin, 'La justicia después del juicio: legados y desafíos em la Argentina postdictatorial', in C. Fico, M.D.F. Moraes et al. (eds), *Ditadura e Democracia: balanço e perspectivas* (Rio de Janeiro: FGV, 2008), 341–60.
47. Jelin, 'La Justicia', 344, 347.
48. Grandin, 'The Instruction of Great Catastrophe', 49.
49. Ibid.
50. Ibid., 1–2.
51. G. Grandin and T.M. Klubock, 'Editor's Note', *Radical History Review* 97 (2007), 4.
52. Though not related to truth commissions but to transitional justice in general, one of the key studies emphasizing the benefits of a diffusion of global norms is K. Sikkink's *The Justice Cascade: How Human Rights Prosecutions Are Changing World Politics* (New York: Norton, 2011). For predominantly critical views, see Brooks, 'The New Imperialism'; and Nagy, 'Transitional Justice'.
53. F. Kastner, 'Weder Wahrheit noch Recht: Zur Funktion von Wahrheitskommissionen in der Weltgesellschaft', *Mittelweg* 36(16) (2007), 31–50.
54. See A.K. Krüger, *Wahrheitskommissionen* (Frankfurt and New York: Campus, 2014), 17–19.

55. Oettler, 'Der Stachel der Wahrheit'.
56. For a very good survey, see K. Cmiel, 'The Recent History of Human Rights', in A. Iriye, P. Goedde, and W.I. Hitchcock (eds), *The Human Rights Revolution: An International History* (New York: Oxford University Press, 2012), 27–51. Key studies include L. Hunt, *Inventing Human Rights: A History* (New York: W.W. Norton & Company, 2007); S. Moyn, *The Last Utopia: Human Rights in History* (London and Boston: Harvard University Press, 2010); S.-L. Hoffmann (ed.), *Human Rights in the Twentieth Century* (New York: Cambridge University Press, 2011); and Iriye, Goedde, and Hitchcock, *The Human Rights Revolution*.
57. For recent examples, see A. Karn, 'Switzerland's Independent Commission of Experts: State-Sponsored History and the Challenges of Political Partisanship', in Bevernage and Wouters, *The Palgrave Handbook*, 757–71.
58. E. Barkan, *The Guilt of Nations: Restitution and Negotiating Historical Injustices* (New York and London: W.W. Norton & Company, 2000), xi, xvii, xi.
59. Ibid., xxi–xxii.
60. Ibid., x.
61. Grandin, 'The Instruction of Great Catastrophe', 46–47; Grandin and Klubock, 'Editor's Note', 4.
62. See, for example, the work by L. Rüsing, 'Truth Commissions in Postcolonial Societies: The Cases of Canada and Mauritius', paper presented at the International Symposium on the Brazilian Truth Commission, Hannover, October 2015.
63. To name but a few: D. Mendeloff, 'Truth-Seeking, Truth-Telling and Post-Conflict Peacebuilding: Curb the Enthusiasm?', *International Studies Review* 6(3) (2004), 355–80; M.B.-J. Hirsch, M. MacKenzie, and M. Sesay, 'Measuring the Impacts of Truth and Reconciliation Commissions: Placing the Global "Success" of TRCs in Local Perspective', *Cooperation and Conflict* 47(3) (2012), 386–403; Wiebelhaus-Brahm, *Truth Commissions and Transitional Societies*; O.N.T. Thoms, J. Ron, and R. Paris, 'State-Level Effects of Transitional Justice: What Do We Know?', *International Journal of Transitional Justice* 4(3) (2010), 329–54; Olsen, Payne, and Reiter, *Transitional Justice in Balance*.
64. For two concise and more complete summaries of assumed aims and effects of truth commissions, see Tristan Anne Borer, 'Truth Telling as a Peace-Building Activity: A Theoretical Overview', in Borer (ed.), *Telling the Truths: Truth Telling and Peace Building in Post-Conflict Societies* (South Bend: University of Notre Dame Press, 2006), 1–57; and O. Bakiner, 'Truth Commission Impact: An Assessment of How Commissions Influence Politics and Society', *International Journal of Transitional Justice* 8 (2014), 6–30.
65. Many authors have covered the supposed benefits. See, for example, Rothberg and Thompson, *Truth v. Justice*; and Hayner, *Unspeakable Truths*. On commissions' role as a healthy platform from which to tell unacknowledged stories of suffering, see M. Minow, *Between Vengeance*

and Forgiveness: Facing History after Genocide and Mass Violence (Boston, MA: Beacon, 1998). For detailed bibliographic reference, see Wiebelhaus-Brahm, 'Truth Commissions and the Construction of History'.

66. The impunity question has long been discussed elsewhere. While Bakiner stresses that only two commissions have explicitly recommended amnesties (South Africa and Liberia), this sidelines the much more complex question of truth commissions' indirect contribution to impunity. See Bakiner, 'Truth Commission Impact', 7.
67. Schneider and Almeida, 'Brazilian Truth Commission', 640.
68. Grandin, 'The Instruction of Great Catastrophe', 46; Grandin and Klubock, 'Editor's Note', 6.
69. See the work of H.M. Weinstein, L.E. Fletcher, P. Vinck, and P.N. Pham, 'Stay the Hand of Justice: Whose Priorities Take Priority?', in R. Shaw and L. Waldorf (eds), *Localizing Transitional Justice: Justice Interventions and Local Priorities after Mass Violence* (Stanford, CA: Stanford University Press, 2010), 27–48; A.L. Hinton, 'Introduction: Toward an Anthropology of Transitional Justice', in Hinton (ed.), *Transitional Justice: Global Mechanisms and Local Realities after Genocide and Mass Violence* (Newark: Rutgers University Press, 2010), 1–22; and Schneider and Esparza, 'Introduction'.
70. Hirsch, MacKenzie, and Sesay, 'Measuring the Impacts'. For an overview of a similar kind of criticism levelled against transitional justice, see Schneider and Esparza, 'Introduction'.
71. Hirsch, MacKenzie, and Sesay, 'Measuring the Impacts', 388.
72. This point of criticism has been put forward by numerous scholars including P. Clark and N. Palmer, 'Introduction: Challenging Transitional Justice', in Palmer, Clark, and Granville, *Critical Perspectives*, 4–6; and Wiebelhaus-Brahm, 'Truth Commissions and the Construction of History'.
73. Hirsch, MacKenzie, and Sesay, 'Measuring the Impacts', 300.
74. Wiebelhaus-Brahm, 'Truth Commissions and the Construction of History'; and Bakiner, 'Truth Commission Impact'. A good example is the different results produced by Olsen, Payne, and Reiter, on one hand, and Hunjoon Kim and Kathryn Sikkink, on the other (who have recently joined up for a new cooperative project). Using different methods to evaluate truth commissions, the former find that truth commissions on their own have 'a significant, negative effect'. See Wiebelhaus-Brahm, *Truth Commissions and Transitional Societies*, 153–54n12. Wiebelhaus-Brahm, too, finds a minor negative effect (*Truth Commissions and Transitional Societies*, 153–54n12). By contrast, Kim and Sikkink claim that truth commissions have positive effects. However, others argue that it is impossible to observe any kind of impact. See Bakiner, 'Truth Commission Impact', 9n21.
75. Wiebelhaus-Brahm, 'Truth Commissions and the Construction of History'.
76. While it is beyond the scope of this volume, evaluation criteria include human rights statistics, democracy indexes and rule of law performance, and are often based on major aggregated data like the Freedom House

database and other similar sources. For an overview of related studies, see Bakiner, 'Truth Commission Impact', 9nn12–15, 10.

77. M.D. Jobson, 'Commentary on Transitional Justice after Transition', in Palmer, Clark, and Granville, *Critical Perspectives in Transitional Justice*, 485–91.
78. C.E. Milton, 'The Truth Ten Years On: The CVR in Peru', in E.A. Montaño and E. Crenzel (eds), *The Struggle for Memory in Latin American Recent History and Political Violence* (London: Palgrave Macmillan, 2016), 126–27.
79. L. Kent, 'Local Memory Practices in East Timor: Disrupting Transitional Justice Narratives', *The Journal of Transitional Justice* 5 (2011), 434–55.
80. Ibid., 446–38.
81. Schneider and Esparza, 'Introduction'.
82. This dialogues with Bakiner's claim that the impact of truth commissions depends on a complex set of relations between politicians, national and global human rights protagonists and commissioners. See Bakiner, 'Truth Commission Impact', 29.
83. For another recently published assessment of the Brazilian National Truth Commission, see M. Torelly, 'Assessing a Late Truth Commission: Challenges and Achievements of the Brazilian National Truth Commission', *International Journal of Transitional Justice* 12(2) (2018), 194–215, retrieved 20 January 2018 from https://doi.org/10.1093/ijtj/ijy002.

Bibliography

Abrão, P., and Torelly, M. 'As dimensões da Justiça de Transição no Brasil', in L.A. Payne, P. Abrão, and M.D. Torelly (eds), *A anista na era da responsibilização: o Brasil em perspectiva internacional* (Oxford: Oxford University Press, 2011), 212–49.

Allier-Montano, E. 'Exploration – the Peace Commission: A Consensus on the Recent Past in Uruguay?' *European Review of Latin American and Caribbean Studies* 81 (2006), 87–96.

Archdiocese of Sao Paulo. *Torture in Brazil*. Austin: University of Texas, 1998.

Arthur, P. 'How Transitions Reshaped Human Rights: A Conceptual History of Transitional Justice'. *Human Rights Quarterly* 31(2) (2009), 321–67.

Atencio, R. *Memory's Turn: Culture and Transitional Justice in Brazil*. Madison: University of Wisconsin Press, 2014.

Bakiner, O. 'Truth Commission Impact: An Assessment of How Commissions Influence Politics and Society'. *International Journal of Transitional Justice* 8 (2014), 6–30.

Bakiner, O. *Truth Commissions: Memory, Power, and Legitimacy*. Pennsylvania: University of Pennsylvania Press, 2016.

Barkan, E. 'AHR Forum: Truth and Reconciliation in History. Introduction: Historians and Historical Reconciliation'. *American Historical Review* 114(4) (2009), 899–913.

Barkan, E. *The Guilt of Nations: Restitution and Negotiating Historical Injustices*. New York and London: W.W. Norton & Company, 2000.

BBC. 'Brazil Far-Right Politician Enters Presidential Race'. Retrieved 25 July 2018 from https://www.bbc.co.uk/news/world-latin-america-44919769.

Bell, C. 'Transitional Justice, Interdisciplinarity and the State of the "Field" or "Non-Field"'. *The International Journal of Transitional Justice* 3 (2009), 5–27.

Benites, A. 'Intervenção federal no Rio desperta fantasmas sobre o papel do Exército'. *El País (Brasil)*. Retrieved 21 February 2018 from https://brasil.elpais.com/brasil/2018/02/20/politica/1519155351_378130.html.

Bezerra, G., and Pozzebom, F.R. 'Bolsonaro é inocente no caso da apologia ao estupro'. *Veja*. Retrieved 1 March 2018 from https://veja.abril.com.br/blog/o-leitor/bolsonaro-e-inocente-no-caso-da-apologia-ao-estupro.

Borer, T.A. 'Truth Telling as a Peace-Building Activity: A Theoretical Overview', in Borer (ed.), *Telling the Truths: Truth Telling and Peace Building in Post-Conflict Societies* (South Bend: University of Notre Dame Press, 2006), 1–57.

Bragon R. 'Conselho de Ética livra Bolsonaro de processo por homenagem a Ustra'. *Folha de S. Paulo*. Retrieved 15 May 2018 from https://www1.folha.uol.com.br/poder/2016/11/1830828-conselho-de-etica-livra-bolsonaro-de-processo-por-homenagem-a-ustra.shtml.

Brooks, R.E. 'The New Imperialism: Violence, Norms, Rule of Law'. *Michigan Law Review* 101(7) (2003), 2275–340.

Carneiro, J. 'Marielle Franco: Vivacious Fighter Shaped by the Favela'. BBC. Retrieved 25 March 2018 from https://www.bbc.com/news/world-latin-america-43484449.

Chaves, F. 'Tribuna: Marielle Franco e o futuro do Brasil'. *El País (Brasil)*. Retrieved 21 June 2018 from https://brasil.elpais.com/brasil/2018/06/13/opinion/1528925943_158923.html.

Clark, P., and Palmer, N. 'Introduction: Challenging Transitional Justice', in N. Palmer, P. Clark, and D. Granville (eds), *Critical Perspectives in Transitional Justice* (Cambridge, Antwerp, and Portland: Intersentia, 2012), 1–16.

Cmiel, K. 'The Recent History of Human Rights', in A. Iriye, P. Goedde, and W.I. Hitchcock (eds), *The Human Rights Revolution: An International History* (New York: Oxford University Press, 2012), 27–51.

Comissão Nacional da Verdade (CNV). 'The Final Report of the Brazilian Truth Commission'. Retrieved 20 December 2014 from http://www.cnv.gov.br/index.php/outros-destaques/574-conheca-e-acesse-o-relatorio-final-da-cnv.

Crenzel, E. *Memory of the Argentina Disappearances: The Political History of Nunca Más*. New York and London: Routledge, 2017.

D'Araújo, M.C.D. 'Taking Stock (with Discomfort) of the Military Dictatorship Fifty Years after the 1964 Coup: A Bibliographical Essay'. *Brazilian Political Science Review* 9(3) (2015), 143–63.

De Souza, A. 'Bolsonaro cogitou acordo com PGR para suspender processo sobre incitação ao estupro, mas desistiu'. *O Globo*. Retrieved 21 June

2018 from https://oglobo.globo.com/brasil/bolsonaro-cogitou-acordo-com-pgr-para-suspender-processo-sobre-incitacao-ao-estupro-mas-desistiu-22549281#ixzz5MACU7CCg.

Dinges, J. *The Condor Years: How Pinochet and His Allies brought Terrorism to Three Continents*. New York: New Press, 2004.

Elster, J. *Closing the Books: Transitional Justice in Historical Perspective*. Cambridge: Cambridge University Press, 2004.

Ferrara, A. *Assessing the Long-Term Impact of Truth Commissions: The Chilean Truth and Reconciliation Commission in Historical Perspective*. London and New York: Routledge, 2015.

Fico, C. 'Brazilian Military Dictatorship: Theoretical and Historiographical Approximations'. *Tempo e Argumento* 9(20) (2017), 400–67.

Freeman, M. *Truth Commissions and Procedural Fairness*. Cambridge: Cambridge University Press, 2006.

Gairdner, D. *Truth in Transition: The Role of Truth Commissions in Political Transition in Chile and El Salvador*. Bergen: CMI, 1999.

Grandin, G. 'The Instruction of Great Catastrophe: Truth Commissions, National History, and State Formation in Argentina, Chile, and Guatemala'. *American Historical Review* 110(1) (2005), 46–67.

Grandin, G., and Klubock, T.M. 'Editor's Note'. *Radical History Review* 97 (2007), 1–10.

Hayner, P. *Unspeakable Truths: Facing the Challenge of Truth Commissions*. New York: Routledge, 2002.

Hinton, A.L. 'Introduction: Toward an Anthropology of Transitional Justice', in Hinton (ed.), *Transitional Justice: Global Mechanisms and Local Realities after Genocide and Mass Violence* (Newark: Rutgers University Press, 2010), 1–22.

Hirsch, M.B.-J., MacKenzie, M., and Sesay, M. 'Measuring the Impacts of Truth and Reconciliation Commissions: Placing the Global "Success" of TRCs in Local Perspective'. *Cooperation and Conflict* 47(3) (2012), 386–403.

Historical Clarification Commission (CEH). *Guatemala: Memory of Silence*. Guatemala City: CEH, 1999.

Hoffmann, S.-L. (ed.). *Human Rights in the Twentieth Century*. New York: Cambridge University Press, 2011.

Hunt, L. *Inventing Human Rights: A History*. New York: W.W. Norton & Company, 2007.

Iriye, A., Goedde, P., and Hitchcock, W.I. (eds). *The Human Rights Revolution: An International History*. New York: Oxford University Press, 2012.

Jelin, E. 'La justicia después del juicio: legados y desafíos em la Argentina post-dictatorial', in C. Fico, M.D.F. Moraes et al. (eds), *Ditadura e Democracia: balanço e perspectivas* (Rio de Janeiro: FGV, 2008), 341–60.

Jelin, E. *State Repression and the Labors of Memory*. Minnesota: University of Minnesota Press, 2003.

Jobson, M.D. 'Commentary on Transitional Justice after Transition', in N. Palmer, P. Clark, and D. Granville (eds), *Critical Perspectives in*

Transitional Justice (Cambridge, Antwerp, and Portland: Intersentia, 2012), 485–91.

Karn, A. 'Switzerland's Independent Commission of Experts: State-Sponsored History and the Challenges of Political Partisanship', in B. Bevernage and N. Wouters (eds), *The Palgrave Handbook of State-Commissioned History after 1945* (London: Palgrave MacMillan, 2018), 757–71.

Kastner, F. 'Weder Wahrheit noch Recht: Zur Funktion von Wahrheitskommissionen in der Weltgesellschaft'. *Mittelweg* 36(16) (2007), 31–50.

Kent, L. 'Local Memory Practices in East Timor: Disrupting Transitional Justice Narratives'. *The Journal of Transitional Justice* 5 (2011), 434–55.

Kritz, Neil. *Transitional Justice: How Emerging Democracies Reckon with Former Regimes*, 3 vols. Washington, DC: Institute of Peace Press, 1995.

Krüger, A.K. *Wahrheitskommissionen*. Frankfurt and New York: Campus, 2014.

Laplante, L., and Theidon, K. 'Truth with Consequences: Justice and Reparations in Post-Truth Commission Peru'. *Human Rights Quarterly* 29 (2007), 228–50.

Maier, C.S. 'Doing History, Doing Justice: The Narrative of the Historian and the Narrative of the Truth Commission', in R. Rothberg and D. Thomson (eds), *Truth v. Justice: The Morality of Truth Commissions* (Princeton, NJ: Princeton University Press, 2000), 261–78.

McEvoy, K., and McGregor, L. *Transitional Justice from Below: Grassroots Activism and the Struggle for Change*. Portland, OR: Hart, 2008.

McSherry, P. *Predatory States: The Operation Condor and Covert War in Latin America*. Boulder, CO: Rowman & Littlefield, 2005.

Mendeloff, D. 'Truth-Seeking, Truth-Telling and Post-Conflict Peace-building: Curb the Enthusiasm?' *International Studies Review* 6(3) (2004), 355–80.

Milton, C.E. 'The Truth Ten Years On: The CVR in Peru', in E.A. Montoño and E. Crenzel (eds), *The Struggle for Memory in Latin American Recent History and Political Violence* (London: Palgrave Macmillan, 2016), 111–28.

Minow, M. *Between Vengeance and Forgiveness: Facing History after Genocide and Mass Violence*. Boston, MA: Beacon, 1998.

Mnewabe, N. 'Truth Commissions', in L. Stan and N. Nedelsky (eds), *Encyclopedia of Transitional Justice*, Vol. 1 (Cambridge: Cambridge University Press, 2013), 98–106.

Mouralis, G. 'The Invention of "Transitional Justice" in the 1990s', in L. Israel (ed.), *Dealing with Wars and Dictatorships* (The Hague: Asser Press, 2014), 83–100.

Moyn, S. *The Last Utopia: Human Rights in History*. London and Boston: Harvard University Press, 2010.

Nagy, R. 'Transitional Justice as Global Project: Critical Reflections'. *Third World Quarterly* 29(2) (2008), 275–89.

Napolitano, M. *1964: História do regime militar brasileiro*. São Paulo: Contexto, 2014.

Oettler, A. *Erinnerungsarbeit und Vergangenheitspolitik in Guatemala*. Frankfurt/M: Vervuert, 2004.

Oettler, A. 'Der Stachel der Wahrheit: Zur Geschichte und Zukunft der Wahrheitskommission in Lateinamerika'. *Lateinamerika Analysen* 9 (2004), 93–126.

Olsen, T.D., Payne, L.A., and Reiter, A.G. *Transitional Justice in Balance: Comparing Processes, Weighing Efficacy*. Washington, DC: United States Institute of Peace, 2010.

Palmer, N., Clark, P., and Granville, D. (eds). *Critical Perspectives in Transitional Justice*. Cambridge, Antwerp, and Portland: Intersentia, 2012.

Rothberg, R., and Thomson, D. (eds). *Truth v. Justice: The Morality of Truth Commissions*. Princeton, NJ: Princeton University Press, 2000.

Rüsing, L. 'Truth Commissions in Postcolonial Societies: The Cases of Canada and Mauritius'. Paper presented at the International Symposium on the Brazilian Truth Commission, Hannover, October 2015.

Schneider, N. 'Professional Historical Writing and Human Rights Engagement in the Twenty-First Century: Innovative Approaches and Their Dilemmas', in S. Berger (ed.), *The Engaged Historian: Perspectives on the Intersections of Politics, Activism and the Historical Profession* (New York: Berghahn, forthcoming in 2019).

Schneider, N. 'The Supreme Court's Recent Verdict on the Amnesty Law: Impunity in Post-Authoritarian Brazil'. *European Review of Latin American and Caribbean Studies* 90(2011), 39–54.

Schneider, N. '"Too Little Too Late" or "Premature"? The Brazilian Truth Commission and the Question of "Best Timing"'. *Journal of Iberian & Latin-American Research* 19(1) (2013), 149–62.

Schneider, N. 'Truth No More? The Struggle over the National Truth Commission in Brazil'. *Iberoamericana* 42 (2011), 164–70.

Schneider, N., and Almeida, G.I.D. 'The Brazilian Truth Commission (2012–2014) as a State-Commissioned History Project', in B. Bevernage and N. Wouters (eds), *The Palgrave Handbook of State-Commissioned History after 1945* (London: Palgrave MacMillan, 2018), 637–52.

Schneider, N., and Esparza, M. 'Introduction', in Schneider and Esparza (eds), *Legacies of State Violence and Transitional Justice in Latin America: A Janus-Faced Paradigm?* (Lanham, MD: Lexington Books, 2015), xi–xxviii.

Sikkink, K. *The Justice Cascade: How Human Rights Prosecutions Are Changing World Politics*. New York: Norton, 2011.

Sikkink, K., and Walling, C.B. 'Argentina's Contribution to Global Trends in Transitional Justice', in N. Roht-Arriaza and J. Mariezcurrena (eds), *Transitional Justice in the Twenty-First Century: Beyond Truth versus Justice* (Cambridge: Cambridge University Press, 2006), 301–25.

Sriram, C.L., and Pillay, S. (eds). *Peace versus Justice? The Dilemma of Transitional Justice in Africa*. Cape Town: University of KwaZulu-Natal Press, 2009.

Teitel, R. *Transitional Justice*. New York: Oxford University Press, 2000.

Teitel, R. 'Transitional Justice Genealogy'. *Harvard Human Rights Journal* 16 (2003), 69–94.

Thoms, O.N.T., Ron, J., and Paris, R. 'State-Level Effects of Transitional Justice: What Do We Know?' *International Journal of Transitional Justice* 4 (3) (2010), 329–54.

Torelly, M. 'Assessing a Late Truth Commission: Challenges and Achievements of the Brazilian National Truth Commission'. *International Journal of Transitional Justice* 12(2) (2018), 194–215. Retrieved 20 January 2018 from https://doi.org/10.1093/ijtj/ijy002.

Weinstein, H.M., Fletcher, L.E., Vinck, P., and Pham, P.N. 'Stay the Hand of Justice: Whose Priorities Take Priority?', in R. Shaw and L. Waldorf (eds), *Localizing Transitional Justice: Justice Interventions and Local Priorities after Mass Violence* (Stanford, CA: Stanford University Press, 2010), 27–48.

Wiebelhaus-Brahm, E. 'Truth Commissions and the Construction of History', in B. Bevernage and N. Wouters (eds), *The Palgrave Handbook of State-Commissioned History after 1945* (London: Palgrave MacMillan, 2018), 599–621.

Wiebelhaus-Brahm, E. *Truth Commissions and Transitional Societies: The Impact on Human Rights and Democracy*. New York: Routledge, 2009.

Wiebelhaus-Brahm, E., García-Godos, J., and Skaar, E. (eds). *Beyond Words: Latin American Truth Commissions' Recommendations* (forthcoming).

Wilcken, P. 'The Reckoning: Investigating Torture in Brazil'. *New Left Review* 78 (2012), 73–90.

Part I

The Brazilian National Truth Commission

Section 1

Emergence and Context

Chapter 1

Dear Madame President

A Never-Delivered Speech and a Never-Ending Story

Vera Paiva

'Victim' is the term used by the United Nations to name persons subjected to cruel, inhuman or degrading treatment or punishment, including torture. Victims are entitled to compensation and rehabilitation.[1]

I was invited to be part of this edited volume because my family is 'victim'. My father was detained by agents of the military government and 'disappeared' in 1971. Without any prior accusation, my mother and fourteen-year-old sister were also arrested at home, one day later, and deprived of due process. Being the voice of the 'victims' in this collection makes this contribution a moment of testimony. Giving testimony is an important part of the process of rehabilitation and psychosocial reparation, so for this opportunity I am thankful.

I must say that as a professor and researcher in the psychosociological field working within a human rights framework for almost four decades on the global response to AIDS, I found that a dramaturgic perspective of social life is quite productive for inspiring both academic and activist imaginations. By understanding everyday life through scenes and their scenarios, and by decoding each scene and embodied actor's perspective (as *sujeitos em cena*), we help people to comprehend their lives, changing the way they live their scenes. This dramaturgic approach has helped mitigate unnecessary psychosocial suffering in my area of scholarship. Understanding and changing scenes and scenarios – that is how we have moved on from unacceptable oppression and humiliation, from naturalized inequalities that deny the humanity of many people on the basis of their ethnicity, gender or sexual orientation, territory or economic status, or religious or political beliefs.

So, I will share my views of this *never-ending story* through some real episodes and scenes that I lived and observed, and will offer some interpretation. I will begin with the Brazilian National Truth Commission (the CNV) sanction act.

Scene 1: Invitation to the Palace (16 November 2011)

Our family had been invited to attend the ceremony at which Presidenta Dilma would sanction the CNV law. We decided that I would go with my son, João Henrique, to represent our family. The night before, I got a phone call inviting me to speak at the ceremony on behalf of all families and significant others of ex-political prisoners and the missing. It was quite unexpected, a task that involved some hours of work that night, with no time to discuss it with other families.

Scene 2: Waiting for the Emblematic Event (17 November 2011)

It was a typical sunny day in Brasília. I had travelled from São Paulo to the Palácio do Planalto, the working place of the president-elect. The room was filled with people for the special ceremony. You could cut the tension with a knife. While we waited and waited for the ceremony to begin, many of us gave interviews to the press.

Scene 3: Unexpected Reactions... (17 November 2011)

The president-elect begins to descend the ramp, apparently still debating with ministers at her side. All presidents elected since the democratization were there, of different parties: José Sarney (PMDB/Partido do Movimento Democrático Brasileiro), Collor de Mello (PSC/Partido Social Cristão), Fernando Henrique Cardoso (PSDB/Partido da Social Democracia Brasileira) and Luiz Inácio 'Lula' da Silva (PT/Partido dos Trabalhadores). The chiefs of the army, the navy and the air force were sitting side by side with congressmen and congresswomen, as well as many of us – the affected families, friends and partners.

It was not a long session. Many of us kept looking at the military for their reaction. Even now, twenty-six years after the military had stepped down from power, and twenty-three since the new human rights-based Constitution had been declared, among the president's own military cabinet there was no applause, not a single change in facial expression.

Figure 1.1. Military officials during the official signing of the law to instate the Brazilian Truth Commission. Palácio do Planalto, Brasília. Photo: Wilson Dias/ABr. Wikimedia Commons, CC BBY 3.0.

A few ministers gave speeches, followed by a representative of the amnesty movement, and then, finally, the president. Since the president is always the last speaker, it was then that I realized that none of us, the affected families, would be given the opportunity to speak.

I was happy with that political moment. Just after the end of the ceremony, while wishing my mother could have been there to witness it, I received a warm hug from the president and from the Minister for Human Rights, Maria do Rosário, who said only: 'I am so sorry'.

Scene 4: Would They Defend...? (18 November 2011)

The next day, the 'so sorry' became clear. Journalists called me the next morning to get my reaction to the press coverage, claiming that, following negotiations with the military, I had been 'prevented' from talking. *If a so-called victim [i.e. me] talks, they [the military people] would have to talk....*[2] I had not read the papers, but my answer was simple: the military wanted to talk? Why not let them talk? What were they going to say...? Would they defend the dictatorship or the torture sponsored by their now-retired ex-superiors? Would they defend the 'disappearing-technology' that the Brazilian dictatorship inaugurated in Latin America to destroy the political opposition who had turned into the 'enemy of the people' (*inimigos da pátria*)? That afternoon, I decided to disseminate my speech, and my brother, Marcelo Paiva, published it on his blog.[3]

I invite you now to imagine yourself in that scenario, embodying any participant in a scene that never happened. Let us imagine we are now at the Palácio do Planalto, I am facing you from the podium, Presidenta Dilma is on my right, as is the ramp that she had descended. The huge windows of the Palácio are behind me, through which you can see the Praça dos Três Poderes, Niemeyer's architectural monument to the three branches of government. Choose any 'character' you would like to be – an affected family member, a member of the armed forces, a member of Congress, a journalist, a government official, the coffee lady, the security guard, one of the past presidents. Here we are, and I am giving you and the president this speech for the first time.

A Never-Delivered Speech (Imaginary Scene 5, 17 November 2011)

'Your Excellency Presidenta Dilma,[4] dear Human Rights Minister Maria do Rosário and all ministers present, representatives of the National Congress and the armed forces. Dearest former political prisoners and relatives of the missing who have been in this struggle for such a long time.

João Henrique and I, grandson and daughter of Rubens Paiva, we thank you for the honour of witnessing this historic moment. It is a privilege to speak before you. There are hundreds of families of the killed and the still missing, thousands of teenagers, women and men arrested and tortured during the military regime, and this is a key moment in our history.

We hope that by facing the truth about this period, by preventing human rights violations of any kind from remaining under seal, we are closer to facing the legacy that still today haunts the daily lives of Brazilians. I speak not only of the lives of families marked by periods of dictatorship. Countless Brazilian families today, in 2011, still suffer abductions, torture and arbitrary arrests, and humiliation – with no defence lawyer, without bail. Is it not unacceptable to hear, almost every day, about the burdens of the citizens of the *favelas* in every city, the massacres of civilians by the military police, or to see on TV the 'war' scenes in Rio de Janeiro?

Hard data indicate that especially the poorest and blackest Brazilians are still routinely abused in the streets, are still arbitrarily detained without any respect for their civil rights.[5] The same never-ending story happens with those men and women perceived as homosexuals or identified as non-gender-normative, deprived of any guarantee of their most basic rights to non-discrimination, and the physical and moral integrity guaranteed by the 1948 Declaration of Human Rights and by our 1988 Constitution. Yet all this keeps happening, most excellent Presidenta. It is still being carried out by public servants who disregard their constitutional obligation and perpetuate actions inherited from the state of exception that we lived from 1964 to 1988. Respect for human rights, democratic respect for differing opinions, as well as building the peace, must be worked on every day and by every generation! All of us, civilians and military, must commit ourselves to support this effort.

My own family's history is only one of many, and the myriad other stories out there should continue to be recorded for posterity. Today in Brasília, a remarkable public exhibition illustrates the horrible ordeal of Frei Tito, a much-beloved Catholic priest. His emblematic case offers another lesson about the period, and ought to be investigated by this commission being established today so that cases like it never happen again. We hope many other similar initiatives will multiply the work of the commission. Establishing memorials (*marcas da memória*) is reparatory and healing, not only for those directly affected but also for the communities that choose not to live those experiences again. They are a way to reframe the collective memory and to build the future.

In March, exactly forty years after we had last seen him or last heard his voice, an exhibition about my father was inaugurated in the National Congress. It would soon travel to four capitals. The young Rubens Paiva, my father, had been an activist as a university student, leading the fight to nationalize our soil. '*O petróleo é nosso!* The oil is ours!', he used to make us sing whenever we passed Petrobras oil power plants. To put the abundance of the Brazilian soil to use and mitigate inequality among the Brazilian people, rather than enriching only a few, was his dream. He was a civil engineer, building roads and bridges, and he participated in the construction of a mythical Brasília – a dream of many in the 1950s to integrate the country around a geographical centre. In 1962, he was elected to the National Congress by the people, only to be impeached and exiled in 1964 by the military-civil coup. By 1971, he was once again a successful engineer, democratically concerned as a citizen about his country, and the father of five children. On 20 January 1971, he returned from the Leblon beach, happy to have played volleyball and ready to have lunch with his family on a holiday. Immediately upon his arrival, he was arrested. He must have negotiated to drive his own car to his destination. This car, which my mother would later locate at a military precinct, would for decades be the only proof that he had been arrested. My mother was arrested the next day with my fourteen-year-old sister, along with two young men who had passed by to visit us. They were held for days in the DOI-CODI (Departamento de Operações de Informações – Centro de Operações de Defesa Interna), one of the most notorious locations of that period of horror. When I finally met them after their release, I found my sister with her soul gone and my mother squalid. From barracks to barracks, headquarters to headquarters, Eunice Paiva, my mother, spent years trying to find my father, or at least have news of him. No news.

It was only at the opening of the exhibition in São Paulo, forty years later, that we, for the first time, held a memorial where family and friends came together to honour his memory. After that, we were finally able to talk to each other and break the silence, a silence typical of those whose lives have been held in the suspension that forestalls the experience of mourning. To finally accept that my father had been murdered was to kill him once again. On that Memorial Day, at the newly inaugurated Museum of Resistance (Museu da Resistência), we found that the date on which each of us had accepted that Rubens Paiva was dead varied widely, by months and even years.

This scar can be less painful now. With the installation of a National Truth Commission (CNV), Brazil may consolidate its democracy and its path to peace.

Most excellent Presidenta, besides the marks on the soul from the dictatorship period, we have many things in common: we are women, mothers and public servants. We share the view that human rights and ethics should serve as the foundation for public policies in Brazil. When I was nineteen years old, I also got involved with the youth movement that wanted to change the country. While waiting for this ceremony to begin and preparing what I was going to say, I remembered how this mobilization for transitional justice had begun.

On the board of the newly founded autonomous students' union at my university, which had been named after Alexandre Vannucchi Leme (one of our young colleagues killed by the dictatorship in 1973),

I helped to organize the first mobilization in the streets since the 1968 movements.[6] We organized peacefully against the arbitrary imprisonment of arrested colleagues and for amnesty for political prisoners and the exiled. It was May 1977 and until we, thousands of students, were stopped by the bombs of Colonel Erasmo Dias, we walked peacefully through downtown, distributing an open letter whose slogan was: *today, silence equals consent.*[7]

I think this letter is absolutely appropriate for expressing our convictions today, at this very event approving the National Truth Commission, that *those who remain silent will still be consenting!*

If this truth commission does not have the autonomy and sovereignty to investigate, and a large team that helps carry out its work, we will be consenting. By consenting, I emphasize, people will be complicit in the suffering of thousands of families still affected by this legacy of horror. The socially organized culture of state violence continues unquestioned.

Brazil was the last country to end the period of slavery, and recent data confirm that we are among the ten most wealthy countries in the world, where inequality is still absurd. Indigenous and black people, the young above all, suffer most heavily the burdens of inequality and state violence. Today, with the establishment of this commission, we are also the last country, very timidly but with glimmerings of hope, to begin to do what other countries that lived through dictatorships in the same period have been doing.

We have already been charged by the UN and by international organizations to move forward in this process of transitional justice. Re-establishing the truth and preserving the memory of our country's past does not constitute 'revenge', as many are still calling it. Those deemed responsible for the barbarity should be tried in court, albeit with the right to due process – a right that the political prisoners or assassinated opposition, like my father, never had. This is fundamental, so that the torturers of today should not feel impunity for their daily role of obstructing peace and justice. Chile and Argentina have done it. South Africa, moreover, gave the world an example of how to face truth and rescue memory through principles of 'remorse', 'regret', 'reconciliation', 'rehabilitation' and 'reintegration', so that the years of terror would not be repeated, and so that each generation could appreciate it anew.

I conclude by insisting that democracy is built and rebuilt day by day, every day. It should be valued and reconstructed by each generation. From today on, those who stay silent, again will consent.

Thank you!

Subsequent Episodes of this Never-Ending Story

I hope you got some sense of the drama that in 2011 was just beginning.

Social and political processes are successful firstly through the symbolic domain, and depend on psychosocial interventions that challenge the cultural scenario to offer new interpretations, provide new understanding of everyday life, tell new stories and offer new narratives about the past. Beyond simply changing people's minds, these interventions have an impact on policies, politics and structures. What changed with the instalment of the National Truth Commission?

The CNV members assumed office on 16 May 2012. Meanwhile, I had received a full apology from the Minister for Human Rights and was present at this public ceremony together with my other son, João Francisco. Presidenta Dilma, a tortured political prisoner herself, spoke emotionally, saying that the CNV should not support resentment or hate.[8]

The subsequent political conflicts were about the 'two sides' notion. Businessmen and the judicial hierarchies, public and military servants, as well as all segments that had supported the repression and torture, have framed the dictatorship as resulting from a war: the state versus terrorist enemies. These beneficiaries of the dictatorship had received full amnesty from the military regime in 1979, succeeding in preventing the implementation of transitional justice.[9] After twenty-five years of authoritarian rule, most of the surviving media – remarkably, radio and TV – helped to popularize the idea that those who were fighting for human rights were essentially supporting delinquents.[10] Brazil is the only Latin American country where such a notion circulates. Since the 1980s, radio and TV have channelled this cultural war on human rights. Consequently, the harassment of human rights advocates has never stopped, and continues to serve both the torturers and the beneficiaries of the coup.

The first challenges were overcome by the 'memory and truth' social movement, as one could name it, alongside the convictions of CNV members. It was determined that the Brazilian state violence between 1964 and 1988 was unacceptable and should be investigated. Only 'this side' would matter.

Affected families – the children and grandchildren of those killed, imprisoned and tortured, the families of people still missing after all those years – were surprised by the support they received from younger generations, from men and women in their twenties who had not lived through the dictatorship themselves. Many of these young men and women became active in public debates in communities, universities, schools, labour unions, churches, NGOs and social media. Mainstream media could not ignore these debates. In this scenario, my favourite statement was: 'What country do you want to leave for your children? Do you feel good with torture, will you be happy if your children live near the torturers out there?'

My brother, Marcelo Paiva, addressed the military more than once in his column and blog:

> You belong to a new generation of generals, admirals, lieutenant-generals ... You were young during the dictatorship ... Why not clean up the reputation of the organization? You are not the same! Are you indebted to those who sullied the name of the armed forces? You must follow a tradition that honours us, that has guaranteed the integrity of the Republic, the end of the Getúlio Vargas dictatorship, after fighting the fascists in Italy, and which is now leading the international campaign in Haiti.[11]

The commission, as we argued in interviews and public debates, would become whatever the social movements would make of it. The collective memory that had been established in previous debates about how to frame the dictatorship period – the 'cadre' in Halbwachs' (1952) terminology – was challenged again.[12] All 'sides' aimed at different Brazilian generations that, for decades, had been socialized by an all-encompassing media, a deeply censored educational system and a chronic lack of information.

In my view, it was at that moment that we were able to clearly link the past and the current state violence: it had never ended. A new 'memory and truth' social movement grew with black and young people's participation. A growing segment of this movement aimed at expanding the understanding of the past and its *conscientization* through its tragic legacies.[13]

As an apt illustration of this link, military police violence increased, repeatedly in uneven violent repression, tackling human rights and leftist social movements. After 2013, this happened across all federation states, including those governed by ex-exiled or imprisoned people of *all* parties.[14] As I had mentioned in my 'non-speech' the year before, the state police involvement in massacres in poor neighbourhoods, against indigenous peoples as well as against rural workers and forest people, never ended.

Political reactions from authorities and the mainstream media would claim that police 'escaped' governmental control, or that the violence was enacted against 'delinquents without human rights'. An alternative perspective could question: were they responding to the

CNV memory and truth process? Human rights-based social movements have adopted 'Pelo fim da Policia Militar' ('End the military police') as a slogan in social movements, large parades and meetings.

In view of the CNV support, however, many of the most affected institutions, such as universities, some professional councils and unions, state congresses and city councils, ended up establishing their own truth committees to investigate the dictatorship period. International networks for transitional justice supported the investigation of multinational companies that had been involved with the regime, including the media.[15] The direct participation of the United States government in the military coup following and infusing the Cold War spirit was again an issue in local discussions.

The CNV process occurred as massive and unprecedented rallies and protests, aimed at implementing or expanding citizenship rights, produced scenes that were rarely registered by mainstream media. When the media did register them, they reinterpreted a great deal of it. Symbolic and embodied battles in the streets of Brazilian cities revealed how beneficiaries of the dictatorship led the backlash against human rights and in subsequent years furthered it through Presidenta Dilma's impeachment process. Overturning human rights as a goal for global governance was also developing in the international arena, linked in some of the scenes I lived.

Scene 6: An Invitation to the Palace (17 October 2013)

I was working on a paper when I received a phone call from 'Palácio do Planalto'. The presidenta's staff person was inviting me and my brother Marcelo to view a documentary with Presidenta Dilma at Palácio da Alvorada. They would be showing *O Dia que Durou 21 Anos* (The Day that Lasted 21 Years), directed by Flavio Taváres (2012).[16] Marcelo is tetraplegic; to travel on short notice was not possible for him, and I had a full agenda. It took me some time to realize that one does not refuse a president's invitation.

We knew that Taváres' documentary was about the direct involvement of the US government in the 1964 coup, and that my father had been a critical actor in this issue during his two years as an elected congressman in Brasília. Rubens Paiva headed the investigation that proved that a variety of US funds had sponsored the election of dozens of members of the Brazilian Congress. Many would assume that this was one reason he was impeached by the military and, some years later, killed.

Scene 7: US–Brazil Relations, Espionage, Resistance and Foreseeing the Palace Assault (18 October 2013)

There was additional meaning to the scenes we were about to live. This concerned the American espionage on Presidenta Dilma and Petrobras, the national oil company, that had recently been disseminated by WikiLeaks. Presidenta Dilma was supposed to be in Washington meeting with President Obama but had cancelled her trip on account of this espionage event.[17] Chancellor Merkel, who had also been spied upon, offered her solidarity.

A full moon illuminated the iconic Itamarati Palace garden, the official residence of the Brazilian president, the icon of Brasilia.[18] After watching the film, invitees engaged in an hour of spontaneous and candid debate. Presidenta Dilma participated in the group discussion. It was above all about how the US had been directly involved in the '64 coup; the evidence shown in the documentary was undisputable. Since the author of a book about João Goulart was among the nineteen invited to that session, the following half an hour focused on the actions of Goulart. Goulart, who had served as president of Brazil since 1961, had left the country when he noticed that there was no substantial resistance to the military coup.

In a vivid moment during the debate, Presidenta Dilma said that 'leaving the palace' was something that should not have happened: 'Allende did not do it!' and she put her hands and arms over her chest in a gesture that I interpreted as putting herself in the Chilean leader's position.

While I am writing this chapter, I realize that this scene occurred before we had access to a tape recovered during the memory and truth movement on which Rubens Paiva can be heard calling for the resistance. The family, as well as many of his partners in Congress or in the federal government who were exiled or imprisoned after the coup, knew about it, but no one had ever heard it. It is now public.[19] As you might imagine, family and friends experienced deeply emotional moments when they heard Paiva's voice for the first time in four decades, or in the case of his grandchildren, for the first time ever.

Thirty months later, in 2016, Presidenta Dilma remained in the palace until the last possible minute, refusing to renounce the presidency. Through live TV coverage, the country saw her defending herself for more than twenty hours. Many liberals were embarrassed by the absence of any proof substantiating the accusation of corruption, as the mainstream media wanted to frame it. In her impeachment movement, ex-torturers and the beneficiaries of the dictatorship were allowed to be key actors. She was impeached by the most conservative Congress since the transition to democracy, but there was much resistance on Brazilian streets.

Did Presidenta Dilma foresee the difficulties soon to be confronted, or know that the CNV she had dared to inaugurate would provoke the demons that had been lurking in the closet since the democratic period? I did.

Inconclusion: The Never-Ending Story

Since 2013, the backlash has shown its face as the national youth movement has been on the rise. Fed up with the high expenditures of the World Cup and the Rio Olympics, it has been fighting instead for progressive urban mobility policies (free-pass), public health and education. After being violently repressed, youth movements won the sympathy of poor people, the primary commuters who have also been troubled by policies of urban mobility. Even the media was made to retract. The Globo media network, which had been labelling the movement's participants 'delinquents and criminals', was accused of compliance with dictatorship legacies once more and, surprisingly, apologized. In a successful psychosocial intervention to change the movement's meanings, its editorial stated that they had been wrong about the movements, reframing them as an 'anti-corruption case against the Lula/Dilma government'. Now the streets are free, parades count on police and media support. Previous youth free-pass movement leaders understood this, leaving the streets to be immediately subjugated by members of the white middle class wearing Brazilian football national team t-shirts and crying out against the corruption of the Workers Party's (PT).

Cold War discourses gained momentum: 'all' against 'enemies of the country', 'all' against 'reddish' people. Ex-torturers, as well as those defending the military rule, had their space guaranteed in the big white middle-class parades encouraging the impeachment of Presidenta Dilma. These parades were not only supported but convoked by the media. The most emblematic and horrifying moment was when Congressman Bolsonaro, a homophobic, misogynistic, racist ex-military who had defended the dictatorship period, voted for Presidenta Dilma's impeachment 'in the name of' her torturer, live on TV.

Scene 8: Our Own Bolsonaro Scene (Congresso Nacional, 1 April 2014)

The National Congress[20] was inaugurating a bust of my father, a public homage to the congressmen killed by the dictatorship. It was the first memory mark for family and friends to visit and pay their respects, as he was not buried. Bolsonaro interrupts the ceremony to pass through us, booing the bust, Rubens Paiva, and making it a never-ending story.

Did human rights violators win the symbolic and embodied political dispute about the truth regarding the past? Is it still possible to promote transitional justice and the end of arbitrary imprisonment, injustice and torture in Brazil?

The contribution to peace and democracy of the CNV and the memory and truth commissions and movements that multiplied should be stressed for at least five reasons. First, the CNV's reports and debate on state terror deepened the understanding of Brazil's violent past and its links to the enslavement of black Africans and indigenous people, still the primary target of police violence and injustice.[21] The involvement of a younger generation, the second reason to value CNV outcomes, fostered the consolidation of a new narrative, through existing documents and further investigations. It touched upon the ordeal of poor people, as well as those living in rural areas: they had been tortured, put in prisoners' camps and killed to open their territory to agribusinesses that continued to enact racism of the worst dehumanizing category – sponsoring people's massacres. Never-ending unacceptable stories.[22]

The debate on missing and killed people has usually been led by white, urban, middle-class established leftists who, appropriately, have demanded transitional justice. My family highly appreciated this move, also because my mother, Eunice Paiva, who became a lawyer after her and my father's imprisonment, dedicated part of her life to defending many ethnicities in danger, as my brother tells in his book about her and this period of our lives.[23]

Third, the debate on how to conceive human rights and promote justice, including for non-heterosexual and non-gender-normative persons, reached poor and peripheral communities – those most affected by the popular media propaganda against LGBT rights.[24] The noisy silence about state terror spoke. New generations no longer feel that everyday state violence is 'natural' or acceptable, and they understand that it has a long history marked by skin colour, ethnicity, gender/sexuality and class. Fourth, another important legacy of this period is the alternative media expansion through youth initiatives, such as

Media NINJA or *Jornalistas Livres*, which were founded at this very moment. Nearly absent in any news media coverage, massive human rights-based resistance movements, during and after the impeachment, were registered and shown live on the internet.

Many new stories and new details of known cases were told, while a very important step – support for psychological healing and reparation through official political amnesty – was offered by a governmental programme called Testimony Clinics (*Clinica dos Testemunhos*), a fifth reason to value the CNV legacy.

In my family, this was a deeply emotional period that reopened our mourning. Two scenes are emblematic.

Scene 9: The Assassination of Dictatorship Torturers, Most Probably by Their Peers

I was leaving the Medical School after giving a class when a journalist called to get my impression about the discovery of documents related to the disappearance of Rubens Paiva. They had been found in the house of Army Colonel Molinas who had just been killed. It was November 2012. The colonel had coordinated the DOI-CODI military division in which dozens of political prisoners had been tortured and killed, including my father. The journalist brought me to tears with the detailed description of personal belongings registered in the death quarter – my father's watch, his wallet, his keyring... I had never visualized it so clearly, and I missed him a lot... *Saudades*....

Another assassination was a scary moment for me and provided many painful scenes: Colonel Malhães had defended the practice of making people's bodies disappear. He assumed the responsibility for the disappearance of my father's body and gave two different versions of what happened. Malhães was murdered before he could clarify it.

Both episodes are discussed in the *Folha de São Paulo* of 24 April 2014.[25] The next scene provides an international perspective on the legacies of the CNV.

Scene 10: President Obama Declassifies a Document about Rubens Paiva (July 2015)

Again, a phone call woke me up in the middle of the night in Stellenbosch, South Africa, where I was attending a conference. The caller wanted to tell the family before the newspapers broke the story the next morning that President Obama had declassified documents to hand over to Presidenta Dilma, who would finally visit Washington. As can be seen in Figures 1.2 and 1.3, the US embassy knew, within about three weeks of my father's arrest, that he had been murdered. The only

OPTIONAL FORM NO. 10
MAY 1962 EDITION
GSA FPMR (41 CFR) 101-11.6
UNITED STATES GOVERNMENT

Memorandum

~~CONFIDENTIAL~~

Declassified
Authority: 43265 By:
Brewer Thompson
Date: 05-06-2015

TO : The Ambassador

DATE: February 11, 1971

FROM : John W. Mowinckel

SUBJECT: Disappearance of Rubens Paiva

The continued disappearance of former Deputy Rubens Paiva after his arrest two or three weeks ago is causing profound concern to his many friends and associates. [redacted] Paiva died under interrogation either from a heart attack or other causes. When this becomes known (as it eventually will) it is certain that his friends will generate a violent and emotional campaign against the Brazilian government by every means possible --international press, letters to Senators Fulbright, Church, Kennedy, etc.

Many of Paiva's friends still have a slim hope that he may still be alive although they admit that this may be wishful thinking. They suspect that, since he was a fat man, he may have died of a heart attack under torture.

While I had never heard of Paiva before his arrest he is apparently very well known in Brazil as a physically and intelligently courageous man of the left who was a deputy during the Goulart regime and cassated in 1964. He was a wealthy man who inherited money from his well-to-do family and made a good deal on his own as an engineer. His family owns land in the Valle Ribeira [illegible] Paulo. While Carlos Lamarca did not have his guerrilla [illegible] Paiva's land, it was close by.

All Paiva's friends are convinced that he has had no sympathy at any time with the terrorist movement or with violence as a means of opposing the Brazilian military. They say, however, that as a leader of left-wing thought in Brazil it is possible he may at some time or another have given assistance to political fugitives related to friends of his.

I further understand that Paiva was a very successful engineer and after his cassation did a lot of construction work for both the Castello Branco and Costa e Silva governments. He is tremendously respected, particularly by his friends and also by many of those who disagree with him politically.

~~CONFIDENTIAL~~

Buy U.S. Savings Bonds Regularly on the Payroll Savings Plan

5010-108

NW 43265 DocId:31246616 Page 1

Figure 1.2. Declassified archival material first page. National Archives and Records Administration, United States. Published with permission.

~~CONFIDENTIAL~~

.2.

It is known to his friends that he was arrested because of a letter addressed to him by someone in Chile which arrived here in the hands of some woman.

Comment: This is another example of irresponsible strong arm tactics and bungling by Brazilian security forces. The difference is that this time, when the facts become known, it will not be possible to sweep them under the rug. Confirmation of his death will raise one hell of a stink and once again embarrass the U.S. Government in its relationship with the GOB.

In my opinion every effort should be made by you and other members of this mission to convince the GOB that something must be done to punish at least some of those responsible--punished by public trial. If the GOB does not do this fairly soon, it is certain that the GOB's sins will rub off on us, thereby causing one more problem on the Hill and in the press for the Nixon administration.

Enclosure:
copy of Feb. 2nd N.Y. Times article

cc: Minister Boonstra
Col. Moura
Mr. Phillips
Mr. Low (Mr. Walker)

~~CONFIDENTIAL~~

NW 43265 DocId:31246616 Page 2

Figure 1.3. Declassified archival material second page. National Archives and Records Administration, United States. Published with permission.

thing I could think of was my mother's suffering and the fact that, for four decades, nobody had been kind enough to tell the family.

Was this an act of reparation on the part of the US government for the espionage scandal on Presidenta Dilma, herself a former political prisoner and already facing the impeachment process?

Finally, as Paulo Abrão (2014) said about the Testimony Clinics initiative: we do not measure the terrible effects of a dictatorship by the piles of corpses it produced.[26] When terror becomes a state practice, it affects the whole society. As we all now know, there were global state connections for the disregarded fundamental rights of the victims, aiming to influence their people.

Abrão also reminds us that the victim's pain expresses the collective trauma of the breaking and vanishing, the loss of the institutional protections of life and liberty. So, 'if there is no mourning without recognizing death, neither will reparation be possible without official recognition of the crime'.[27]

Many people who for decades had kept silent were now mobilized by this environment and began to tell their stories in the company of trained psychologists. Some were able to cope with the trauma, even if, as we used to say in my family, it was an insurmountable one. But I saw my sister, who had been arrested alongside my father and mother when she was fourteen, and who had long been confined to her trauma, finally begin to elaborate it through the Testimony Clinics after four long decades of ineffectual treatments and much psychological suffering.

So, my last scene is an excerpt of a testimony I was invited to give at the Sesc-Pompéia Theater Stage/SP (25 August 2013) in the middle of beautiful play – 'Cantata para um bastidor de utopias'. This is how I ended it:

> Amarildo de Souza[28] was arrested and disappeared.
> He was 43 in 2013 – Rubens Paiva was 41 years old in 1971.
> Amarildo was 1.74 m tall – Rubens Paiva was 1.76 m.
> Amarildo was a bricklayer – Rubens Paiva was a civil engineer.
> Amarildo was a Rocinha favela resident – Rubens Paiva's house faced the Leblon beach.
> Amarildo was one of 12 siblings, married, father of 6 children – Rubens Paiva was one of 6 siblings, married, father of 5 children.
> Amarildo's sister was named Eunice – my mother's name is Eunice.
> Amarildo was black – my father was white.

The Brazilian process may be illustrative of similar political and psychosocial phenomena, stories observed on all continents. The question we have in common, the never-ending challenge, is how to better resist the backlashes that may curtail democracy and repeat the cycle of violence and unnecessary suffering.

Vera Paiva is Professor in the Social Psychology Department at the University of São Paulo (USP) and coordinator of the Study Nucleus of AIDS Prevention (NEPAIDS-USP) since 1991, where she developed a human rights-based conceptualization and set of practices. Paiva represents civil society in the Special Commission for the Dead and Disappeared (Comissão Especial de Mortos e Desaparecidos Políticos) and has been a human rights activist since the struggle against dictatorship.

Notes

1. United Nations, *Convention against Torture and Other Cruel, Inhuman or Degrading Treatment or Punishment* (1984).
2. F. Gallo, 'Família de Rubens Paiva critica governo', *O Estado de S. Paulo*, 21 November 2011.
3. M.R. Paiva, 'Comissão da 1/2 Verdade', *O Estado de São Paulo*, blog, 20 November 2011.
4. Although the speech was never officially delivered, it has enjoyed an interesting afterlife. My original speech first appeared in Portuguese on my brother's blog. An English translation by John Catalinotto, whom I never met, was then shared on the *Tlaxcala* blog forty days after the event, on 26 December, the day my father would have turned eighty-two. Tlaxcala is an international network of translators for linguistic diversity that allows translations to be freely reproduced on a 'copyleft' basis. For the translation of the speech, see J. Catalinotto, 'The Censored Speech at the Ceremony Establishing the Brazilian Truth Commission', *Tlaxcala*, 26 December 2011. This version here is a significantly amended and extended translation of that speech. For the original speech in Portuguese, see V. Paiva, 'Discurso de Vera Paiva na cerimônia de criação da Comissão da Verdade', *Sul21* (2011).
5. This number continued to grow and got worse after the impeachment of Presidenta Dilma, as detailed in B. Maia, 'A violência tem cara, cor e endereço', *Com Ciencia. Revista Eletrônica de Jornalismo Científico. Dossiê Violência* 192 (2017).
6. In 1968, Brazilian students led the fight and marches for civil and political rights and freedom. This period was followed by a second and even bloodier phase of the military dictatorship.
7. We filled the streets in 1977, expressing outrage at the lack of democracy and social justice. The letter was published on the front page of *O Estado de Sao Paulo* the next day, to our amazement. All press that survived the years of military government had supported the dictatorship, including *Globo* and *Folha de São Paulo*, which only acknowledged this and apologized during or after the memory and truth movement. Their networks are still the only traditional media available in Brazil; all heavily supported President Dilma's impeachment.

8. M. Savarese, 'Dilma instala Comissão da Verdade e diz que não haverá ressentimento, ódio nem perdão, *UOL*, 16 May 2012.
9. In the *Estado de São Paulo*, 28 April 2010, retrieved 20 January 2018 from http://politica.estadao.com.br/noticias/geral,entenda-a-polemica-sobre-a-lei-da-anistia,544229.
10. S. Varjão, *Violações de direitos na mídia brasileira: ferramenta prática para identi car violações de direitos no campo da comunicação de massa*, Vol. 1 (Brasilia: ANDI, 2015).
11. M.R. Paiva, 'Limpar o nome do exército', *O Estado de São Paulo*, blog, 9 February 2014.
12. M. Halbwachs, *On Collective Memory* (Chicago: University of Chicago Press, 1992).
13. P. Freire, *Pedagogy of the Oppressed* (New York: Continuum, 1971).
14. Brazil has two police forces: the civil police and the military police (the PM). Both are state-governor controlled. 'Law enforcement' is still skewed, and remains, in typical fashion, a legacy of the dictatorship. Its institutional power has never been touched.
15. Business and Human Rights Resource Center, 'Volkswagen (re Military Dictatorship, Brazil)' (2017).
16. F. Taváres, *O Dia que Durou 21 Anos* (2012).
17. T. Hardy, 'Dilma não deverá viajar aos Estados Unidos em outubro', *O Globo*, 14 September 2013.
18. P.V. Chagas, 'Dilma recebe convidados para sessão de filme sobre a ditadura', *Empresa Brasileira de Comunicaçao*, 18 October 2013.
19. A group of journalists found this long-lost tape of the Radio Nacional, the most important national radio station in 1964, on which was recorded a call to resistance spoken by Rubens Paiva. Retrieved 20 January 2018 from https://www.youtube.com/watch?v=mONaXFy98ys.
20. E. Éboli and L. Washington, 'Inauguração de busto de Rubens Paiva vira ato pela revisão da Lei da Anistia', *O Globo*, 1 April 2014.
21. Comissão Nacional da Verdade (CNV), 'The Final Report of the Brazilian Truth Commission' (2014).
22. Ministério dos Direitos Humanos, Conselho Nacional de Direitos Humanos, 'CNDH manifesta preocupação quanto ao aumento da violência em conflitos no campo' (2018).
23. M.R. Paiva, *Ainda estou aqui* (Rio de Janeiro: Alfaguara, 2015).
24. See CNV, 'Final Report' and also J.N. Green and R. Quinalha (eds), *Ditadura e Homossexualidades: Repressão, Resistência e a Busca da Verdade* (São Carlos: EdUFSCar, 2014).
25. In *Folha de São Paulo*, retrieved 20 January 2018 from http://www1.folha.uol.com.br/poder/2014/04/1445454-coronel-paulo-malhaes-que-assumiu-torturas-e-encontrado-morto-no-rio.shtml.
26. P. Abrão, 'Prefácio', in Sigmund Freud Associação Psicanalítica (ed.), *Clínicas do testemunho: reparação psíquica e construção de memórias* (Porto Alegre: Criação Humana, 2014), 15–24.
27. Ibid., 17.

28. In Rio alone, ten thousand Amarildos were killed between 2001 and 2011. For a good synthesis of Amarildo's story, see Wikipedia, *Case of Amarildo de Souza*, https://pt.wikipedia.org/wiki/Caso_Amarildo.

Bibliography

Abrão, P. 'Prefácio', in Sigmund Freud Associação Psicanalítica (ed.), *Clínicas do testemunho: reparação psíquica e construção de memórias* (Porto Alegre: Criação Humana, 2014), 15–24.

Business and Human Rights Resource Center. 'Volkswagen (re Military Dictatorship, Brazil)' (2017). Retrieved 31 January 2018 from https://business-humanrights.org/en/volkswagen-re-military-dictatorship-brazil.

Catalinotto, J. 'The Censored Speech at the Ceremony Establishing the Brazilian Truth Commission'. *Tlaxcala*. Blog. 26 December 2011. Retrieved 25 August 2018 from http://www.tlaxcala-int.org/article.asp?reference=6484.

Chagas, P.V. 'Dilma recebe convidados para sessão de filme sobre a ditadura'. *Empresa Brasileira de Comunicaçao*, 18 October 2013. Retrieved 20 May 2015 from http://www.ebc.com.br/cultura/2013/10/dilma-recebe-convidados-para-sessao-de-filme-sobre-a-ditadura.

Comissão Nacional da Verdade (CNV). 'The Final Report of the Brazilian Truth Commission' (2014). Retrieved 20 January 2018 from http://www.cnv.gov.br/index.php/outros-destaques/574-conheca-e-acesse-o-relatorio-final-da-cnv.

Éboli, E., and Washington, L. 'Inauguração de busto de Rubens Paiva vira ato pela revisão da Lei de Anistia'. *O Globo*, 1 April 2014. Retrieved 20 May 2015 from https://oglobo.globo.com/brasil/inauguracao-de-busto-de-rubens-paiva-vira-ato-pela-revisao-da-lei-de-anistia-12060616#ixzz56oaqzvDz.

Freire, P. *Pedagogy of the Oppressed*. New York: Continuum, 1971.

Gallo, F. 'Família de Rubens Paiva critica governo'. *O Estado de S. Paulo*, 21 November 2011. Retrieved 20 May 2015 from http://politica.estadao.com.br/noticias/geral,familia-de-rubens-paiva-critica-governo,801277.

Green, J.N., and Quinalha, R. (eds). *Ditadura e Homossexualidades: Repressão, Resistência e a Busca da Verdade.* São Carlos: EdUFSCar, 2014.

Halbwachs, M. *On Collective Memory*. Chicago: University of Chicago Press, 1992.

Hardy, T. 'Dilma não deverá viajar aos Estados Unidos em outubro'. *O Globo*, 14 September 2013. Retrieved 20 May 2014 from https://oglobo.globo.com/brasil/dilma-nao-devera-viajar-aos-estados-unidos-em-outubro-9963764.

Maia, B. 'A violência tem cara, cor e endereço'. *Com Ciencia. Revista Eletrônica de Jornalismo Científico. Dossiê Violência* 192 (2017). Retrieved 20 January 2018 from http://www.comciencia.br/a-violencia-no-brasil-tem-cara-cor-e-endereco.

Ministério dos Direitos Humanos, Conselho Nacional de Direitos Humanos. 'CNDH manifesta preocupação quanto ao aumento da violência em conflitos no campo' (2018). Retrieved 2 February 2018 from http://www.mdh.gov.br/sobre/participacao-social/cndh/noticias/cndh-manifesta-preocupacao-quanto-a-aumento-da-violencia-em-conflitos-no-campo.

Paiva, M.R. *Ainda estou aqui*. Rio de Janeiro: Alfaguara, 2015.

Paiva, M.R. 'Comissão da 1/2 Verdade'. *O Estado de São Paulo*. Blog. 20 November 2011. Retrieved 20 January 2018 from http://cultura.estadao.com.br/blogs/marcelo-rubens-paiva/comissao-da-12-verdade/.

Paiva, M.R. 'Limpar o nome do exército'. *O Estado de São Paulo*. Blog. 9 February 2014. Retrieved 20 January 2018 from http://cultura.estadao.com.br/blogs/marcelo-rubens-paiva/limpar-o-nome-do-exercito/.

Paiva, V. 'Discurso de Vera Paiva na cerimônia de criação da Comissão da Verdade'. *Sul21* (2011). Retrieved 25 September 2018 from https://www.sul21.com.br/opiniaopublica/2011/11/discurso-de-vera-paiva-na-cerimo nia-de-criacao-da-comissao-da-verdade/.

Savarese, M. ' Dilma instala Comissão da Verdade e diz que não haverá ressentimento, ódio nem perdão...' *UOL*, 16 May 2012. Retrieved 20 January 2018 from https://noticias.uol.com.br/politica/ultimas-noticias/2012/05/16/dilma-chora-ao-instalar-comissao-da-verdade.htm?cmpid=copiaecola&cmpid=copiaecola.

Taváres, F. *O Dia que Durou 21 anos* (2012). Retrieved 20 January 2018 from https://www.youtube.com/watch?v=v-HhhdgYOa.

United Nations. *Convention against Torture and Other Cruel, Inhuman or Degrading Treatment or Punishment* (1984). Retrieved 20 January 2018 from http://www.ohchr.org/Documents/ProfessionalInterest/cat.pdf.

Varjão, S. *Violações de direitos na mídia brasileira: ferramenta prática para identi car violações de direitos no campo da comunicação de massa*. Vol. 1. Brasília: ANDI, 2015.

Chapter 2

The Public Prosecutor's Office of São Paulo and the Legacy of the Dictatorship

A Brief Report on Activities Prior to the Truth Commission

Eugenia Augusta Gonzaga

Brazil was one among many countries whose legal order was shattered in the Cold War context. In 1964, the military launched a coup with the support of most of the middle and upper classes. This support was given because of fearmongering. With the help of conservative media outlets, news was spread that the elected government was weak and associated with left-wing movements, which could lead to the establishment of a communist government in Brazil, as had occurred in Cuba in the 1950s. Therefore, civilians took to the streets demanding a coup. With the financial and strategic support of the business class and the US government, the army took over the presidency on 1 April 1964.[1]

From that moment onwards, individual rights and legal procedures were increasingly suspended. People seen as opponents of the military government were dismissed, illegally imprisoned, tortured, exiled or murdered. Very often their bodies would be withheld from their relatives.

Persecution and military violence spread to the whole country, but the majority of the population knew very little about these incidents. The only thing they could be sure of was that it was dangerous to oppose the government. Few Brazilians knew that the deaths of the so-called 'terrorists', declared to have occurred during armed conflicts, were in fact deaths that occurred under torture and without any means of resistance.

Silence about these crimes was made possible due to the support of the country's major media organizations, which was later complemented by the targeted persecution of dissident journalists and media outlets. This widespread ignorance of these past crimes has made it very difficult to find consistent support for transitional justice measures in Brazil.

Resistance to the dictatorship was concentrated in capital cities such as São Paulo, Rio de Janeiro, Salvador and Recife. All of the urban guerrilla cells in these cities were dismantled, and their leaders (for example Carlos Marighella and Carlos Lamarca) and hundreds of other guerrilla fighters were killed. There was also some organized resistance in rural areas, mainly in the Araguaia region between the states of Pará and Tocantins. The main leader of the Araguaia Guerrilla, Maurício Grabois, and almost all members of this group were killed.

Civilians who had no connection with political resistance movements were also killed, either by mistake or for expressing dissident ideas, or even because they presented some form of embarrassment to the dictatorial government.[2] This was the case with the deaths of thousands of indigenous people killed between 1960 and 1980 in the central and northern regions of Brazil. At the time when the Trans-Amazonian Highway and hydroelectric plants were being constructed, some indigenous people were killed by mining companies and individual miners.

Most of the bodies were hidden in the cemeteries of capital cities, buried without identification, under fake names and without notifying family members. Consequently, many of these bodies could not be retrieved and ended up being lost. It is estimated that many of these bodies have been buried in cemeteries in Ricardo Albuquerque in Rio de Janeiro and Vila Formosa and Perus in São Paulo. Most of the bodies of the Araguaia Guerrilla were either left in the open or destroyed.

It is believed that the last political activist was killed in 1985, even if most of the guerrilla groups had been dismantled before then, in the mid 1970s. By this time, the main leaders had already been wiped out and news of the violence committed by public officials had become more widespread in the Brazilian and international press.

A movement to return to the democratic legal order began in response to the appeal of many families of victims and pressure from international agencies. In 1979, the Amnesty Law was imposed by the government. While it continued to exclude some political crimes, it allowed the release of some political prisoners and the recovery of job posts, and exiles could return to the country.

However, despite this small political opening, the Brazilian dictatorship continued to collaborate with repressive military governments in other South American countries. Brazil became one of the main protagonists of the Condor Operation, a transregional military network established in the 1970s and 1980s in the Southern Cone. The countries involved (Brazil, Argentina, Chile, Paraguay, Uruguay and Bolivia) established a mutual cooperation agreement aiming to jointly suppress any resistance to their dictatorial regimes. The entry of military officers into other countries' territory was allowed (which, in a normal situation, would be considered an insult to national sovereignty). They could arrest individuals and take them back to their country of origin. As we know, for example, members of the Montonero Peronist Movement, who were resisting the dictatorship in Argentina, were kidnapped at Galeão Airport in Rio de Janeiro by Argentinian agents in 1980 and never seen again.

In the early 1980s, security agents of the Brazilian military regime were responsible for two bombings in Rio de Janeiro (at Riocentro and at the headquarters of the Brazilian Bar Association [OAB/RJ]). These terrorist events occurred at a politically tense moment, as members of the armed forces disagreed over a political opening of the regime. Even if the president at the time considered himself committed to the opening of political power, important military leaders believed that Brazil was still threatened by communists and required ever more repression. In that moment, paramilitary organizations carried out bombings so they could blame left-wing groups for the terrorist actions and justify the functioning of national security structures.

It is important to note that brutal acts continued to occur, although from 1974 onwards the regime liberalized its politics. Furthermore, the military made sure that the Amnesty Law was interpreted in a way that guaranteed that the crimes committed by state agents against political activists would be pardoned. On account of this interpretation (the law is not clear in that sense), no cases against regime agents have been brought before the courts for nearly thirty years.

In 1985, indirect elections were held and a civilian president took power. The first direct presidential elections, however, were held in 1989. With the political opening, the family members of the disappeared – it has always been the family members who pushed this justice and memory agenda forward – engaged in the struggle for the recovery of the bodies of their loved ones, the opening up of archives and the punishment of those responsible for the killings and torture.[3] In 1990, they discovered a mass grave in the Perus cemetery in São Paulo; more than a thousand bodies were exhumed from that grave. The bodies of three political activists have been identified, but it is estimated that up to twenty political activists could still be buried in that location. In the same period, another mass grave was located at the Ricardo Albuquerque cemetery in Rio de Janeiro, but the remains found there were jumbled together and degraded, and it has not been possible to proceed with the identification of those remains. In the Araguaia guerrilla case, a number of initiatives were undertaken to locate the bodies of those who died there, including judicial processes, but to no avail. The family members filed a lawsuit at the Inter-American Court on Human Rights (IACHR) against the Brazilian federal government in 1995. The request was accepted and submitted to the Court in 2009, in what became known as the 'Gomes Lund' or the Araguaia Guerrilla case. The Inter-American Court on Human Rights decided against the Brazilian state and in favour of the families in November 2010.

In 1995, the families achieved the enactment of Law 9140, which established the Special Commission on the Political Dead and Disappeared (CEMDP). At first, when family members were more involved with this initiative, the Commission was dedicated to the recognition of individuals as dead and/or political disappeared, which enabled the production of death certificates and compensation to be offered to their families. The CEMDP has produced a wealth of documents, including a well-documented report that is still used as a basis for different reports on the subject. It can be considered a first truth commission in Brazil.[4]

Another step forward was the creation of the Amnesty Commission in 2002, with the task of advising the Justice Minister in granting compensation to victims of political persecution. It has analysed more than fifty thousand applications, and has granted financial compensation to approximately thirty-five thousand people persecuted by the Brazilian dictatorship. Whether by the competence of its leaders or because the country clearly opted for the payment of compensation and a politics of forgetting and no accountability for its agents, the Amnesty Commission was set up with a good structure and is fulfilling its role very well. On the other hand, the CEMDP, which should not be restricted to compensation but should also continue the search for missing bodies, has not, until now, had the structure and skilled workforce necessary to carry out its mandate successfully.

In September 1999, Civil Public Inquiry no. 06/99 was introduced to the Prosecutor's Office in São Paulo, under the leadership of the then Regional Attorney for Citizens' Rights, Marlon Alberto Weichert. This took place following the requests made by representatives of the Grupo Tortura Nunca Mais (Torture Never Again Group) from Rio de Janeiro and the Commission of Family Members of the Political Dead and Disappeared from São Paulo. The request was made because of the excessive delay in the processing and identification of the remains that had been exhumed from the Perus cemetery in São Paulo. The inquiry was taken over by myself, also in my position as Regional Attorney for the Protection of Citizens' Rights. At the request of the family members, even after leaving this function, I and Marlon Weichert continued to handle these procedures for as long as possible at the level of the Public Prosecutor's Office.

We have taken actions that have been considered ground-breaking in the history of transitional justice in the country, but the goals of family members and other stakeholders (such as the location of bodies, the opening up of archives and the punishment of criminals) are still far from completed. Even so, some progress has been made.

I shall now report on the events that took place following the actions of the Public Prosecutor's Office. The bones exhumed from the Perus cemetery in 1990, that were still waiting for identification at Unicamp, in the city of Campinas, were transferred in 2001 to the Araça cemetery in the city of São Paulo. Work continued under the direction of representatives of the state of São Paulo and the University of São Paulo but with no results. In 2005, it was demanded that a private laboratory was hired. Two more political activists were identified, and a DNA bank started to be established based on agreements between the Human Rights Secretariat and the laboratory that was hired.

In 2006, the Attorney General of the Republic, Antonio Fernando de Souza, answered our request and notified the then President Lula about the possibility of opening up archives by presidential decree. No decree was issued, but in 2007 the Brazilian government published the book *The Right to Memory and Truth*.[5] This was a valuable step but the book also demonstrated the lack of knowledge about the contents of missing documents that are still necessary to restore truth.

In May 2007, the conference 'South American Debate on Truth and Justice' was held in Brasília. It was attended by legal experts from Argentina, Chile and Peru, countries where accountability actions were already underway, based on principles of international law on crimes against humanity. From this event, the 'Letter from São Paulo' ('Carta de São Paulo') was issued. It concluded that punishment of those deemed responsible was possible in Brazil, despite the existence of the Amnesty Law and the supposed prescription of crimes.

Based on this understanding, from 2008 onwards, the first civil liability cases were presented. Because we lacked the power to deal with criminal assignments in the Public Prosecutor's Office, we were forced to ask colleagues working in that area to start the first criminal prosecutions. They refused to cooperate, and our requests were stalled. The prosecutions filed in the judiciary have not yet been successful either. However, these attempts were very important to trigger public debate.

Since then, the problem of impunity has gained impetus and other advances have occurred.

Demands to open the archives increased, a National Truth Commission was implemented in 2012, and the Brazilian Bar Association took a case before the Supreme Court which involved ruling on the Amnesty Law. Unfortunately, in April 2010, the Supreme Court confirmed the validity of the Amnesty Law, including crimes committed by state agents against political activists.

In the same year, however, shortly afterwards, the IACHR reached its decision on the already mentioned 'Gomes Lund' (or Araguaia) case, and Brazil was sentenced to locate the victims' remains and prosecute those responsible.[6] The Inter-American Court has ruled that the Amnesty Law is not applicable for the gross human rights violations that occurred during the dictatorship and therefore these crimes cannot be prescribed.

Following this rule, a working group was formed within the Public Prosecutor's Office in a modus operandi that has become common practice in this institution. More than one hundred criminal investigations were launched nationwide and around a dozen criminal cases were presented. The judiciary, however, remained uncooperative, and very few favourable decisions have been reached. So far, no agent of the dictatorial period has been arrested or convicted. Another legal action taken before the Supreme Court awaits trial, in which a new statement on the Amnesty Law is requested, in light of the Inter-American Court's decision.

In 2011, the Brazilian government issued Law no. 12.527, which regulates access to information contained in public documents and provides that 'no access to information necessary for the judicial or administrative supervision of fundamental rights can be denied' and that 'information or documents that deal with actions involving the violation of human rights practiced by public officials or under the authority of public authorities may not be the object of restricted access'. Most of the documents of this nature have been transferred to the National Archive and have been made available for consultation.

The problem of unidentified archives, however, remains unsolved, because the military continues to deny the existence of documents from that period. Whenever asked, the armed forces claim the documents were destroyed. I do not believe that is what happened, but until now it has not been possible to counter this claim with hard evidence.

In the same vein, in view of the decision of the Inter-American Court and existing claims in the country, the Brazilian government published Law 12.528/2011 and, on 16 May 2012, it established the

National Truth Commission (NTC). The NTC operated from 2012 to 2014 and produced an extensive report with twenty-nine recommendations.[7] The NTC recognized and confirmed the existence of 434 cases of deaths and disappearances of political activists by state agents and indicated the names of 377 public officials responsible for these crimes.

This apparently 'small' number of deaths is due to the fact that the NTC was restricted to counting the number of deaths of political activists in situations of resistance or armed conflict. The deaths of indigenous populations, peasants, miners or child victims of epidemics are not calculated. If they were, the number of deaths would easily exceed thirty thousand. It should also be remembered that more than thirty-five thousand people in the country have been compensated by the Amnesty Commission due to political persecution and, in most cases, torture, as I have already mentioned.

Because of its brief period in operation, I would refrain from saying that the National Truth Commission brought to light a great deal of new information, but it can be said that it has made a substantial compilation of existing information. Its recommendations are also very important, suggesting the creation of a permanent body to follow up and monitor compliance with its recommendations, as well as strengthening existing commissions such as the CEMDP and the Amnesty Commission. Among the recommendations are also included the withdrawal of the Amnesty Law for agents of the state for accountability purposes, intensifying search efforts for the bodies of political activists, and the demilitarization of the police.

With regard to the demand to search for the bodies, the Brazilian government has engaged more fully in searching for the Araguaia bodies due to the international conviction. These explorations have had different institutional formats over time. At first, they were led by the army itself. Only recently have these examinations been organized by the Human Rights Secretariat (HRS). Since 2016, they have been held by a working group coordinated by the HRS in cooperation with Ministry of Justice and Defence.[8] The result is that more than five million reais have already been spent in the Araguaia region, but no bodies of political militants have been found in these phases (two bodies were identified prior to the international conviction). Searches of other sites have received little or no financial resources for their implementation.

During all these years of experience in the field, it has been learned that these searches are technically extremely challenging, and also that they have been largely neglected in the past. For this reason, in 2009, we proposed a lawsuit seeking the accountability of public agencies, universities and doctors involved in the identification of the remains found in the Perus cemetery, because that work was carried out in a sloppy manner. This claim also calls for the creation of a specific budget for search and analysis teams. The case has not yet been tried, but in 2014 the city of São Paulo, the Human Rights Secretariat and Unifesp (the Federal University of São Paulo) made an agreement and resumed the investigation of the remains found in the Perus cemetery, forming the Perus Work Group (GTP, in Portuguese).

This means that those remains are finally being analysed by a multidisciplinary team composed of doctors, dentists, archaeologists and anthropologists. The work is being carried out with extreme caution. More than one thousand skeletons have been cleaned and anthropometrically analysed. The collection of samples for DNA tests and the DNA bank has been completed, respecting international protocols and techniques.

During the political decision to resume the analyses, the Human Rights Secretariat invited me to preside over the CEMDP, and in July 2014, President Dilma Rousseff appointed me to that role.

Since then, the CEMDP has developed the following activities:

- coordinating the analysis of the remains found in the Perus cemetery;
- monitoring the search activities in the Araguaia region;
- establishing the CEMDP's internal policies;
- obtaining an appointment with the president to nominate new members to the commission;
- presenting projects to obtain funding and establish permanent working groups;
- implementing administrative procedures that document the work of the commission and all measures related to the search for the bodies of each individual political disappeared;
- working with (ongoing) local truth commissions in the country;
- establishing a joint agenda with the Amnesty Commission in order to fully comply with the recommendations of the National Truth Commission, in particular regarding the reinterpretation of the Amnesty Law, the demilitarization of the military police and other measures to combat police violence, a legacy of the dictatorship.

Our priority now is to reconstitute the Special Commission on the Political Dead and Disappeared and work towards the completion of its pioneering role as a protagonist for the search of the bodies of the political disappeared – always with an eye to the future, to ensure that 'we do not forget, so it does not happen again' ('para que não se esqueça, para que não se repita').

Eugenia Augusta Gonzaga holds the office of Regional Public Prosecutor, as part of the Federal Prosecutions Office, and is the President of the Special Commission of the Political Dead and Disappeared (CEMDP). She holds a Masters in Constitutional Law from Pontifícia Universidade Católica de São Paulo, and has published extensively on disability rights. She co-authored the first legal initiatives to press for accountability of public officials involved in serious human rights violations during the Brazilian dictatorship.

Notes

1. The US had supported a military coup in Paraguay ten years earlier and would support many others in Latin America during the 1970s.
2. Such as the example of Zuleika Angel Jones, a stylist with no history of political activities who was murdered for conducting an international campaign to find her son, Stuart Angel Jones, killed by the military because of his political activities.
3. Even before the complete transition to civil power, in 1980, a group of families went to the Araguaia region in order to search for the bodies of their relatives, who had disappeared in the guerrilla context, between 1972 and 1974.
4. Comissão Especial sobre Mortos e Desaparecidos Políticos (Special Commission on Political Dead and Disappeared). *Direito à verdade e à memória*. Brasília: Secretaria Especial dos Direitos Humanos, 2007.
5. Comissão Nacional da Verdade (CNV). 'The Final Report of the Brazilian Truth Commission'. Retrieved 20 January 2018 from http://www.cnv.gov.br/index.php/outros-destaques/574-conheca-e-acesse-o-relatorio-final-da-cnv.
6. Gomes Lund and others (Araguaia Guerrilla) vs. Brasil, Series C, No. 219 (Inter-American Court of Human Rights 2010). Retrieved 20 January 2018 from http://www.corteidh.or.cr/docs/casos/articulos/seriec_219_ing.pdf.
7. Comissão Nacional da Verdade (CNV). 'The Final Report of the Brazilian Truth Commission'. Retrieved 20 January 2018 from http://www.cnv.gov.br/index.php/outros-destaques/574-conheca-e-acesse-o-relatorio-final-da-cnv.
8. The Araguaia Work Group (GTA, in Portuguese) resumed its activities in 2016 after a period with no expeditions to the region.

Bibliography

Comissão Especial sobre Mortos e Desaparecidos Políticos (Special Commission on Political Dead and Disappeared). *Direito à verdade e à memória*. Brasília: Secretaria Especial dos Direitos Humanos, 2007.

Comissão de Familiares de Mortos e Desaparecidos Políticos (Relatives Commission on Political Dead and Disappeared). *Dossiê Ditadura: Mortos e Desaparecidos Políticos no Brasil (1964–1985)*. São Paulo: Imprensa Oficial do Estado de São Paulo, 2009.

Comissão Nacional da Verdade (CNV). 'The Final Report of the Brazilian Truth Commission'. Retrieved 20 January 2018 from http://www.cnv.gov.br/index.php/outros-destaques/574-conheca-e-acesse-o-relatorio-final-da-cnv.

Gomes Lund and others (Araguaia Guerrilla) vs. Brasil, Series C, No. 219 (Inter-American Court of Human Rights 2010). Retrieved 20 January 2018 from http://www.corteidh.or.cr/docs/casos/articulos/seriec_219_ing.pdf.

Chapter 3

The Censorship of History and Fact-Finding in Brazil (1964–2018)

Antoon De Baets

History was censored in multiple ways in Brazil between 1964 and 2018, and specifically between 1964 and 1985, the period of the military dictatorship. In a broad sense, history encompasses not only the work of historians but also the work of truth commissions and similar initiatives. These commissions, in producing reports about past injustices, often act as protohistorians who write a first draft of history. This brief overview, consequently, provides some insight into the constraints within which historians and fact-finders had to work in Brazil.[1] It mines a database of cases of censorship of history that was compiled over the last three decades and covers most countries in the world for the postwar period until today. Part of it is available on the website of the Network of Concerned Historians. This summary overview is far from exhaustive but sufficiently representative to give a reliable impression of the restrictions placed on historians and human rights data collectors in Brazil since 1964.

Historical Writing

The military coup of 1964 installed a dictatorship that would last until 1985, although a period of relaxation was initiated in 1979. This was a time of harsh repression, especially during the first decade when the work climate in the universities abruptly changed. Hours after the military coup on 31 March 1964, Eremildo Luiz Viana, historian and director of the National School of Philosophy of the University of Brazil in Rio de Janeiro, occupied Radio MEC (the radio of the Ministry of Education and Culture) with the support of military troops. The radio's director, historian Maria Yedda Linhares of the same university, was removed from her post on the accusation of being a 'fanatic communist' and of 'having invited two known communists to be her instructors', including historian Hugo Weiss (who was dismissed himself). A commission of inquiry, created in May 1964 to investigate this alleged communist infiltration, did not find any evidence. The university's historians, however, would experience an atmosphere of denouncement and persecution until 1979, when the historians who had been expelled together with Linhares – Eulália Lahmeyer Lobo, a historian of the Americas living in exile, and Manoel Maurício de Albuquerque (Weiss was by now deceased) – were rehabilitated.[2]

Linhares herself was subjected to seven investigations by the military police. At a certain moment, she received permission to work in France and Britain. After her return in 1965, she participated in the anti-dictatorial movement. She was then arrested and imprisoned three times. In addition, she was dismissed in April 1969 under Ato Institucional 5 (Institutional Act 5, a military decree) of December 1968. Following protests from French historians, she was released and she went into exile in France where she worked as a historian until 1974. After her return, she was unemployed until 1977 when she started working as a historian of Brazilian agriculture. In the 1980s and 1990s she twice became secretary of education under the governor of Rio de Janeiro.[3]

A famous episode of history textbook censorship began in February 1964, just weeks before the military coup, and exploded in the weeks after it. The Ministry of Education and Culture had published five volumes of a new ten-volume history textbook series for secondary schools, *História nova do Brasil* (A New History of Brazil). The books had been written by a group of mostly young history teachers under the supervision of General Nélson Werneck Sodré. Sodré was a Marxist military historian and head of the history department at the Instituto Superior de Estudos Brasileiros (ISEB; Higher Institute of Brazilian Studies). He was considered by many as the official historian of the Partido Comunista Brasileiro (PCB; Brazilian Communist Party). The controversial textbook series focused on the Brazilian people and emphasized the economic dimension of history. Several newspapers and television channels gave voice to fierce protest against the plan to make the textbook obligatory reading throughout Brazil. In March, ISEB's premises were broken into, and documents relevant to future volumes stolen. Then came the coup. A decision to reprint two volumes that were out of stock and publish subsequent volumes with the Editora Brasiliense in São Paulo met with a hostile reception. The books were indeed edited but seized afterwards because they were said to blacken national heroes and propagate Marxist ideas. As they were deemed subversive, the ministry now withdrew its support. The military police investigated the matter, imprisoned and tortured the textbook authors and deprived them of all opportunities to lecture. With the exception of Sodré, they were exiled for many years. The textbooks were confiscated from bookshops, burned and banned, and the ISEB was closed.[4]

According to my estimate, in 1964 alone, at least nineteen professional historians were dismissed, persecuted or exiled, especially those suspected of left-wing sympathies. The newly installed military censorship affected contemporary history above all: the government did not welcome unofficial analytical studies of current conditions, and publishers consequently shifted to more distant history or issued little on contemporary Brazil. In 1972, for example, journalist and historian Hélio Silva, director of the Centro de Memória Social Brasileira (Centre for Brazilian Social Memory), interrupted the chronological order of the publication plan of his multivolume series on twentieth-century Brazilian political history, in order to avoid description of the sensitive Getúlio Vargas years (1930–45 and 1951–54), especially the period between 1937 and 1945 during which the Vargas government, inspired by Portugal's Estado Novo (New State), had taken an authoritarian turn. Instead, a volume about the year 1889 (when Brazil turned from an empire into a republic) appeared. Later, in 1977, Silva was one of the intellectuals who presented an anti-censorship petition to the minister of justice.[5]

Many of the leading historians did not escape the dictator's grip. Four of the better-known cases were those involving Jânio Quadros, Celso Furtado, José Honório Rodrigues and Caio Prado Jr. Quadros, a lawyer, historian and former president of Brazil (serving in 1961), was deprived of his political rights from 1964 to 1979. Nevertheless, *História do povo brasileiro* (History of the Brazilian People), a six-volume work of which he was the co-editor, was allowed to be published in São Paulo in 1967. In spite of this, he spent four months in internal exile in 1968 because of his public statements. After the dictatorship, he made a comeback as the mayor of São Paulo.[6] Furtado was a dependency economist internationally renowned for his retrospective studies. A minister of planning before the coup, he was forced out of his post and expelled. He went into exile and became a professor at the Sorbonne in Paris. Meanwhile, his work *La economía iberoamericana desde la conquista ibérica hasta la revolución cubana* (The Ibero-American Economy from the Iberian Conquest until the Cuban Revolution) was banned in Chile after Pinochet's coup in 1973. Furtado was granted amnesty in 1979 and returned to Brazil, where he eventually became minister of culture.[7] Around the time of the 1964 coup, director of the National Archives and historian of historiography José Honório Rodrigues was also removed from his post; he went to the United States for brief stints. Despite dire circumstances, he remained a prolific author. His collection of essays, *História combatente* (Combative History), published in 1982 when dictatorial control had become weaker, included previously banned articles on the role of chance in the historical process and the military in the era of Pedro I (1822–31).[8]

As early as the Vargas era, communist historian and politician Caio Prado Jr had clashed with the powers that be, for which he suffered frequent harassment, interrogation and imprisonment before 1964. His 1966 book *A revolução brasileira* (The Brazilian Revolution) was understood to have inspired a new generation of urban guerrillas. In 1968, he competed for a chair of Brazilian history, with a thesis entitled *História e desenvolvimento: A contribuição da historiografia para a teoria e prática do desenvolvimento brasileiro* (History and Development: The Contribution of Historiography to the Theory and Practice of Brazilian Development). According to many, Prado was the best candidate but the contest was never completed because of political interference. In the same year, he was deprived of his political rights and sentenced by a military court to four years and six months of imprisonment for a 'subversive' interview in a student magazine. The court was reportedly in doubt about whether the word 'struggle' used in the interview actually meant 'armed struggle'. The sentence was reduced on appeal. Eventually, Prado was imprisoned for almost eighteen months until his acquittal by the Supreme Military Court in 1971.[9]

Many students and staff of the history and geography department of São Paulo University were purged under the dictatorship. They were accused of participating in so-called 'parity committees for educational reform', set up in 1968. One of the victims was Maria Emília Viotti da Costa. In an inquest carried out in 1969, the military police of São Paulo accused her of spreading subversive propaganda in her classes. She was dismissed.[10] In protest against this mass dismissal of his colleagues in 1969, leading historian Sérgio Buarque de Holanda, author of *Raízes do Brasil* (Roots of Brazil; twenty-two editions by 1995), resigned from his post as a professor of the history of Brazilian civilization. Later he declared that, in the absence of a free press, he wanted the departmental minutes to bear witness to these arbitrary official acts. This was the second time that Buarque de Holanda had lost his position. The first time was in 1939, during the Vargas dictatorship, when he was an assistant professor of economic history at the University of the Federal District in Rio de Janeiro: he was dismissed for his socialist sympathies.[11]

Some historians and history teachers became actively involved in political or military resistance. One of them was Dulce Pandolfi, who in 1968 was a politically active student of social sciences at the Federal University of Pernambuco in Recife. She joined the Ação Libertadora Nacional (National Liberation Action), a left-wing armed organization led by Carlos Marighella. Persecuted, she fled to Rio de Janeiro, where she was arrested in August 1970. During her detention at the Destacamento de Operações de Informações – Centro de Operações de Defesa Interna (DOI-CODI; Department of Information Operations – Centre for Internal Defence Operations), the intelligence and repression agency, she was tortured for more than three months. She was used as a guinea pig to demonstrate torture techniques and simulated executions during classes for DOI-CODI recruits. In late 1970, she was transferred to other prisons until her conditional release in December 1971. She became a historian specializing in Brazilian political history and political sociology. In May 2013 she testified about her experiences before the Comissão Nacional da Verdade (National Truth Commission).[12] Jacob Gorender's fate was similar. A leader of the Partido Comunista Brasileiro Revolucionário (PCBR; Revolutionary Brazilian Communist Party), he was imprisoned in January 1970 and tortured by the DOI-CODI in Rio de Janeiro before his release a year later. In 1978 he published *O escravismo colonial* (Colonial Slavery), reportedly largely written in prison.[13]

Pandolfi and Gorender survived but others were killed for their political or armed resistance. One of them, in 1972, was history teacher Antonio Benetazzo, also a member of the Ação Libertadora Nacional.[14] Among those who disappeared were Ivan Mota Dias, a history student who was also a member of an armed group, in 1971, and Vandick Reidner Pereira Coqueiro, a history teacher and guerrilla fighter, in 1974.[15] History professor Afonso Henrique Martins Saldanha, president of the teachers' union of Rio de Janeiro, was imprisoned in 1970; he died in 1974 when he was released from prison after complications resulting from the torture he had undergone.[16]

Two examples of historians who went into exile were Ciro Cardoso and Ângela de Castro Gomes. While he was completing his PhD thesis in France, Marxist-inspired historian Cardoso was named in military police investigations; he decided not to return and spent the years from 1971 to 1979 in Costa Rica and Mexico.[17] De Castro was registered and watched by the police because of her (nonviolent) political activism; in 1971 she went to France for about a year.[18]

The case of Luiz Basílio Rossi, although fairly typical of what could happen with historians actively interested in politics, deserves special mention. In 1972–73 the human rights organization Amnesty International decided to expand its mandate with an international campaign against torture. Not only did it publish an influential report against torture worldwide and lead a successful lobby for what was to become the United Nations Convention against Torture in 1984, it also started the quick distribution of casesheets regarding individuals at immediate risk of torture. The first ever such campaign worldwide was for Rossi. A professor of Brazilian history at various higher education institutions, he was abducted by the military in 1973 and tortured, apparently because of his friendship with politically active persons. He was released on bail in October, and in February 1974 went into exile to Belgium. Meanwhile, his trial took place in March 1975; he was not sentenced but an arrest order was issued.[19]

As the dictatorship waned in the 1980s, more democratic conditions gradually prevailed. This was not always the case, however, as demonstrated by the suspension in 2001 of part 15 of the series *Sociedade e história do Brasil* (Society and History of Brazil). Written by historian Marco Antonio Villa and distributed to public schools and libraries, this booklet criticized the government of President Fernando Henrique Cardoso (in office 1995–2002). Other parts of the series were also attacked. Part 1, about Brazil's independence in 1822, for example, met with criticism by the governor of Minas Gerais state because it maintained that the Inconfidência Mineira (Minas Gerais conspiracy), a rebellion in 1789, had been organized by the elite in that state for economic reasons. Part 13, about the 1964–85 dictatorship, was criticized by Member of Parliament Yeda Crusius – after she had sought the advice of two historians who remained anonymous – and by a group of ex-military, apparently because the text mentioned the thousands of victims of human rights violations in that period and because it defended the thesis that fear of initiating reforms under President João Goulart (in office 1961–64) was the principal reason for the coup in 1964.[20]

The dictatorial past lingers on in the collective memory until the present day. In the run-up to the presidential elections of 28 October 2018, historian Janaína de Almeida Teles and her mother Maria Amélia de Almeida Teles were interviewed on television about their experience as victims of torture under the military dictatorship during the broadcast time of one of the two presidential candidates, Fernando Haddad. Both were promptly subjected to a wave of attacks on social media, including death threats, by adherents of the other presidential candidate, Jair Bolsonaro (who won the elections). In December 1972 Maria Amélia de Almeida Teles and her husband, two members of the

Partido Comunista do Brasil (PCdoB), had been imprisoned and tortured in the DOI-CODI detention centre in São Paulo, including by the prison's director, colonel Carlos Alberto Brilhante Ustra. Janaína Teles and her brother, then five and four years respectively, were kidnapped by the Operação Bandeirante (Oban), also under Ustra's command, and forced to attend the torture sessions of their parents. In 2008, the Tribunal de Justiça (Court of Justice) in São Paulo declared that Ustra had been a torturer. Punishment of his crimes, however, was prevented by the 1979 amnesty law. Janaína Teles specialized in the history of the military dictatorship.[21]

More distant periods of Brazilian history were generally less subject to public controversy, although the situation did sometimes become tense. In 2000, for example, the police impeded a protest march organized by two thousand indigenous leaders from across Brazil during the quincentenary of the arrival of the first Portuguese explorers to Brazil in 1500. The violence employed by shock troops against the indigenous activists led the president of the official indigenous institute Fundação Nacional do Índio (FUNAI; National Indian Foundation) to resign in protest.[22]

The writing of biographies was seriously hampered when the civil code was reformed in 2002, making it mandatory for biographical films and books to receive authorization from the biographee prior to their public release. This caused many authors to practice self-censorship. In addition, several celebrities – such as Garrincha, Pelé, Roberto Carlos, Vinicius de Moraes, Ruy Castro, Teixeirinha and Di Cavalcanti – initiated defamation cases against journalists and historians who risked publishing their unauthorized biographies. After several failed attempts to have the clause repealed on the grounds that it encouraged censorship, the Chamber of Deputies passed the so-called 'biographies law' in 2014, allowing the disclosure of biographical information without prior authorization.[23]

Like the historians discussed above, fact-finding commissions encountered similar obstacles when they tried to cope with the violent past.

Fact-Finding

Specifics about fact-finders between 1964 and 1979, when a certain relaxation of the dictatorship set in, are virtually unknown to this author, but from 1979 onwards their history was quite eventful. During the twilight years of the dictatorship (1979–85), an almost unbelievable secret operation of source collection and fact-finding took place. It started when an amnesty law, promulgated in August 1979, gave lawyers piecemeal access to the records of the Supreme Military Court in order to enable them to prepare amnesty requests on behalf of political prisoners. In collaboration with the Catholic Church and the World Council of Churches, a team of these lawyers patiently and secretly photocopied and microfilmed the court's complete archives and stored duplicates abroad for safekeeping. The files contained complete records of all 707 political cases tried in military courts between 1964 and 1979 – 850,000 pages in total. The copying was done secretly because the amnesty law deterred investigation. In addition, when caught, the lawyers faced reprisals and the archives risked being destroyed. The analysis of the materials led to a twelve-volume, 6,946-page report, indicated as 'Project A'. A summary of this material was published as *Brasil: Nunca mais* (Brazil: Never Again) in July 1985, a few months after the return to democracy. The report became the top nonfiction bestseller in Brazilian literary history. It described 1,918 accounts of torture from 1964 to 1979. A list with the names of 444 torturers was made public separately in November 1985. The team of authors maintained its anonymity even after the book was published. Years later, in August 2013, a website containing all the 'Project A' materials was launched.[24]

Once the dictatorship had fallen, the files that contained or could contain incriminating evidence of the two decades of repression became the subject of heated controversy. Human rights groups and relatives of those tortured, disappeared and assassinated under the dictatorship sought unimpeded access to personal files – and sometimes risked death threats for their efforts.[25] In 1988, the relatives of forty disappeared submitted a petition to the Supremo Tribunal Federal (Supreme Court) under the new *habeas data* constitutional provision, which established the right of access to personal files, including those held by the security services.[26]

This lack of access to the repression archives also stalled the historical debate about recent Brazilian history, as one leading historian, Carlos Fico, repeatedly signalled. The Brazilian Historical Association protested against an executive order, issued in late 2002, which extended the classification of many official documents for an additional thirty to fifty years.[27] In another development, thousands of pages of documents believed to have been destroyed were rediscovered in 2004. The military and state intelligence agencies had alleged that these documents had been legally incinerated after the return to democracy in 1985, but they had in fact been kept in secret archives.

Although they were rescued, it later transpired that many of these files were kept in deplorable circumstances.[28]

An official report published by the Secretaria Especial dos Direitos Humanos (SEDH; Special Secretariat for Human Rights) in 2007 after eleven years of research by its Comissão Especial sobre Mortos e Desaparecidos Políticos (CEMDP; Special Commission on Political Deaths and Disappearances), *Direito à memória e à verdade* (Right to Truth and Memory), shed light on 475 cases of torture and disappearance during the dictatorship. It was an official recognition that human rights violations had been committed during that era.[29] However, many armed forces archives on other disappearances or on the suppression of the communist guerrilla uprising in the Araguaia region, state of Pará, in 1967–74, remained closed. A short time later, the Supreme Court ordered the armed forces to open these secret files.[30]

In 2009, the Inter-American Commission on Human Rights intervened in the controversy. It stated that neither time bars nor the 1979 amnesty could be applied to the crimes against humanity committed under the dictatorship – a view examined but not shared by the Supreme Court in 2010.[31] However, six months later, the Inter-American Court of Human Rights found that Brazil had violated the right to the truth ('direito à verdade') by not adequately investigating the disappearances of sixty-eight peasants and Araguaia guerrillas and that the amnesty law could not be used to block prosecutions in cases of grave human rights violations.[32]

In July 2012, around the time that the newly installed National Truth Commission again fuelled discussions about the dictatorial past, the office of Tortura nunca mais (Torture Never Again), a civil society group raising awareness of the repression during the dictatorship, was burglarized and archives containing reports on torture victims were stolen.[33] In its 2014 report, the National Truth Commission endorsed the Inter-American Court of Human Rights' view on the amnesty law. The report identified 377 individuals responsible for human rights violations under the dictatorship. As of December 2018, the Supreme Court's re-examination of the validity of the amnesty law is pending.

More recently, other setbacks have been noted. In September 2016, the newly installed government of President Michel Temer appointed twenty new members to and removed six members from the Amnesty Commission (established to propose laws and reparations for the victims of the dictatorship). Among the new members was Paulo Lopo Saraiva, a former army sergeant during the military regime who had participated in repression activities during the 1964 coup against Goulart. The Movimento por verdade, memória, justiça e reparação (Movement for Truth, Memory, Justice and Reparation) called this a dismantling of the commission. It was the first time since its establishment that commission members had been removed.[34]

Impunity was not limited to dictatorship-era crimes, as two cases from the 1990s prove. The first involved a historian; the second a centre for popular memory. Although the cases were related to neither history nor memory, they throw light on the activism of historians in the first case, on an organization that focuses on memory, among other things, in the second case, and on the level of violence in both cases (the victims were killed). In June 1994, poet and historian Hermógenes da Silva Almeida Filho and lawyer Reinaldo Guedes Miranda were shot dead in Rio de Janeiro. They were members of the human rights commission of the local council that monitored the investigation into two massacres of street children. Both had also reported that they had received threatening notes, apparently relating to their activities on behalf of black people and homosexuals.[35] In 1996, Francisco Gilson Nogueira de Carvalho, a lawyer of the Centro de Direitos Humanos e Memória Popular (Centre for Human Rights and Popular Memory) in Natal, was shot dead because he had looked into the connections between a death squad ('the golden boys') and local authorities in Rio Grande do Norte. An official investigation into his killing was discontinued a year later because sufficient evidence could not be found. In 1997, the parents sued the state for lack of due diligence while investigating the facts surrounding their son's death. In 2006, however, the Inter-American Court of Human Rights ruled that it had not been demonstrated that Brazil had violated the right to a fair trial and the right to judicial protection in view of the limited factual support available to it.[36]

From this quick survey, it is clear that fact-finding efforts alternated between success and failure.

Epilogue: Brazil's Dancing Procession

It is difficult to draw general conclusions from this overview. Some of the developments described here have been summarized or illustrated with only a few examples taken from many. In addition, a major problem is that censorship is a phenomenon that by definition censors want to hide. Much stays in the dark. We can be certain that for every development described here, another has stayed under the radar, especially in a country with such a wide array of theatres as Brazil. No firm trends can be distilled from it, except for the most general (and obvious) one: historical writing and fact-finding wither in dictatorial conditions and flourish in democratic ones. But even in democracies, little can be taken for granted. For every triumph in terms of openness and understanding, there is a setback when human rights archives are inaccessible, reports withheld, findings distorted and authors intimidated or dismissed. The road to truth, justice and reparation is long and winding.

Antoon De Baets is Professor of History, Ethics and Human Rights at the University of Groningen, the Netherlands. He has written 185 publications, including *Responsible History* (Berghahn, 2009) and *Crimes against History* (Routledge, 2019). Since 1995, he has coordinated the Network of Concerned Historians. He is also writing about the relationship between historical writing and democracy, the legal framework of historical writing, and a human rights approach to the past. A full biography can be found at http://www.concernedhistorians.org/va/cv.pdf.

Notes

1. I am grateful to the following colleagues for their personal communications: Estevão de Rezende Martins (1995, 2010), Nanci Leonzo (1995), Ciro Cardoso (2000), Norbert Duys (2001), Pedro Caldas (2010), Patricia Santos Hansen (2013), Rodrigo Sá Motta Patto (2013), Johnny Roberto Rosa (2013), Meize Lucas (2013) and Nina Schneider (2018). All links were last checked on 10 December 2018.
2. M. de Moraes Ferreira, 'The Dark Side of the Force: The Military Dictatorship and the History Course of the National School of Philosophy of the University of Brazil (FNFi/UB)', *História da historiografia* 11 (April 2013), 75–79.
3. J.G. Moreas and J.M. Rego (eds), *Conversas com historiadores brasileiros* (São Paulo, 2002), 35; V. Saul and T. Murillo, 'Maria Yedda Linhares: sua trajetória, suas histórias e opiniões', *Humanas* (interview, July 1998), URL link is no longer functional.
4. P.T. Johnson, 'Academic Press Censorship under Military and Civilian Regimes: The Argentine and Brazilian Cases, 1964–1975', *Luso-Brazilian Review* 15(1) (1978), 22–23; Moraes Ferreira, 'Dark Side of the Force', 71–72; C.A. Carneiro Benevides, L.M. Paschoal Guimarães and N. Leonzo, 'Nationalisme et marxisme dans l'enseignement de l'histoire du Brésil', paper presented at the 18th International Congress of Historical Sciences, Montréal, 1995); R.A. Gorman (ed.), *Biographical Dictionary of Marxism* (Westport, CT, 1986), 312–13; J.N. Green, 'Facing the Past', *Hemisphere: A Magazine of the Americas* 15 (2005), 22–25; C. Moura, 'Climate of Terror',

Index on Censorship 4 (1979), 8–10; D. Jones (ed.), *Censorship: A World Encyclopedia*, vol. 1 (London and Chicago, 2001), 288; S.B. Liss, *Marxist Thought in Latin America* (Berkeley and Los Angeles, 1984), 123–26; T.E. Skidmore, 'The Historiography of Brazil, 1889–1964', *Hispanic American Historical Review*, part 1, 55(4) (1975), 727; B.A. Tenenbaum (ed.), *Encyclopedia of Latin American History and Culture* (New York, 1996), 5: 139–40; Comissão Nacional da Verdade, *Relatório* (Brasília, 2014), 2: 22–23, 33.

5. R.M. Levine, *Historical Dictionary of Brazil* (Metuchen, 1979), 198; Comissão Nacional da Verdade, *Relatório*, 1: 654.
6. I. Beloch and A. Alves de Abreu, *Dicionário histórico-biográfico brasileiro, 1930–1983* (Rio de Janeiro, 1984), 2854–55; R.J. Alexander (ed.), *Biographical Dictionary of Latin American and Caribbean Political Leaders* (New York, 1988), 371–72; L. Mooney (ed.), *Annual Obituary 1992* (Chicago and London, 1993), 38–41; Levine, *Historical Dictionary*, 177; Skidmore, 'Historiography of Brazil', 1: 729; Tenenbaum, *Encyclopedia*, 4: 503–4.
7. G. Martinière, 'Problèmes du développement de l'historiographie brésilienne', *Storia della Storiografia* 19 (1991), 137, 139; Beloch and Alves de Abreu, *Dicionário histórico-biográfico*, 1414–17; M. Sanders, 'Book Burning and Brutality', *Index on Censorship* 1 (1974), 10; J.L. Love, *Crafting the Third World: Theorizing Underdevelopment in Rumania and Brazil* (Stanford, CA, 1996), 153–71; T.E. Skidmore, 'The Historiography of Brazil, 1889–1964', *Hispanic American Historical Review*, part 2, 56(1) (1976), 89–90; Tenenbaum, *Encyclopedia*, 2: 631.
8. J.H. Rodrigues, *História da História do Brasil* (São Paulo, 1979), 1: ix–x; J.D. Wirth, 'An Interview with José Honório Rodrigues', *Hispanic American Historical Review* 64(2) (1984), 227; S.J. Stein, 'José Honório Rodrigues (1913–1987)', *Hispanic American Historical Review* 68(3) (1988), 573–76; Tenenbaum, *Encyclopedia*, 4: 589–90.
9. Amnesty International, *Report* (London), (1969–70), 20 and (1970–71), 62; J. Dassin (ed.), *Torture in Brazil: A Report by the Archdiocese of São Paulo* (originally Portuguese 1985; translation J. Wright) (New York, 1986), 133; Gorman, *Biographical Dictionary*, 268–69; F. Iglésias (ed.), *Caio Prado Júnior* (São Paulo, 1982), 13–21, 29, 32–34, 36; *Index on Censorship* 4(10) (1979); 5 (1981), 14; Liss, *Marxist Thought*, 116–19; Love, *Crafting the Third World*, 178–80; Skidmore, 'Historiography of Brazil', 2: 99; Tenenbaum, *Encyclopedia*, 4: 464–65.
10. Dassin, *Torture in Brazil*, 116–17.
11. L. Boia (ed.), *Great Historians of the Modern Age: An International Dictionary* (Westport, CT, 1991), 86–88; R.M. Morse, 'Sérgio Buarque de Holanda (1902–82)', *Hispanic American Historical Review* 63(1) (1983), 147–50; Tenenbaum, *Encyclopedia*, 3: 200–201. During the Vargas dictatorship (1937–45), historians and sociologists such as Gilberto Freyre, Octávio Tarquínio de Sousa, Caio Prado Jr and Buarque de Holanda were watched as political suspects – and silenced, dismissed or exiled. At the end of this authoritarian period (in 1945), the archives of the political

police were deliberately burned. When Vargas's second presidency ended with his suicide in 1954, the historian José María de Albuquerque Bello abstained from investigating it in the updated 1958 version of his *História da República,* claiming 'insurmountable difficulties in clarifying ... mysteries'. 'Gilberto Freyre', in P. Burgess et al., *Annual Obituary 1987* (Chicago and London, 1990), 351; Dassin, *Torture in Brazil,* xv, 5 (Müller); Boia, *Great Historians,* 85 (Bello).

12. Comissão Nacional da Verdade, *Relatório,* 1: 153–54, 729; Dassin, *Torture in Brazil,* 14–15.
13. Comissão Nacional da Verdade, *Relatório,* 1: 552.
14. Comissâo dos Familiares dos Mortos e Desaparecidos Políticos, Instituto de Estudo da Violência do Estado (IEVE) and Grupo Tortura Nunca Mais-RJ e PE, *Dossiê dos mortos e desaparecidos políticos a partir de 1964* (Recife, 1995), 135–36; Comissão Nacional da Verdade, *Relatório,* 3: 1071–73.
15. Comissâo dos Familiares, *Dossiê,* 311–12, 396; Comissão Nacional da Verdade, *Relatório,* 3: 608–10, 1587–89.
16. Comissâo dos Familiares, *Dossiê,* 235; Comissão Nacional da Verdade, *Relatório,* 3: 1739–40.
17. V. Saul and T. Murillo, 'Entrevista com Ciro Flamarion Cardoso', *Humanas* (interview, June 1998).
18. A.H. Lopes, I. Lustosa and J. Rouchou, 'Ângela de Castro Gomes: Entrevista', *Escritos III* ([2011]), 313–42.
19. Amnesty International, *Report* (London) (1972–73), 47; (1973–74), 38; and (1974–75), 66; *Index on Censorship* 2 (1973).
20. R. Ulhôa, 'PSDB suspende livro sobre era FHC', *Folha de São Paulo,* 3 November 2001; 'Fascículo 15 tinha críticas à gestão FHC', *Folha de São Paulo,* 3 November 2001; 'Historiador se diz censurado', *Folha de São Paulo,* 3 November 2001.
21. Comissão Nacional da Verdade, *Relatório* (Brasília 2014), 1: 368–369, 385, 407, 410, 954; 'Edson e Janaína Teles,' *Memórias da Ditadura* (no date); A. Palmar, 'Mortos e desaparecidos políticos: reparação ou impunidade?' *Documentos Revelados* (29 June 2012); R. Domingos, 'Julgamento mostra que ferida do regime militar ainda não sarou' (1 November 2006).
22. Amnesty International, *Report 2001* (London, 2001), 56; Human Rights Watch, *World Report 2001* (New York, 2000), 105.
23. P. Araújo, 'Editora aceita recolher livro de Roberto Carlos, que desiste de indenização', *Notícias da Globo,* 7 April 2007; R. Spuldar, 'No History Lessons', *Index on Censorship* 42(3) (2013), 133–35; S. Marques, 'Brazil's Banned Biographies: When Public Figures Want to Control the Message', *Index on Censorship,* 16 July 2014.
24. All documents can be found at http://bnmdigital.mpf.mp.br/pt-br. See also Dassin, *Torture in Brazil,* ix–xviii, 4–7; Green, 'Facing the Past', 22–25; Jones, *Censorship,* 1: 281–82; L. Weschler, *A Miracle, a Universe: Settling Accounts with Torturers* (New York, 1990), 7–79.

25. I.X. Pereira, *O direito à nossa história: a luta dos familiares dos mortos e desaparecidos políticos* (Brasília, 1996); Amnesty International, *Report 1999* (London, 1999), 106.
26. Amnesty International, *Report* 1989 (London, 1989), 110; Human Rights Watch, *World Report 1999* (New York, 1998), 107; Pereira, *O direito*.
27. Green, 'Facing the Past', 22–25; C. Fico, 'Ditadura militar brasileira: aproximações teóricas e historiográficas', *Tempo & Argumento: Revista de história do tempo presente* 9(20) (2017).
28. Amnesty International, *Report 2006* (London, 2006), 76; Green, 'Facing the Past', 22–25; Human Rights Watch, *World Report 2006* (New York, 2006), 171; L. Rohter, 'Hidden Files Force Brazil to Face Its Past', *New York Times*, 31 January 2005, 6.
29. Comissão Especial sobre Mortos e Desaparecidos Políticos, *Direito à memória e à verdade* (Brasília, 2007).
30. See also Associação Nacional de História (ANPUH), *O STF não sabe o que é história* (2012); Amnesty International, *Report* (London) (2005), 60, 63 and (2008), 74; Human Rights Watch, *Brazil: Prosecute Dictatorship-Era Abuses: Landmark International Decision Provides Powerful Push for Accountability* (14 April 2009); Human Rights Watch, 'Brazil: Report on Past Atrocities a Key Step Forward' (31 August 2007); Human Rights Watch, *World Report 2008* (New York, 2008), 193–94; M. Osava, 'The Long Shadow of the Dictatorship', Inter Press Service News Agency, 30 September 2009; M. Sandy, 'Digging up the Bodies: Brazil's Long Path to Justice after Military Rule', *Aljazeera America*, 7 October 2015.
31. Inter-American Commission on Human Rights, 'IACHR Takes Case against Brazil to the Inter-American Court' (press release 16/09, 8 April 2009); Inter-American Court of Human Rights, *Gomes Lund and Others (Guerrilha do Araguaia) versus Brazil: Judgment* (2010); Human Rights Watch, *Brazil: Prosecute Dictatorship-Era Abuses*; Sandy, 'Digging up the Bodies', N. Schneider, 'Impunity in Post-authoritarian Brazil: The Supreme Court's Recent Verdict on the Amnesty Law', *European Review of Latin American and Caribbean Studies* 90 (2011), 39–54.
32. Inter-American Court of Human Rights, *Gomes Lund*; Amnesty International, *Report 2011* (London, 2011), 87.
33. Simon Romero, 'Leader's Torture in the '70s Stirs Ghosts in Brazil', *New York Times*, 4 August 2012.
34. 'Temer Appoints Dictatorship Defender to Amnesty Commission', *Telesur*, 4 September 2016; *Nota pública do Movimento por verdade, memória, justiça e reparação*, Blog do Juca Kfouri, 4 September 2016.
35. Amnesty International, *Urgent Action 239/94* (17 June 1994); Amnesty International, *Report 1995* (London, 1995), 80; *Index on Censorship* 4–5 (1994), 232.
36. Inter-American Court of Human Rights, *Nogueira de Carvalho versus Brazil: Judgment* (2006); A. De Baets, 'Truth Commissions', in Jones, *Censorship*, 4: 2459–62. See also A. De Baets, 'A organizaçâo do esquecimento: Historiadores perseguidos e censurados na Africa, Asia e América

Latina', *Revista de história* (São Paulo) 134 (1996), 95–103; A. De Baets, 'Uma teoria do abuso da história', *Revista Brasileira de História* 33(65) (2013), 17–60.

Bibliography

Alexander, R.J. (ed.). *Biographical Dictionary of Latin American and Caribbean Political Leaders*. New York, 1988.

Amnesty International. *Reports*. London, 1961–.

Associação Nacional de História (ANPUH). *O STF não sabe o que é história* (2012). Retrieved 10 December 2018 from http://www.concernedhistorians.org/le/304.pdf.

Beloch, I., and Alves de Abreu, A. *Dicionário histórico-biográfico brasileiro, 1930–1983*. Rio de Janeiro, 1984.

Boia, L. (ed.). *Great Historians of the Modern Age: An International Dictionary*. Westport, CT, 1991.

Brasil: Nunca Mais (website). Retrieved 10 December 2018 from http://bnmdigital.mpf.mp.br/pt-br.

Burgess, P., et al. *Annual Obituary 1987*. Chicago and London, 1990.

Carneiro Benevides, C.A., Paschoal Guimarães, L.M., and Leonzo, N. 'Nationalisme et marxisme dans l'enseignement de l'histoire du Brésil'. Paper presented at the 18th International Congress of Historical Sciences, Montréal, 1995.

Comissão Especial sobre Mortos e Desaparecidos Políticos. *Direito à memória e à verdade*. Brasília, 2007.

Comissâo dos Familiares dos Mortos e Desaparecidos Políticos, Instituto de Estudo da Violência do Estado (IEVE) and Grupo Tortura Nunca Mais-RJ e PE. *Dossiê dos mortos e desaparecidos políticos a partir de 1964*. Recife, 1995. Retrieved 10 December 2018 from http://www.dhnet.org.br/dados/dossiers/dh/br/dossie64/br/dossmdp.pdf.

Comissão Nacional da Verdade. *Relatório*. 3 vols. Brasília, 2014. Retrieved 10 December 2018 from http://cnv.memoriasreveladas.gov.br.

Dassin, J. (ed.). *Torture in Brazil: A Report by the Archdiocese of São Paulo* (originally Portuguese 1985; translation J. Wright), New York, 1986.

De Baets, A. 'A organizaçâo do esquecimento: Historiadores perseguidos e censurados na Africa, Asia e América Latina'. *Revista de história* (São Paulo) 134 (1996), 95–103.

De Baets, A. 'Truth Commissions', in D. Jones (ed.), *Censorship: A World Encyclopedia*, vol. 4 (London and Chicago, 2001), 2459–62.

De Baets, A. 'Uma teoria do abuso da história'. *Revista Brasileira de História* 33(65) (2013), 17–60. Retrieved 10 December 2018 from http://www.scielo.br/scielo.php?script=sci_pdf&pid=S0102-01882013000100002&lng=en&nrm=iso&tlng=pt.

Domingos, R. 'Julgamento mostra que ferida do regime militar ainda não sarou' (1 November 2006). Retrieved 10 December 2018 from http://

g1.globo.com/Noticias/Politica/0,,AA1346783-5601,00-JULGAMENTO+MOSTRA+QUE+FERIDA+DO+REGIME+MILITAR+AINDA+NAO+SAROU.html.

'Edson e Janaína Teles'. *Memórias da Ditadura* (no date). Retrieved 10 December 2018 from http://memoriasdaditadura.org.br/biografias-da-resistencia/edson-e-janaina-teles/index.html.

Fico, C. 'Ditadura militar brasileira: aproximações teóricas e historiográficas'. *Tempo & Argumento: Revista de história do tempo presente* 9(20) (2017). Retrieved 10 December 2018 from http://revistas.udesc.br/index.php/tempo/article/view/2175180309202017005/6755.

Gorman, R.A. (ed.). *Biographical Dictionary of Marxism*. Westport, CT, 1986.

Green, J.N. 'Facing the Past'. *Hemisphere: A Magazine of the Americas* 15 (2005), 22–25.

Human Rights Watch. *Brazil: Prosecute Dictatorship-Era Abuses: Landmark International Decision Provides Powerful Push for Accountability*. 14 April 2009. Retrieved 10 December 2018 from https://www.hrw.org/news/2009/04/14/brazil-prosecute-dictatorship-era-abuses.

Human Rights Watch. *Brazil: Report on Past Atrocities a Key Step Forward*. 31 August 2007. Retrieved 10 December 2018 from https://www.hrw.org/news/2007/08/30/brazil-report-past-atrocities-key-step-forward.

Human Rights Watch. *World Reports*. New York, 1990–.

Iglésias, F. (ed.). *Caio Prado Júnior*. São Paulo, 1982.

Iglesias, F. 'Situation de l'histoire et des historiens du Brésil', in R. Rémond (ed.), *Être historien aujourd'hui* (Paris, 1988), 47–66.

Index on Censorship, 1972–.

Inter-American Commission on Human Rights. 'IACHR Takes Case against Brazil to the Inter-American Court'. Press release 16/09, 8 April 2009.

Inter-American Court of Human Rights. *Nogueira de Carvalho versus Brazil: Judgment* (2006). Retrieved 10 December 2018 from http://www.concernedhistorians.org/le/562.pdf.

Inter-American Court of Human Rights. *Gomes Lund and Others (Guerrilha do Araguaia) versus Brazil: Judgment* (2010). Retrieved 10 December 2018 from http://www.concernedhistorians.org/le/224.pdf.

Johnson, P.T. 'Academic Press Censorship under Military and Civilian Regimes: The Argentine and Brazilian Cases, 1964–1975'. *Luso-Brazilian Review* 15(1) (1978), 3–25.

Jones, D. (ed.). *Censorship: A World Encyclopedia*, vol. 1. London and Chicago, 2001.

Levine, R.M. *Historical Dictionary of Brazil*. Metuchen, 1979.

Liss, S.B. *Marxist Thought in Latin America*. Berkeley and Los Angeles, 1984.

Lopes, A.H., Lustosa, I., and Rouchou, J. 'Ângela de Castro Gomes: Entrevista'. *Escritos III* ([2011]), 313–42.

Love, J.L. *Crafting the Third World: Theorizing Underdevelopment in Rumania and Brazil.* Stanford, CA, 1996.

Marques, S. 'Brazil's Banned Biographies: When Public Figures Want to Control the Message'. *Index on Censorship*, 16 July 2014. Retrieved 10

December 2018 from https://www.indexoncensorship.org/2014/07/forbidden-books-brazil-biographies-law-can-put-end-previous-censorship-may-bring-post-censorship.

Martinière, G. 'Problèmes du développement de l'historiographie brésilienne'. *Storia della Storiografia* 19 (1991), 117–46.

Mooney, L. (ed.). *Annual Obituary 1992*. Chicago and London, 1993.

Moraes Ferreira, M. de. 'The Dark Side of the Force: The Military Dictatorship and the History Course of the National School of Philosophy of the University of Brazil (FNFi/UB)'. *História da historiografia* 11 (April 2013), 65–84. Retrieved 10 December 2018 from https://www.historiadahistoriografia.com.br/revista/article/download/631/346.

Moreas, J.G., and Rego, J.M. (eds). *Conversas com historiadores brasileiros*. São Paulo, 2002.

Morse, R.M. 'Sérgio Buarque de Holanda (1902–82)'. *Hispanic American Historical Review* 63(1) (1983), 147–50.

Moura, C. 'Climate of Terror'. *Index on Censorship* 4 (1979), 8–10.

Network of Concerned Historians. *Annual Reports*, 1995–. Retrieved 10 December 2018 from http://www.concernedhistorians.org/content/ar.html.

Nota pública do Movimento por verdade, memória, justiça e reparação. Blog do Juca Kfouri. 4 September 2016. Retrieved 10 December 2018 from http://blogdojuca.uol.com.br/2016/09/nota-publica-do-movimento-por-verdade-memoria-justica-e-reparacao.

Osava, M. 'The Long Shadow of the Dictatorship'. Inter Press Service News Agency, 30 September 2009. Retrieved 10 December 2018 from http://www.ipsnews.net/2009/09/rights-brazil-the-long-shadow-of-the-dictatorship.

Palmar, A. 'Mortos e desaparecidos políticos: reparação ou impunidade? *Documentos Revelados* (29 June 2012). Retrieved 10 December 2018 from http://www.documentosrevelados.com.br/livros/mortos-e-desaparecidos-politicos-reparacao-ou-impunidade.

Pereira, I.X. *O direito à nossa história: a luta dos familiares dos mortos e desaparecidos políticos*. Brasília, 1996.

Rodrigues, J.H. *História da História do Brasil*. São Paulo, 1979.

Rohter, L. 'Hidden Files Force Brazil to Face Its Past'. *New York Times*, 31 January 2005. Retrieved 10 December 2018 from http://www.nytimes.com/2005/01/31/world/americas/hidden-files-force-brazil-to-face-its-past.html.

Sanders, M. 'Book Burning and Brutality'. *Index on Censorship* 1 (1974), 7–13.

Sandy, M. 'Digging up the Bodies: Brazil's Long Path to Justice after Military Rule'. *Aljazeera America*, 7 October 2015. Retrieved 10 December 2018 from http://america.aljazeera.com/multimedia/2015/10/brazil-victims-of-military-see-measure-of-justice.html.

Schneider, N. 'Impunity in Post-authoritarian Brazil: The Supreme Court's Recent Verdict on the Amnesty Law'. *European Review of Latin American and Caribbean Studies* 90 (2011), 39–54.

Skidmore, T.E. 'The Historiography of Brazil, 1889–1964'. *Hispanic American Historical Review*, part 1, 55(4) (1975), 716–48; part 2, 56(1) (1976), 81–109.
Spuldar, R. 'No History Lessons'. *Index on Censorship* 42(3) (2013), 133–35.
Stein, S.J. 'José Honório Rodrigues (1913–1987)'. *Hispanic American Historical Review* 68(3) (1988), 573–76.
'Temer Appoints Dictatorship Defender to Amnesty Commission.' *Telesur* (4 September 2016). Retrieved 10 December 2018 from https://www.telesurenglish.net/news/Temer-Appoints-Dictatorship-Defender-to-Amnesty-Commission-20160903-0023.html.
Tenenbaum, B.A. (ed.). *Encyclopedia of Latin American History and Culture*. 5 vols. New York, 1996.
Weschler, L. *A Miracle, a Universe: Settling Accounts with Torturers*. New York, 1990.
Wirth, J.D. 'An Interview with José Honório Rodrigues'. *Hispanic American Historical Review* 64(2) (1984), 217–232.

Chapter 4

Democratic Transition and Conciliation

Human Rights and the Legacy of the Brazilian Dictatorship

Janaína de Almeida Teles

The Political Disappeared and the Imposition of Silence and Forgetting

The dictatorship period in Brazil was marked by practices that alternated between hiding and revealing political repression, combining the regime's intention to legitimize itself with the need to spread fear. Repression was selective and posed a permanent threat. This policy was made clear through exemplary cases of persecuted people who were harshly tortured in clandestine centres. The repressive apparatus also made use of public cemeteries and prisons where murdered dissidents were buried under false names and causes of death.[1]

The formation of a network of clandestine units intensified gradually after the 1964 coup and the socio-political pressures that followed from the repressive Institutional Act no. 5/AI-5 of December 1968, giving rise to the repression system known as the DOI-Codi system (Department of Information Operations – Centre for Internal Defence Operations). The DOI-Codi was controlled by the army but had a certain degree of operational autonomy.[2] The DOI-Codi system combined several modalities of repression and included such broad and diverse spheres as clandestine extermination centres, the prison system and the military justice system. Implementing this system required the structuring of a sophisticated bureaucratic state apparatus and high levels of collaboration between civilians and military personnel. This structuring made it possible to share responsibilities and left a certain margin for managing power and disputes within and outside the state.[3]

Thus, an extensive legislation of exception was passed and a broad administrative and institutional structure instated that often lacked efficiency. It gave 'juridical significance to a sphere of action that is itself extrajuridical', proper to the state of exception, the extreme condition of which is the suspension of the juridical order.[4] The dictatorship knew how to skilfully weave its way through the zone of indistinction between the *de jure* situation and the *de facto* situation. The maintenance of a public sphere that kept some democratic devices lent an appearance of normality and legitimacy to the regime. In spite of being a state of exception, it kept the National Congress, a moderate opposition party and a justice system in place.

The legality of the state of exception made possible the coexistence of bodies and institutions such as the concentration camps of the Araguaia Guerrilla (1972–74), the DOI-Codi, the network of clandestine extermination centres, the political police (DOPS; Department of Political and Social Order), the military justice system and prisons, one of the keys to the dictatorship's success for a relatively long period of time. These overlapping hierarchies were part of the logic of repression, which, in spite of its extent, centralized decisions about the life or death of the politically persecuted.[5]

The DOI-Codi system became the main setting for the dehumanization and depersonalization of political prisoners. There, agents of the state operated on the threshold of the laws of exception, supported by the Law of National Security (LSN). These legal loopholes opened possibilities for all kinds of clandestine practices by the organs of repression, especially the use of torture – not legalized torture, but allowed, nonetheless, given the generalization of this zone of indistinction and the huge expansion of the Executive's power.

The military justice system, in its turn, was based on several legislative acts that overlapped and were muddled with one another. The legal framework of exception became a bloated system where, in addition to the 1967 and 1969 Constitutions, more than 366 different legislative acts overlapped, among them acts of exception and supplementary and ordinary laws and acts. This legality was vital for legitimizing the regime and demobilizing political contestation.[6]

In this period, thousands of people were kidnapped and imprisoned, but only guerrilla leaders and members of the armed resistance lost their lives. The data show the selectiveness of the legal repression. In the military justice system, of the 17,420 people investigated by the police based on the LSN, 42.3 per cent were prosecuted.[7] The number of victims of extrajudicial repression followed an even more selective pattern – at least 453 people were killed or disappeared for political reasons during the dictatorship.[8]

Police violence increased with the creation of the Military Police (PM), conceived as an auxiliary and reserve force for the army, establishing extensive control of society. Trained by the army since 1969 to carry out regular policing using machine guns, its target of choice was the young, black suburban population.[9] In addition, hundreds of peasants and indigenous people were murdered as a result of land disputes. At least 1,196 peasants and 8,350 indigenous people died or disappeared during the dictatorship.[10]

In 1971, with the adoption of the DOI-Codi system at a national level and the consolidation of a centralized apparatus of repression, there began a strategic change in the repression methods of the dictatorship, which gained force in the combat of the Araguaia Guerrilla and culminated in 1974. That year, the Ernesto Geisel government (1974–79) changed its strategy and started what was called a phase of 'slow, gradual and safe' political opening. This so-called opening earned Ernesto Geisel the label of a 'moderate' military president.[11]

The opening sought to create mechanisms to ensure the regime's legitimacy and stability, heralding a new stage of institutionalization. It took place in the context of a change from the official slogan of 'development with security' of the Médici government to 'continuity without immobility'.[12] Geisel sought to carry out repressive policies more palatable to the *status quo*, which initially threatened his legitimacy because of increasing denunciations of human rights abuses, and subsequently pressured him due to the decline of the 'economic miracle' (a period of significant economic growth, which, however, was distributed in a highly unequal manner).

Up until then, the tendency of the Brazilian repressive apparatus was to murder dissidents (under torture). Later it was claimed that the killed had died as a result of shootings, being run over, or suicide. This was replaced in 1974 by 'forced disappearances', which by nature did not have to be 'explained' by the government and would later become common in Argentina and other Latin American countries.[13]

The claiming of deaths as results of shootings and suicides carried on, in accordance with Geisel's ambiguous attitude. He continued to give signs that he would eliminate any threat to his project of controlled political opening, as demonstrated by the arrest of hundreds of militants of the Brazilian Communist Party (PCB) across the country from 1974 to 1976. The PCB, however, was not part of the armed struggle and therefore did not fit in the government's main target group.

It was Geisel's intention to ensure a reduction of social tension, increasing the levels of political participation in a controlled fashion in order to co-opt elite sectors of the regime opposition. In this regard, another decisive facet of his project was an agreement that ensured that censorship was gradually removed from the newsrooms of the mainstream press. These were indications to both regime dissidents and to those who rejected his process of political opening, including military staff. The latter were wary of its consequences, especially due to their involvement with torture. They preferred that political repression would not be jettisoned, but that state violence would simply not be reported about. Censorship was entirely suspended from certain newspapers, became more selective in the case of other outlets like the *Veja* magazine, and concentrated instead on the so-called alternative press (more critical press).

Another set of measures was passed to maintain an appearance of legality that related to the voting system. By passing Act AI-2 (1965), which established indirect presidential elections and the extinction of political parties, a system was created based on bipartisanship. It was based on the idea of a 'reliable' opposition party – the Brazilian Democratic Movement (MDB), deliberately allowed by the regime. From then on, intricate laws and forms of electoral control instituted indirect elections in some executive spheres, interspersed with manipulated direct elections.[14]

With this ambiguous design, Geisel's opening strategy was not able to avoid a weakening of the dictatorship (for example a rise in denunciation campaigns and significant electoral setbacks), but was effective in laying the groundwork for a long political transition, including impunity. In the 1974 elections, the remaining left-wing Brazilians supported the MDB and the elections took a referendum-like character, which resulted in a clear victory for the opposition. This defeat, along with the rise of new social movements, threatened the government's ability to control the opening process.

Denunciations at Home and Abroad

The campaigns denouncing human rights abuses both in Brazil and abroad played a vital role in the resistance to the dictatorship. The struggle of the relatives of the political dead and disappeared was particularly important in this quest. At a national level, the Council for the Defence of Human Rights (CDDPH) created by the deposed president João Goulart demanded the investigation of human rights abuses from its foundation in 1968. The demands were encouraged by the institutional pressure exerted by the Brazilian Bar Association (OAB) and the protests against the regime that had spread across the country.

The CDDPH was contacted regarding the case of Olavo Hansen, a Trotskyist militant and trade union leader arrested on 1 January 1970 and murdered under torture at DOPS/São Paulo. The case was then widely publicized due to pressure from Brazilian and foreign unions, progressive sectors of the Catholic Church, intellectuals and students, and even reached the National Congress. However, in line with the version given by the authorities, the investigation by the Council concluded that it had been suicide, dashing the hopes of civil society and parliamentarians of the opposition.

In 1971, other cases of forced disappearance such as those of federal congressman Rubens B. Paiva, who had been stripped of his political rights, and Stuart Angel Jones (son of the famous fashion designer Zuzu Angel, murdered by the regime in 1976) were denounced at the CDDPH and filed. The Médici government changed the makeup of the Council and determined that its meetings were to be secret in order to guarantee a government majority and compliance with the regime's guidelines. In March 1972, the MDB left the CDDPH, claiming that the Council did not investigate denunciations and that by remaining in it, the party was legitimizing the dictatorship. The OAB, however, remained in the CDDPH even though it was known to be ineffective.[15]

From 1973 onwards, certain murders galvanized the public's indignation. Church services celebrated in honour of murdered regime opponents turned into mass demonstrations against the violence of the dictatorship. Those celebrated at Sé Cathedral by the Archbishop of São Paulo, Dom Paulo Evaristo Arns, became important political events. The church service held in March 1973 in remembrance of the student Alexandre Vannucchi Leme of the University of São Paulo, who was murdered under torture at the DOI-Codi/São Paulo on 17 March 1973, was one such event. The singer Sérgio Ricardo (who sang the song 'Calabouço' [Dungeon]) and three thousand people attended the ceremony in spite of intense police repression.[16]

The reaction to Vannucchi Leme's death laid the groundwork for a reorganization of the student movement, which mobilized sectors of civil society and occupied previously stifled institutional spaces. These protests helped to strengthen the networks of solidarity with political prisoners, which gradually gained public visibility and held emblematic church services such as those for journalist Vladimir Herzog in October 1975 and Santo Dias da Silva, a labour leader murdered in November 1979.

In the international sphere, in June 1970, the Inter-American Commission on Human Rights (IACHR) of the Organization of

American States (OAS) received a petition from the Latin American Confederation of Christian Trade Unions and other union bodies to investigate Hansen's death. The appeals made to the IACHR were some of the few options left for those attempting to organize denunciation campaigns against the Brazilian dictatorship.[17]

The appeals were in alignment with the denunciations of torture that had gained international publicity from 1969 to 1971, thanks to campaigns led by those in exile and banished political prisoners exchanged for kidnapped ambassadors. The main aim of these campaigns was to hit the Brazilian government where it hurt so as to overcome the obstacles to investigating the violent crimes of state repression.

Under pressure from the campaigns, the IACHR assessed thirty-three denunciations of human rights violations involving the murder and forced disappearance of Brazilian dissidents in the 1970s, but still failed to secure any sentences.[18] The exceptions were the cases of Hansen and Father Henrique (murdered in 1969), in which the Commission found the Brazilian state responsible. In its annual 1973 report, the IACHR reproached the Brazilian government for its lack of collaboration with the investigations, declaring that it had found indications of grave human rights violations in the country and advising the punishment of those responsible. Because censorship still existed, this historic decision was not made public in Brazil.[19]

In not making Brazil an actual target of pressure and criticism, the IACHR failed, but it did establish jurisprudence for other countries affected by dictatorships such as Chile and Argentina.[20] At that time, the Commission had a low profile and was not very effective. Its activities were often dictated by the logic of the Cold War and of the United States' agenda.[21]

In Europe, Amnesty International had investigated human rights violations in Brazil since 1969. After attempting several times to obtain authorization from the Brazilian government to examine on-site the denunciations it had received, in September 1972 it published a *Report on Allegations of Torture in Brazil* in London.[22] In response, the government forbade any mention of it in Brazil.[23]

From March to April 1974, denunciations of abuses in Brazil gained publicity as a result of Russell Tribunal II. Held in Rome, the second version of the tribunal began with a report read by Italian judge Salvatore Sense, in which he presented a panorama of the situation of law in Brazil. Miguel Arraes read the accusation against the country and former political prisoners and relatives testified. The tribunal found that the scope of human rights violations verified in Brazil meant that they qualified as crimes against humanity.[24]

The 'Crisis of the Disappeared' and the Removal of Parliamentarians' Political Rights

In 1974, the relatives of the politically persecuted started to organize themselves as a result of an escalation of cases of forced disappearance. The fact that there were no bodies to bury, the impossibility of mourning and the absence of a grave increased and prolonged their uncertainty and suffering.

Ever since leaders of the PCB and Ação Popular (AP), among others, had disappeared, their relatives had started to meet in lawyers' offices or in the Catholic Church's Justice and Peace Commissions (CJPs) to try and organize the search for information. The disappearances were denounced through petitions for *habeas corpus* (abolished by the AI-5) and letters addressed to the authorities and to national and international human rights bodies. In this way, the Family Members' Commission was established with the aim of denouncing and investigating these crimes.

In August 1974, Dom Paulo Evaristo Arns and the family members met confidentially with General Golbery do Couto e Silva, the Presidency's Chief of Staff, to request information about their relatives. He heard the stories of the arrests and kidnappings of twenty-two political disappeared case by case and promised to provide an answer.

As there was still no answer by January 1975, Dom Paulo began a campaign in all the churches of the diocese of São Paulo requesting information on the disappeared. The relatives then published a letter sent to military President Geisel, which led the Minister of Justice, Armando Falcão, to publish an official statement on the matter. They also went to the federal capital to ask MDB parliamentarians to support a proposal for a Parliamentary Committee of Investigation (CPI) to investigate human rights violations in the country.

The government's answer was a written statement and a speech by the Minister of Justice broadcast nationally in February, in which vague explanations were given about twenty-seven people, some of whom had not even been arrested. The OAB, sectors of the Catholic Church and liberal newspapers such as *O Estado de S. Paulo* spoke in favour of respecting human rights. The relatives appealed to the MDB in writing, reiterating their request for a CPI.

The party was split, but Lysâneas Maciel (MDB/Rio de Janeiro), a deputy from the so-called 'authentic' (more active and critical) group, obtained the necessary signatures to set up the CPI. The Minister of Justice, however, went on TV to talk about Maciel's supposed links with the PCB, which led several signatories to withdraw their signatures.

Maciel insisted, but new attempts to move the project forward to a vote were thwarted by procedural manoeuvres and pressure from the Executive, led by Arena (National Renewal Alliance) senators Jarbas Passarinho and José Sarney, who reacted in a threatening tone.[25]

The majority of the MDB retreated and changed the debate into a discussion about a CPI on multinationals and criticism of the regime's economic policy. The government did not intend to let go of its powers of exception so soon and hinted that investigations of human rights violations would be met with reprisals. The Chamber of Deputies followed in the steps of the Senate, where the two parties had come to an understanding initiated by the MDB and put 'institutional criticism' (that is, denunciations of crimes by the dictatorship) on hold, focusing instead on social and economic problems. Their silence was the outcome of the 'crisis of the disappeared'. However, the denunciations had placed a strain on the dictatorship.[26]

The creation of the CPI of the multinationals partly reflected a change in the business community's position and the beginning of a rupture in its alliance with the military. With the end of the 'economic miracle', criticism of the government's economic policy became the main argument of the opposition. The understanding coordinated by the MDB moderates, which replaced the human rights CPI with the multinationals CPI, sought to disassociate the political model from the economic model. By depoliticizing the parliamentary dispute, direct confrontation with the military was avoided, as was a possible investigation of the link between business and the 1964 coup and the repressive apparatus. Moderates and government supporters thus sought to keep their distance from the demonstrations and demands made by civil society and social movements.

The 'authentic' group continued to search for institutional loopholes to deal with the problem of human rights abuses. In the midst of this climate of terror, however, some parliamentarians protested in the National Congress. In January 1976, Geisel stripped the political rights and terms of office of two MDB deputies accused of having been helped by the PCB in the 1974 elections and criticizing the organs of repression. A fresh wave of removal of political rights included state and federal deputies such as Lysâneas Maciel. The MDB protested and demanded the end of the AI-5, but according to the party's moderates, the tone of their statement had to take into consideration that they could not 'give pretexts' for the elections at the end of that year to be cancelled.[27]

Although the arrests, threats, removal of political rights, and even murder of mothers of the disappeared – such as Zuzu Angel – continued, the phase of reorganization of the student movement had begun.[28] In 1976, Geisel continued curtailing parliamentary opposition with the Falcão Law. In April 1977, he shut down the National Congress and imposed the 'April Package', which included increasing the president's term of office to six years; indirect elections for governor; appointing a third of all senators, known as 'bionic senators'; and a change in how the number of seats per state in the Federal Chamber was calculated. In addition, the Military Police was allowed to have its own internal justice system. Although this affected the credibility of the project of political opening, the package managed to contain the opposition's electoral force, thus ensuring a government majority in Congress.[29]

In June 1977, Geisel removed the political rights of another parliamentarian, this time the leader of the MDB caucus and the 'authentic' group Alencar Furtado (MDB/Paraná) because of the impact of his recent statement given on TV and radio. In it, Furtado had paid homage to parliamentarians whose political rights had been taken away, political prisoners and the exiled, and to the disappeared and their relatives – the 'maybe, who knows?' orphans and widows.[30]

In August that year, in a context of aggravated confrontations surrounding the presidential succession, a 'Letter to the Brazilian people' by University of São Paulo Law School professor Gofredo da Silva Telles Jr, in which he demanded the end of the state of exception, marked the distancing between the military and liberals. A considerable part of the opposition, civil society and the press grew interested in campaigns for a Constituent Assembly and amnesty for political prisoners.

The Partial Amnesty and Disputes about Its Legal Interpretation

In line with the ambiguous dynamic that sustained the law of exception, Brazil fostered a peculiar process of partial amnesty in 1979. This happened as a result of political and social pressures that challenged the dictatorship's self-amnesty project. The struggle for amnesty for the politically persecuted was linked to an attempt to expose the regime's violence and involved the participation of relatives of the dead and disappeared, which proved decisive. Initially, Dom Paulo Evaristo Arns presented this political agenda at a meeting organized at the São Paulo Metropolitan Curia in December 1974. The following year, wives, mothers and sisters of political prisoners, dead and disappeared created the Women for Amnesty Movement on the occasion of International Women's Year.[31] The movement grew in size with a campaign for a broad, general and unrestricted amnesty that began in February 1978 when the first Brazilian Amnesty Committee (CBA) was created in Rio de Janeiro. The campaign achieved a certain degree of popular support as a result of the extensive public dissemination of the dictatorship's crimes. Some of the pro-amnesty rallies in state capitals such as São Paulo and Rio de Janeiro were attended by up to twenty or thirty thousand people.[32]

Their aim was amnesty for all the politically persecuted and a systematization and dissemination of the denunciations of human rights abuses in order to undermine the regime, which was showing signs of weakness. The CBAs were a legal movement to fight against the dictatorship and its ideological framework, the National Security Doctrine.

Initially, the CBAs were made up of groups of survivors of state repression and their solidarity networks. They took on the family members' demands as their political platform, which was based on the following points: clarification about the torture and political deaths and disappearances; return of mortal remains; accountability and punishment for torturers; dismantling of the repressive apparatus; and the end of the 'laws of exception'. The movement sought to broaden its alliances, establishing relations with the MDB's progressive sectors and the new social movements.[33]

In December 1978, the government revoked the AI-5 with a Constitutional Amendment. In contrast, it furthered the regime's institutionalization by incorporating measures of exception into the legislation in force and introducing a device into the Constitution that relieved any act by the dictatorship from judicial review.[34]

In March 1979, a CBA caravan went to the National Congress taking an Open Letter and a memorandum to MDB parliamentarians containing denunciations of the torture and murder of dissidents and a demand for explanation and accountability for the crimes. They also demanded the creation of a human rights CPI, going back to the proposal made in 1975.

The MDB approved the CPI proposal at its National Convention in May that year. It was a narrow vote, held during a meeting that saw many interventions by deputies. The victory was influenced by the relatives' testimonials. Deeply moved, his mother Egle Vannucchi Leme stated: 'We have no illusions about its [the CPI's] limitations, but it's a way in which to fight and we all need to keep on fighting'. Rosalina Santa Cruz concluded by saying: 'it's easy to say that we should forget everything in the name of national conciliation when there are so many families searching for their children, not knowing if they're dead or alive and what cemetery they're in. We don't want revenge, we want justice'.[35]

Those in favour of the CPI, accused of being 'revanchists' or ingenuous, asserted that it was not possible to bring torturers to the dock but that the CPI's implementation could mean the creation of a thorough record of the violence committed by the dictatorship. PCB representatives, among others, were against the proposal, arguing that the CPI could prevent the Amnesty Law from being approved. The project was vetoed by the Arena, which proposed a different CPI, thus reaching the constitutional limit allowed.[36]

In July 1979, political prisoners in Rio de Janeiro went on hunger strike to pressure the National Congress to approve a more comprehensive amnesty bill. There were differences among them over what strategies to adopt, but the hunger strike ended up spreading across the country.[37]

During this period, discussions between the MDB and the CBAs evolved into an agreement on Amendment no. 7 to the government bill presented on 9 August 1979.[38] The amendment explicitly rejected any reciprocity in the amnesty (art. 1 § 2), and proposed amnesty for the politically persecuted and an inquiry to investigate the circumstances surrounding the political disappearances (art. 15).[39]

The bill was approved in a session marked by casuism on 22 August 1979. In the morning, the National Congress was surrounded by the Military Police and demonstrators attempted to enter the gallery of the plenary hall, which ended up being opened. Due to the majority attained as a result of electoral casuism, a government victory was highly likely.

The first few votes took place in order to highlight/give preference to the MDB's bill (and, as a last resort, to deputy Djalma Marinho's [Arena/Rio Grande do Norte] amendment). They came as a surprise as they revealed a partial loss of control by the government and the adhesion of dissidents. Finally, the roll-call vote was scuppered and the military's amnesty bill was approved by the leaders of the two parties. This attitude caused criticism, but only twenty-nine of the 189 MDB deputies voted against the bill, complaining about the lack of equitability in the amnesty.[40]

The Amnesty Law was sanctioned in August 1979 by General Figueiredo. Considered 'reciprocal', it included victims and perpetrators in the light of what was considered to be a period of 'war' in which both sides had 'overstepped the mark', thus equating the violence by agents of the state with that of the guerrilla fighters. However, between 1979 and 1981, militants, relatives, jurists and lawyers such as Nilo

Batista, Seabra Fagundes and Samuel MacDowell, among others, questioned this interpretation.[41]

The law's text determines that amnesty be granted to 'political crimes or those connected to them' (§ 1 of art. 1), that is, crimes of any nature related to those committed with a political motivation – those provided in the LSN. A connected crime might be a bank robbery or car theft by militants, those who supposedly committed crimes against the regime, to support the armed struggle. However, the interpretation that the 'connected crimes' also referred to those committed by the torturers prevailed. Jurists explained that in order to characterize a connection between crimes, those who commit them must be the same people, with the same objectives and motivation, which does not apply to those who tortured and killed political prisoners and their families.[42]

Furthermore, the law did not include those who were convicted of terrorism, robbery, kidnapping or assault (§ 2 of art. 1). They were set free as a result of a reduction in the sentences stipulated by the LSN, which was reformulated in 1978, and were released from prison on probation. The amnesty was not reciprocal; it was just that the torturers remained immune to prosecution. Since the 1988 Constitution, its scope has been extended as part of a peculiar process of compensation for the victims of the dictatorship, but what was prescribed in the article was kept intact.[43]

In December 1979, the government passed a party law with a view to encouraging the creation of new parties and fragmenting the opposition, thus doing away with the bipartisan system and the plebiscitary nature of the previous elections. This strategy was successful and by the end of 1981 five parties had already been provisionally registered.[44]

Meanwhile the debate about punishing torturers came back on the political scene in February 1981, when a clandestine torture centre organized by the Army Information Centre (CIE) known as '*Casa da Morte*' ('House of Death') was found to be located in Petrópolis, in the state of Rio de Janeiro. The news provoked a harsh reaction from the military, which covered the front pages of news publications.[45] In a threatening tone, a televised statement by the armed forces made it clear that they would not admit any investigations, which rendered the debate about amnesty for torturers inviable.

Civil Accountability and the Araguaia Guerrilla Lawsuits

In the 1970s, some lawsuits were filed by relatives of the dead and disappeared to obtain information and hold the Brazilian state responsible for the crimes. These lawsuits became famous, especially after the state was found guilty of murder in the Vladimir Herzog case. The declaratory judgement action by the family requested that the state be held responsible for his arbitrary arrest, torture and death. This was the way the family found to break through the wall surrounding the judiciary. A young judge named Márcio José de Moraes issued the pioneering sentence that found the state guilty in October 1978.[46]

After the sentence was made public, another two cases were reopened, inspiring more relatives to file declaratory judgement actions in order to find out the truth in cases of disappearance or murder. The course of these suits, however, revealed the difficulty in achieving definitive sentences in the vast majority of cases.[47]

In June 1979, relatives of the disappeared of the Araguaia Guerrilla unsuccessfully attempted to question President Figueiredo in the justice system about the armed conflict in southeastern Pará that led to the disappearance of sixty-nine fighters. In the statement of claim, the families requested that the graves of their relatives be revealed, that their death certificates be handed over, transportation of their mortal remains, clarification on the circumstances surrounding their deaths and that the final report by the Ministry of War on the suppression of the guerrilla, dated January 1975, be made public.

In October 1980, the CBAs helped to organize the first expedition of relatives to the guerrilla region with the aim of finding clues as to the whereabouts of the fighters' mortal remains and obtaining testimonies from residents. Finally, in 1982 they managed to file a 'lawsuit for provision of facts' against the state in the federal justice system.[48]

In the statement of defence, the federal state did not recognize the guerrilla, denied the existence of a final report, pointed out supposed flaws in the suit and asked that it be denied based on the legal impossibility of the claim and the defendants' legitimacy, as well as the nonexistence of interest in the suit, the impropriety of punishment and because of the five-year limitation period, without considering the merits of the case.

Between 1982 and 1993, the state made all the appeals possible to postpone the trial on merits. Once the preliminary allegations were rejected, the judge granted the production of documentary and testimonial evidence, ordering the state to provide a list of civilians killed, activities carried out and the fate of the bodies, as well as all the documents regarding civilian casualties, whether official or unofficial, with indication as to the authorship of and responsibility for said documents. All the state did was attach the opinion of the Ministry of the

Army's Legal Department to the records. The plaintiffs, on the other hand, gathered a large number of documents and several testimonies.[49]

In 1993, the justice system recognized the family members' rights.[50] The state, however, argued that the plaintiffs' claims could not be considered because of the Law of the Dead and Disappeared (Law 9.140/95).[51] This was not accepted by the justice system, which stipulated a deadline by which to present the guerrilla report.[52] In the trial of merits, Judge Solange Salgado recognized that given the great amount of evidence presented, the occurrence of the Araguaia Guerrilla was undeniable. In addition, she stated that the administrative procedure established by Law 9.140/95 did not meet the plaintiffs' claims, as they were demanding their fundamental rights, such as the right to truth and to hold traditional services for the deceased.

She considered that forced disappearance is a permanent violation happening in the present, and that it only comes to an end when the victim's fate is found out and the circumstances in which the facts occurred are revealed. She also observed that the case concerned a multiple, ongoing violation of several rights recognized by Brazilian constitutional norms, with prolonged effects over time, and that disappearance is a cruel crime against humanity that goes beyond any limitation period and is meant to evade the law.[53]

Thus, she ordered a breach of the confidentiality of military information regarding all operations related to the guerrilla and established that there was to be a rigorous investigation in the armed forces in order to paint a detailed and precise picture of the operations carried out in the fight against the Araguaia Guerrilla.[54]

Over the course of this unfinished legal battle, the relatives continued to mobilize, contacting human rights defence entities in Brazil and abroad. In 1995, they resumed their practice of transnational legal mobilization and, alongside international NGOs, forwarded the case to the IACHR. The sluggishness of the Brazilian justice system was replicated by the OAS, however. Only in March 2001 did the IACHR publish its admissibility report on the claim and analyse the merit of the application, forwarding the case to the Inter-American Court of Human Rights, which led to Brazil being found guilty in 2010. The court's sentence corroborated the national legal decision and considered the Brazilian state responsible. It ordered a criminal investigation into the facts, having considered that the 'provisions of the Law of Amnesty preventing the investigation and sanction of grave human rights violations are incompatible with the American Convention on Human Rights and lack any legal effect'. At the same time, it recommended the creation of a Law of Information and a truth commission.[55] As of today, the Brazilian state has only complied with these two recommendations by the Inter-American Court.[56]

Torture and the Legacy of the Dictatorship

Despite the economic crisis, the transition to democracy – the *Diretas Já* (Direct Elections Now) campaign and the indirect election of the first civil president in 1984 – lacked an evident rupture with the dictatorial past.[57] The 'conciliation in the upper echelons' and transition controlled by the civil and military elites prevailed. However, the echoes of the dictatorship's traumas played a crucial role in the transition's institutional design and the assessment of the authoritarian legacy. Human rights defence became one of the main underpinnings of the political debate.

The relatives of the dead and disappeared and the Torture Never Again groups (especially the Rio de Janeiro group founded in 1985) became consolidated as political actors and stewards of the memory of the recent past. The military and the right remained in protagonist roles, ensuring impunity and that devices of the law of exception were kept in place. Old and new left-wing parties adopted ambiguous postures towards the defence of human rights.[58]

In the interval between the publication of *Brazil: Never Again* (1985) and the digging up of the Perus mass grave (1990) – two 'inaugural' moments of the memory of the dictatorship – came the Constituent Congress and approval of the Constitution (1988), a moment in which a rupture with the past became more evident. The new Constitution included a number of progressive rights, but also kept authoritarian elements in place, especially regarding the relationship between political authorities and the armed forces.[59]

Once the Constituent Congress began, the family members launched a campaign for the inclusion of paragraphs on torture and the legacy of authoritarianism in the Constitution.[60] The proposal was not accepted, however, and regulation of the law on torture only happened in 1997, without any devices regarding the punishment of the torturers of the dictatorship period. More importantly, torture failed to be characterized as a crime against humanity.

The Commission of Party-Electoral Organization and Guarantee of Constituent Institutions (responsible for the new political structure and the role of the military and public security institutions) was chaired by Colonel Jarbas Passarinho, former minister of the military governments and a signatory of the AI-5.[61] The result of this commission's actions was that the army's control of the public security forces was ensured, as was tutelage of legitimately instituted political authorities by the armed forces.

In the item on 'Defence of the State and of the Democratic Institutions' in the Constitution, article 142 speaks of military interference in civil matters and the political sphere, stating: 'The armed forces are intended for the defence of the country, for the guarantee of the constitutional powers, and, on the initiative of any of these, of law and order'.[62] In a state that abides the rule of law, the military cannot abide by constitutional powers and guarantee them at the same time. By making the armed forces guarantors of law and order, they ended up being established as one of society's political spheres. Thus, they play a central role in maintaining internal security and not just border protection, introducing measures of exception in society's daily life. The exception gradually becomes the rule, as seen by the violent repression of the protests against the 2014 World Cup and 2016 Olympics.[63]

The Amnesty Law was an emblematic moment, marked by the joy of a victory, which, although partial, opened up possibilities, projecting the survivors' efforts into the future. However, it also signified a denial of the torture, murder and disappearance, strengthening memories and narratives of conciliation.

The reparation policies for the victims did not go hand-in-hand with a guarantee of the right to truth and justice.[64] This demand has remained marginalized and limited to organizations of relatives, survivors and sectors of the human rights movement. Despite diligent efforts by members of the CNV and some state attorneys, little progress has been made in uncovering facts or achieving justice.[65] Nevertheless, relatives and survivors insist on remembering the recent past, stimulating debate and political participation with the goal to change the meaning of Brazilian history and citizenship.

If on one hand the survivors and those who remained of the left understood that this heritage was relevant and an important political capital, an analysis of the Workers' Party's (PT) resolutions, on the other, indicates that the party distanced itself from what was left pending from the dictatorial past. This topic is highlighted in PT documents until 1994.[66]

It becomes clear that the main determinations of the OAS's sentence on the Araguaia Guerrilla have not been followed. The PT governments neither broke with the legal and political limits imposed by the controlled transition nor changed the interpretative norms and frameworks inherited from that period. The Supreme Federal Court's (STF) 2010 decision, for example, confirmed the interpretation that the 1979 amnesty was 'reciprocal', given the importance of not breaking the supposed 'historical agreement', which allowed a 'peaceful and harmonious' transition in the country.[67] It is a well-known fact that on the day of the trial, one of the STF ministers took the lawyer Fábio K. Comparato aside to tell him that on the previous evening all of the ministers had dined with then President Lula and a military authority. The STF ministers had been pressured to vote against the OAB's lawsuit, whose interpretation of the Amnesty Law was that according to the 1988 Constitution the torturers had not been granted amnesty.

The demand for a return of the military, as seen in the pro-impeachment demonstrations against President Dilma Rousseff, along with other recent backward steps, indicates that the strategy of prioritizing past 'agreements' to the detriment of human rights has failed. The reconstruction of Brazil's democracy requires directly confronting this responsibility that the dictatorship has left us.[68]

Janaína de Almeida Teles holds a PhD in Historiography from the University of São Paulo (USP) and has published widely advocating for the families of the dead and disappeared in Brazil. Her parents and aunt survived imprisonment and torture, and she and her brother were briefly kidnapped at the age of five and four years old, respectively, by military agents and kept at a torture centre where their parents were held. Their case constituted the most notorious episode of repression involving children during the military regime in Brazil.

Notes

1. J. de A. Teles, *Os herdeiros da memória: a luta dos familiares de mortos e desaparecidos políticos por 'verdade e justiça' no Brasil* (Master's thesis in Social History, São Paulo, FFLCH/USP, 2005).
2. C. Fico, *Além do golpe: versões e controvérsias sobre 1964 e a ditadura militar* (Rio de Janeiro: Record, 2004), 83.
3. J. de A. Teles, *Memórias dos cárceres da ditadura: os testemunhos e as lutas dos presos políticos no Brasil* (PhD in Social History, São Paulo, FFLCH/USP, 2011).
4. G. Agamben, *Estado de exceção* (São Paulo: Boitempo, 2004), 24.
5. Teles, *Os herdeiros da memória*, 75.
6. A.W. Pereira, *Ditadura e repressão: o autoritarismo e o estado de direito no Brasil, no Chile e na Argentina* (São Paulo: Paz e Terra, 2010), 125.
7. A total of 38.3 per cent of the defendants were found guilty, of which 26.4 per cent were sentenced to less than five years in prison, while guerrilla fighters were found guilty on multiple counts with sentences of up to ninety years or more. However, many suffered torture and long periods of

confinement with no formal record. See Teles, *Memórias dos cárceres da ditadura*; Arquidiocese de São Paulo, *Perfil dos atingidos* (Rio de Janeiro: Vozes, 1987), 11–13; and Arquidiocese de São Paulo, *Projeto 'Brasil: Nunca Mais'. As leis repressivas* (1985), Vol. 4, 338.

8. See data compilation of the Dossiê Ditadura and the Comissão Nacional da Verdade (CNV) report in C.A.S. de Almeida et al., *Dossiê Ditadura: mortos e desaparecidos políticos no Brasil, 1964–1985* (São Paulo: Imprensa Oficial, 2009); and Comissão Nacional da Verdade (CNV), *Relatório da Comissão Nacional da Verdade*, Vols I and II (Brasília/DF: Brazilian Presidency, 2014).
9. Particularly from 1973 onwards. See data on the city of São Paulo in C. Barcellos, *Rota 66: a história da polícia que mata* (Rio de Janeiro: Record, 1992), 250.
10. The CNV did not ascertain the state's direct responsibility for these crimes and published the data in the annex of its report. It also did not add them to the official figures. The number of indigenous people refers only to what took place in part of the northern region. See CNV, *Relatório*, Vol. II, 205, 248. In this way, the CNV shed light on political and civil rights violations, neglecting the economic, social and cultural rights violations of the dictatorship period. See A. Pádua Fernandes, 'Justiça de Transição e fundamento nos direitos humanos: perplexidades do relatório da Comissão Nacional da Verdade brasileira', in C. Kashiura Jr, O. Akamine Jr, and T. Melo (eds), *Para a crítica do Direito: reflexões sobre teorias e práticas do direito* (São Paulo: Outras expressões/Editorial Dobra, 2015), 723–26. In addition, Army Commander Enzo Martins Peri forbade the CNV from perusing his records and was not reprimanded for this.
11. Teles, *Os herdeiros da memória.*
12. M.H.M. Alves, *Estado e oposição no Brasil (1964–1984)* (Petrópolis: Vozes, 1984), 185–86.
13. In 1974, fifty-four militants disappeared but only two were considered 'dead'. Almeida et al., *Dossiê Ditadura*, 591–92, 600. Disappearances also became a strategy to cover up for police officers posing as militants. Teles, *Os herdeiros da memória*.
14. Alves, *Estado e oposição no Brasil*, 187–97.
15. All cases presented to the CDDPH were shelved. See Teles, *Os herdeiros da memória*, 88–95, 105–12.
16. See Almeida et al., *Dossiê Ditadura*, 427–31.
17. See J.N. Green, *Apesar de vocês: oposição à ditadura nos Estados Unidos (1964–1985)* (São Paulo: Companhia das Letras, 2009), 286, 277.
18. See Teles, *Os herdeiros da memória*, 107. There are records of 119 petitions accepted by the IACHR from 1970 to 2015. See R.A. Lima and M. Maia, 'O ativismo de direitos humanos brasileiro nos relatórios da Comissão Interamericana de Direitos Humanos (1970–2015)', *Revista Direito e Praxis* 8(2) (2017), 1419–54.
19. Teles, *Os herdeiros da memória*, 110.
20. Green, *Apesar de vocês*, 305–6.

21. B.B. Bernardi, 'O Sistema Interamericano de Direitos Humanos e a Justiça de Transição: impactos no Brasil', paper presented at the 3rd International Relations Seminar of the Brazilian Association of International Relations (ABRI), Florianópolis (SC), 29 and 30 September 2016, 1.
22. Amnesty International (Europe), *Report on Allegations of Torture in Brazil* (London; Amnesty International, 1972).
23. E. Biocca, *Estratégia do Terror: A face oculta e repressiva do Brasil* (Lisbon: Iniciativas Editoriais, 1974), 9.
24. G. Tosi and L.F. Guerra (eds), *Brasil, violação dos direitos humanos: Tribunal Bertrand Russell II* (João Pessoa: Ed. UFPB, 2014), 323–34.
25. Teles, *Os herdeiros da memória*, 142.
26. Ibid.
27. Ibid.
28. Almeida, *Dossiê Ditadura*, 649–51.
29. Alves, *Estado e oposição no Brasil*.
30. Teles, *Os herdeiros da memória*, 172.
31. Ibid., 145.
32. Ibid., 202.
33. H.A. Greco, *Dimensões fundamentais da luta pela anistia* (PhD in History, Belo Horizonte, FAFICH/UFMG, 2003), 268.
34. Constitutional Amendment (EC) no. 11/78 ruled that the prerogative to declare a state of siege, among other measures of exception, was exclusive to the Executive. See Alves, *Estado e oposição no Brasil*.
35. Teles, *Memórias dos cárceres da ditadura*, 192.
36. Ibid., 193–94.
37. Ibid., 434–36.
38. Amendment 7 (9 August 1979); Comissão Mista sobre a Anistia, *Anistia* (Brasília/DF, 1982), Vol. 1, 71–74. Initially, the CBAs had supported Amendment 1. Ibid., 53–57.
39. Comissão Mista, *Anistia*, Vol. 1, 71–74.
40. Greco, *Dimensões fundamentais da luta pela anistia*, 254–55.
41. N. Batista, 'Aspectos Jurídico-Penais da Anistia', *Revista Encontros com a Civilização Brasileira* 19 (1980); Teles, *Os herdeiros da memória*, 243.
42. See F.K. Comparato, 'O que fizeste de teu irmão?' and 'A responsabilidade do Estado brasileiro na questão dos desaparecidos durante o regime militar', in J. Teles (ed.), *Mortos e desaparecidos políticos: Reparação ou impunidade?* (São Paulo: Humanitas, 2001).
43. The interpretation of what reciprocity meant created obstacles to investigating the dictatorship's crimes and was confirmed by the Supreme Federal Court (STF) in 2010. Retrieved 15 December 2017 from http://www.jusbrasil.com.br/noticias/2167601/oab-julgamento-da-adpf-153.
44. See Law no. 6.767 of 20 December 1979. Retrieved 15 December 2017 from http://www2.camara.leg.br/legin/fed/lei/1970-1979/lei-6767-20-dezembro-1979-357280-publicacaooriginal-1-pl.html.
45. See Teles, *Memórias dos cárceres da ditadura*, 145–50.
46. See P. Brossard, *O caso Herzog* (Brasília/DF: Senado Federal, 1978).

47. We know that in 1973, the widow of former Sergeant Manoel R. Soares filed a suit requesting damages for his murder in 1966 in the 'Tied Hands Case'. She died in 2009 without there ever having been a definitive sentence. I compiled twenty-two lawsuits of this kind. See Teles, *Os herdeiros da memória*, 296–331.
48. See L.E. Greenhalgh and F.A.B. Paranhos, *Interpelação Judicial* (Brasília/DF, 25 June 1979).
49. S. Salgado, *Sentença da Ação Ordinária dos familiares de desaparecidos da Guerrilha do Araguaia*, Case no. I-44/82-B (Brasília/DF, 2003).
50. Ibid., 7.
51. See Law 9.140 of 4 December 1995. Retrieved 15 December 2017 from https://presrepublica.jusbrasil.com.br/legislacao/104145/lei-9140-95.
52. Salgado, *Sentença da Ação Ordinária*, 8–9.
53. Ibid., 15–21.
54. Ibid., 45–46.
55. Corte Interamericana de Direito Humanos, *Caso Gomes Lund e Outros ('Guerrilha do Araguaia') Vs. Brasil. Sentença de 24 de Novembro de 2010 (Exceções Preliminares, Mérito, Reparações e Custas).*
56. In the 21,319 pages of documents of the SNI (National Information Service) on the Araguaia Guerrilla sent to the justice system, no information was found about what happened to the guerrilla fighters. See Corte Interamericana de Direito Humanos, *Caso Gomes Lund e Outros*, 73 and 106. The CNV's work did not change this panorama.
57. EC no. 26/85 established the date of the Constituent Assembly and expanded the amnesty. EC no. 11/78 only ceased to have legal effect once the Constitution was promulgated, as the prerogatives regarding the measures of exception of the Executive Branch were then annulled.
58. In creating a specific justice system for the Military Police, the 'April Package' greatly increased the scope of impunity imposed by the regime.
59. The Law of the Press (revoked in 2009) and the current LSN (1983), among others. See T. Skidmore, *Brasil: De Castelo a Tancredo* (Rio de Janeiro: Paz e Terra, 1988), 506. The SNI was abolished only in 1991.
60. G. Patriota, 'Proposta à Assembléia Nacional Constituinte', Câmara dos Deputados, Sala de Sessões, 27 April 1987, author's files.
61. Passarinho wrote that the military would not apologize because they did not regret what they did during the dictatorship. See J. Passarinho, 'A tortura e o terrorismo', *Folha de S. Paulo*, 28 November 2006, 3.
62. J. Zaverucha, *FH, Forças Armadas e Polícia. Entre o autoritarismo e a democracia (1999–2002)* (Rio de Janeiro: Record, 2005), 63–64, 93–95, 122.
63. The federal intervention in Rio de Janeiro's public security under the command of the armed forces suggests an augmentation of measures of exception in the country. See M. Dias et al., 'Intervenção no Rio cria imbróglio legal para votação da Previdência', *Folha de S. Paulo*, 17 February 2018, A23–24.

64. The Brazilian state discharged itself from having to provide details of the dictatorship's crimes, leaving the victims with the responsibility of ascertaining them in procedures implemented by the Executive such as the CEMDP and Amnesty Commission. See Teles, *Memórias dos cárceres da ditadura*, 2011.
65. By March 2017, the Prosecution Service had filed twenty-seven criminal cases against thirty-seven agents of the dictatorial state. Out of this total, at least nineteen cases are underway or awaiting an answer to their appeal. See Ministério Público Federal, *Crimes da Ditadura Militar*, 2ª Câmara de Coordenação e Revisão, Criminal (Brasília/DF, 2017).
66. Teles, *Memórias dos cárceres da ditadura*.
67. Conselho Federal da OAB, *Arguição de Descumprimento de Preceito Fundamental (ADPF) nº 153* (Brasília/DF, 2008).
68. Prosecutor General Raquel Dodge, however, has requested from the STF that the complaint made in 2014 by five military personnel accused of involvement in the murder of former federal deputy Rubens B. Paiva in January 1971 be reopened. According to Dodge, the merits of the case were not examined. Regarding the issue of connections between crimes, she recalls that the permanent nature of the crime of concealment of a body means that the statute of limitations does not apply. E. Barretto, 'Perfil: o novo homem forte de Temer', *O Globo*, 25 June 2017. Furthermore, the CNV considered that repression by the dictatorship was the result of a state policy, thus concluding that the grave human rights violations committed by agents of the state during this period amount to crimes against humanity, which are indefeasible. M. Weichert, 'O relatório da Comissão Nacional da Verdade: conquistas e desafios', *Projeto História* (São Paulo) 50 (2014), 94–95. The backward steps go a lot further than cuts in funding and the end of public policies for human rights. In addition, the person appointed as Chief of the Office of Institutional Security was General Sérgio Etchegoyen, who sued the CNV in 2014 for stating that his father was a torturer during the dictatorship. See Barretto 'Perfil'.

Bibliography

Agamben, G. *Estado de exceção*. São Paulo: Boitempo, 2004.

Almeida, C.A.S. de, Teles, J. de A., Teles, M.A. de A., and Lisbôa, S.K. (eds). *Dossiê Ditadura: mortos e desaparecidos políticos no Brasil, 1964–1985*. São Paulo: Imprensa Oficial, 2009.

Alves, M.H.M. *Estado e oposição no Brasil (1964–1984)*. Petrópolis: Vozes, 1984.

Amnesty International (Europe), *Report on Allegations of Torture in Brazil*. London: Amnesty International, 1972.

Arquidiocese de São Paulo. *Projeto 'Brasil: Nunca Mais'. As leis repressivas*. Vol. 4. São Paulo: Arquidiocese de São Paulo, 1985.

Arquidiocese de São Paulo. *Perfil dos atingidos*. Rio de Janeiro: Vozes, 1987.

Barcellos, C. *Rota 66: a história da polícia que mata*. Rio de Janeiro: Record, 1992.

Barretto, E. 'Perfil: o novo homem forte de Temer'. *O Globo*, 25 June 2017. Retrieved 18 December 2017 from https://oglobo.globo.com/brasil/perfil-novo-homem-forte-de-temer-21516812#ixzz57U59RVdd.

Batista, N. 'Aspectos Jurídico-Penais da Anistia'. *Revista Encontros com a Civilização Brasileira* 19 (1980).

Bernardi, B.B. 'O Sistema Interamericano de Direitos Humanos e a Justiça de Transição: impactos no Brasil'. Paper presented at the 3rd International Relations Seminar of the Brazilian Association of International Relations (ABRI), Florianópolis (SC), 29 and 30 September 2016.

Biocca, E. *Estratégia do Terror: A face oculta e repressiva do Brasil*. Lisbon: Iniciativas Editoriais, 1974.

Brossard, P. *O caso Herzog*. Brasília/DF: Senado Federal, 1978.

Comissão Mista sobre a Anistia. *Anistia*. Vols I and II. Brasília/DF, 1982.

Comissão Nacional da Verdade (CNV). *Relatório da Comissão Nacional da Verdade*. Vols I and II. Brasília/DF: Brazilian Presidency, 2014.

Comparato, F.K. 'O que fizeste de teu irmão?' and 'A responsabilidade do Estado brasileiro na questão dos desaparecidos durante o regime militar', in J. Teles (ed.), *Mortos e desaparecidos políticos: Reparação ou impunidade?* (São Paulo: Humanitas, 2001).

Conselho Federal da OAB. *Arguição de Descumprimento de Preceito Fundamental (ADPF) n° 153*. Brasília/DF, 2008.

Corte Interamericana de Direito Humanos. *Caso Gomes Lund e Outros ('Guerrilha do Araguaia') Vs. Brasil. Sentença de 24 de Novembro de 2010 (Exceções Preliminares, Mérito, Reparações e Custas)*. Retrieved 18 May 2017 from http://www.corteidh.or.cr/docs/casos/articulos/seriec_219_por.pdf.

Dias, M., et al. 'Temer fala em medidas extremas e inicia intervenção inédita no Rio' (Capa, p.B1, B4–B6); 'Intervenção no Rio cria imbróglio legal para votação da Previdência'. *Folha de S. Paulo*, 17 February 2018, A23–24.

Fico, C. *Além do golpe: versões e controvérsias sobre 1964 e a ditadura militar*. Rio de Janeiro: Record, 2004.

Greco, H.A. *Dimensões fundamentais da luta pela anistia*. PhD in History, Belo Horizonte, FAFICH/UFMG, 2003.

Green, J.N. *Apesar de vocês: oposição à ditadura nos Estados Unidos (1964–1985)*. São Paulo: Companhia das Letras, 2009.

Greenhalgh, L.E., and Paranhos, F.A.B. *Interpelação Judicial*. Brasília/DF, 25 June 1979.

Kucinski, B. *A síndrome da antena parabólica: ética no jornalismo brasileiro*. São Paulo: Fundação Perseu Abramo, 1998.

Lima, R.A., and Maia, M. 'O ativismo de direitos humanos brasileiro nos relatórios da Comissão Interamericana de Direitos Humanos (1970–2015)'. *Revista Direito e Praxis* 8(2) (2017), 1419–54.

Ministério Público Federal. *Crimes da Ditadura Militar*. 2ª Câmara de Coordenação e Revisão, Criminal. Brasília/DF, 2017.

Pádua Fernandes, A. 'Justiça de Transição e fundamento nos direitos humanos: perplexidades do relatório da Comissão Nacional da Verdade brasileira', in C. Kashiura Jr, O. Akamine Jr, and T. Melo (eds), *Para a crítica do Direito: reflexões sobre teorias e práticas do direito* (São Paulo: Outras expressões/ Editorial Dobra, 2015), 717–45.

Passarinho, J. 'A tortura e o terrorismo'. *Folha de S. Paulo*, 28 November 2006, 3.

Patriota, G. 'Proposta à Assembléia Nacional Constituinte', Câmara dos Deputados, Sala de Sessões, 27 April 1987. Author's files.

Pereira, A.W. *Ditadura e repressão: o autoritarismo e o estado de direito no Brasil, no Chile e na Argentina*. São Paulo: Paz e Terra, 2010.

Presidência da República/Secretaria de Direitos Humanos. *Habeas Corpus: que se apresente o corpo*. Brasília/DF: SDH, 2010.

Salgado, S. *Sentença da Ação Ordinária dos familiares de desaparecidos da Guerrilha do Araguaia*. Case no. I-44/82-B. Brasília/DF, 2003.

Skidmore, T. *Brasil: De Castelo a Tancredo*. Rio de Janeiro: Paz e Terra, 1988.

Teles, J. de A. *Os herdeiros da memória: a luta dos familiares de mortos e desaparecidos políticos por 'verdade e justiça' no Brasil*. Master's thesis in Social History, São Paulo, FFLCH/USP, 2005.

Teles, J. de A. *Memórias dos cárceres da ditadura: os testemunhos e as lutas dos presos políticos no Brasil*. PhD in Social History, São Paulo, FFLCH/USP, 2011.

Tosi, G., and Guerra, L.F. (eds). *Brasil, violação dos direitos humanos: Tribunal Bertrand Russell II*. João Pessoa: Ed. UFPB, 2014.

Turollo, R. Jr. 'Dodge pede que Supremo rediscuta anistia'. *Folha de S. Paulo*, 15 February 2018, A8.

Weichert, M. 'O relatório da Comissão Nacional da Verdade: conquistas e desafios'. *Projeto História* (São Paulo) 50 (2014), 86–137.

Zaverucha, J. *FH, Forças Armadas e Polícia. Entre o autoritarismo e a democracia (1999–2002)*. Rio de Janeiro: Record, 2005.

Section 2

Noveltics of the Brazilian Model

The National Commission, Local Committees and Corporate Complicity

Chapter 5

The National Truth Commission (NTC)

Truth and Responsibility

Carolina de Campos Melo and André Saboia Martins

In February 2018, in an extraordinary joint meeting of the National Defence and the Republic Council, the commander of the Brazilian army affirmed that the armed forces needed a guarantee to act in the maintenance of domestic order and public security without the risk of a 'new truth commission'.[1] This demand for a 'guarantee' refers specifically to the use of military force during the federal intervention in the state of Rio de Janeiro, decreed on 16 February 2018 to last until the end of December 2018, the first time this exceptional measure has been used since the enactment of the democratic Constitution of 1988.

Brazil is one of the very few, if not the only country in the Americas where members of the police and armed forces have not been criminally sanctioned for human rights violations committed under a military dictatorship that came to power during the Cold War period. In 1979, the National Congress passed an amnesty law, which exempted from criminal responsibility both members of opposition groups and state actors involved in 'political crimes' and 'crimes of any nature related to political crimes', in what has long been understood by Brazilian authorities, in spite of its elliptical legal formulation, as a provision that effectively prevents sanctions for gross human rights violations committed by the military regime and its agents.

The nongovernmental report *Brasil: Nunca Mais*[2] was edited in 1985 under the auspices of the Catholic Archdiocese of São Paulo and the World Council of Churches. It received important civil society support and first systematized gross human rights violations. Ten years of democratic rule were necessary for institutional advances such as the adoption of Law no. 9.140/1995, which recognized the state's liability for deaths and disappearances during the military regime. Moreover,

Law no. 10.559/2001 recognized state responsibility for cases of 'political persecution' and authorized the Amnesty Commission to conduct reparations for people who were hindered from undertaking economic activities, expelled from universities, put into jail, and submitted to gross human rights violations for political reasons. These initiatives, however limited in their scope, have contributed to questioning the official military versions of what happened in the authoritarian past and to providing reparations for the victims of the regime.

From May 2012 until December 2014, the National Truth Commission (NTC) directed its efforts towards accomplishing the aim legally established in art. 1 of Law 12.528: to examine and clarify the gross human rights violations implemented during the 1946–88 period, in order to make effective the right to memory and to historical truth and to promote national reconciliation. Composed of three volumes, the NTC final report was published on 10 December 2014. The first volume has eighteen chapters and deals with themes such as organs and procedures of political repression employed by the authoritarian government, the participation of the Brazilian state in gross human rights violations that occurred abroad, human rights violation methods and practices, emblematic cases, institutions and places related to violations, individual responsibility, the participation of the judicial power in the dictatorship and, finally, the commission's conclusions and recommendations for the prevention of human rights violations. The second volume is composed of seven chapters that demonstrate how the dictatorship violated the human rights of specific social groups, such as members of the armed forces who resisted the military coup, urban workers and labour unions, peasants and rural workers, indigenous peoples, Christian churches, university professors and students as well as non-heterosexual activists (LGBT groups). This volume's chapters are also dedicated to the uncovering of civil society and private corporation collaboration with the dictatorship and to the description of social and cultural forms of resistance to authoritarian rule in Brazil. The third volume is dedicated to historical case profiles of each of the 434 individually identified victims of murder or enforced disappearance committed by state actors. As the NTC concludes, the number of 191 dead, 210 missing and thirty-three missing whose mortal remains were later located – four of them in the course of the NTC – remains below the estimated total number of victims of lethal state violence during the investigated period, referring only to cases in which evidence collected due to the performed work made possible the individual identification of such victims.

The refusal by the Brazilian armed forces to fully recognize their responsibility for the gross human rights violations ascertained during the NTC's investigations underscored the NTC's conclusion that 'national reconciliation' – effective reconciliation between military forces and Brazilian civil society – shall only be achieved when the former recognize their institutional responsibility concerning past violations, thus consolidating, on a permanent basis, their commitment to a democratic rule of law.[3]

Therefore, this chapter discusses the work of the NTC and the writing up of its final report, mainly through the lenses of responsibility. First, it addresses one of the NTC's main conclusions, that the gross human rights violations investigated by the commission, especially those committed during the period of military dictatorship, were the result of a state policy of widespread and systematic character, therefore constituting crimes against humanity. Second, the text discusses the recommendations edited by the NTC, with special attention to the definition of institutional responsibility by the armed forces and personal responsibility of state agents. Third, it analyses the NTC's conception of individual responsibility of perpetrators (in Portuguese: 'authorship') that contemplated three levels: political-administrative responsibility; responsibility for the management of repression structures; and responsibility of agents directly involved in gross human rights violations. Fourth, the text explores how the idea of responsibility had an extraterritorial scope, since the NTC systematized information concerning participation of foreign state agents in investigated episodes related to human rights violations perpetrated in Brazil and abroad.

Gross Human Rights Violations as Crimes against Humanity

The NTC refuted the explanation sustained by the armed forces for the last five decades that tortures, executions and disappearances occurred in the military regime due to the voluntary 'excesses' of a reduced number of military personnel. Two concepts were key for the NTC to come to a different conclusion, both part of its legal mandate: the clarification of 'gross human rights violations' implemented during the 1946–88 period, mainly during the dictatorship, in order to turn effective, the 'right to memory and to historical truth'.

Following the standards set by the UN and the Inter-American System of Human Rights, the NTC report has defined the right to truth as an inalienable and autonomous right to conduct effective investigation, which implies knowing the full and complete truth about events, including their specific circumstances, who participated in them, the circumstances in which the violations took place, as well as the reasons for them.[4] The NTC incorporated two dimensions of the right to truth in its daily investigations: individual, considering the obligation of the state to present information specifically about the circumstances of a case, including the identity of the authors and, in the case of death and disappearance, the locations of the remains; and collective, including the state obligation to inform the society about the circumstances and the reasons for what occurred.

The use of the expression 'gross human rights violations' by the legislator – rather than 'crimes' or 'abuses' – guided the NTC to look for a normative framework offered by international human rights treaties and case law. The law established a list of four distinct types of gross human rights violations that deserved special treatment by the NTC: torture, death, enforced disappearance and concealment of corpses. Considering the reality imposed by the repressive regime on Brazilian society, and also abiding by international standards, especially concerning the violation of non-derogable rights recognized by international human rights law (IHRL), the NTC also considered illegal/arbitrary detentions and sexual violence as gross human rights violations to be investigated, as well as references to genocide and ethnocide in the case of violations against the human rights of indigenous peoples. By using the state responsibility landmark, the NTC members adopted Resolution no. 2, in August 2012, which established that it would examine and clarify the gross human rights violations practised by 'public agents, persons acting in their behalf, with support or in the interest of the state'. This meant the examination of actions and omissions by state agents that have resulted in violations of state obligations established by international treaties or by imperative norms of international law (*jus cogens*). The NTC understood that this normative framework bound the Brazilian authorities at the time the events occurred, even in the case of treaties that were signed only after the return to civil democratic rule.[5] In the case of enforced disappearances, the option for the international standard was crucial, since Brazil had not ratified the treaties on this issue.[6]

As a result of its work, the NTC came to four main conclusions, as described in Chapter 18 of the final report. First, the NTC confirmed the occurrence of gross human rights violations, as exposed in the report as a result of research activities, with evidence obtained by public institutions, civil society entities, and victims of the regime and their family members.

Second, the NTC has proven that the gross human rights violations had a widespread and systematic character. During the dictatorship, according to the NTC, repression and elimination of political opponents became a state policy, conceived and implemented due to decisions emanating from the presidency and the military ministries. Operationalized through chains of command that extend from these governing bodies, reaching the organs responsible for the installations and the procedures directly involved, this state policy mobilized public officials for the systematic repression. Chapter 9 ('Torture') of the NTC Report is particularly important in this affirmation, since it situates the practice of torture in the context of the doctrine of national security, used in a standardized approach, demonstrating how it was transmitted to militaries as knowledge through printed manuals and practical demonstrations in military units, and how it counted on medical services that would evaluate the limit of resistance of the detainees to torture.

Third, the NTC examined whether crimes against humanity occurred. This configuration results from the association of such acts with a number of elements that render them particularly serious: to be inhumane acts committed in the context of an attack against the civilian population, in a widespread or a systematic way, and with authors' knowledge of their extension and impact. Thereby, considering evidence registered in this report indicating that gross human rights violations committed by the military regime occurred in a widespread and systematic context of state attack against civilians, linked to many different social groups such as urban workers, peasants, students, clerics and many others, the NTC found that the practice of illegal and arbitrary detention, torture, executions, enforced disappearance and concealment of corpses perpetrated by state agents during the military dictatorship characterized the committing of crimes against humanity.[7]

Fourth, the NTC concluded that this situation still persists today. Despite not occurring in the context of political repression – as occurred during the military dictatorship – the practice of illegal and arbitrary detention, torture, executions, enforced disappearances and even concealment of corpses is part of the current Brazilian reality. The NTC understands that this framework is derived from the fact that the perpetration of gross human rights violations that occurred in the past was not properly denounced, and authors were not held legally responsible for their acts, thus creating the conditions for its perpetuation.

The Recommendation of Institutional and Individual Responsibility

In the process of establishing recommendations that would contribute to the prevention of gross human rights violations, ensure their non-recurrence and enhance the democratic rule of law, the NTC opened a public consultation mechanism, which received 399 recommendation suggestions between August and September 2014. In its final report, more precisely in Chapter 18 of the first volume, the NTC published a set of seventeen institutional measures, eight initiatives for constitutional and legal reformulations, as well as four measures to ensure the continuation of its actions and recommendations:

(A) *Institutional measures*: besides the first three, which will be emphasized below; [4] The prohibition of official events commemorating the military coup of 1964; [5] The reformulation of entrance examinations and continuous processes of assessment in the military and public security sector in order to enhance the knowledge of the precepts inherent to democracy and human rights; [6] The modification of the curricular content of military and police academies in order to promote democracy and human rights; [7] The rectification of the annotation referent to the cause of death in the death certificates of persons victimized by gross human rights violations; [8] The rectification of information in the National Integration Network of Public Safety Information, Justice and Enforcement (INFOSEG Network) and, in general, all public records; [9] The creation of mechanisms to prevent and to combat torture; [10] The decoupling of the legal medical institutes, as well as the criminal forensics organs, from the public security departments and Civil Police; [11] The strengthening of public defenders; [12] To ensure more dignity for the prison system and for the treatment of the arrested persons; [13] The legal provision of an external ombudsman for the prison system and organs related to this system; [14] The provision of Community Councils to strengthen the monitoring of prisons; [15] The guarantee of permanent medical and psychosocial care for victims of gross human rights violations; [16] The promotion of democratic values and human rights in education; [17] Support for the creation and the functioning of an organ designed to protect and promote human rights.

(B) *Constitutional and legal reforms*: [18] The repeal of the National Security Law; [19] The improvement of Brazilian legislation in order to typify the criminal acts corresponding to crimes against humanity and the crime of enforced disappearance; [20] The demilitarization of the State Military Police; [21] The dissolution of the State Military Justice; [22] The exclusion of civilians from the jurisdiction of the Federal Military Justice; [23] The suppression of discriminatory references to homosexuality in current legislation; [24] To change the criminal procedure law in order to eliminate the registration of 'resistance killings'; [25] The introduction of custody hearings, to prevent the practice of torture and illegal detention.

(C) *Follow-up measures to the NTC's actions and recommendations*: [26] The establishment of a permanent body to follow up on CNV actions and recommendations; [27] The pursuance of activities aimed at locating, identifying and delivering to family members or legitimated people the mortal remains of the disappeared persons to provide a dignified burial; [28] The preservation of the memory of gross human rights violations; and [29] The pursuance and the strengthening of the location policy and the openness of the military dictatorship files.

Once it had demonstrated that the commitment of gross human rights violations became a state policy, with the participation of the military command, infrastructure and units, the NTC considered the acknowledgement by the armed forces of its institutional responsibility as 'imperative', assuming it as Recommendation number 1. More than that, the NTC understood that this attitude had to be 'clear and direct', an 'essential element to the national reconciliation', in order 'not to repeat this history'.[8] The idea of clear and direct responsibility arose from the answers of the army, navy and air force to the NTC's request to self-investigate the use of military units in which gross human rights violations had occurred. The request provided a preliminary report that considered cases already evaluated by the Special Commission on the Dead and Politically Disappeared and by the Amnesty Commission, organs of the Brazilian state, with the participation of representatives of the armed forces. When the armed forces answered that the acts described in the request and recognized by the commissions were not contested, the NTC made a public statement that the Ministry of Defence and the military commands needed to move away from the denial of gross human rights violations in military units to the acknowledgement of the armed forces' engagement in these crimes.[9]

Recommendation number 2 deals with the determination of legal responsibility – criminal, civil and administrative. It deals with public officials who gave rise to gross human rights violations during the period investigated by the CNV. Among all recommendations, the repeal of the 1979 Amnesty Law and the persecution of those culprits was the only one not taken by consensus. The divergent position taken by one of the members – exposed in Chapter 18 of the final report – was based on the same line of argument taken by the Brazilian Supreme Federal Court in April 2010, claiming that the Amnesty Law is compatible with the 1988 Constitution.

Here, the NTC made one of its most important compromises regarding the idea of responsibility, guided by international standards. The Inter-American Court of Human Rights case law is clear on considering that all amnesty provisions, provisions on prescription and the establishment of measures designed to eliminate responsibility are inadmissible.[10] The reason for this is that they are intended to prevent the investigj142

ation and punishment of those responsible for gross human rights violations.[11] Analysing the responsibility of the Brazilian state for the disappearance of political opponents of the 1970 Araguaia Guerrilla, the court had affirmed in 2010 – the same year as the Supreme Federal Court decision – that provisions of the Brazilian Amnesty Law that prevent the investigation and punishment of gross human rights violations are not compatible with the American Convention, lack legal effect, and cannot continue as obstacles for the investigation of the facts of the case, or for the identification and punishment of those responsible, nor can they have equal or similar impact regarding other gross violations of human rights enshrined in the American Convention that occurred in Brazil.[12] Once the NTC had conceived that crimes against humanity were committed, it assumed the impact of the 'legal regime of imprescritibility and the impossibility of amnesty'.[13]

Oriented by the provision of Law no. 12.528, which required the NTC to observe Law no. 6.683 of 28 August 1979, the NTC proposed, by Recommendation number 2, a new interpretation of amnesty, not applying its provisions in cases of gross human rights violations. The idea of responsibility inherent to the first recommendations seems crucial, in the NTC's perspective, to connect impunity in the past and the persistence of gross human rights violations and to enhance the democratic rule of law.

Between 2012 and 2017, the Federal Public Prosecution Office (MPF) offered twenty-seven criminal charges against forty-seven public agents engaged in forty-three crimes. In a significant number of these charges – 81 per cent by single judges, 78 per cent by courts of appeal and 100 per cent of the cases analysed by the Supreme Federal Court

– the judicial power dismissed the cases by applying amnesty provision or prescription arguments.[14] In February 2018, the Prosecutor General of the Republic, Rachel Dodge, asked the STF to revisit the question of application of amnesty provisions to public agents engaged in gross human rights violations.[15] The Brazilian Amnesty Law has held strong since 1979, but it is time for the judiciary to accept that responsibility may deter human rights violations in the present. As Sikkink and Marchesi suggest, the key test for the impact of the NTC is whether it can not only provide public acknowledgement to victims and a record for collective memory, but also contribute to making the Brazilian state hold offenders accountable.[16]

The Perpetrators of Gross Human Rights Violations

Besides institutional and individual responsibility, the final report dedicates Chapter 16 to the 'persons responsible for gross human rights violations'.[17] Understanding that these violations have mostly occurred under a military chain of command, the NTC opted to identify three levels of participation by state actors. The first level, pertinent to political and institutional responsibility, implies the actions of conceiving, planning or deciding on policies concerning the repression and persecution of political opponents of the regime, and it applies to the military presidents, armed forces ministers as well as the heads of the presidency, navy, air force and army information services. The second level of responsibility refers to the administrative control of structures and procedures related to the practice of gross human rights violations, a category that applies to the agents who, by action or omission, directed activities in military units where gross violations took place. Finally, the third level – direct responsibility – applies to those individuals identified as immediate authors of gross human rights violations.

A total of 377 state agents – 191 of whom were still alive at the time the report was issued – were identified by the NTC in the chapter on individual responsibility. They were indicated according to their respective level of participation, in a series of entries where some lines were saved for information specifically concerning individual state functions, conducts, professional training and decorations related to the practice of human rights violations, as well as the names of identified victims. In the identification of responsible persons of gross human rights violations, the NTC proceeded cautiously, always seeking to substantiate its findings with documents and testimonies of victims, witnesses, experts and public agents. All agents listed in

Chapter 16, or the units that were under their direction or supervision, are mentioned in other sections of the report, especially in the third chapter, dedicated to the historical profiles of the victims of murder and forced disappearance by state actors, whose conduct is described in thorough detail in the report.

It is important to stress that due to the legal constraints preventing the NTC from exercising activities of jurisdiction or legal persecution, the identification of individual responsibility by the NTC did not imply, by itself, the attribution of individual legal responsibility – criminal, civil or administrative – to the persons listed in Chapter 16 of the NTC report.

In spite of the cautious approach adopted by the NTC in the exercise of its legal prerogative of identifying chains of command and immediate responsibility of gross human rights violations, the commission's decision to effectively name names and recommend the sanctioning of state perpetrators was received with apprehension by the government of then President Dilma Rousseff. In the days immediately following the issuing of the NTC's final report, it was soon made clear that the government was not only unwilling to implement the accountability measures recommended by the NTC, but it feared a 'torrent' of judicial actions questioning the report's conclusions and recommendations.[18] Governmental fears concerning the judicial questioning of the NTC's conclusions and recommendations were later proven to be disproportional, since only two judicial actions were proposed against the NTC's conclusions on those made responsible for the gross human rights violations, along with another action against the recommendation of demilitarizing the military police in Brazil, and all the demands were rejected by Brazilian federal justice.[19]

Extraterritorial Responsibility: National and Foreign State Agents' Participation in Gross Human Rights Violations

According to the law that created the NTC, its goal involved a detailed clarification of gross human rights violations 'notwithstanding its occurrence abroad'; hence, it authorized the NTC to investigate outside of Brazil through means of international cooperation. In order to gain access to records kept by foreign governments and international organizations, which could be a valuable source of information for the research and writing of the Truth Commission's report, the NTC made direct requests of cooperation to around twenty foreign governments as well as to the Office of the UN High Commissioner on Human Rights (OHCHR), the UN High Commissioner on Refugees (UNHCR) and the Inter-American Commission on Human Rights (IACHR). Through this particular modality of international cooperation, the NTC was granted access to documentation in public institutions in Argentina, Chile, the Czech Republic, Germany, Paraguay, the United Kingdom, the United States and Uruguay, as well as files concerning communications of human rights violations in Brazil presented to the UNHCR, the IACHR and the former UN Human Rights Commission during the period between 1964 and 1985. In addition to this access to foreign documents, the NTC's research in the archives of the Ministry of Foreign Relations and the Brazilian National Archive was of the utmost importance in clarifying the international dimensions of human rights violations committed with participation of Brazilian state agents.

The results of the investigations concerning gross human rights violations outside of Brazil's borders are presented primarily in Chapter 5 ('Brazilian state participation in gross violations abroad') and Chapter 6 ('International connections: the repressive alliance in the Southern Cone and Operation Condor') of the first volume of the commission's final report. Chapter 9 ('Torture') and Chapter 14 ('Guerrilla in Araguaia') of the commission's report present thorough descriptions of the influence of doctrine and military training provided by France, Britain and the United States in the institutionalization of Brazil's methods and structures of political repression in the period of state terror. Together with an account of the influence of foreign services in the institutionalization of systems of torture and state terror in Brazil, the NTC's final report also provides some information concerning the participation of foreign state agents in episodes of human rights violations perpetrated in Brazil and abroad.

Conclusions

The NTC adds to the discussion of the role of truth commissions by affirming that national reconciliation presumes recognition of institutional responsibility concerning past violations. In this sense, the idea of reconciliation does not imply compromise between victims and state perpetrators, but calls attention to the historical and institutional connections involving impunity in the past and the persistence of gross human rights violations, assuming that responsibility may prevent human rights violations in the present. The idea of responsibility was handled by the NTC in multiple ways. First, it affirmed that the gross human rights violations were the result of a widespread and systematic state policy that constituted crimes against humanity. Second, it called for recognition of institutional responsibility by the armed forces and personal responsibility of state agents as two distinct matters. Considering that Brazilian society continues to struggle with a deeply rooted authoritarian culture, the process of recognition by the armed forces of their responsibility for past violations would be a decisive step to consolidate republican commitment to a democratic rule of law. The NTC also described the conception of individual responsibility (in Portuguese: authorship) on three levels: political-administrative responsibility; responsibility for the management of repression structures; and responsibility of agents directly involved in gross human rights violations. Finally, the NTC systematized information concerning the participation of foreign state agents in specific episodes of human rights violations perpetrated in Brazil and abroad.

The Brazilian army commander's unsettling remarks in 2018 have confirmed, to some degree, the effectiveness of the NTC's efforts to intertwine truth-telling and the rationale of responsibility. What remains a major challenge for democracy in Brazil is the unfinished task of institutional recognition of past human rights violations.

Carolina de Campos Melo was a member of the Final Report Executive Team of the NTC. She is a Professor of International Law at PUC-Rio and a member of the Human Rights Center at the Law School. She is also a Union Attorney (Advocacia-Geral da União – AGU).

André Saboia Martins was the Executive Secretary of the NTC and a member of the Special Commission for the Dead and Politically Disappeared.

Notes

The positions taken by the authors are of their personal responsibility. Some of them were also discussed in C. Melo, 'Truth versus/and Justice: The Case of the Brazilian National Truth Commission', in C. Julio and P. Drumond (eds), *Human Rights and Conflict Resolution: Bridging the Theoretical and Practical Divide* (London and New York: Routledge, 2018), 123–39.

1. *Folha de São Paulo*, '"Militares precisam ter garantia para agir sem o risco de surgir uma nova Comissão da Verdade", diz comandante do Exército', retrieved 20 February 2018 from https://g1.globo.com/politica/blog/cristiana-lobo/post/general-vilas-boas-militares-precisam-ter-garantia-para-agir-sem-o-risco-de-surgir-uma-nova-comissao-da-verdade.ghtml.
2. Arquidiocese de São Paulo. *Brasil Nunca mais: um relato para a história.* 34 ed. (Petrópolis, RJ: Vozes, 1985).
3. Comissão Nacional da Verdade (CNV), 'The Final Report of the Brazilian Truth Commission', retrieved 20 December 2014 from http://www.cnv.gov.br/index.php/outros-destaques/574-conheca-e-acesse-o-relatorio-final-da-cnv, 962–67. See also *Folha de São Paulo*, 'Verdade, Memória e Reconciliação', *Folha de São Paulo*, 10 December 2014, signed by José Carlos Dias, José Paulo Cavalcanti Filho, Maria Rita Kehl, Paulo Sérgio Pinheiro, Pedro Dallari, Rosa Cardoso.
4. CNV, 'The Final Report', 35.
5. Ibid., 279.
6. The UN and the Inter-American Treaties on Enforced Disappearances were promulgated after the work of the NTC, on the day before the official notification of the impeachment of President Dilma Rousseff, in May 2016. The NTC considered the Inter-American Court case law on enforced disappearances, pointing out three characteristics of this violation: (1) it is plurioffensive, since it violates several rights, including the right to juridical personality; (2) it is an autonomous crime, as it has to be codified and as such distinguished from other conducts; and (3) it is permanent, as it starts when the liberty of the disappeared is violated and lasts until the identity of the whereabouts of the remains is certified. This last aspect was important to review official versions that were built on narratives from the repression. CNV, 'The Final Report', 292–93.
7. CNV, 'The Final Report', 964.
8. Ibid., 965.
9. Comissão Nacional da Verdade (CNV), 'Nota da CNV sobre ofício do Ministério da Defesa de 19 de setembro de 2014', retrieved 20 December 2014 from http://cnv.memoriasreveladas.gov.br/images/pdf/nota_CNV_22_09_2014_esclarecimentos.pdf.
10. Inter-American Court of Human Rights (IACtHR), Case of Barrios Altos v. Peru. Merits. Judgement of 14 March 2001, par. 2.
11. Inter-American Court of Human Rights (IACtHR), Case of Almonacid Arellano et al. v. Chile. Preliminary Objections, Reparations, and Costs. Judgement of 26 September 2006, Rule 6.
12. Inter-American Court of Human Rights (IACtHR), Case of Gomes Lund et al. ('Guerrilha do Araguaia') v. Brazil. Preliminary Objections, Reparations, and Costs. Judgement of 24 November 2010, Declaration 3. These conclusions were recently ratified by the tribunal on the Herzog case, when it considered the occurrence of crimes against humanity by the military dictatorship. Inter-American Court of Human Rights (IACtHR), Case of

Herzog et al. v. Brazil. Preliminary Objections, Merits, Reparations, and Costs. Judgement of 15 March 2018.
13. CNV, 'The Final Report', 965.
14. Ministério Público Federal, Câmara de Coordenação e Revisão, 2, *Crimes da ditadura militar* (Brasília: MPF, 2017), 25.
15. *Folha de São Paulo*, 'Dodge pede ao STF para reabrir caso que discute anistia a militares: Procuradoria quer julgar reclamação de militares acusados por morte de Rubens Paiva', retrieved 20 February 2018 from https://www1.folha.uol.com.br/poder/2018/02/dodge-pede-ao-stf-para-reabrir-caso-que-discute-anistia-a-militares.shtml.
16. K. Sikkink and B. Marchesi, 'Nothing but the Truth: Brazil's Truth Commission Looks Back', *Foreign Affairs* 26 (February 2015).
17. M. Freeman, *Truth Commissions and Procedural Fairness* (Cambridge: Cambridge University Press, 2006); P. Hayner, *Unspeakable Truths: Facing the Challenge of Truth Commissions* (New York: Routledge, 2011).
18. On governmental apprehension concerning an expected 'torrent of actions' questioning the NTC report, see the records of the '44ª Reunião (Extraordinária) da Comissão Permanente de Direitos Humanos e Legislação Participativa do Senado Federal', which took place on 25 June 2015 in Brasília. Diário do Senado Federal de 04/08/2015, Suplemento "B", p. 595, retrieved from https://legis.senado.leg.br/diarios/PublicacoesOficiais.
19. C. Osmo, Judicialização da justiça de transição na América Latina = Judicialización de la Justicia de Transición en América Latina. Tradução para o espanhol: Nathaly Mancilla Órdenes. Brasília: Ministério da Justiça, Comissão de Anistia; Rede Latina Americana de Justiça de Transição. Brasília, 2016. p. 97.

Bibliography

Arquidiocese de São Paulo. *Brasil Nunca mais: um relato para a história*. 34 ed. Petrópolis, RJ: Vozes, 1985.

Comissão Nacional da Verdade (CNV). 'The Final Report of the Brazilian Truth Commission'. Retrieved 20 December 2014 from http://www.cnv.gov.br/index.php/outros-destaques/574-conheca-e-acesse-o-relatorio-final-da-cnv.

Comissão Nacional da Verdade (CNV). 'Nota da CNV sobre ofício do Ministério da Defesa de 19 de setembro de 2014'. Retrieved 20 December 2014 from http://cnv.memoriasreveladas.gov.br/images/pdf/nota_CNV_22_09_2014_esclarecimentos.pdf.

Folha de São Paulo. 'Verdade, Memória e Reconciliação'. *Folha de São Paulo*, 10 December 2014. Signed by José Carlos Dias, José Paulo Cavalcanti Filho, Maria Rita Kehl, Paulo Sérgio Pinheiro, Pedro Dallari, Rosa Cardoso.

Folha de São Paulo. 'Dodge pede ao STF para reabrir caso que discute anistia a militares: Procuradoria quer julgar reclamação de militares acusados por morte de Rubens Paiva'. Retrieved 20 February 2018 from https://www1.folha.uol.com.br/poder/2018/02/dodge-pede-ao-stf-para-reabrir-caso-que-discute-anistia-a-militares.shtml.

Folha de São Paulo. '"Militares precisam ter garantia para agir sem o risco de surgir uma nova Comissão da Verdade", diz comandante do Exército'. Retrieved 20 February 2018 from https://g1.globo.com/politica/blog/cristiana-lobo/post/general-vilas-boas-militares-precisam-ter-garantia-para-agir-sem-o-risco-de-surgir-uma-nova-comissao-da-verdade.ghtml.

Freeman, M. *Truth Commissions and Procedural Fairness*. Cambridge: Cambridge University Press, 2006.

Hayner, P. *Unspeakable Truths: Facing the Challenge of Truth Commissions*. New York: Routledge, 2011.

Inter-American Court of Human Rights (IACtHR). Case of Barrios Altos v. Peru. Merits. Judgement of 14 March 2001.

Inter-American Court of Human Rights (IACtHR). Case of Almonacid Arellano et al. v. Chile. Preliminary Objections, Reparations, and Costs. Judgement of 26 September 2006.

Inter-American Court of Human Rights (IACtHR). Case of Gomes Lund et al. ('Guerrilha do Araguaia') v. Brazil. Preliminary Objections, Reparations, and Costs. Judgement of 24 November 2010.

Inter-American Court of Human Rights (IACtHR). Case of Herzog et al. v. Brazil. Preliminary Objections, Merits, Reparations, and Costs. Judgement of 15 March 2018.

Melo, C. 'Truth versus/and Justice: The Case of the Brazilian National Truth Commission', in C. Julio and P. Drumond (eds), *Human Rights and Conflict Resolution: Bridging the Theoretical and Practical Divide* (London and New York: Routledge, 2018), 123–39.

Ministério Público Federal. Câmara de Coordenação e Revisão, 2. *Crimes da ditadura militar*. Brasília: MPF, 2017.

Osmo, Carla. Judicialização da justiça de transição na América Latina Judicialización de la Justicia de Transición en América Latina. Tradução para o espanhol: Nathaly Mancilla Órdenes. Brasília: Ministério da Justiça, Comissão de Anistia; Rede Latina Americana de Justiça de Transição. Brasília, 2016.

Sikkink, K., and Marchesi, B. 'Nothing but the Truth: Brazil's Truth Commission Looks Back'. *Foreign Affairs* 26 (February 2015).

Chapter 6

Repression, Resistance and the Intergenerational Dialogue

Establishing a Truth Commission at the University of Brasília

Cristiano Paixão and José Otávio Guimarães

Acceleration of Transitional Justice in Brazil

During the 2000s, transitional justice initiatives gained momentum in Brazil. This acceleration destabilized the pact built by Brazilian political elites who tried to control the redemocratization process after the military regime (1964–88). In Brazil, the struggle for reparation and justice was not initially regarded as a national priority. Brazilian society took little interest in the violence suffered by political prisoners and citizens who were murdered or disappeared. Two laws passed in 1995 and 2002 made significant advancements: they recognized the human rights violations perpetrated by the state during the state of exception and created two new institutions, the Special Commission for the Political Dead and Disappeared (CEMDP) and the Amnesty Commission. Although these advances guaranteed economic reparations for the victims and their families, they failed to confront the 1979 Amnesty Law granting *de facto* impunity. The silence and oblivion of past repression was further reinforced by the difficult access to documents related to the political repression. This scenario only started to change from the year 2000 onwards.

Over the last ten years, several initiatives have triggered public debate on former human rights violations. They include: (1) the Amnesty Commission's strategic shift to symbolic reparations and public memory and truth policies; (2) the attempt to judicially review the Amnesty Law of 1979 in order to allow investigation, prosecution and conviction of the military staff involved in crimes during the dictatorship; (3) the creation of a National Truth Commission following the recommendation of the third National Human Rights Plan, published in 2009; and (4) the ruling of the Inter-American Human Rights Court, which sentenced the Brazilian state in the case of *Gomes Lund and Others* (the Araguaia Guerrilla), in December 2010.

After numerous efforts to negotiate with different political sectors and with representatives of the armed forces, these initiatives led to the enactment of two laws on 18 November 2011: the law that created the National Truth Commission (CNV) and the Freedom of Information Law (LAI) that guaranteed easier access to files related to human rights violations. In this context, an interesting phenomenon occurred. All over the country, truth and memory commissions were created at diverse organizational levels of Brazilian society. The commissions were organized by both federal entities (state assemblies and municipal chambers) and civil society organizations (universities, unions, the National Bar Association and the National Student Union).

Establishment and Objectives of the Anísio Teixeira Commission

On 10 August 2012, the rector of the University of Brasília, José Geraldo de Sousa Junior, created the Anísio Teixeira Truth and Memory Commission (CATMV-UnB). José Geraldo is a well-known jurist recognized for his commitment to social movements. The commission initially had ten members, a number that was later increased to fourteen (ten professors and four former students). The commission's objectives were presented in the second article of the constitutive document.[1]

> I) to locate and produce an inventory of documental collections regarding violations of human rights and individual liberties that occurred in the period between 1 April 1964 (military coup) and the first military intervention at the UnB, and 5 October 1988 (enactment of the Brazilian Democratic Constitution);
> II) to locate, produce and gather new documents relating to the period referred to in item I;
> III) to analyse the documentation and collections located;
> IV) to present information that supports the work of the National Truth Commission, the Ministry of Justice's Amnesty Commission, and the Special Commission for the Political Dead and Disappeared;
> V) to produce and publish a final report presenting a detailed analysis of violations of human rights and individual liberties of the academic community and society at large.

Once the CATMV-UnB was inaugurated, the research work started. The commission signed cooperation agreements with the Amnesty Commission and the National Truth Commission in order to enhance an exchange of information. It also organized two significant public events: the handing over of a dossier from Anísio Teixeira's family to the CNV and the CATMV that could potentially offer relevant insights into the professor's suspicious death; and a public homage to Honestino Guimarães, a noted student leader at the university, who was disappeared in 1973.[2] Another partnership was established with the Public Archives of Brasília. The commission held public audiences, took statements from teachers and students who were persecuted and/or affected by the military regime, and conducted time-consuming research for documents in the National Archives (ASI/UnB fund, CISA fund, SNI fund), the Brasil Nunca Mais Digital archive and in newspaper archives (*Folha de São Paulo, Folha da Tarde, Correio Braziliense, Jornal do Brasil, O Globo* and *Última Hora*). The commission also engaged in joint initiatives with other commissions and took part in the National Network of University Commissions.

The CATMV finished its activities on 22 April 2015. At the final ceremony, the rector, Ivan Camargo, son of a colonel who played an important part in the regime's official propaganda agencies, made a formal apology for the human rights violations committed between 1964 and 1985 at the university. On the same day, the commission delivered a preliminary 350-page report as the result of almost three years of investigative work. The CATMV made this preliminary report available online and invited readers to comment on it. This was a pioneering initiative; no university truth commission had ever invited the public to comment on its final report. After a thorough evaluation of the comments, the commission adopted and inserted many of the suggestions into the final report, which was eventually published in September 2015.[3] The final report's historical narrative was thus shaped by the community's critical participation. From the start, the CATMV was aware that the report would only be a first step in the ongoing struggle for truth and memory, not a definite closure.

The University of Brasília's Vanguard Project and Post-1964 Repression

The creation of the University of Brasília (UnB) in 1962 took place in a context marked by the country's increasing modernization and intense social debate, which, however, excluded large parts of the population.

The creation of a university in the country's new capital was tied to a much larger project: to rethink the foundations of education in Brazil. The University of Brasília and the entire public education system were essential parts of the country's reconstruction.

As various historical works and important Brazilian films have registered, the creation and establishment of the UnB were followed closely by the national scientific community of the time. The mentors of the university, Anísio Teixeira and Darcy Ribeiro, invited many leading academics to join the faculty, most of whom accepted the invitation.

The many innovations of the university project include: interdisciplinarity both in teaching and research; the 'transversal' distribution of courses into themed branches, which allowed for more flexibility in the curricula; many extension activities, for which a strong relationship between the university and the community was a prerequisite; and, finally, the freedom given to professors in elaborating their courses.[4]

The proposals contained in the UnB's political-pedagogical project were clearly vanguard, especially considering the condition of higher education in Brazil in the early 1960s.[5] The traditional university, masterminded by Gustavo Capanema during the Estado Novo, was a clear-cut system of chairs allied to a rigid fixation of the curriculum.

The reformatory character of the UnB may have particularly stimulated the fierce repression suffered from the earliest moments of the coup. Anísio Teixeira, the rector at the time, was discharged from office, and the Directive Council was ousted. Dismissals, persecutions and interventions of all sorts followed, culminating in the October 1965 crisis. On this occasion, after the firing of a total of fifteen professors, 223 colleagues sympathized with them and resigned from their professorships. The university lost 80 per cent of its faculty. The arduous work of attracting important Brazilian intellectuals to the new capital had been in vain.

Some of the teachers who remained at the university still pursued the original education project despite the hostile environment, while many professors collaborated. The student movement organized itself and created bastions of protest and resistance. The campus was invaded by military forces in August 1968, a traumatic event both for the academic community and the city of Brasília. Many arrests were made, followed by the customary internal processes of expulsion. Other invasions would take place later, always followed by the same level of violence.

As time went by, the national situation worsened. On 13 December 1968, the National Congress was shut down, Institutional Act no. 5 was enacted, quickly followed by the Decree Law no. 477 of 1969, all of which facilitated the escalation of repressions against students. The regime entered its most aggressive, authoritarian and violent phase. The systematic persecution and torture of students persisted throughout the 1970s.

Characteristics of the Repression at the University of Brasília

From the moment of the first interventions at UnB, acts violating the human rights of students, professors and staff took place, and the repression gradually gained a systematic character. The tentacles of the National Information Service (SNI) were well rooted inside the Rector's Office, sheltered under the Security and Information Department (ASI). In practical terms, this department assured the functionality of a repressive apparatus that had resources such as infiltration, active inducement of informants, and espionage.[6] This structure was operational for many years, at least up to 1984, the year in which the rector-intervener José Carlos Azevedo, a Brazilian Navy officer, was forced to resign.

Many documents relating to the waves of repression against the UnB's academic community circulated in the ASI: disciplinary procedures, internal investigations, reports from security sectors and many other records.[7] With the ratification of Law no. 6683/1979 and, especially, Constitutional Amendment no. 26/1985, the amnesty claims of professors who were punished with acts of exception during the regime started to be analysed, leading to the return of some of those who had been fired or forced to quit the university's faculty.

The history of the UnB shows that many international human rights laws were violated on its site by the Brazilian state. Students and professors were submitted to repeated torture sessions in compounds of the armed forces or the Federal District's security agencies. Three students have been missing since then: Honestino Guimarães, Paulo de Tarso Celestino and Ieda Delgado. Honestino Guimarães, one of the greatest symbols of the resistance of the student movement, had his political amnesty recognized post-mortem by the Amnesty Commission in September 2014, in an Amnesty Caravan jointly organized with the Anísio Teixeira Commission, in the symbolic Darcy Ribeiro Memorial Auditorium on the University of Brasília's campus.[8]

The agents of these grave violations of human rights at the University of Brasília have never been judged. The Anísio Teixeira Truth Commission's final report criticizes the state agencies constitutionally charged with criminal prosecution and civil responsibility and forced them to open investigations and examine the possibility of reparations for victims and family members.[9]

The Term of Cooperation that was signed with the Amnesty Commission allowed the CATMV to have access to the commission's extensive and unique collection, the foundation of which is made up by amnesty case files, uniting a variety of important documents brought by the claimants themselves.[10] This Term of Cooperation also enabled joint efforts to clarify specific incidents of grave violations of human rights, such as the disappearance of the three previously mentioned students and various uses of torture. At the CATMV inauguration ceremony, a public accusation was made referring to the circumstances surrounding the death of Anísio Teixeira. João Augusto de Lima Rocha, a professor at the Federal University of Bahia and a biographer of Anísio Teixeira, provided elucidating information. This was complemented with a dossier presented by the educator's family. The documents were handed to both commissions (the CNV and the CATMV) for further inquiry.

These new documents, which had not previously been fully analysed, offer a new understanding of the manifestations at the UnB during the military regime. Public hearings were held in the years 2013, 2014 and 2015 to register statements from those who had been targeted by these repressive acts in the many waves of repression felt in university life. Documents and hearings (both public and private) formed the basis for a final report, which might contribute to the enforcement of the fundamental right to memory and truth. We equally hope that the work carried out by the CATMV stimulates the university's community to build practices of knowledge that can guarantee visibility to the suffering of those who resisted the regime. The campus ought not be taken over by forgetfulness.

Repression and Resistance in an Intergenerational Perspective

One of the ways in which to understand the different forms of repression and resistance of the student movement is to take an intergenerational approach. It is convenient to use the 1988 Constitution as a clear temporal threshold. The eighth article of the Transitory Constitutional Provisions establishes that the reparations for human rights violations cover the period between September 1946 and October 1988. The large reparations programme goes beyond the temporal limits conventionally accepted as the beginning and end of the dictatorship (1964–85).

How is it possible to understand this article? This provision should be read – and thus applied – in an intergenerational perspective. By expanding the reparation period, the Constitutional Assembly offered a dialogue between generations. It allowed communist militants who were persecuted by agencies of repression under the Dutra government (1945–50) to be amnestied at the same time as union leaders who were involved in strikes in the second half of the 1980s. These are different generations of politically repressed, formed by groups and people with different trajectories and timelines. The Amnesty Commission enlarged this already amplified reparation programme further. It decided that the children, grandchildren, descendants and family members of victims of repression should also be recognized for their resistance while in exile and leading a clandestine life.

In this regard, the case of Paulo Fonteles Filho is significant. His parents, then students at the University of Brasília, were imprisoned and tortured by army officers at the Criminal Investigations Platoon (PIC), located in the Urban Military Sector of Brasília. His mother, Hecilda Fonteles, was pregnant when she was subjected to repression, and the Amnesty Commission recognized that her son was tortured while still in his mother's womb.[11] For many years, until his death in 2017, Paulo Fonteles Filho was an active militant defending populations who suffered the effects of the dictatorship's repressive apparatus in the Araguaia region. He was also a member of the Pará State Truth Commission.[12]

The case of Joaquim Eduardo de Alencar is equally emblematic. A doctor, teacher and communist militant, he started being persecuted by the security apparatus in May 1946. He was registered by DOPS (the Social and Political Order Department) in 1948 and monitored in 1949, 1955, 1960, 1961 and 1962. It is clear that his indictment at a Military Police inquiry in May 1964 related to his political activism prior to the military coup. During the democratic interregnum (1945–64) he had already been regarded as an 'enemy'.[13]

Joaquim Alencar was born in 1912. Paulo Fonteles Filho was born in prison in 1972. These two trajectories, which go far beyond the period from 1964 to 1985, reveal the complexity and reach of the authoritarian culture that was constructed in Brazil throughout the twentieth century. In addition, they show today's generations the diversity, importance and integrity of the fight against dictatorial regimes. The histories of these people are connected to the university. Joaquim Alencar was a well-known tropical disease specialist, having been a founding professor of the Medical College of the Federal University of Ceará. Paulo Fonteles Filho's parents, Hecilda and Paulo Fonteles, were University of Brasília students, and were engaged in the student movement there in the 1970s.

What do these trajectories tell us? Initially, they promote intergenerational dialogue. From a legal standpoint, it is important to remember a particularly talked-about article of the Brazilian Constitution, which refers to the guardianship of the environment. It stipulates that it is the duty of the state and society, in general, to defend and preserve an ecologically balanced environment 'for present and future generations' (art. 225, *caput*). Could we not understand this message and extend it to the field of transitional justice?

Currently, one of the biggest challenges in this field involves institutional reform. Our armed forces and police are still structured in a manner very similar to their structure during the authoritarian period. Abuses such as state violence, kidnappings, disappearances and torture are still practised throughout Brazil. Students who protest still suffer all sorts of violent treatment, as some dramatic episodes demonstrate. In March 2014, for example, the Federal Police invaded the campus of the Federal University of Santa Catarina.

The violence, the deaths and disappearances, the torture and disciplinary action that occurred during the dictatorship's repression of the universities, if well recorded and publicized, can become a 'bridge' between the persecuted students of the past and present. The knowledge of what happened at the UnB may help younger advocates of democracy to oppose those colleagues who are ignorant of the barbarous acts that afflicted their country and university and who now take to the streets and call for a new military intervention.

The student movement, which was severely targeted and practically dismantled by the military regime, was reborn during the political opening and played an important role in the consolidation process towards democracy. This endless consolidation work continues, and the dream of the students from the 1960s, committed to freedom and universal education, feeds the dreams of those who fight today for tomorrow's students.[14]

The Honestino Guimarães Bridge

We would like to conclude by revisiting the idea of a 'bridge' as a metaphor for intergenerational dialogue and by highlighting the sixth recommendation of the CATMV final report: 'to rename places which currently pay homage to champions of the military dictatorship in order to clearly demarcate the desired rupture with the military regime and pay homage to the struggle for democratic freedom'. On 2 August 2017, the governor of the Federal District sanctioned the law that renamed a bridge after Honestino Guimarães.[15]

Like every authoritarian regime, the Brazilian dictatorship took care to ensure that important figures would not be forgotten. During the state of exception, many public places were named after powerful military figures. One such place was a bridge connecting Brasília's central area with the Lago Sul (Southern Lake), one of the capital's most upmarket neighbourhoods. The name chosen for this bridge was Costa e Silva, the general-president, who in 1968 ordered a violent invasion of the UnB and signed the infamous Institutional Act no. 5 (AI-5), which curtailed fundamental rights and radicalized the repression of those who resisted the militarily imposed order.

Thirty years of civil government were needed to finally create the conditions under which the bridge could be renamed, as recommended by the CATMV. The choice of the new name, Honestino Guimarães, the UnB student leader who in 1969 became president of the National Students' Union, reveals the importance and influence of the university in the life of Brasília, an icon of modernism and innovation, a bearer of hope, renovation and regeneration. Honestino had been educated in the Federal District's government schools, supporting the idea of education as a synonym for inclusion, citizenship and self-reliance. Finally, his fate was tragic: Honestino disappeared under the regime. Family members, friends, colleagues and society in general remain unaware of his whereabouts. There is no grave, no body.

But the process of renaming the bridge was not a consensual one. After the Brasília City Council put it into law, the Honestino Guimarães Bridge became a place of political struggle. When the signs were replaced, right-wing political groups connected with the military defended the former name of the bridge. The rallies failed to receive major support, and the groups were relatively small, but they managed to attract the attention of local newspapers. They were also successful in presenting a legal complaint against the renaming of the bridge. When this chapter was being concluded, a district judge had repealed the City Council Law that renamed the bridge, and there was an appeal pending analysis by a Circuit Court.[16] It is beyond the scope of this chapter to present the technicalities involved in the lawsuit, which will likely be submitted to higher courts, but the controversy exemplifies the current political disputes over the legacy of the dictatorship.

Before the formal renaming, a collective of youth movements called Levante Popular da Juventude (often translated as Popular Uprising of the Youth) conducted an 'intervention' and manipulated the public signs on the bridge. They covered its ancient name with Honestino Guimarães banners and put other signs alongside the road.[17] Interestingly, when the district law was on the books, the supporters of Costa e Silva used the same strategy, painting the dictator's name on the new sign.[18] The urban space turned into a sort of public stage in a struggle over the meaning of the past. Connecting time and space, the rebaptizing of a public monument has generated diverse protests and claims.[19]

The action of naming the bridge after Honestino Guimarães is deeply meaningful. A bridge, by definition, is an expression of humanity, a mark upon nature, conveying the civilizing sign of urban life (as is the city of Brasília, with the Plano Piloto's foundational geometric design). As Walt Whitman said, the bridge is a modern emblem of movement. The bridge may, then, be understood as a metaphor for the passing of one generation to the next, from a period of obscurity to a transparent present that may announce a fully democratic future.

Honestino is the protagonist of this connection. He represents the transformative role that societies play in their own construction. In connecting different parts of the city, as well as the past and the future (open to democratic and inclusive practices), the Honestino Guimarães Bridge presents itself as a mediator. It thus establishes itself both as an expression of a struggle against the legacy of arbitrariness and as a promise of a free and democratic life. The final report of the University of Brasília's Anísio Teixeira Truth and Memory Commission also wishes to function in this way.

Cristiano Paixão is a professor at the University of Brasília Law School. He was Coordinator of Institutional Relations of the Anísio Teixeira Truth and Memory Commission (2012–15) and a member of the Amnesty Commission of the Brazilian Ministry of Justice (2012–16).

José Otávio Guimarães is a professor in the History Department at the University of Brasília. He was Research Coordinator of the Anísio Teixeira Truth and Memory Commission (2012–15) and a member of the advisory board of the Latin American Transitional Justice Network (2014–15).

Notes

We thank Claudia Paiva Carvalho, Nina Schneider, José Flávio Nogueira and John Wilson for suggestions and discussion.

1. 'Resolução da Reitoria n. 0085/2012', issued 10 August 2012, retrieved 8 January 2019 from http://www.comissaoverdade.unb.br/images/docs/rr_85_2012.pdf.
2. C. Paixão and J.O. Guimarães, 'Comissão da Verdade na UnB: entre o passado e o futuro', retrieved 8 January 2019 from http://www.comissaoverdade.unb.br/noticias/108-comissao-da-verdade-na-unb-entre-o-passado-e-o-futuro; see also P.E.C. Parucker, 'Um passo a mais na luta pelo direito à memória e à verdade', retrieved 8 January 2019 from http://www.comissaoverdade.unb.br/noticias/98-um-passo-verdade.
3. Retrieved 2 April 2018 from www.comissaoverdade.unb.br.
4. R.A. Salmeron, 'A Universidade de Brasília e sua história', *Humanidades* (EdUnB) 56 (2009), 168–79.
5. See R.A. Salmeron, *A universidade interrompida: Brasília 1964–1965* (Brasília: EdUnB, 2007).
6. R.P.S. Motta, 'Os olhos do regime militar brasileiro nos *campi*. As assessorias de segurança e informações das universidades', *Topoi* 9(16) (2008), 30–67; R.P.S. Motta, *As universidades e o regime militar* (Rio de Janeiro: Zahar, 2014), 193–241.
7. G.D. Aparecida, 'Os olhos e os ouvidos da repressão na Universidade de Brasília', *Quadrilátero – Revista do Arquivo Público do Distrito Federal* 1(1) (1998), 13–26.
8. BRASIL, Ministério da Justiça, Comissão de Anistia, Requerimento no. 2013.01.72431, sentenced in Brasília on 20 September 2013; D. Faria, 'Em memória de Ieda Santos Delgado', retrieved 2 August 2015 from http://www.comissaoverdade.unb.br/noticias/109-em-memoria-de-ieda-santos-delgado; M.C. Vasconcelos, 'Honestino', in *Unb 30 anos* (Brasília: EdUnB, 1992), 311–18.
9. See the first two recommendations of the CATMV's final report.
10. P. Abrão and T. Genro, *Os direitos da transição e a democracia no Brasil* (Belo Horizonte: Fórum, 2012), 33–80, 109–20.
11. BRASIL, Ministério da Justiça, Comissão de Anistia, Requerimento no. 2010.01.66508, sentenced in Brasília on 6 September 2012.
12. 'Ex-vereador Paulo Fonteles Filho morre em Belém', Portal G1, 26 October 2017, retrieved 1 April 2018 from https://g1.globo.com/pa/para/noticia/ex-vereador-paulo-fonteles-filho-morre-em-belem.ghtml.
13. BRASIL, Ministério da Justiça, Comissão de Anistia, Requerimento no. 2009.01.65097, sentenced in Fortaleza on 3 August 2012.
14. V. Langland, *Speaking of Flowers: Student Movements and the Making and Remembering of 1968 in Military Brazil* (Durham, NC and London: Duke University Press, 2013).
15. 'Ponte Costa e Silva troca de nome e termina homenagens à ditadura no DF', Correio Braziliense, 2 July 2015, retrieved 2 May 2017 from https://

www.correiobraziliense.com.br/app/noticia/cidades/2015/07/02/interna_cidadesdf,488697/ponte-costa-e-silva-troca-de-nome-e-terminam-homenagens-a-ditadura-no.shtml.

16. BRASIL, Tribunal de Justiça do Distrito Federal e Territórios, Processo no. 2015.01.1.113133-4, sentenced on 9 June 2017.
17. See images of this intervention on the website of ABAP (Associação Brasileira de Anistiados Políticos), retrieved 2 May 2017 from http://anistiapolitica.org.br/abap/index.php?option=com_content&view=article&id=710:lpj-renomeia-ponte-em-brasilia.
18. 'Grupo quer nome de Costa e Silva de volta à ponte do Lago Sul', Portal Metrópoles, 3 October 2015, retrieved 2 May 2017 from https://www.metropoles.com/distrito-federal/grupo-quer-nome-de-costa-e-silva-de-volta-na-ponte-do-lago-sul.
19. See A. Huyssen, *Present Pasts: Urban Palimpsests and the Politics of Memory* (Stanford, CA: Stanford University Press, 2003).

Bibliography

Abrão, P., and Genro, T. *Os direitos da transição e a democracia no Brasil*. Belo Horizonte: Fórum, 2012.

Aparecida, G.D. 'Os olhos e os ouvidos da repressão na Universidade de Brasília'. *Quadrilátero – Revista do Arquivo Público do Distrito Federal* 1(1) (1998), 13–26.

Faria, D. 'Em memória de Ieda Santos Delgado'. Retrieved 2 August 2015 from http://www.comissaoverdade.unb.br/noticias/109-em-memoria-de-ieda-santos-delgado.

Huyssen, A. *Present Pasts: Urban Palimpsests and the Politics of Memory*. Stanford, CA: Stanford University Press, 2003.

Langland, V. *Speaking of Flowers: Student Movements and the Making and Remembering of 1968 in Military Brazil*. Durham, NC and London: Duke University Press, 2013.

Motta, R.P.S. *As universidades e o regime militar*. Rio de Janeiro: Zahar, 2014.

Motta, R.P.S. 'Os olhos do regime militar brasileiro nos *campi*. As assessorias de segurança e informações das universidades'. *Topoi* 9(16) (2008), 30–67.

Paixão, C., and Guimarães, J.O. 'Comissão da Verdade na UnB: entre o passado e o futuro'. Retrieved 8 January 2019 from http://www.comissaoverdade.unb.br/noticias/108-comissao-da-verdade-na-unb-entre-o-passado-e-o-futuro.

Parucker, P.E.C. 'Um passo a mais na luta pelo direito à memória e à verdade', retrieved 8 January 2019 from http://www.comissaoverdade.unb.br/noticias/98-um-passo-verdade.

Salmeron, R.A. 'A Universidade de Brasília e sua história'. *Humanidades* (EdUnb) 56 (2009), 168–79.

Salmeron, R.A. *A universidade interrompida: Brasília 1964–1965*. Brasília: EdUnB, 2007.

Vasconcelos, M.C. 'Honestino', in *Unb 30 anos* (Brasília: EdUnB, 1992), 311–18.

Chapter 7

Truth Commissions in the Digital Age

An Analysis of the Brazilian Case

Ana Lúcia Migowski

The establishment of Truth Commissions (TCs) is one of the most common mechanisms of transitional justice processes.[1] In Brazil, this measure was implemented twenty-six years after the opening of the military dictatorship that ruled the country from 1964 to 1985. Other nations that also experienced mass violence and human rights violations have acted much faster in this regard. In the paradigmatic case of South Africa, for example, a Truth and Reconciliation Commission was installed in 1996, two years after the official end of apartheid. Brazil's neighbours, Argentina and Chile, also established TCs shortly after democratic governors assumed their seats. The time gap between the beginning of the transition in Brazil and the official installation of a TC raises a series of questions, such as the role of historical distance and its impact on the analyses of crimes, the absence of the participation of relevant actors, witnesses, victims and perpetrators who passed away in the meantime, and the effects of structural amnesia in civil society.[2]

A delayed TC also involves shifts within media environments. From the opening in 1985 to the start of the work of commissioners in 2012, the available media technologies changed radically. This is especially true considering the emergence of the networked society in the early 2000s and digital communication platforms like social network sites and environments based on user-generated content (the so-called Web 2.0). Information circulates in unprecedented ways throughout digital networks and its resonance with political, economic and social issues is more than evident. Take, for example, the recent impact of social media in the organization of mass protests in different countries, from the Arab Spring in 2010/11 to the election of the American President, Donald Trump, in 2016. According to Castells:[3]

> We live with the Internet and in the Internet, in all the spheres of our everyday lives. The new generations continue to watch television selectively, but via the Internet. They keep reading newspapers (more than ever), but different ones (and in fragments) through the Internet. They have constructed their own spaces of relationship, information, interaction and debate in the so-called social media – the multimodal social networks of the Internet – while accessing the most diverse assortment of contents through mobile technologies.[4]

In fact, it is not just 'new generations' that are affected by the use of the internet and web platforms. The reach of digital communication technologies is nowadays pervasive; it is everywhere and almost unavoidable. Public institutions, like TCs, also have to deal with the transformations that digital media cause to its activities.

> This interactivity, whilst a challenge for the traditional news economy and for media regulators, offers a genuinely transformative shift in terms of participation in human rights campaigns, discourse and awareness. ... human rights activists, scholars and the media themselves have begun to adapt to these changes and to use many of these new technologies to document abuses, to publicize and co-ordinate their campaigns for change, to advocate for remedial action, and to lobby governments and international institutions.[5]

One of the aims of this chapter is to provide an overview and a comparative analysis of the online presence of TCs and a more in-depth examination of the specific case of the Brazilian TC. I propose an exploration of the ways in which official attempts at investigating the truth about past human rights violations interact with popular knowledge in public debates on historical events.

TCs are crucial for memory processes as they fuel public debates on national history and trauma. Media promote access to the activities of these institutions and consequently the reception of their findings and investigations. The mediation of memories and engagement of debates over the past through different media brings about specific regimes of representation and arenas where memories can be shared, elaborated and also put into question.

In this chapter, I examine the manners by which an institution dedicated to the investigation and popularization of findings about past human rights violations acts in this context. First, I discuss the relationship between media (in a broader sense) and transitional justice. Then, I describe how different TCs make use of digital media. Last but not least, I look at the specific case of the Brazilian Truth Commission in order to understand how the Brazilian Truth Commission has interacted with the public via digital media platforms. These reflections will help explore the potential of Facebook for debates on the transitional process in Brazil.

Media in Transitional Justice Settings

A few scholars have addressed the relationship between media and transitional justice processes. The main focus so far has been on the role of local media in enabling public debate, and promoting discussions on national identities, as well as on the resonance of news coverage of international politics. Concerning TCs more specifically, experts posit that the agency of media is often overlooked and that this attitude can be harmful to transitional processes. Media may be important in 'selling' or 'explaining' transitional justice processes to the public in the form of news reports and publicity campaigns, and it can also have an even more central role by negotiating matters of identity.[6] The framing, agenda-setting and circulation promoted by the press usually form the primary objects of analysis. The South African case is an example of the symbiotic relationship between TCs and national broadcasting media.[7]

It is important to consider that very often media outlets covering transitional processes maintain structural connections to those that existed during the authoritarian or totalitarian period. The way that media supported or fought – voluntarily or not – the previous regime may influence the way they frame the new democratic state:

> Yet, a transition process does not begin with a whole new media system, but rather inherits whatever media institutions existed before and inevitably played a role during the period in question. Thus, countries embarking on a transitional justice project must also inevitably consider how to address any long-term damage to national media institutions and cultures.[8]

Societies experiencing transitional processes are usually polarized. Opinions very often diverge, and media impact the negotiation of meanings, being sometimes responsible for exacerbating such controversial positions: 'Thus, just as media can be a factor in negotiations leading to conflict resolution, they can also lead to further polarization'. Training journalists to cover post-conflict matters, as in the Liberian case, and 'the creation of independent media outlets and information campaigns', like in Bosnia and Herzegovina, are some of the strategies deployed to promote a plurality of voices.[9]

Digital and social media, however, add new layers of complexity, as through them official institutions and the public can potentially interact beyond the mediation of major mass media outlets. In the Brazilian case, private companies that were connected to the dictatorial past used to mediate such relationships. Public TV channels, radio stations and newspapers funded by the governments that decide on establishing Truth Commissions have always been players in this game, but their popularity within Brazilian society is still very low according to recent public opinion surveys. Nonetheless, digital media enable other regimes of interaction in a rather emergent and spontaneous way. Scholars studying media in the context of transitional justice processes recognized that the impact of social media has been undertheorized so far. Price and Stremlau point out: 'Social media have demonstrated the capacity to intensify aspects of separation and hostility as well as modes of increasing harmony and understanding. A major difference has been the complexity or appropriateness of intervention and control'.[10]

If examining the link between the traditional press and reckoning procedures with a violent past already posed significant analytical and political tasks, social media present further challenges to public institutions like TCs. In this context, they may deal with the widening of communication channels and possibilities of interaction with civil society. TCs commonly create specific public relations departments and communication teams responsible for reporting in official channels of communication. At the same time, civil society and independently organized initiatives also find on social media space to react to or reflect on the work of public institutions. Promoting dialogue and spreading the word about investigations and findings within these environments becomes a task to be accomplished by TCs in order to allow 'patterns of past violence, and causes and consequences of these destructive events' to be widely known and discussed. According to Bakiner: 'Truth commissions have emerged in political contexts where societies' conventional mechanisms for investigating serious crimes and writing unbiased accounts of the past (the judiciary and the media chief among them) had ceased to function'. As a means of overcoming these constraints, most TCs work to combine political, social and memorial issues related to multiple temporalities, especially to present and future uses of the past. It necessarily implies understanding the agency and consciously making use of media environments where TCs can reach society.[11]

TCs in the Digital Age

According to the list of the Truth and Reconciliation Commissions provided by the United States Institute of Peace (USIP), twelve TCs have been established since 2006. This year is a milestone for talking about the presence of TCs on social media as it marks the opening of Facebook to public access. In 2009, Facebook also made possible the creation of fan pages, the most common format used by public institutions like TCs. Facebook is, at the time of writing, the leading social network site worldwide, and TCs have been using it to report and interact with civil society.[12] By following the links provided by some of these TCs on their official websites, I have identified that six of them were officially present on Facebook: Brazil, Canada, Colombia, Kenya, Paraguay and Tunisia. These TCs, however, have deployed different strategies concerning their presence on Facebook.

Considering the ephemerality of digital media and the limited time of the mandate of TCs themselves, it is hard to precisely describe how they were using their Facebook pages while the investigations were running. Just two of the TCs currently present on Facebook were active at the time of writing – the Tunisian and the Colombian one. The other commissions remained present on Facebook through different approaches. Two main patterns have been identified. While the Brazilian and Kenyan TCs left their Facebook pages without any further changes after the release of their final reports, Canada adopted a different strategy. The page representing this TC during its mandate has been converted into a new page reflecting its new institutional status as it was turned into the National Centre for Truth and Reconciliation. New policies regarding the continuity and implementation of recommendations of TCs foster such modifications in the status of TCs, and their Facebook pages follow the same path. Paraguay deleted its Facebook page, yet its link is still present on the official website.

Further research using Facebook's search engine revealed other unofficial and independent initiatives referring to the work of these TCs or related to the general topic of truth-seeking in post-conflict societies. The Facebook group Víctimas Comisión Valech, from Chile, organized by victims who suffered during Pinochet's rule, is one example. Ecuador and Honduras did not create official pages on Facebook – as far as this research could trace –, but they are present online through civil society initiatives. Taking such initiatives into consideration offers a more inclusive way of understanding the role of digital media in processes of transition.[13]

Gready and Robins stress the importance of civil society engagement rather than considering only official mechanisms and traditional social movements (such as NGOs) in transitional processes. The authors outline various modes of action taken by the 'new civil society', such as the attempt to influence formal mechanisms by calling for resistance or documenting it, mobilizing and empowering social actors. Such modes of action have the potential to impact official decisions, and these 'new' ways depend highly on the connectivity provided by social media. Activists and other actors directly or indirectly involved in past conflicts use social network sites, mainly Facebook, YouTube and Twitter, to engage and actively exhibit their opinion on reckoning processes.[14]

Assessing the impact of social media on contemporary transitional justice processes requires further methodological and conceptual tools not entirely covered here. This overview, based on the few cases identified so far, is meant to introduce the broader topic and demonstrate that other countries have also made use of digital environments for communicating and fostering transitional processes. In the following, I will concentrate on the Brazilian case and analyse both the official and unofficial ways of producing meaning over the transitional process; the Facebook page of the National Truth Commission (hereafter NTC); and the pages and groups reacting and responding to the NTC, respectively.

The Brazilian Truth Commission Facebook Page

The Brazilian government established the Brazilian National Truth Commission in 2012, almost fifty years after the 1964 civil-military coup. Its main achievements have been to intensify the public debate on the dictatorship in Brazil, and to disclose information about former human rights violations. Hundreds of news reports, special issues of magazines and newspapers, documentaries, movies, novels and academic books have since been released. Public hearings and testimonies given to the NTC by military officers, political activists, victims and their relatives have also offered new means of looking at this period of Brazilian history.[15]

Traditional media have paid little attention to the activities of the NTC, according to researchers from the field of journalism, especially in the initial stages. Several studies show that the news coverage, which is vital for citizens to follow the commission's work, has been insufficient. To Abreu, 'the news coverage has been weak, full of obliterations, which did not translate the importance of creating a TC in the political history of Brazil. On the contrary, news companies have been constantly suspicious of its goals and purposes'. Sanglard demonstrated that the news coverage 'was dominated by mainstream press companies and by those aligned to a more left-wing ideology'. According to this scholar, the presence of the NTC in the news was intensified in the final year, 2014, especially because: '(1) it was in the final stages that results of the investigation were presented; (2) there was massive and special coverage because of the fiftieth anniversary of the civil-military coup; and (3) the NTC developed new communication strategies in its final months'.[16]

This unstable news coverage was challenging for the NTC, particularly in terms of making its findings and activities visible and accessible to the general public. 'Historically, truth commissions emerged when social communication over the meaning of the past failed', so taking a consistent approach in this regard is essential for the success of the transitional justice process.[17]

As part of its public relations strategies the NTC also created its own communication channels. Apart from reports, interviews, videos and documents made available on its institutional website, the commission also created profiles on social network sites. Facebook, which is currently the most popular digital platform in Brazil, played an important role in this context. The use of digital environments has increased the possibilities of dialogue and diversification of publics reached by the commission. The Facebook page has been liked more than 250,000 times; the Twitter profile counts about thirteen thousand followers; and the YouTube channel remains as a repository of testimonies and documentaries. Thousands of comments and responses to messages published by the NTC can be found on these platforms.[18]

Brazilians are among the most active internet users nowadays. They rank sixth in the world in terms of time spent online, and second regarding time spent on social media such as Facebook. This shows how decisive it is to be present online in order to engage with civil society. The political formation of many Brazilians is largely based on information they access on social media. Opinions presented on their timelines, as well as news reports, blog posts and videos, are used as arguments for public debate. Malini identified how strong these 'distributed nets of information' are for the formation of public opinion in Brazil. Two massive protests organized in 2013 and 2015 are robust examples of social and political mobilizations online.[19]

Bichara conducted an extensive content analysis of the NTC Facebook page covering different periods from 2014 and 2015. She found that the communication department responsible for updating the page concentrated mostly on publishing information about the activities of the commission, giving accounts of the investigations, events and meetings promoted by the commissioners. The researcher also highlighted that comments and reviews left on the page represent the memory and political culture in Brazil: they reproduce a polarized view on the topic, with some users defending and others criticizing the NTC's work as well as a continuous reference to current political fights.[20]

After the end of the commission in December 2014, documents produced by the NTC, including the website, were integrated into the project Memórias Reveladas (Uncovered Memories) hosted by the National Archives in Rio de Janeiro. The changes made on the official webpage include the addition of the item 'Facebook' on its main menu. Demonstrating the relevance of the social network site to the legacy of the NTC, here one finds the following statement:

> The Facebook page of the National Truth Commission gave accounts of the activities of its working groups since its installation on 12 May 2012, until the submission of the final report to President Dilma Rousseff, on 10 December 2014. As a legacy, the material published throughout these two years and seven months of activities remains available.
>
> These are pictures, videos and news reports produced by the NTC and the press, visual communication pieces and the complete coverage of events, visits to historical settings, testimonies and many other facts that were part of the National Truth Commission research and investigation process.[21]

Officially, it serves as an archive of contents and interactions produced within Facebook while it was updated (from 2012 to 2015). Even after the end of the commission in 2014, new interactions among Facebook users and reactions to the NTC's work continue to take place, both on the page, especially in the comments and reviews areas, and in the form of pages and groups that refer to the transitional process covered by the commission.

In what follows, I describe the methodology employed for understanding how the Brazilian National Truth Commission made use of Facebook for publicizing the activities performed and the results of its investigations, as well as promoting public debate. At the same time that the Facebook page made the work of the NTC more transparent through media, it also attracted reactions from multiple publics. The establishment of the NTC had already been the target of controversies, above all from the military sector, which did not want to share details on the topic, and social movements that fought for the punishment of perpetrators. Digital communication channels provide a fertile ground for the manifestation of these and other publics.

Methodology

I collected and qualitatively analysed the last fifty posts published on the NTC Facebook page and their respective comments. These data cover contents published over the last three months in which the page was updated (November 2014 to January 2015). According to the broader analysis conducted by Bichara, the most intensive interactions took place during the last months, above all regarding comments and likes. The small sample selected for the study presented here (considering the total number of 1,405 posts published since 2012) offers an overview of the resonance of a transitional justice mechanism on social media. I also looked for other pages and groups that make reference to official state-sponsored mechanisms and briefly analysed how they reflect civil society initiatives that also respond to the transitional process. In methodological terms, I employed grounded theory and content analysis in order to identify the main topics addressed in the sample. This strategy allowed for the recognition of the main patterns of interaction that exhibit the engagement of Facebook users around the topic and with transitional justice mechanisms. By combining these two approaches, I propose a comprehensive overview of the unfolding processes regarding the use of digital media with respect to how Brazilian society and institutions have been dealing with the recent dictatorial past. For ethical reasons, I translated all comments into English and deleted usernames. Considering the potential harmful implications of identifying users who have given statements on this contentious political and historical topic, hiding such sensitive information is currently the recommended methodological strategy.[22]

Engagement, Conflict and Memories on the National Truth Commission Facebook Page

The most common topics approached in the fifty analysed posts were about the work developed by the commission (visits to archives, prisons and hospitals, awards received), the publication of the final report, and testimonies and news reports regarding missing and dead victims. Most of the total number of more than six hundred comments had a supportive character, with messages addressed to the commissioners. The second most expressive category articulated dissatisfaction or opposing remarks towards the commission's activities. Also, several comments presented public doubts regarding the NTC's work in general.

Despite the common-sense idea that digital and social media potentially democratize the public debate around political and memorial issues, their cultural appropriation has shown different facets. As Papacharissi states, 'The ability to discuss any political subject at random, drifting in and out of discussions and topics on a whim, can be very liberating, but it does not create a common starting point for political discussion. Ultimately, there is a danger that these technologies may overemphasize our differences and downplay or even restrict our commonalities'.[23]

This seems to be the case with messages left by certain users on the NTC Facebook page. As seen previously, the number of supportive messages demonstrating an empathetic relationship between users and institution is notable. However, at the same time, opposing comments are also numerous. A sequence of two videos in comments on a post about the result of an investigation into the circumstances of the death of a victim of the dictatorship illustrates such polarized use of digital media. While the first commenter posted a link pointing to a 1971 video featuring testimonies of torture victims, a subsequent commenter made use of the same space to publish a documentary supportive of the civil-military coup. These dynamics reveal a debate based on the reinforcement of prior ideas or, in Papacharissi's words, something that 'overemphasizes differences'.[24]

Exposing contradictory opinions is certainly part of a democratic environment, but the problem here is that little or no constructive exchange of ideas seems to occur. Instead of a dialogical environment, the Facebook page becomes an arena where citizens try to reinforce their own convictions, especially regarding their memories and historical knowledge based on first- or second-hand experiences. Violent acts and harsh words are frequently employed for these means.

Users answer most of the questions and aggressive messages. The commission staff replied only to very direct comments, such as: 'Is the final report going to be published online?' In this sense, the page can be understood mainly as a unidirectional channel in terms of communication, where the institution puts forward its findings, reports its activities and provides the public with a space for debate. Kansteiner identified this same practice in his analysis of the US Holocaust Museum Facebook page.[25]

This lack of feedback can also be interpreted as the common policy of not 'feeding the trolls' usually adopted by public institutions. 'The phrase "Don't feed the trolls!" is commonly used by "legitimate" forum users, warning each other not to give the troll the attention he seeks.' Trolls, in a broader sense, can be defined as 'people who genuinely wish to be part of the group, but seek to influence the forum negatively, by continually starting arguments, criticizing or complaining'. By following such a definition, trolling acts can be traced in the comments area, especially those based on repetitive statements and vague argumentation. Not replying to them tends to minimize the harmful effect to the general debate. As Prince and Stremlau warn, the 'complexity or appropriateness of intervention and control' is a major challenge for human rights and transitional justice institutions.[26]

Links to news websites and online versions of printed magazines and newspapers are frequently included in comments left on the NTC Facebook page. These contents are used as arguments from authority, confirming and supporting users' preconceived ideas about the topic. A link to a column by Reinaldo Azevedo, a famous Brazilian journalist, entitled 'Truth Commission Report Hides 121 Corpses; It's About Mystification, Revenge and Farce', for example, was published by a user in response to the post in which the NTC announces the release of its final report. Without any further comments, the user left this link in an effort to both criticize the NTC and make other commenters aware of this source. Traditional media keep on framing and setting parameters for the interpretation of transitional justice mechanisms.

It is also possible to reflect on the use of this public space for calling attention to problems Brazilians experience in the present. This relationship between past and present is crucial for understanding processes of memory labour. A user, for example, wrote on all posts analysed and on different dates the following message: 'Right now there are political prisoners in Rio de Janeiro'. These inheritances of the authoritarian past persist and shape the memorial debate. Violence and human rights violations in Brazil are, unfortunately, chronic conditions that persist despite democracy. The repetition of the same statement in various posts seeks to put this topic onto the national agenda.

The presence of the NTC on social network sites can also emerge from non-official initiatives, as seen in regards to the Chilean case. I found eight pages and groups referring to and unfolding the meanings produced by the NTC. In order to find these occurrences, I searched using the keyword 'Comissão da Verdade' (Truth Commission, in Portuguese) through the Facebook built-in search engine. Setting aside the results for pages and groups dedicated to local and institutional TCs, I selected a total of five pages and three groups concerning the topic.

The goals and contents produced within these pages and groups are manifold, demonstrating different attitudes towards the work of the NTC. In this respect, it is worth mentioning 'The Leftists' Truth' (A Verdade das Esquerdas) and 'The Truthful Truth: Terrorism Never Again' (A Verdadeira Verdade: Terrorismo Nunca Mais), with more negative manifestations towards the TC and supportive of the military regime. On the other hand, the group 'Truth Commission: I Support!!' (Comissão da Verdade: Eu apoio!!) assumes a positive position. Journalists and activists interested in following the developments and impact of the NTC created another group called the 'National Truth Commission: Repercussion and Information'. This initiative focuses on objectively reporting and assessing outcomes of the NTC. Yet the most recent posts published on the group seem more aligned with the agenda of human rights and current political struggles in Brazil. Along these lines, the 'National Truth Commission: Indigenous Peoples' Rights Violations' is a page used to report a specific event promoted by the NTC in order to investigate crimes committed against indigenous peoples. Administrators continue to add updates about the struggles and achievements of indigenous people to this page. One last case worth mentioning is the page 'National Truth Commission – 2nd Part Democracy', which appropriates the name 'National Truth Commission', adding '2nd Part' as if to propose a continuation of the work of investigation within the democratic regime.

In sum, the interactions within and beyond the Brazilian TC Facebook page reveal many facets of present cultural, memorial and political attitudes in Brazil. Looking at how civil society and public institutions engage in this kind of phenomenon is key to understanding contemporary transitional justice.

Final Remarks

Digital media represent an arena where TCs can potentially publicize and promote public debate. Some TCs created over the last decade worldwide have employed social media in order to report their activities and engage civil society in transitional processes.

Nevertheless, they can also serve as a stage for polarization and reinforcement of preconceived ideas. This finding is in line with Kansteiner's analysis of other public institutions addressing historical and memorial contents: 'The users ... appear to expect and accept this miscommunication, perhaps because they are not looking at institutions ... for historical and political guidance. Apparently, they simply like to be part of the group and share its values'. The comparative analysis initiated in this chapter may require further developments so that this assertion can be extrapolated to other cases.[27]

In the Brazilian case, however, this scenario seems a natural outcome of periods of silence and lack of public debate about the origins and consequences of the authoritarian regime preceding the NTC. This has given room for all sorts of speculation and multiplication of narratives in many sectors of civil society. Despite the extensive work of historians, archivists, artists and social movements working on the clarification of the circumstances of the dictatorship, especially with regard to human rights violations, questions remain, and many 'truths' circulate within the public sphere. The Brazilian Truth Commission makes these dissonant voices and perspectives even more explicit as it emphasizes the relevance of reckoning with the past and is targeted by multiple and clashing manifestations.

Ana Lúcia Migowski is a PhD candidate at the Justus-Liebig Universität Giessen and a former grantholder at the Graduate Centre for the Study of Culture (GCSC). She received her Master's degree in Communication and Information from the Federal University of Rio Grande do Sul (PPGCOM-UFRGS), where she is currently a member of the research group Laboratory of Digital Artefacts (LAD/UFRGS).

Notes

1. Transitional justice as a concept refers generally to 'processes of trials, purges, and reparations that take place after the transition from one political regime to another'. See J. Elster, *Closing the Books: Transitional Justice in Historical Perspective* (Cambridge: Cambridge University Press, 2004), 1. Scholars have criticized this definition, contrasting theory and practice, and relativizing the overemphasis on legal rather than cultural and educational matters. See N. Roht-Arriaza, 'The New Landscape of Transitional Justice', in N. Roht-Arriaza and J. Mariezcurrena (eds), *Transitional Justice in the Twenty-First Century: Beyond Truth versus Justice* (Cambridge: Cambridge University Press, 2006), 1–16. In Brazil, it is commonly used

to describe 'available mechanisms to deal with legacies of past violence: truth, reparation, justice and the restoration of institutions justice'. See P. Abrão and M.D. Torelly, 'Justiça de Transição no Brasil: a dimensão da reparação', in B.V.S. Santos, P. Abrão, C.M. Santos, and M.D. Torelly (eds), *Repressão e Memória Política no Contexto Ibero-Brasileiro: estudos sobre Brasil, Guatemala, Moçambique, Peru e Portugal* (Brasília: Ministério da Justiça, Comissão de Anistia; Portugal: Universidade de Coimbra, Centro de Estudos Sociais, 2010), 27. Here, I provide insights on how social media have been appropriated for the attainment of such mechanisms, especially Truth Commissions. I argue that besides legal and truth-seeking efforts, social media are also crucial for understanding contemporary transitional justice processes.

2. In this chapter, I use the term 'Truth Commission' (abbreviated as TC) when referring generically to this transitional justice mechanism. When writing about specific cases, however, I preserve their original names. This is the case with the Brazilian 'National Truth Commission' (Comissão Nacional da Verdade, in Portuguese), hereafter the NTC.
3. For an overview of economic, political and social implications of the networked society, see M. Castells, *The Network Society*: *The Rise of the Network Society* (Oxford: Wiley-Blackwell, 2010), 500–509.
4. M. Castells, 'Democracy in the Age of the Internet', *Transfer: Journal of Contemporary Culture* 6 (2011), 99.
5. D. Joyce, 'Media Witnesses: Human Rights in an Age of Digital Media', *Intercultural Human Rights Law Review* 8 (2013), 234.
6. See the work of L.J. Laplante, 'The Role of Media in Transitional Justice', in J. Hoffmann and V. Hawkins (eds), *Communication and Peace: Mapping an Emergent Field* (Abingdon: Routledge, 2015), 265–76; M.E. Price and N. Stremlau, 'Media and Transitional Justice: Toward a Systematic Approach', *International Journal of Communication* 6 (2012), 1077–99; L.J. Laplante and K. Phenicie, 'Mediating Post-Conflict Dialogue: The Media's Role in Transitional Justice Processes', *Marquette Law Review* 93(1) (2009), 251–83. Atencio also provides a comprehensive analysis of the 'cycles of cultural memory' in the Brazilian transitional process that are marked by the relationship between cultural products – some of them media products, like book, film and TV series – and institutional mechanisms. See R. Atencio, *Memory's Turn: Culture and Transitional Justice in Brazil* (Madison: University of Wisconsin Press, 2014), 27.
7. R. Krabill, 'Symbiosis: Mass Media and the Truth and Reconciliation Commission of South Africa', *Media, Culture and Society* 23 (2001), 567–85.
8. Laplante and Phenicie, 'Mediating Post-Conflict Dialogue', 279.
9. For more insights on polarization, see Price and Stremlau, 'Media and Transitional Justice', 1080. On the Liberian case, see L. Randall and C.R. Pulano, Jr, 'Transitional Justice Reporting Audit: A Review of Media Coverage of the Truth and Reconciliation Process in Liberia', International Center for Transitional Justice, 2008, retrieved 10 February 2018 from

https://www.ictj.org/sites/default/files/ICTJ-Liberia-Truth-Reconciliation-2008-English.pdf. Refer to Price and Stremlau, 'Media and Transitional Justice', 1091 for more details on the Bosnian and Herzegovinian case.

10. Chagas wrote a news report on the perception of Brazilians in regard to public media. See P.V. Chagas, 'Mídia pública ainda não é lembrada por brasileiros', EBC: Agência Brasil, 2014, retrieved 10 January 2018 from http://agenciabrasil.ebc.com.br/geral/noticia/2014-03/midia-publica-ainda-nao-e-lembrada-por-brasileiro. Remarks on the challenges and potentials of social media for human rights institutions can be found in Price and Stremlau, 'Media and Transitional Justice', 1094.
11. This definition of TCs is based on United Nations, 'Guidance Note of the Secretary-General: United Nations Approach to Transitional Justice', March 2010, retrieved 2 January 2018 from https://www.un.org/ruleoflaw/files/TJ_Guidance_Note_March_2010FINAL.pdf. The second quotation refers to O. Bakiner, 'One Truth among Others? Truth Commissions' Struggle for Truth and Memory', *Memory Studies* 8(3) (2015), 345–60.
12. The twelve countries that established TCs from 2006 onwards are: Brazil (National Truth Commission, 2011–14), Canada (Truth and Reconciliation Commission, 2009–15), Chile (Comisión Valech II, 2010–15), Colombia (Comisión para el Esclarecimiento de la Verdad, la Convivencia y la no Repetición, 2014 and Comisión de la Verdad 2017) Congo (Truth and Reconciliation Commission, 2003–07), Ecuador (Truth and Reconciliation Commission, 2003–07), Honduras (Truth and Reconciliation Commission, 2010–11), Kenya (Truth and Reconciliation Commission, 2008–?), Mauritius (Truth and Justice Commission, 2009–11), Paraguay (Truth and Justice Commission, 2004–08), Solomon Islands (Truth and Reconciliation Commission, 2009–11) and Tunisia (Truth and Dignity Commission, 2014–). For more information on this matter, see United States Institute of Peace, 'Truth Commission Digital Collection', 16 March 2011, retrieved 12 January 2018 from https://www.usip.org/publications/2011/03/truth-commission-digital-collection. For complementary information, also refer to Wikipedia, 'List of Truth and Reconciliation Commissions', retrieved 12 January 2018 from https://en.wikipedia.org/wiki/List_of_truth_and_reconciliation_commissions. Find statistics on the popularity of Facebook on We Are Social, '2018 Digital Yearbook', 2018, 9, retrieved 1 February 2018 from https://www.slideshare.net/wearesocial/2018-digital-yearbook-86862930.
13. Non-official pages of the Truth Commissions from Chile, Honduras and Ecuador were found through the research methods used in this chapter. These methods consisted of (1) looking for links to the Facebook pages on the official websites of each commission; and (2) searching Facebook for references to the Truth Commissions. I have also focused the research on Truth Commissions that have been established from 2006 onwards. Examples mentioned in the text: Victimas Comisión Valech (V.C.V), Facebook, retrieved 1 December 2017 from https://www.facebook.com/groups/227901763929400/; Red Salvadoreña de Solidaridad con la

Resistencia Popular de Honduras, retrieved 1 December 2017 from https://www.facebook.com/RED-SALVADORE%C3%91A-DE-SOLIDARIDAD-CON-LA-RESISTENCIA-POPULAR-DE-HONDURAS-110389065660768/; Comisión de la Verdad and Justicia de Ecuador, retrieved 1 December 2017 from https://www.facebook.com/Comisiondelaverdadec/.

14. P. Gready and S. Robins, 'Rethinking Civil Society and Transitional Justice: Lessons from Social Movements and "New" Civil Society', *International Journal of Human Rights* 21(7) (2017), 966.
15. President Dilma Rousseff signed the law (n. 12.528) authorizing the creation of a National Truth Commission in 2011. The NTC was then established in 2012 and its mandate continued until 2014. For an updated analysis of the achievements and limitations of the work of the Brazilian Truth Commission, see C.S. Bauer, *Como será o passado? História, historiadores e a Comissão Nacional da Verdade* (Jundiaí-SP: Paco Editorial, 2017).
16. See the work of C.R. Abreu, 'O discurso jornalístico da Comissão Nacional da Verdade', *Rumores (USP)* 7(1) (2013), 348; and F.N. Sanglard, 'Jornalismo e Ditadura: Análise da Cobertura Midiática durante os trabalhos da Comissão da Verdade', *Porto Alegre: Anais do Congresso Compolítica* 7 (2017), 21.
17. Bakiner, 'One Truth among Others?', 356.
18. The number of comments and reviews continues to grow, even after the end of the commission in 2015, when the communication team stopped updating the Facebook page.
19. For statistics on the habits of Brazilian internet users, see A. Pariona, 'Countries Where People Spend the Most Time Online', Worldatlas, 2017, retrieved 12 January 2018 from https://www.worldatlas.com/articles/top-countries-which-spend-the-greatest-amount-of-time-online.html; and S. Kemp, 'Digital in 2017: Global Overview', We Are Social, 2017, retrieved 1 February 2018 from https://wearesocial.com/special-reports/digital-in-2017-global-overview. Malini is an outstanding Brazilian scholar who deals with political uses of social media. In this chapter, I quote F. Malini, 'A opinião pública distribuída: blogs e jornalismo nas eleições brasileiras de 2006', *e-compós* 9(1) (2007), 1–21.
20. M. Bichara, 'O Dever de Memória no Facebook', *Mosaico* 6(9) (2015), 73–89.
21. Comissão Nacional da Verdade, 'Facebook CNV', retrieved 10 January 2018 from http://cnv.memoriasreveladas.gov.br/depoimentos.html.
22. See the work of P. Reilly and F. Trevisan, 'Researching Protest on Facebook: Developing an Ethical Stance for the Study of Northern Irish Flag Protest Pages', *Information, Communication and Society* 19(3) (2016), 27–28; A. Markham and E. Buchanan, 'Ethical Decision-Making and Internet Research: Recommendations from the AoIR Ethics Working Group (Version 2.0)', Association of Internet Researchers, 2012, retrieved 10 December 2017 from https://aoir.org/reports/ethics2.pdf.
23. Z. Papacharissi, 'The Virtual Sphere: The Internet as a Public Sphere', *New Media & Society* 4(1) (2002), 9.

24. Ibid.
25. W. Kansteiner, 'Transnational Holocaust Memory, Digital Culture and the End of Reception Studies', in T.S. Andersen and B. Törnquist-Plewa (eds), *The Twentieth Century in European Memory: Transcultural Mediation and Reception* (Leiden: Brill, 2017), 323–24.
26. For an analysis of the action of trolls, see A. Binns, 'DON'T FEED THE TROLLS! Managing Troublemakers in Magazines' Online Communities', *Journalism Practice* 6(4) (2012), 548; see also Price and Stremlau, 'Media and Transitional Justice', 1077.
27. Kansteiner, 'Transnational Holocaust Memory', 324.

Bibliography

Abrão, P., and Torelly, M.D. 'Justiça de Transição no Brasil: a dimensão da reparação', in B.V.S. Santos, P. Abrão, C.M. Santos, and M.D. Torelly (eds), *Repressão e Memória Política no Contexto Ibero-Brasileiro: estudos sobre Brasil, Guatemala, Moçambique, Peru e Portugal* (Brasília: Ministério da Justiça, Comissão de Anistia; Portugal: Universidade de Coimbra, Centro de Estudos Sociais, 2010), 26–56.

Abreu, C.R. 'O discurso jornalístico da Comissão Nacional da Verdade'. *Rumores (USP)* 7(1) (2013), 336–52.

Atencio, R. *Memory's Turn: Culture and Transitional Justice in Brazil*. Madison: University of Wisconsin Press, 2014.

Bakiner, O. 'One Truth among Others? Truth Commissions' Struggle for Truth and Memory'. *Memory Studies* 8(3) (2015), 345–60.

Bauer, C.S. *Como será o passado? História, historiadores e a Comissão Nacional da Verdade*. Jundiaí-SP: Paco Editorial, 2017.

Bichara, M. 'O Dever de Memória no Facebook'. *Mosaico* 6(9) (2015), 73–89.

Binns, A. 'DON'T FEED THE TROLLS! Managing Troublemakers in Magazines' Online Communities'. *Journalism Practice* 6(4) (2012), 547–62.

Castells, M. 'Democracy in the Age of the Internet'. *Transfer: Journal of Contemporary Culture* 6 (2011), 96–103.

Castells, M. *The Network Society: The Rise of the Network Society*. Oxford: Wiley-Blackwell, 2010.

Chagas, P.V. 'Mídia pública ainda não é lembrada por brasileiros'. EBC: Agência Brasil, 2014. Retrieved 10 January 2018 from http://agenciabrasil.ebc.com.br/geral/noticia/2014-03/midia-publica-ainda-nao-e-lembrada-por-brasileiros.

Elster, J. *Closing the Books: Transitional Justice in Historical Perspective*. Cambridge: Cambridge University Press, 2004.

Gready, P., and Robins, S. 'Rethinking Civil Society and Transitional Justice: Lessons from Social Movements and "New" Civil Society'. *The International Journal of Human Rights* 21(7) (2017), 959–75.

Joyce, D. 'Media Witnesses: Human Rights in an Age of Digital Media'. *Intercultural Human Rights Law Review* 8 (2013), 231–80.

Kansteiner, W. 'Transnational Holocaust Memory, Digital Culture and the End of Reception Studies', in T.S. Andersen and B. Törnquist-Plewa (eds), *The Twentieth Century in European Memory: Transcultural Mediation and Reception* (Leiden: Brill, 2017), 305–44.

Kemp, S. 'Digital in 2017: Global Overview'. We Are Social, 2017. Retrieved 1 February 2018 from https://wearesocial.com/special-reports/digital-in-2017-global-overview.

Krabill, R. 'Symbiosis: Mass Media and the Truth and Reconciliation Commission of South Africa'. *Media, Culture and Society* 23 (2001), 567–85.

Laplante, L.J. 'The Role of Media in Transitional Justice', in J. Hoffmann and V. Hawkins (eds), *Communication and Peace: Mapping an Emergent Field* (Abingdon: Routledge, 2015), 265–76.

Laplante, L.J., and Phenicie, K. 'Mediating Post-Conflict Dialogue: The Media's Role in Transitional Justice Processes', *Marquette Law Review* 93(1) (2009), 251–83.

Malini, F. 'A opinião pública distribuída: blogs e jornalismo nas eleições brasileiras de 2006'. *e-compós* 9(1) (2007), 1–21.

Markham, A., and Buchanan, E. 'Ethical Decision-Making and Internet Research: Recommendations from the AoIR Ethics Working Group (Version 2.0)'. Association of Internet Researchers, 2012. Retrieved 10 December 2017 from https://aoir.org/reports/ethics2.pdf.

Papacharissi, Z. 'The Virtual Sphere: The Internet as a Public Sphere'. *New Media & Society* 4(1) (2002), 9–27.

Pariona, A. 'Countries Where People Spend the Most Time Online'. Worldatlas, 2017. Retrieved 12 January 2018 from https://www.worldatlas.com/articles/top-countries-which-spend-the-greatest-amount-of-time-online.html.

Price, M.E., and Stremlau, N. 'Media and Transitional Justice: Toward a Systematic Approach'. *International Journal of Communication* 6 (2012), 1077–99.

Rundall, L., and Paluma, C.R. Jr. 'Transitional Justice Reporting Audit: A Review of Media Coverage of the Truth and Reconciliation Process in Liberia'. International Center for Transitional Justice, 2008. Retrieved 10 February 2018 from https://www.ictj.org/sites/default/files/ICTJ-Liberia-Truth-Reconciliation-2008-English.pdf.

Reilly, P., and Trevisan, F. 'Researching Protest on Facebook: Developing an Ethical Stance for the Study of Northern Irish Flag Protest Pages'. *Information, Communication and Society* 19(3) (2016), 419–35.

Roht-Arriaza, N. 'The New Landscape of Transitional Justice', in N. Roht-Arriaza and J. Mariezcurrena (eds), *Transitional Justice in the Twenty-First Century: Beyond Truth versus Justice* (Cambridge: Cambridge University Press, 2006), 1–16.

Sanglard, F.N. 'Jornalismo e Ditadura: Análise da Cobertura Midiática durante os trabalhos da Comissão da Verdade'. *Porto Alegre: Anais do Congresso Compolítica* 7 (2017), 1–23.

United Nations. 'Guidance Note of the Secretary-General: United Nations Approach to Transitional Justice'. March 2010. Retrieved 2 January

2018 from https://www.un.org/ruleoflaw/files/TJ_Guidance_Note_March_2010FINAL.pdf.

United States Institute of Peace. 'Truth Commission Digital Collection'. 16 March 2011. Retrieved 12 January 2018 from https://www.usip.org/publications/2011/03/truth-commission-digital-collection.

Chapter 8

Corporate Complicity in the Brazilian Dictatorship

Leigh A. Payne

'Do you have any idea who Henning Boilesen was?' A recent documentary film depicts interviews with residents of a street in São Paulo bearing that name. One neighbour ventures a guess that he was German, given his name. Another confidently identifies him as a business manager, pointing to a plaque near the street sign indicating those bare bones of his past. Most have no idea.[1]

Several years later, and as a result of a network of researchers investigating past political violence in Brazil, the filmmakers might now find at least a few more residents who can identify Boilesen and what he did to get his name on a street sign in São Paulo in 1973. Because of that new knowledge, a group of students started a petition to remove his name from the street sign.[2]

Boilesen, a Brazilian of Dutch extraction, and the chief executive officer at the Ultragas company, represents corporate complicity in the 1964 coup and the dictatorship it implanted. He is widely believed to have coordinated the financing of the coup and repressive apparatus along with an estimated 123 other members of the business community. His company, along with others, allegedly provided the repressive equipment used in the torture centres installed after the coup. Some claim he participated in that torture along with other business leaders. His open support for the coup and the dictatorship distinguishes him from the many other members of the business community who remain hidden in the background. As the recognizable face of complicity, Boilesen was assassinated in 1971, gunned down in broad daylight near his home, by the ALN (Ação Libertadora Nacional) urban guerrilla group.[3]

With figures like Boilesen, the story of business involvement in the coup and dictatorship is hardly a secret. But as the residents of Henning Boilesen Street attest, until recently little attention has been paid to the question of corporate complicity in past political violence.

Several events converge to explain the new interest. First, the 2012 National Truth Commission (NTC) included businesses' human rights violations in its final report. Recognizing that the military did not act alone but that civil society forces participated in supporting the coup and the dictatorship has thus extended the truth-gathering beyond the state sector and into what is now referred to as the 'civil-military dictatorship' or more pointedly the 'business-military dictatorship'. The Brazilian Secretary of Justice called on the NTC to 'investigate the corporations that financed the dictatorship' and acknowledge the private sector's responsibility for repression.[4] The NTC created a task force to do so. NTC member and criminal lawyer Rosa Cardoso claimed that the group could establish 'institutional accountability' for business behaviour during the coup and the dictatorship, showing that Brazil faced 'not a military coup, but a civil-military coup that involved the entire business class'.[5] Several of the more than one hundred subnational truth commissions also took up the call to investigate corporate complicity. The president of the Rubens Paiva São Paulo State Truth Commission, Adriano Diogo, expressed the view that business leaders had carried out the same activities as state actors, and thereby shared responsibility for those violations.[6] Official and unofficial truth commissions called on academic, legal and media researchers to conduct investigations, and documents, articles, videos, studies and seminars have proliferated as a result.[7]

These investigations have revealed multiple layers of corporate complicity in Brazil. Brazilian and transnational business elites actively supported the coup itself and sustained the dictatorship through legal and illegal (corrupt) financing.[8] Companies in Brazil benefited with ill-gotten gains from their collaboration with the regime.[9] More direct participation in the violence involved the creation of blacklists of workers considered to be 'subversive elements', who faced subsequent detention, torture, and death or disappearance in the repressive apparatus. Manoel Fiel Filho, for example, was picked up in the middle of the day at his job in the Metal Arte factory, taken to the torture centre, and was dead within an hour or so due to blows to his head. As in the case of Boilesen, businesses also supplied the instruments of repression, such as vehicles, weapons, installations, and torturers themselves.[10]

The study of transitional justice mechanisms to address corporate complicity in past human rights violations has begun.[11] The prosecutorial model is not necessarily new, having been used by the Allied Forces in Germany and Japan following World War II.[12] Recent efforts are underway in Argentina, Chile and Colombia.[13] With nearly half of the respondents to a Brazilian public opinion poll responding that those who carried out repression should face punishment, evidence suggests that a major civil society barrier to prosecution might be lifting in Brazil.[14] Indeed, one civil case against Volkswagen has begun. Nonetheless, the amnesty law, a very reluctant judiciary, along with the difficult burden of proof fifty years after the coup when few protagonists are still alive, suggest that criminal prosecutions are unlikely.[15]

In terms of truth commissions' advances in the area of corporate complicity for past human rights abuses, however, Brazil could be said to be a leader. The Corporate Accountability and Transitional Justice project based at the University of Oxford documents Brazil's NTC outpacing all other commission reports in the number of economic actors identified for their human rights abuses: 123 or 38 per cent of all of the companies named in all of the final reports in the world.

When Brazil is noted for its slow adoption of transitional justice mechanisms, why would it lead in the area of corporate complicity? My research in Brazil during the 1980s involving more than 155 interviews with business elites regarding corporate complicity in the coup and dictatorship provides some insights.[16] It suggests that the knowledge of a diverse business community involved in the repressive apparatus has catalysed an innovative process in Brazil.

Brazilian Industrialists and the 1964 Coup and Dictatorship

There is no doubt that Brazilian industrialists played an important role in the 1964 military coup that toppled President João Goulart. Some even claimed sole responsibility for the coup. According to Paulo Ayres Filho, of Universal Consultores, 'the 1964 Revolution was made in my living room' (22 October 1987).[17] The Brazilian president of a multinational corporation's large Brazilian operation said: 'The 1964 Revolution was made by me. The military didn't want to come in. They did it because they were begged to do so by the business community. ... It isn't that the business community supported the military in their coup, but that the military supported us in our coup' (6 October 1987). Business elites, particularly São Paulo industrialists, thus take credit for the prominent role they played in the coup. Journalists even referred to the coup as the 'Paulista revolt'.[18]

The major organizing force behind business leaders' support for the coup was the Institute for Economic and Social Research (IPES), which was formed on 29 November 1961.[19] Although there was no formal relationship between IPES and pre-existing business organizations, some of IPES's members were also directors of key business associations, including the Federation of Industries of the State of São Paulo (FIESP), the Centre of Industries of the State of São Paulo (CIESP), the National Confederation of Industries (CNI), the National Council of Producing Classes (CONCLAP) and the American Chamber of Commerce. IPES also coordinated the activities of, and received funds from, existing broad-based pressure groups such as the Brazilian Institute for Democratic Action (IBAD). IBAD was formed in 1959 to 'defend democracy', but it mainly united several industrial, commercial, military, Catholic and middle-class groups to fight what its members perceived as the growing threat of communism in Brazil.

In an interview in 1987, one of the most active IPES defenders, Paulo Ayres Filho, described the organization's formation. Initially, IPES's membership consisted of ten businessmen in Rio de Janeiro and São Paulo who were concerned with the 'leftist tendency in political life' in Brazil[20] and were anxious to find 'democratic solutions' to the country's problems.[21] Despite its clear anti-communist bent, the group attempted to appear apolitical. It suspected that a 'radical right' image might block widespread support within the Brazilian population.[22] Thus it professed to study the 'reforms proposed by João Goulart and the left, from a free enterprise, technical, business point of view'. By advocating open political participation and endorsing 'moderate reform in the existing political and economic institutions',[23] it aimed to broaden its appeal to include individuals in the political centre.

These efforts failed, at least as far as the press was concerned. Ayres accused the 'communist press' of labelling IPES 'reactionary' and calling it an agent of 'imperialism' (22 October 1987). Attacks in the media, Ayres claimed, initially hindered IPES's recruitment efforts; members of the business community were reluctant to join an overtly anti-communist organization. They feared reprisals from a left-leaning government, Ayres contended, that could include the denial of government credits and subsidies. Other IPES members claimed to have received threatening telephone calls from the 'communists'.

To overcome those fears, IPES took its recruitment efforts and political activities underground.[24] It re-emerged in 1963 as a much stronger organization, claiming five hundred enterprises in São Paulo and Rio de Janeiro, key business leaders, and branches in other parts of the country.[25]

A fortified due-paying membership base enabled IPES to expand its activities. It created an intelligence division with investigators inside and outside of the government, 'to collect, classify and correlate information on the extent of Red infiltration in Brazil'.[26] IPES allegedly spent between $200,000 and $300,000 on intelligence-gathering and distribution, aimed at increasing anti-communist sentiment among the public.[27] To directly influence government, IPES lobbied Congress and the executive branch on various economic policies. IPES also contributed to the campaigns of pro-free market and anti-communist candidates for political office.[28] The importance placed on electoral efforts was reflected in a poll at the time, in which 95 per cent of CIESP members confirmed that business should have representatives in government (2 per cent felt this was unnecessary, and 3 per cent were indifferent), and 96 per cent believed that only individuals with first-hand knowledge of industry could adequately represent industrialists' interests.[29]

IPES also extended its network to include technocrats and the military. Many IPES members had been trained along with military officers and technocrats at the Superior War College (ESG). General Golbery do Couto e Silva joined IPES and directed the organization's intelligence-gathering operations.

To win support from urban workers, IPES attempted to improve the image of private enterprise. It promoted the idea of the 'social function and responsibility of private property', alongside its standard courses on leadership and its anti-communist and pro-private property campaign. IPES developed social welfare projects, including literacy campaigns, legal, medical, dental and hospital assistance, and consumer, credit and housing cooperatives. It set up job and skills training in a variety of fields.

IPES's labour activities received organizational and financial support from the American Institute for Free Labor Development (AIFLD), an American Federation of Labor and Congress of Industrial Organizations (AFL-CIO) affiliated group with connections to the Central Intelligence Agency. Many of the union leaders whom IPES supported had been trained in the United States.[30] These conservative union leaders defended material gains for workers and an alliance with business behind industrial growth, and eschewed militancy and class struggle. IPES supported the Democratic Union Movement (MSD), bearing the slogan 'God, private property, and the free market'.[31] By the end of 1964, IPES's officials claimed that the organization had trained two thousand workers, including heads of trade unions.

The struggle to unite the business community behind IPES proved difficult because of ideological differences. According to one of the organization's publications, of the six ideological groups within the business community (1% Communists, 3% Criminals, 10% Useless

Innocents, 12% Reactionaries, 70% Unconscious, and 4% Conscious), IPES could only draw from the 'conscious elements', members willing to lead the class against the 'communist threat' and whose interests go beyond the narrow terrain of their business and enter into politics.[32]

Eventually IPES claimed support from a broad base of business leaders. This was only partially due to the organization's efforts, however. President Goulart's policies and practices were perceived by industrialists as threatening their interests, prompting them to join IPES as a form of self-defence.[33]

By far the most important of IPES's activities was its role in the 1964 coup. IPES, Ayres contends, never planned to participate in a military coup. Its initial aim was only to create a broad-based opposition movement that would pressure the Goulart government to modify its radical posture. Some IPES members, however, felt constrained by the organization's emphasis on education and information, as well as its lack of direct action. One such industrialist from the São Paulo IPES group allegedly 'organized vigilante cells to counter left-wing hecklers at anti-Communist meetings with "intellectual methods-like a kick in the head"'. A group of industrialists carried this further; they set up a hand grenade factory and launched guerrilla operations against leftists.[34]

According to the president of a multinational corporation's Brazilian operation, IPES altered its tactics to include direct involvement in the coup conspiracy after two 1964 events: Goulart's 13 March rally[35] and the 25 March navy mutiny.[36] These events catalysed IPES and the armed forces to mobilize jointly.[37] It strengthened 'long cultivated friendships' in the military services, convincing the various branches to carry out the 'revolution' and reinstate 'morals and justice, freedom and democracy'.[38] It called on the armed forces to help organize 'a revolution to depose Goulart, re-establish the hierarchy and discipline in the Armed Forces, and lead the economy … along a normal course again'.[39]

After the coup succeeded, Ayres (22 October 1987) continued to call on industrialists to support IPES and remain vigilant against the threat of communism in Brazil. He failed in this endeavour. IPES ceased operations shortly after the 1964 coup. The capacity to set aside ideological and corporate differences within the business community to carry out a political project thus proved short-lived.

Who Supported the Coup and Why?

Consistent with existing explanations for the wave of coups in the most industrially advanced countries of Latin America, the original leaders of IPES had significant ties to foreign, particularly United States, capital.[40] Although all of IPES's founders were Brazilian, they had strong links to United States businesses: they managed subsidiaries of United States firms, received technical assistance or investment capital from United States corporations, sat on the boards of United States corporations, or belonged to the American Chamber of Commerce.[41] This is not surprising. After all, Goulart threatened multinational corporations with his controls over profit remittance, and his expropriation and nationalization plans. The United States government had stopped foreign aid except to the 'islands of administrative sanity', namely the conservative state governments that opposed Goulart.[42]

Focusing only on the strong international business support for the coup downplays IPES's appeal among private domestic businesses that lacked ties to foreign capital. Goulart's strategies also threatened these businesses. For example, Brazilian entrepreneurs owned all of the oil companies that would have been nationalized under Goulart's 13 March decree. In addition, IPES attacked the Goulart government on a wide range of political and economic issues of concern to private domestic businesses. Thus, IPES was able to capitalize on Goulart's policies to unite a diverse set of businesses in favour of the coup.[43]

My interviews with 132 industrialists confirm this view: while a majority (64 per cent) stated that they had supported the coup, they represent a diverse group.[44] Age, business activity, and the nationality of the firm proved significant in determining industrialists' support for the coup. The data do not support the hypothesis that multinational firms and firms with extensive ties abroad were the strongest supporters of the coup. Neither the percentage of foreign capital in a firm, the percentage of the firm's products that were exported, nor industrialists' experience abroad proved statistically significant in determining industrialists' support for the coup. The nationality of the firm proved significant, but the data challenge rather than confirm the transnational hypothesis. I found that 71 per cent of the industrialists from Brazilian firms whom I interviewed supported the coup, as opposed to 46 per cent of the industrialists from foreign firms.[45]

Before rejecting the transnational hypothesis altogether, several factors warrant consideration. For example, because of host governments' sensitivity towards multinational corporations' involvement in domestic political affairs, executives (especially non-Brazilians) at foreign firms probably concealed their support when I interviewed them, thus skewing the results. In addition, owing to turnover, many foreign executives may not have been in Brazil, in which case they could not have supported the coup. Like Brazilian executives, a majority of the multinational executives who had business ties in Brazil in 1964 supported the coup. Rather than confirming the international ties hypothesis, business involvement in Brazil at the time of the coup, whether with a multinational or a Brazilian company, proved to be the determining factor.

The data further indicate that ideology played an important role in determining industrialists' support for the coup, although only for executives at Brazilian firms. Those Brazilian industrialists who identified themselves as being on the right were most likely to state that they had supported the coup (79 per cent of this group did so), followed by those who defined themselves as centrists (68 per cent), and lastly by those who defined themselves as left of centre (44 per cent). It is not surprising that those who associate themselves with the right and even with the centre supported the coup. However, such significant support from those who consider themselves to be left of centre was surprising. It may indicate either that support for the coup was shared by reactionary and progressive elements within the business community, or that reactionary industrialists who had supported the coup in 1964 altered their political views (and identified with more progressive political viewpoints) during the twenty-year dictatorship.

In sum, this analysis of business leaders' involvement in the 1964 coup reveals insights into corporate complicity. Under normal conditions, business elites are not likely to unite and mobilize against the democratic government. The convergence of factors in Brazil in the 1960s forced business leaders out of their innately competitive, individualistic and fragmented attitudes to act collectively. The perception of threat to private sector investments was so great that industrialists with a range of ideological views and management perspectives nevertheless shared a fear of the Goulart government, although for different specific reasons. Whereas business leaders typically use individual political pressure to eliminate threats to their firms, their perception of the extent and severity of the threat, and Goulart's apparent indifference to their needs, convinced them that they had little individual leverage over the government. Finally, their perception that Goulart would postpone elections and disband Congress eliminated, in their eyes, the possibility that he could be replaced, or collectively influenced, via democratic methods. The motives behind support for the coup emerged not primarily from a concern over economic growth or social unrest, as existing theory proposes, but rather from a desire for political and economic stability.

Many studies of the Goulart government explore the causes of its breakdown. The business community was affected by some of these, particularly the failure of the government to resolve the nation's economic problems (e.g. the mounting foreign debt, high rates of inflation, and balance-of-payments deficits). Whereas Goulart did not cause these problems, and his policies were often constrained by external factors (e.g. reduction in United States aid to Brazil), he nonetheless proved incapable of managing the economy. Goulart's attempts to carry out reforms proved ineffective: they heightened the perception of government incompetence, intensified opposition to the government, empowered the anti-government conspirators and increased political instability. Business leaders felt that Goulart's proposed reforms dramatically altered the status quo. Their fears were shaped as much by Goulart's reforms, however, as by the prevailing international fear of socialist revolution.

International factors thus also played an important role in mobilizing business leaders in 1964. More than the direct leadership by transnational elites, as existing theory suggests, my study contends that the prevailing international fear of socialist revolution shaped both domestic and transnational business leaders' perceptions.

Furthermore, the coup had broad societal support, which ensured a successful outcome. Other social sectors, particularly the military, shared business leaders' ultimate goal of ousting Goulart, although they did not necessarily share their specific motivations for it. This convergence of factors allowed business elites to effectively mobilize their rich reserve of financial, organizational and social assets to undermine the Goulart government. They thus demonstrated the potential political power of Latin American business elites, a power that eroded in the subsequent phase of the dictatorship.

Who Supported the Dictatorship and Why?

Some scholars have suggested that IPES business leaders developed the blueprint for the military regime, including specific educational reforms, foreign investment strategies and labour legislation.[46] Evidence of post-coup links between business elites and the military regime are at best tenuous, however. While IPES members replaced many of the government officials ousted, and assumed positions in ministries, advisory committees, government-owned banks and credit institutions, these individuals were economists and military personnel, rather than business leaders.[47] Although they shared private sector interests, a direct role of business elites in the governing coalition demands further proof.

The highly beneficial policies for business during the dictatorship would be one reason why businesses would support it. The so-called 'economic miracle' (1968–73) with average annual growth rates of 13 per cent in the industrial sector, stimulated business through subsidies and credits, low inflation rates, wage repression, foreign investment, relaxed profit remittance laws, infrastructure development, and devaluation and tax concessions to stimulate exports.[48]

The regime's repression of workers further benefited businesses by removing the threat from the left and expropriation of private property. IPES's leaders allegedly participated in the 'effectiveness' of the repression by giving to the regime's intelligence apparatus the dossiers IPES had created on alleged subversives during the Goulart government. These dossiers were apparently used to identify many of the individuals detained, stripped of political rights, fired, imprisoned, tortured and killed during the dictatorship.

The regime's intervention in labour disputes also benefited business leaders. After two major strikes in 1968, the Costa e Silva government nearly abolished the right to strike. As a result, the regime successfully eliminated production stoppages due to strikes during its first fourteen years in power.[49] Some industrialists publicly praised and defended the regime's strike restrictions and argued that control over strike activity was essential to national security and the common good.[50] Business leaders applauded the regime's harsh repression of major strike activity in 1968.[51]

These benefits, however, did not guarantee unified support for the regime from the business community. While those I interviewed strongly approved of the Castello Branco government – 47 per cent considered him to be the best president in Brazilian history – they did not endorse the military regime as a whole. Particularly surprising, for example, is the response to General Médici, the military president in power during the economic miracle and who carried out the most extensive repression. He received endorsement as the best president in Brazilian history from only 4 per cent of industrialists. A majority of newer industrial leaders indicated a strong preference for the democratic government of Kubitschek. These aggregate data provide a glimpse of the great diversity of opinion in the business community towards the military regime. The unity among reactionary, democratic, politically uncommitted industrialists for the coup fell apart during the military regime.

Support among a minority of reactionary elements remained strong throughout the regime. The reactionaries held that authoritarian rule was necessary to protect national security, specifically against a left-wing overthrow of the capitalist order. They criticized Castello Branco for failing to establish security, thereby requiring subsequent military leaders to extend and intensify repression. According to Paulo Ayres Filho (22 October 1987), the Castello Branco government was too reluctant to crack down on subversives, thus enabling the subversives to continue threatening the nation even after the military took over.

Castello Branco's rhetoric cautioned against extremes: 'The extreme right is reactionary; the extreme left is subversive. Brazil must steer an honest middle course ... The answer to the evils of the extreme left does not lie in the birth of a reactionary right'.[52] Moreover, he criticized wealthy industrialists and large landowners for pressing him for self-interested gains. Despite his rhetoric, Castello Branco took measures that went well beyond eliminating the 'extreme left'. The anti-subversive net he cast covered individuals who could hardly be considered extreme leftists or subversives, such as former presidents Kubitschek and Quadros.[53]

Reactionary industrialists not only embraced the military regime, they actively bolstered the regime's repressive practices by forming anti-communist vigilante cells such as the Brazilian Anti-Communist Alliance (AAB) and financing and implementing Operation Bandeirantes (OBAN). Formed in November 1974, the AAB issued death threats to key individuals on the left and claimed responsibility for planting bombs in the headquarters of the Brazilian Press Association (ABI) and the Organization of Brazilian Lawyers (OAB).[54] OBAN was a semi-clandestine organization founded by the regime in September 1969 to consolidate civilian and military efforts to fight subversion. OBAN, and its 1970 successor the Information Operations Detachment-Centre for Internal Defence Operations (DOI-CODI), detained labour leaders, urban guerrillas and other so-called 'subversive' individuals, and tortured and sometimes killed them.

Whether business contributions to OBAN were voluntary remains in dispute. An executive at a United States multinational corporation claimed that a United States consular official encouraged members of the business community to make these contributions.[55] The multinational firms rumoured to have contributed to OBAN include Nestlé, General Electric, Mercedes Benz, Siemens and Ford.[56] Large Brazilian firms and their directors were also allegedly important donors to OBAN. The domestic firms and directors rumoured to have contributed include an enormous São Paulo agribusiness firm, Copersucar; an extremely successful construction company, Camargo Correia; and Paulo Maluf, a politician in the military regime's party and the director of his family's wood and pulp firm, Eucatex.[57] Funding also came from certain social groups to which business leaders belonged, including the ultraconservative Catholic lay organization Tradition, Family, and Property (TFP), which was run by Adolpho Lindenberg, the founder of a large civil engineering and construction firm.[58]

Other members of the business community contend that OBAN contributions were obtained through a form of extortion. If they refused to make a 'voluntary' contribution, they faced threats. One industrialist recounted to me that his firm's bank account at the Banco do Brasil was closed and he was threatened with physical harm as reprisal for failing to contribute. For others the decision was pragmatic: they had something to gain (e.g. control over radical social movements) if they did contribute, and potentially much to lose (e.g. financial constraints imposed on them by the regime, physical harm from right-wing forces within the regime, and increased subversion) if they did not. Thus, most industrialists provided the funds or equipment OBAN requested.[59]

There is no incontrovertible proof that any of the industrialists rumoured to have financed OBAN or formed the AAB actually did so. Lists of contributors and founders do not exist and those identified deny involvement. A journalist investigating OBAN argued that secrecy prevailed partly because of the illegality of the operation, but more importantly because industrialists feared retribution from the left for participating, even indirectly, in torture.[60] Their fears were apparently justified by Boilesen's murder.[61] Another plausible argument is that these businesspeople have been falsely accused of promoting torture and repression. This is highly unlikely, however, since some of the industrialists I interviewed, while denying their own involvement, acknowledged that businesspeople had indeed contributed funds, cooperated with the regime's repressive apparatus and formed anti-communist vigilante groups.

Little public information exists about strident advocates of authoritarianism who engaged in violence against 'subversives', the reactionaries. My own research suggests that during the coup and the dictatorship they were a small group with disproportionate power because of their linkages to the military and technocrats. They included heads of multinational firms and domestic firms. They were engaged in diverse sectors of the economy, including industry, construction and agribusiness. And while some were active in conservative religious organizations, others were not religious.

They certainly had disproportionate power compared to the small number of democrats within the business community. This group also supported the coup because they believed Goulart threatened democracy and that military intervention was necessary to restore democratic order. While this view appears naive now, these industrialists expected the military to intervene to defend the Constitution and remain in power only long enough to restore order and call elections.[62] Once it became clear that the military planned to stay in power and impose authoritarian rule, they withdrew their support from the regime.[63] They thus had a principled objection to military-authoritarian rule and to the violation of human and civil rights, specifically democratic political participation. Several of these individuals claimed that they had attempted to voice opposition to the military regime during its early years but were silenced through the military's effective use of intimidation, threats and reprisals. Some industrialists even went into exile owing to their fear of retribution from the military government. Thus, the democrats within the business community played virtually no role during the first decade of the military regime. It was only with the political opening that they publicly voiced their opposition to the regime.

The majority of industrialists within the business community fall into the 'uncommitted' category. They supported the coup and accepted the military regime and most of its policies. Despite their generally supportive attitude, they cannot be labelled authoritarian. Indeed, most of their comments about the military regime suggest that they simply ignored the distinctions between political systems. They expressed a rhetorical preference for democracy over authoritarianism, but also considered the type of political system irrelevant as long as the government provided stability. They valued stability, particularly with regard to investments, more highly than the democratic values of 'opposition, public contestation, or political competition'.[64] Indeed, they tended to equate democracy with governments that protected political order and promoted economic growth, even if they repressed democratic rights and freedoms. More accurately, the politically uncommitted generally accepted the political status quo, whether authoritarian or democratic, unless their interests were severely threatened. Thus, when the military regime began the transition to democracy, these business leaders also accepted that political system.

For the politically uncommitted, therefore, the military regime provided their desired investment stability, proved competent in managing the economy, and eliminated threats to the economic and political order. It was also legitimate, in most industrialists' opinion, owing to its defeat of communism and internal subversion and the re-establishing of authority and obedience. These industrialists accepted the regime's repressive measures as necessary to the stability project. They applauded the regime's efforts when these directly benefited them.

The short-term benefits of the military regime's economic and social order project did not last or lead to a passive or uncritical appraisal of the regime by the business community. As early as 1964, industrialists criticized the government for excluding them from economic decisions. This concern manifested itself in the frequent appearance of writings and speeches by industrialists praising 'collaboration' and asking to be consulted on economic issues. As one industrialist stated, 'It is not only a democratic right or tradition and a law but also a duty, that the state, in order to fulfil its democratic responsibilities, must listen to the thoughts of industry'.[65] Another example of industrialists' concern was their reaction to wage controls. While they obviously benefited from lower wages, they reacted against what they perceived as the regime's attempt to take away their control over labour relations. Industrialists' sense of a loss of influence resulted from the institutional changes that transpired during the course of the military regime. During the early years of the military regime, Brazilian business leaders could influence the regime via four mechanisms: official business associations; extra-corporatist, or parallel, associations representing the interests of specific industrial sectors; bureaucratic rings (informal networks between state agencies and specific industrial sectors); and personal contacts with public officials.[66] After the Castello Branco administration, however, the subsequent military governments greatly reduced the decision-making power of Congress, centralized decisions in the ministries, and excluded business leaders from government councils. In this context, the business community's lobbying efforts via official and parallel business associations had little effect. Instead, industrialists primarily used bureaucratic rings and personal contacts to gain influence. However, even these efforts proved generally ineffective because the government operated in a vacuum and had its own set of economic priorities. Thus, one of the problems industrialists had faced during the Goulart government – the loss of influence over government decisions – reappeared under the military regime. As one scholar writes:

> In its attempt to contain the 'pressure from below', the bourgeoisie supported measures that essentially destroyed its own direct political expression. It is true that the bourgeoisie never had effective political organization and pressure instruments. Now, however, not only the political party system but all other forms of political action open to

> the bourgeoisie became dependent on contacts and alliances with the military and technocratic groups that alone controlled the state apparatus ... The bourgeoisie lost all leverage to shape its more immediate political interests.[67]

Although industrialists were critical of their loss of influence, they retained the protection of private property. As long as the military regime could convince them that property rights would be threatened by political liberalization, most industrialists continued to accept the regime and even their own loss of direct political influence. They were willing to sacrifice direct political participation for protection of the private sector generally.

In short, the uncommitted business leaders neither endorsed nor rejected the authoritarian role; they merely adapted to it. They adapted, in part, because they derived benefits from the regime's effective economic management and enforcement of social order, and its protections for the private sector. Yet, despite the regime's significant advantages, most of these industrialists neither actively endorsed it nor passively acquiesced to it. Instead, they criticized it for not allowing business groups to have direct influence over policies affecting them. As long as the regime's policies reflected industrialists' interests, the conflict over business influence did not develop into open confrontation. During the second phase of the military regime, however, business leaders sensed that even their indirect influence began to erode, intensifying the latent conflict in business–state relations.

Adaptive Industrialists

From the discussion of the business community's reaction to the military coup and the regime it implanted, two incontrovertible facts emerge. First, industrialists widely supported the overthrow of the Goulart government. Second, they benefited greatly from the policies enacted during the first decade of the dictatorship. Political stability and protection of private property were restored. The regime also provided high growth rates, restricted wage increases and labour activity, and excluded the left from national politics.

The theory of the bureaucratic-authoritarian state[68] assumes on the basis of these two facts that business leaders supported the military coup *in order to* install an authoritarian regime capable of bringing social order and economic growth. This study takes a slightly different approach.

Despite industrialists' active support for the 1964 coup, there is no reason to conclude that they knew that a military regime would be installed after the coup. The historical pattern of military intervention in Brazil would have led them to assume that the regime would intervene only long enough to restore order and call democratic elections. There is also no evidence to confirm that industrialists played a role in designing or shaping the policies of the military regime. Indeed, the frustration of some industrialists over their exclusion from the regime's policy decisions suggests the opposite. In other words, business leaders did not support the coup as a means to stimulate economic growth; the dramatic economic growth that followed the coup was a favourable but unanticipated outcome.

There is also no evidence to support the view that business leaders collectively endorsed the regime. Evidence suggests the contrary. As the adaptive actor approach asserts,[69] the business community's diversity prevented such a consensus from emerging. The only strong endorsement of the military regime came from a small minority of reactionary industrialists who were motivated by their fear of subversion and were unconcerned about democratic rights and liberties. They defended and bolstered the regime's repressive policies. In contrast, another small minority within the business community, including some who had supported the 1964 coup, opposed the authoritarian regime and its repressive policies. They had endorsed the coup owing to their perception that Goulart threatened their firms, the private sector and the democratic system. They believed that the military, as in the past, would restore order and call new democratic elections. When the military failed to do so, and instead imposed a military-authoritarian regime, these business leaders eventually withdrew their support.

The majority of business leaders were uncommitted either to democratic or to authoritarian rule. Rather than rigidly adhering to a specific type of regime, they evaluated governments on the basis of the extent to which those governments protected investment stability. Consistent with the adaptive actor approach, business leaders were critical of military presidents, even those who provided the highest levels of economic growth and social order, because of those presidents' exclusion of business influence and their questionable legitimacy.

Final Reflections

This study of business linkages to the Brazilian coup and dictatorship provides several insights into accountability for past corporate complicity. First, it reveals that Brazilian business elites, even by their own admission, hold responsibility for political violence following the 1964 coup. They may not share equal responsibility, but they do share in failing to publicly acknowledge or remedy wrongdoing.

The NTC has taken a step in making the role of the business community in past human rights violations visible. Although Brazil has been a slow and reluctant adopter of transitional justice, its truth commission has gone further than any other in examining corporate complicity and considering follow-up investigations. The NTC named 123 companies and included in its recommendations further investigations to determine possible legal accountability. One of those cases, a civil case against Volkswagen, has already begun. The union movement behind the Volkswagen case has also identified other companies for which sufficient evidence exists to advance legal action.

These advances in Brazil have resulted from civil society demand, particularly from the union movement but also other civil society groups who have mobilized, such as those petitioning for the removal of the Boilesen name from the São Paulo street. In addition, it has depended on institutional innovators, such as those from the São Paulo truth commission who pressured the NTC to include the findings on business and the members of the NTC who agreed to do so. Internationally, members of German civil society have also mobilized to pressure the Volkswagen company to address the claims made about human rights abuses in Brazil. These factors – civil society demand, institutional innovation and international pressure – have proved useful to advancing accountability, particularly where veto actors are weak.[76]

The 'adaptive actor' approach suggests that the NTC and follow-on civil suits potentially raise the costs of corporate complicity and could thus have a significant effect on corporate behaviour not just in Brazil but globally. Given that most businesses adapt to different political environments, they will also adjust to a new domestic and global human rights regime. They will unlikely do so unless they see the benefit, even if that benefit is avoiding legal and reputational costs. Thus, if Brazil, like Argentina and other countries around the world, begins to attach costly penalties to committing human rights violations, most companies will make adjustments and recalculate the business impact of their behaviour. The NTC and follow-on trials have the potential to reveal corporate criminal and civil wrongdoing still hidden in plain sight on Henning Boilesen Street.

Leigh A. Payne is Professor of Sociology and Latin America at the University of Oxford, St. Antony's College. She is the author of many books and articles on legacies of authoritarian rule, human rights and transitional justice that include case studies of Brazil. Her book (with Gabriel Pereira and Laura Bernal-Bermúdez) *Transitional Justice and Corporate Accountability from Below: Deploying Archimedes' Lever*, is forthcoming from Cambridge University Press.

Notes

Parts of this chapter have been previously published in Leigh A. Payne, *Brazilian Industrialists and Democratic Change* (Baltimore, MD and London: Johns Hopkins University Press, 1994. Revised, adapted and reprinted with permission of Johns Hopkins University Press.

1. C. Litewski (dir.), *Cidadão Boilesen: Um dos empresários que financiou a tortura no Brasil* [film], produced by P. Asbeg, 5 January 2013, retrieved 6 May 2016 from https://www.youtube.com/watch?v=yGxIA90xXeY.
2. See M. Brant, 'Projeto Adeus Boilesen – 09/06' [video], YouTube, (recorded n.d., uploaded 13 June 2013), retrieved 6 May 2016 from https://www.youtube.com/watch?v=SDM-PXdAS2w.
3. A.C. Fon, *Tortura: A história da repressão política no Brasil* (São Paulo: Global, 1979), 56–57.
4. J.P. Bohoslavsky and M.D. Torelly, 'Financial Complicity: The Brazilian Dictatorship under the "Macroscope"', in D.N. Sharp (ed.), *Justice and Economic Violence in Transition* (New York: Springer, 2014), 259.
5. M. Gombata, 'Comissão da Verdade quer responsabilizar empresas que colaboraram com a ditadura', *Carta Capital*, 15 March 2014, retrieved 14 December 2018 from https://web.archive.org/web/20170908001647/https://www.cartacapital.com.br/sociedade/comissao-da-verdade-quer-responsabilizar-empresas-que-colaboraram-com-a-ditadura-8874.html.
6. In Diogo's words, 'We accept the punishment of torturers and the military. Yet the companies that we are talking about committed or encouraged crimes against the Brazilian people that were similar to, or were actually the same crimes as, those carrried out by the military'. Gombata, 'Comissão da Verdade'.
7. Examples include: Gombata, 'Comissão da Verdade'; Felipe Amorim and Rodolfo Machado, 'Elite econômica que deu golpe no Brasil tinha braços internacionais, diz historiadora', *Operamundi*, 2 March 2014, retrieved 7 March 2015 from http://m.operamundi.uol.com.br/conteudo/reportagens/34196/elite+economica+que+deu+golpe+no+brasil+tinha+bracos+internacionais+diz+historiadora.shtml; R. Valente and M. Leitão, 'Ministro determinou ajuda para empreiteira durante a ditadura', *Folha Transparencia*, 7 March 2014, retrieved 2 May 2016 from http://www1.folha.uol.com.br/poder/2013/03/1242058-ministro-determinou-ajuda-para-empreiteira-durante-a-ditadura.shtml.

8. See the discussion of journalist D. Assis's investigations of financing in Gombata, 'Comissão da Verdade': 125 individuals, ninety-five business entities, and five main economic groups (Listas Telefônicas Brasileiras, Light, Cruzeiro do Sul, Refinaria e Exploração de Petróleo União and Icomi) providing more than 70 per cent of the financial contributions. For corruption activities, see the study by C. Fico in G. Amado, 'Ditadura foi um oceano de corrupção', *Correio do Povo*, 16 March 2014, retrieved 7 March 2015 from http://www.correiodopovo.com.br/blogs/juremirmachado/?p=5770.
9. Gombata, 'Comissão de Verdade'; Valente and Leitão, 'Ministro determinou ajuda para empreiteira durante a ditadura'.
10. For information about business and the creation of Operação Bandeirante–OBAN, DOI-CODI (Destacamento de Operações de Informação do Centro de Operações de Defesa Interna), and other torture centres, see Gombata, 'Comissão da Verdade' and 'Empresários que apoiaram o golpe de 64 construíram grandes fortunas', *Correio do Brasil*, 27 March 2014, retrieved 6 May 2016 from https://www.correiodobrasil.com.br/empresarios-que-apoiaram-o-golpe-de-64-construiram-grandes-fortunas/.
11. S. Michalowski (ed.), *Corporate Accountability in the Context of Transitional Justice* (New York: Routledge, 2013).
12. L.A. Payne, G. Pereira, and L. Bernal-Bermúdez, *Transitional Justice and Corporate Accountability from Below: Deploying Archimedes' Lever* (Cambridge: Cambridge University Press, forthcoming).
13. Ibid.; H. Verbitsky and J.P. Bohoslavsky (eds), *The Economic Accomplices to the Argentine Dictatorship: Outstanding Debts* (Cambridge: Cambridge University Press, 2016).
14. The 2014 poll showed 46 per cent support for punishment, 37 per cent opposed, and 17 per cent with no opinion. R. Mendonça, 'Maior parte da população quer anular Lei da Anistia, aponta Datafolha', *Folha de São Paulo*, 31 March 2014, retrieved 6 May 2016 from http://www1.folha.uol.com.br/poder/2014/03/1433374-maior-parte-da-populacao-quer-anular-lei-da-anistia-aponta-datafolha.shtml.
15. M. Spohr, researcher at the Núcleo de Documentação da Fundação Getulio Vargas, cited in 'Comissão da Verdade quer identificar empresas que apoiaram golpe de 1964', *Terra*, 26 March 2014, retrieved 6 May 2016 from http://noticias.terra.com.br/brasil/,9444f8aaac8f4410VgnCLD2000000dc6eb0aRCRD.html.
16. L.A. Payne, *Brazilian Industrialists and Democratic Change* (Baltimore, MD and London: Johns Hopkins University Press, 1994).
17. Because of the anonymity granted, interviews are quoted without attribution. One interviewee, Paulo Ayres Filho, gave permission for the use of his name. Translations of interview material and other Portuguese sources are mine unless otherwise noted.
18. P. Siekman, 'When Executives Turned Revolutionaries, a Story Hitherto Untold: How São Paulo Businessmen Conspired to Overthrow Brazil's Communist-Infested Government', *Fortune* 70(3) (1964), 147.

19. The most extensive study of IPES is found in R.A. Dreifuss, *1964: A conquista do estado: Açao política, poder e golpe de classe* (Petrópolis: Vozes, 1986).
20. Ibid., 163.
21. P. Ayres Filho, 'The Brazilian Revolution' (Paper presented at the Georgetown University Center for Strategic Studies, Washington, DC, July 1964), 10. A condensed version of this paper was published in N.A. Bailey (ed.), *Latin America: Politics, Economics, and Hemispheric Security* (New York: Frederick A. Praeger, 1965), 239–60.
22. Dreifuss, *1964*, 163–64, 178.
23. Ibid., 163.
24. Dreifuss writes that the São Paulo branch of IPES was the headquarters for clandestine operations, while the Rio de Janeiro branch carried out more public debates. Ibid., 179. See also C.W. Hall, 'The Country That Saved Itself', *Readers' Digest* (November 1964), 142.
25. IPES had branches in Rio Grande do Sul, Pernambuco, Minas Gerais, Paraná and Amazonas. Dreifuss, *1964*, 173.
26. Hall, 'The Country That Saved Itself', 138.
27. J.K. Black, *United States Penetration of Brazil* (Philadelphia: University of Pennsylvania Press, 1977), 84.
28. Together with IBAD and another pressure group Democratic Popular Action (ADEP), IPES allegedly spent $12.5 million in October 1962 (funnelled through an advertising agency called Sales Promotion, Inc.) to elect 8 governors, 15 federal senators, 250 federal deputies, 600 state deputies, and various candidates to municipal office. Black, *United States Penetration of Brazil*, 73–75; E. Dutra, *IBAD: Sigla da corrupção* (Rio de Janeiro: Civilização Brasileira, 1963), 14.
29. Yet only 5 per cent said that they themselves had belonged to a political party. P.C. Schmitter, *Interest Conflict and Political Change in Brazil* (Stanford, CA: Stanford University Press, 1971), 278–79.
30. Black, *United States Penetration of Brazil*, 111–24.
31. Dreifuss, *1964*, 317.
32. I. Hasslocher, *As classes produtoras diante do comunismo*, quoted in Dreifuss, *1964*, 165–67.
33. Some evidence exists that IPES assailed particular industrialists and members of the press who oppose IPES's ideals or who supported political candidates who opposed IPES's ideals. Dreifuss, *1964*, 167.
34. Siekman, 'When Executives Turned Revolutionaries', 149.
35. The aspects of the 13 March rally that threatened elites included: announcement of a decree expropriating and nationalizing certain private entities; legalizing the Communist Party; enfranchising illiterates; raising taxes; and stabilizing rents. Goulart's adviser, Leonel Brizola, called for the immediate dismissal of Congress, new elections, and increased representation of popular sectors in government.
36. The main concern of business groups over Goulart's response to the 25 March navy mutiny was his disregard for the hierarchy of the armed

forces and the influence of labour and the left on Goulart's decisions. They saw these factors as evidence of the erosion of the traditional structure of authority in the country.

37. For a description of the contacts between IPES and the armed forces, see Dreifuss, *1964*, 179, 361–415.
38. Filho, 'Brazilian Revolution', 16.
39. Ibid.
40. For the theory of the bureaucratic-authoritarian state, see G. O'Donnell, *Modernization and Bureaucratic-Authoritarianism* (Berkeley and Los Angeles: University of California Press, 1973). On Brazilian foreign business links to the coup, see Dreifuss, *1964*, 163; Black, *United States Penetration of Brazil*, 82–94; and M. Bandeira, *O governo João Goulart – as lutas sociais no Brasil 1961–1964* (Rio de Janeiro: Civilização Brasileira, 1977), 64–74.
41. Dreifuss, *1964*, 163.
42. Black, *United States Penetration of Brazil*, 65–72.
43. Dreifuss, *1964*, 146.
44. For the table summarizing these findings, see Payne, *Brazilian Industrialists*, 25.
45. Ibid.
46. T.E. Skidmore, *The Politics of Military Rule in Brazil, 1964–85* (New York: Oxford University Press, 1988), 23.
47. Dreifuss, *1964*, 421–79.
48. See M.H.M. Alves, *State and Opposition in Military Brazil* (Austin: University of Texas Press, 1985), 107, 268, reproduced in Payne, *Brazilian Industrialists*, 41, Table 3.1.
49. See K.P. Erickson, *The Brazilian Corporative State and Working Class Politics* (Berkeley and Los Angeles: University of California Press, 1977), 159; and Alves, *State and Opposition in Military Brazil*, 52. Both sets of figures are reproduced in Payne, *Brazilian Industrialists*, 43, Table 3.3.
50. A.C. Ferreira Reis, *Direito de greve* (Rio de Janeiro: Confederação Nacional da Indústria-Conselho Econômico, 1967) [mimeo]. For a similar opinion voiced by FIESP, see 'Nôvo projeto sôbre direito de greve é inconveniente e danoso', *Boletim Informativo* 962 (1968).
51. *Estado de São Paulo*, 20 July 1960, 12.
52. Hall, 'The Country that Saved Itself', 156.
53. See P.E. Arns (ed.), *Brasil, nunca mais* (Petrópolis: Vozes, 1985) or the abridged compilation in English, J. Dassin (ed.), *Torture in Brazil: A Report by the Archdiocese of São Paulo* (New York: Vintage Books, 1986), 50.
54. *Latin America*, 27 August 1976, 257. This newsletter covers the activities of the AAB during October and November 1976.
55. A.J. Langguth, *Hidden Terrors* (New York: Pantheon Books, 1978), 123.
56. M. Bandeira, *Cartéis e desnacionalização: A experiencia brasileira, 1964–1974* (Rio de Janeiro: Civilização Brasileira, 1975), 205. See also Dassin, *Torture in Brazil*, 64.

57. See Bandeira, *Cartéis e desnacionalização*, 205; *Veja*, 15 January 1986, 27; and *Latin America*, 30 January 1976, 36–37.
58. Fon, *Tortura*, 60.
59. Ibid., 58–59.
60. Ibid., 57.
61. A. Syrkis, *Os carbonários: Memórias da guerrilha perdida* (São Paulo: Global, 1980), 295.
62. See A. Stepan, *The Military in Politics: Changing Patterns in Brazil* (Princeton, NJ: Princeton University Press, 1971), 115–21.
63. For example, P.E. Martins, quoted in 'Chega de intereses carismáticos', *Senhor*, 15 April 1986.
64. R. Dahl, *Polyarchy: Participation and Opposition* (New Haven, CT: Yale University Press, 1971), 4.
65. R. Noschese, quoted in 'A indústria ante a revolução de março', *Estado de São Paulo*, 17 December 1964. See also 'A indústria quer ser co-responsável pelas decisões do govêrno', *O Globo*, 10 March 1965; and 'Posição de coerência da indústria', *Diario de São Paulo*, 30 March 1965.
66. R.R. Boschi, *National Industrial Elites and the State in Post-1964 Brazil: Institutional Mediations and Political Change* (PhD diss., University of Michigan, 1978), 283–86. See also the Brazilian version, Boschi, *Elites industriais e democracia: Hegemonia burguesa e mudança política no Brasil* (Rio de Janeiro: Edições Graal, 1979), 162–79.
67. F.H. Cardoso, 'Associated-Dependent Development: Theoretical and Practical Implications', in A. Stepan (ed.), *Authoritarian Brazil: Origins, Policies, and Future* (New Haven, CT: Yale University Press, 1973), 148.
68. O'Donnell, *Modernization and Bureaucratic-Authoritarianism*.
69. Payne, *Brazilian Industrialists*, 1–15.
70. F. Lessa, L.A. Payne, and G. Pereira, 'Overcoming Barriers to Justice in the Age of Human Rights Accountability', *Human Rights Quarterly* 37 (2015), 728–54.

Bibliography

Alves, M.H.M. *State and Opposition in Military Brazil.* Austin: University of Texas Press, 1985.

Amado, G. 'Ditadura foi um oceano de corrupção'. *Correio do Povo*, 16 March 2014. Retrieved 7 March 2015 from http://www.correiodopovo.com.br/blogs/juremirmachado/?p=5770.

Amorim, F., and Machado, R. 'Elite econômica que deu golpe no Brasil tinha braços internacionais, diz historiadora'. *Operamundi*, 2 March 2014. Retrieved 7 March 2015 from http://m.operamundi.uol.com.br/conteudo/reportagens/34196/elite+economica+que+deu+golpe+no+brasil+tinha+bracos+internacionais+diz+historiadora.shtml.

Arns, P.E. (ed.). *Brasil, nunca mais.* Petrópolis: Vozes, 1985.

Bandeira, M. *Cartéis e desnacionalização: A experiencia brasileira, 1964–1974.* Rio de Janeiro: Civilização Brasileira, 1975.

Bandeira, M. *O governo João Goulart – as Lutas Sociais no Brasil 1961–1964.* Rio de Janeiro: Civilização Brasileira, 1977.

Black, J.K. *United States Penetration of Brazil.* Philadelphia: University of Pennsylvania Press, 1977.

Bohoslavsky, J.P., and Torelly, M.D. 'Financial Complicity: The Brazilian Dictatorship under the "Macroscope"', in D.N. Sharpe (ed.), *Justice and Economic Violence in Transition* (New York: Springer, 2014).

Boschi, R.R. *National Industrial Elites and the State in Post-1964 Brazil: Institutional Mediations and Political Change*. PhD diss., University of Michigan, 1978.

Boschi, R.R. *Elites industriais e democracia: Hegemonia burguesa e mudança política no Brasil.* Rio de Janeiro: Edições Graal, 1979.

Brant, M. 'Projeto adeus Boilesen – 09/06' [video], YouTube (recorded n.d., uploaded 13 June 2013). Retrieved 6 May 2016 from https://www.youtube.com/watch?v=SDM-PXdAS2w.

Cardoso, F.H. 'Associated-Dependent Development: Theoretical and Practical Implications', in A. Stepan (ed.), *Authoritarian Brazil: Origins, Policies, and Future* (New Haven, CT: Yale University Press, 1973).

'Chega de intereses carismáticos'. *Senhor*, 15 April 1986.

'Comissão da Verdade quer identificar empresas que apoiaram golpe de 1964'. *Terra*, 26 March 2014. Retrieved 6 May 2016 from http://noticias.terra.com.br/brasil/,9444f8aaac8f4410VgnCLD2000000dc6eb0aRCRD.html.

Dahl, R. *Polyarchy: Participation and Opposition.* New Haven, CT: Yale University Press, 1971.

Dassin, J. (ed.). *Torture in Brazil: A Report by the Archdiocese of São Paulo.* New York: Vintage Books, 1986.

Dreifuss, R.A. *1964: A conquista do estado: Açao política, poder e golpe de classe.* Petrópolis: Vozes, 1986.

Dutra, E. *IBAD: Sigla da corrupção*. Rio de Janeiro: Civilização Brasileira, 1963.

'Empresários que apoiaram o golpe de 64 construíram grandes fortunas'. *Correio do Brasil*, 27 March 2014. Retrieved 6 May 2016 from https://www.correiodobrasil.com.br/empresarios-que-apoiaram-o-golpe-de-64-construiram-grandes-fortunas/.

Erickson, K.P. *The Brazilian Corporative State and Working Class Politics.* Berkeley and Los Angeles: University of California Press, 1977.

Ferreira Reis, A.C. *Direito de greve*. Rio de Janeiro: Confederação Nacional da Indústria-Conselho Econômico, 1967 [mimeo].

Filho, P.A. 'The Brazilian Revolution'. Paper presented at the Georgetown University Center for Strategic Studies, Washington, DC, July 1964.

Filho, P.A. 'The Brazilian Revolution', in N.A. Bailey (ed.), *Latin America: Politics, Economics, and Hemispheric Security* (New York: Frederick A. Praeger, 1965), 239–60.

Fon, A.C. *Tortura: A história da repressão política no Brasil.* São Paulo: Global, 1979.

Gombata, M. 'Comissão da Verdade quer responsabilizar empresas que colaboraram com a ditadura'. *Carta Capital*, 15 March 2014. Retrieved 14 December 2018 from https://web.archive.org/web/20170908001647/https://www.cartacapital.com.br/sociedade/comissao-da-verdade-quer-responsabilizar-empresas-que-colaboraram-com-a-ditadura-8874.html.
Hall, C.W. 'The Country That Saved Itself'. *Readers' Digest* (November 1964).
'A indústria ante a revolução de março'. *Estado de São Paulo*, 17 December 1964.
'A indústria quer ser co-responsável pelas decisões do govêrno'. *O Globo*, 10 March 1965.
Langguth, A.J. *Hidden Terrors*. New York: Pantheon Books, 1978.
Lessa, F., Payne, L.A., and Pereira, G. 'Overcoming Barriers to Justice in the Age of Human Rights Accountability'. *Human Rights Quarterly* 37 (2015), 728–54.
Litewski, C. (director). *Cidadão Boilesen: Um dos empresários que financiou a tortura no Brasil* [film], produced by Pedro Asbeg, 5 January 2013. Retrieved 6 May 2016 from https://www.youtube.com/watch?v=yGxIA90xXeY.
Mendonça, R. 'Maior parte da população quer anular Lei da Anistia, aponta Datafolha'. *Folha de São Paulo*, 31 March 2014. Retrieved 6 May 2016 from http://www1.folha.uol.com.br/poder/2014/03/1433374-maior-parte-da-populacao-quer-anular-lei-da-anistia-aponta-datafolha.shtml.
Michalowski, S. (ed.). *Corporate Accountability in the Context of Transitional Justice*. New York: Routledge, 2013.
'Nôvo projeto sôbre direito de greve é inconveniente e danoso'. *Boletim Informativo* 962 (1968).
O'Donnell, G. *Modernization and Bureaucratic-Authoritarianism*. Berkeley and Los Angeles: University of California Press, 1973.
Payne, L.A. *Brazilian Industrialists and Democratic Change*. Baltimore, MD and London: Johns Hopkins University Press, 1994.
Payne, L.A., Pereira, G., and Bernal-Bermúdez, L. *Transitional Justice and Corporate Accountability: Deploying Archimedes' Lever*. Cambridge: Cambridge University Press, forthcoming.
'Posição de coerência da indústria'. *Diario de São Paulo*, 30 March 1965.
Schmitter, P.C. *Interest Conflict and Political Change in Brazil*. Stanford, CA: Stanford University Press, 1971.
Siekman, P. 'When Executives Turned Revolutionaries, a Story Hitherto Untold: How São Paulo Businessmen Conspired to Overthrow Brazil's Communist-Infested Government'. *Fortune* 70(3) (1964).
Skidmore, T.E. *The Politics of Military Rule in Brazil, 1964–85*. New York: Oxford University Press, 1988.
Stepan, A. *The Military in Politics: Changing Patterns in Brazil*. Princeton, NJ: Princeton University Press, 1971.
Syrkis, A. *Os carbonários: Memórias da guerrilha perdida*. São Paulo: Global, 1980.
Valente, R., and Leitão, M. 'Ministro determinou ajuda para empreiteira durante a ditadura'. *Folha Transparencia*, 7 March 2014. Retrieved 2 May

2016 from http://www1.folha.uol.com.br/poder/2013/03/1242058-ministro-determinou-ajuda-para-empreiteira-durante-a-ditadura.shtml.

Verbitsky, H., and Bohoslavsky, J.P. (eds). *The Economic Accomplices to the Argentine Dictatorship: Outstanding Debts*. Cambridge: Cambridge University Press, 2016.

Chapter 9

Volkswagen do Brasil during the Military Dictatorship

An Economic and Political Assessment

Christopher Kopper

Despite popular opinion, the age of right-wing dictatorships did not end in 1945. Eurocentrist perceptions of the world tend to ignore the fact that many right-wing military dictatorships were established in Latin America during the 1960s and 1970s. During these times, journalists in major European nations like Germany started to ask critical questions about the involvement of corporations in these repressive regimes and their potential collaboration with politically motivated crimes against humanity.

Until today, scholarly attention to the history of German foreign direct investments in non-European dictatorships has been significantly low, despite the frequently acclaimed *global turn* of historiography and the growing public interest in transcontinental entanglements.[1] Foreign industrial corporations established manufacturing capacities in non-European markets to open them for exports. This was particularly true for Brazil, which imposed high import tariffs for industrial goods as an incentive for foreign direct investments and as a palliative to shield the balance of payment. Favourable conditions for monetary transfers and for the taxation of profits created a particular incentive for European and North American corporations to invest in Latin America's biggest economy. During the 1950s and 1960s, Brazil became a role model for a protectionist development path that built its hopes on import substitutions through the establishment of a domestically oriented and diversified industrial economy. In the wake of the first oil price crisis of 1974, the Brazilian government shifted its priorities towards the export of manufactured goods in order to balance the aggravating *terms of trade* and to cope with the challenge of steeply rising oil prices.

The particular importance of Brazil for German foreign direct investments is represented in one single number. In 1969, German foreign direct investments in Brazil amounted to 1,238 million Deutschmarks (DM), far exceeding German direct investments in other Latin American, Asian and African nation states.[2] The volume of German direct investments in Brazil nearly reached that of German investments in France, Germany's immediate neighbour, closest ally and biggest trade partner at the time. Among German corporations, Volkswagen (VW) appeared as a pioneer investor on the Brazilian market. Volkswagen opened a small assembly plant in São Paulo in 1953 and established its 80 per cent Brazilian affiliate Volkswagen do Brasil in 1956. A full-scale car factory became operational in 1959. By 1960, Volkswagen was fully compliant with the Brazilian regulatory standard to manufacture cars with a local content of at least 95 per cent. Until the acquisition of the Spanish car manufacturer Seat in 1986, VW do Brasil remained by far the biggest foreign affiliate of the Volkswagen group, even larger than Volkswagen's US affiliate.[3] From the Brazilian perspective, Volkswagen held a similar importance as a foreign investor. In the 1970s, Volkswagen held pole position among non-public industrial investors, trailing only slightly behind nationalized Brazilian corporations like Petrobras, Electrobras and Companhia Vale do Rio Doce.

Unveiling the Truth about Corporate Support for the Military Dictatorship

The impulse to investigate the history of Volkswagen do Brasil and its collaboration with the Political Police (DOPS) and other repressive institutions of the military government was not triggered by the academe or by Volkswagen itself, but originated from Brazil's domestic policy. In November 2011, the Federal Parliament of Brazil voted in favour of a motion by President Dilma Rousseff to investigate crimes against humanity during the military dictatorship (1964–85) through a public research procedure.[4] The establishment of a National Truth Commission (Comissão Nacional de Verdade; CNV) partially followed the example of the South African government. The South African Truth Commission investigated the crimes of the former apartheid regime through an official commission not for the purpose of legal prosecution, but for the public recognition of victims and for the reconciliation of the post-authoritarian society. But the similarities between the South African and the Brazilian truth commissions were not limited to procedural affairs. The South African government did not seek a legal settlement with the political elite of the former apartheid state, whereas the Brazilian government did not have – and does not have – legal means to hold the former elite accountable.[5]

From the perspective of the Rousseff government and significant parts of the Brazilian civil society, the CNV had to serve as a substitute for the lack of opportunity to put the culprits on trial. As all attempts to suspend or revise the Brazilian amnesty law of August 1979 had failed in parliament and in the Supreme Court of Brazil,[6] the truth commission was the last institutional resort for those who did not wish to forgive and forget. The amnesty law of 1979 not only suspended the persecution of former opponents of the military regime, but indemnified the offenders of human rights from the looming threat of a legal prosecution through the forthcoming civilian governments. As the amnesty law of 1979 coincided with the restoration of civic rights and the end of repression, the law was widely accepted as a *quid pro quo* for the normalization of politics. In the long run, however, the amnesty law blocked any legal attempts to sanction crimes against humanity.

During the 1980s, the fear of a potential relapse into the rule of exceptional law and the return of the 'years of lead' (*anos de chumbo*) inhibited the Brazilian civil society from questioning the amnesty and the suspension of legal inquiries. Public criticism of the enforced reconciliation between perpetrators and victims did not begin before the millennium decade.[7] One major reason for the rather low pressure from the civil society was the relatively low number of victims in relation to the population. As a consequence of the severe economic and social disruptions of the post-dictatorial 1980s, a majority of Brazilians perceived the economic boom years of the 1970s as a rather normal era of their lives. The long transition from military rule to a regular parliamentarian democracy and the voluntary retreat of the military elite from politics prevented an escalating conflict, but made a political catharsis unlikely. Since the estimated number of political murders ranked significantly below one thousand, and the number of political arrests at about twenty thousand, the military dictatorship occupied a rather unsuspicious space in the communicative memory of many Brazilians. The Brazilian military rulers ranked on a considerably lower scale of repression and crime than their counterparts in Chile and Argentina, where seven years of military rule (1976–83) claimed between ten thousand and thirty thousand victims. The very high degree of victimization and the resulting public pressure delegitimized the post-dictatorial amnesty laws in Argentina so severely that the Kirchner government had to suspend the amnesty and started a second wave of trials in 2004. For these reasons, the new left-leaning political elite in Brazil and the intellectual opinion leaders had to construct a memorial culture for the victims of the military rule from scratch.

In other post-dictatorial regimes like Germany after 1945 or Central European countries after the demise of communism, trials against leaders and executors of political crimes were instrumental for securing, editing and publishing documentary evidence and testimonies. Since Brazilian state attorneys were not legally committed to this mission, this task was left to a few initiatives from the civil society until the National Truth Commission was established in 2012.

Due to a restrictive law about public archives, historians in Brazil had to wait until 2005 before the files of the most repressive political agencies like the DOPS, the civilian National Information Service (SNI) and the military intelligence were declassified for research. As a consequence of the belated access to formerly classified documents, the author of the most quoted reference work on the dictatorship had to write four of his five volumes without the documentation of perpetrators.[8] Due to his professional background as a journalist, the author, Elio Gaspari, did not choose an analytical approach and instead follows a narration rather than an analytic narrative. His well-written representation focuses on the political history and neglects both the social and the economic aspects of the military dictatorship. An essay collection by the historian Daniel Arao Reis and the renowned economic historians Francisco Vidal Luna (University of São Paulo) and Herbert S. Klein (Columbia University) about social change in Brazil during the dictatorship was published in 2014, at a time when the National Truth Commission had already completed its work.[9] Therefore, the collaborators of the National Truth Commission could not build their work on a solid ground of scholarly research that would have helped them to contextualize the compilation of testimonies and documents in a larger and sharper image of Brazilian society. Due to a lack of human resources, academic historians in Brazil could not make a greater effort to provide a comprehensive overview of Brazil's 'years of lead'.[10]

The National Truth Commission concluded the research process in 2014 and released an extensive three-volume report at the end of the same year.[11] The report confronted some of the biggest Brazilian and foreign enterprises with charges of financial support for the military coup of 1964. According to the report, major enterprises in the state of São Paulo financed a joint interrogation and torture centre of the armed forces and the police and supported the repressive apparatus of the military regime. In addition, the report raised charges against Volkswagen do Brasil of having supported the arrest of a communist worker in their main factory in São Bernardo do Campo and having set up and shared 'blacklists' about allegedly subversive union activists with other industrial employers. The suspicion about cooperation between the DOPS and Volkswagen was mainly based on a key testimony of former VW employee Lucio Bellentani during a hearing by the truth commission of the city of São Paulo.[12]

In addition, the report of the National Truth Commission even suspected Volkswagen of having protected a former Nazi war criminal. Until his arrest by the Brazilian police in 1967, VW do Brasil supposedly employed the commander of the SS extermination camps Treblinka and Sobibor in the corporate security (Segurança Industrial) unit.[13] During the investigations of the National Truth Commission, the state and the city of São Paulo established their own truth commissions. They collected additional testimonies of eyewitnesses and experts and secured documentary evidence in a concerted effort and in close cooperation with the National Truth Commission.[14]

At first, these details from the National Truth Commission report about Volkswagen did not catch any public attention. However, when the State Truth Commission of São Paulo confronted the head of Volkswagen's legal department in a public hearing with critical questions about their collaboration with the military dictatorship, this event attracted considerable attention in the Brazilian media.[15] The head of Volkswagen's legal department gave verbal recognition of the State Truth Commission, but despite the publication of documentary evidence and testimonies against Volkswagen, he denied 'any collaboration with the violation of human rights' and evoked critical questions.[16]

From this moment, the charges against Volkswagen do Brasil began to affect the parent company in Germany. Following the recent charges in the Brazilian media, Germany's biggest TV channel ARD started to research Volkswagen's role under the military dictatorship.[17] During the summer of 2015, a group of Brazilian trade union activists (Trabalhadores por Verdade, Justica e Reparação – Workers for Truth, Justice and Reparations) prepared a lawsuit against Volkswagen and submitted a detailed complaint to the São Paulo State Attorney (Ministério Publico do Estado de São Paulo).[18] In order to generate media coverage in Germany and to put the Volkswagen parent company under pressure, the plaintiffs passed the news to the left-leaning German newspaper *Neues Deutschland* several days before the lawsuit was submitted.[19] Several respected German newspapers with nationwide circulation took up the issue and spread the news even wider in the German public sphere.[20]

The Decision to Research the History of Volkswagen do Brasil

These charges of a collaboration with the military regime in Brazil prompted the German parent company to act. Volkswagen's executive board announced an open and unprejudiced investigation and commissioned the head of Volkswagen's Corporate History Department, Manfred Grieger, with a research project. At the same time, Volkswagen was already under heavy media fire for having defrauded their customers about the toxic emissions of their diesel engines. In regard to their historical communications strategy, Volkswagen acted in defence of its positive reputation as an open communicator of its dark spots in the past. In 1988, Volkswagen was one of the first German corporations to commission a highly respected and independent scholar to investigate the corporate history during the Nazi regime. The voluminous nine hundred-page report by Professor Hans Mommsen and Manfred Grieger was published in 1996 and generated positive reactions in the German media.[21] Since 2000, Volkswagen's Corporate History Department has run two publication series that demonstrate the corporate open-mindedness towards the brighter and the darker sides of their history.

At the same time, the Volkswagen parent company underwent a change of compliance policies. The recently appointed Chief Legal Officer and executive board member Christine Hohmann-Dennhardt pursued a substantial improvement of the compliance regime. As a consequence of the diesel exhaust scandal, the ensuing loss of reputation and heavy fines against Volkswagen, Hohmann-Dennhardt started to implement stricter compliance with legal standards and reputation-saving procedures. Following best practice examples in dealing with corporate history, she decided to commission an external academic historian with a publication record and significant research experience in business history. Hohmann-Dennhardt picked the author of this article for his long-term research experience.[22] At the same time, but for different reasons and without any relation to the Brazilian case, Volkswagen's executive board decided to discontinue Manfred Grieger's employment.[23] After Grieger's dismissal became public, German historians publicly expressed their concerns about a possible relapse into a stage of historical denial and started an open petition in his defence. But their concerns about a looming decline of the corporate history culture at Volkswagen proved to be unfounded.[24]

After the State Attorney of São Paulo began to investigate the history of Volkswagen do Brasil, Volkswagen's managers in Brazil decided to keep a low profile and did not make any efforts to unveil their past, either for internal use or for the public. On 3 November 2016, however, Hohmann-Dennhardt publicly announced that the Volkswagen parent company was going to commission an independent academic historian with the investigation of Volkswagen do Brasil during the military dictatorship.[25] Since Volkswagen's corporate history had already caught the attention of Brazilian and German mass media, journalists observed the historical research from the very start. Several months before the start of Volkswagen's research project, a research collaborative of the German public TV station NDR and the nationwide newspaper *Süddeutsche Zeitung* began production of a TV documentary about Volkswagen do Brasil during the military dictatorship that was released on 24 July 2017. As the TV journalists managed to place short trailers in the main TV news the day before, ratings were considerably higher than expected.[26]

The TV journalists took the chance to film and to interview the author during his research process. The author appeared twice in the documentary when he was filmed doing research at the archive of VW do Brasil and interviewed at his workplace at the Universität Bielefeld. Therefore, the research project on Volkswagen do Brasil had already become an object of media interest before the results were completed and released. However, the author's voluntary collaboration with the TV documentary generated a significant conflict of interest between the journalist and the scholar. The author did not decline the legitimate media interest in his research, but had to deny detailed information about preliminary results in order not to compromise his scholarly integrity.

From the beginning, the author was confronted with the limited quantity and quality of surviving documents about Volkswagen do Brasil. On one hand, the Volkswagen corporate archive in Wolfsburg contains a substantial number of documents on the Brazilian affiliation. On the other hand, the author found a nearly empty corporate archive during his visit to VW do Brasil.[27] Since Brazilian business laws do not stipulate long mandatory terms for keeping corporate files, even the minutes of the executive board meetings and all other relevant sources from the executive level had been destroyed in former decades. Volkswagen do Brasil only established a corporate archive in 2013 on the occasion of its 60th anniversary. The reconstruction of Volkswagen's decision-making procedures in Brazil was based on chance: some evidence survived thanks to original reports, carbon copies or photocopies that had been sent to Germany for approval by Volkswagen's executive board. Only the personal dossiers of the

Human Resources Department still exist, as Brazilian labour laws mandate employers to keep them for an extended period and even beyond the death of employees. In many cases, however, these dossiers contained hardly any information about the political reasons behind dismissals of employees. As a consequence of the ongoing investigations by the Ministério Publico of São Paulo, the archivist collected digitalized documents from the files of the DOPS and the SNI about managers and employees of VW do Brasil.

The rather low quantity of surviving files in Brazil was not the result of a deliberate camouflage strategy. Since Brazilian enterprises were not confronted with public questions about their past until recently, the civil society and stakeholders did not expect them to establish corporate archives. Enterprises like Volkswagen do Brazil had not discovered their history as a resource for their corporate image and their identity until, in 2013, a corporate jubilee was approaching.[28]

The extensive DOPS files in the State Archive of São Paulo (Arquivo do Estado de São Paulo) helped the author to gain a deep impression of the voluntary cooperation of Volkswagen's security unit with the Political Police. The project revealed unexpected results about the intensive collaboration between Volkswagen do Brasil and the repressive institutions of the military dictatorship. From 1969 to 1980, Volkswagen's Segurança Industrial regularly passed information about 'subversive' activities of employees to the police agencies.

A German Multinational during the Military Dictatorship in Brazil. Economic Performance and Political Collaboration

Volkswagen established the first assembly plant in Brazil in 1953, at a time when the country was democratically governed by President Getúlio Vargas.[29] In 1956, right at the beginning of the Kubitschek era, Volkswagen decided to build a full-scale factory to achieve a local content of close to 100 per cent. The decision for this major investment was based on the calculation that VW would lose the emerging but highly protectionist car market in Brazil in the case of non-investment. Volkswagen was lured by tax benefits, subsidized investment loans, favourable exchange rates and the biggest economic growth potential of all Latin American car markets. The protectionist economic policy of Brazil in general and severe tariffs on imported car parts in particular left Volkswagen with the binary decision to invest heavily or to give up the Brazilian market entirely.

The documents in the Volkswagen archive in Wolfsburg do not leave any evidence to support the assumption that Volkswagen do Brasil pledged financial funds for the support of the military coup in 1964. But this fact does not preclude Volkswagen from having paid indirect subsidies to the enemies of the democratically elected president João Goulart and his government. In its position as one of the biggest industrial enterprises in the state of São Paulo, Volkswagen do Brasil was one of the biggest contributors to the São Paulo Federation of Industries (FIESP; Federação das Industrias do Estado de São Paulo), which allegedly endorsed and supported the coup.[30] As the military coup succeeded within just two days, the military elite did not have to draw upon the financial support of the industrial elite or the logistical assistance of the US Navy.

Volkswagen do Brasil's CEO, Friedrich Schultz-Wenk (1914–69), welcomed the military coup enthusiastically. In his long report to the Volkswagen CEO Heinrich Nordhoff, Schultz-Wenk rejoiced about the end of Goulart's allegedly socialist policies and praised the armed forces for the restoration of law and order.[31] Schultz-Wenk even compared the vigour and determination of the military and the political purge with the Nazi takeover of 1933 – not in a terrified tone, but with respect and awe. The Volkswagen CEO advised him to stay away from Brazilian politics and to avoid any public endorsement of the military leadership.[32] Nordhoff was not motivated by discontent about political mass arrests and human rights violations, but by his low confidence in the political stability of Brazil and his general belief that foreign companies should not get politically involved in their host countries.

This neutral wait-and-see attitude of the Volkswagen executive board in Germany soon gave way to an optimistic perception of the Castelo Branco government. The Volkswagen managers in Germany and in Brazil judged the austerity policy of 1964 and 1965 very positively.[33] The rebalancing of the negative balance of payment allowed the Brazilian National Bank to release a greater part of blocked Volkswagen profits for transfer into Germany. Until the first oil price crisis in 1974, Volkswagen benefited from a relatively liberal payment regime allowing them to transfer a substantial fraction of profits, royalties and consultation fees from their Brazilian affiliation to Germany.

Volkswagen do Brasil particularly profited from the rigid governmental control over the Brazilian trade union movement and the rise of wages. Despite the fact that no strikes had taken place in the Volkswagen plant under the Goulart presidency, Volkswagen managers felt reassured that the military government would not allow workers to strike and did its best to deflect union activities to social security issues. The infamous *Ato Institucional* (Executive Order) no. 5 from December 1968 declared strikes illegal and threatened strike leaders with prison sentences of up to one year. Until the repoliticization of unions in the late 1970s, the Volkswagen managers got along with the apolitical and compliant trade union leaders (*pelegos*) very well.

Until the liberalization (*distensão*) of the dictatorship in 1979, real wages stayed considerably behind productivity gains.[34] In addition, the booming car market allowed Volkswagen to pass all price increases in wages, raw materials and finished parts to the customers. Volkswagen clearly profited from the suppression of labour militancy. Since the government and the managers did not recognize the unions as legitimate negotiators of wages, the Federal Ministry of Labour had the power to set wage increases and to keep wage hikes under control. For these reasons, the profit rates on turnover and equity at Volkswagen do Brasil stayed at a considerably higher level than at the German parent company until 1979. The net income of VW do Brazil from 1968 to 1975 alone amounted to 747 million DM.[35]

The high profit rates in the Brazilian market should not be mistaken for secure evidence of the unrestricted validity of the dependency theory. The Brazilian government was not unilaterally dependent on Volkswagen and other multinationals and did not simply act as their political agent. Brazil was not a low tax haven and earned a reputation as an efficient tax collection regime. Generous tax benefits for investments in the developing Amazonas region and in the poor Northeast of Brazil were not particular privileges for multinationals, but an incentive for both domestic and foreign enterprises to invest in underdeveloped areas. Foreign direct investors had to comply with the strict regulatory regime for monetary transfers abroad and needed the consent of the Ministry of Finance (Ministerio da Fazenda) and the Central Bank to transfer profits to their parent companies. However, the Brazilian government did exercise considerable discretion in regard to import duties for machinery and other investment goods and export subsidies. The CEOs of Volkswagen were aware of this fact and always paid the minister of finance and even the president a courtesy visit during their annual business trips to Brazil.

Therefore, the occasional praise of Volkswagen executives for the economic and social policies of the military regime were not merely lip service, but were motivated by serious gratitude and respect. In reaction to growing criticism of human rights violations, mass arrests and torture of political opponents, in the German media, Volkswagen executives spoke up in defence of the Brazilian government.[36]

How was Volkswagen do Brasil involved in political crimes against humanity? The report of the National Truth Commission claimed Volkswagen's involvement in the establishment and financing of a joint interrogation centre of the Political Police and the armed forces in São Paulo, which became a notorious place for the detention, interrogation and torture of political opponents. According to the testimony of a former non-commissioned officer, the Paulista DOI-CODI (Destacamento de Operações de Informação – Operações de Defesa Interna) was equipped with cars and trucks from Brazilian car manufacturers like VW and financed with donations from the Paulistan Federation of Industry (FIESP).[37] Since the FIESP files were destroyed after the end of the military dictatorship, an assessment of their contributions would be impossible. The idea that Volkswagen donated in kind, respectively in cars, does not lack plausibility, but does lack any kind of documentary evidence. Since the evidence of the budget and the financing of the interrogation centre is missing, it would be methodologically dubious to shift immediate moral responsibility for the mistreatment of political opponents to Volkswagen or any other FIESP member.

However, the DOPS files in the State Archive of São Paulo contain sufficient documentary evidence of the cooperation between Volkswagen and DOPS. In 1969, Volkswagen do Brasil hired the army major Ademar Rudge as the new head of the Security Department.[38] Hiring an active officer as the head of a corporate security division was not uncommon in Brazil at this time. Because of his military career, the executive board of VW do Brasil could take Rudge's allegiance with the military rule for granted. Soon after his employment, Rudge established a close collaboration with DOPS. From 1969 onwards, the Segurança Industrial of VW do Brasil kept DOPS closely informed about any allegedly subversive activities in the Volkswagen workforce.

Employees of the Security Department patrolled the bathrooms, changing rooms and toilets and watched for clandestine propaganda flyers. During the 1970s, Volkswagen even installed a camera monitoring system in the factory halls to spot potential work stops and spontaneous assemblies of workers. In 1969, the Security Department reported the names of four employees to DOPS who were under suspicion of having dropped communist flyers. The Security Department acted proactively, without a prior request from DOPS, and reported their names, although they had only caught one of them in the act.[39] From 1970 to 1972, an underground cell of the illegal Communist Party of Brazil (PCB) at Volkswagen occasionally dropped their illegal newspaper *Luta Operaria* ('Workers' Struggle') in toilets and other places that were constantly frequented by workers.[40]

From 1971 onwards, Volkswagen's Security Department constantly exchanged information with DOPS about communist work floor activities. In the spring of 1972, the Security Department provided the Military Police with observations about two workers suspected of communist activities. On request from DOPS, the Security Department forwarded data on twenty-eight employees whom the police were investigating.[41] This information helped DOPS to round up an illegal communist cell of thirty-two persons with two prominent communist leaders at the top: the legendary party chairman Luís Carlos Prestes (1898–1990) and his daughter Anita Leocádia Prestes. Anita's mother, Olga Benário, gained belated posthumous prominence in 2005 through the popular movie *Olga*.

Luís Carlos Prestes and his daughter fled from Brazil in time and found refuge in the Soviet Union. Between 29 July and 8 August 1972, however, DOPS agents arrested six Volkswagen employees under charges of clandestine communist activities on the plant and transported them to the infamous DOPS prison at the Rua Mauá in the centre of São Paulo.[42] One of them, the tool maker Lucio Bellentani, was severely beaten and heavily tortured by the DOPS agents. The police agents even took him to the outskirts of São Paulo and pretended to prepare for his execution in order to extort the names of accomplices. Bellentani and his comrades were released after several months and tried by a military court, but exonerated for lack of evidence. The Attorney General of the Armed Forces appealed the decision for a retrial at the Supreme Military Court. The defendants were sentenced to two years in prison and released on probation several months before the end of their term.[43]

There is an open debate whether the executive board of VW do Brasil did officially authorize Rudge and his subordinates to collaborate with DOPS and to deliver information about 'political subversion' proactively and without any legal obligation. The original reports of the Segurança Industrial in the DOPS files indicate that Rudge forwarded carbon copies to the Human Resources Department and the Chief Human Resources Officer. Since the minutes of the executive board meetings did not survive, historians are unable to establish whether the executive board members officially authorized the collaboration with DOPS or restricted themselves to a tacit approval. As VW do Brasil's CEO Werner P. Schmidt informed the Volkswagen CEO Rudolf Leiding (1914–2003) about the arrest of employees in his monthly report for September 1972, one can conclude that the Chief

Human Resources Officer kept his superior informed about the collaboration with DOPS.[44] But the monthly report to the parent company left the managers at home deliberately in the dark about VW do Brasil's collaboration with DOPS. This does not necessarily mean that the CEO of VW do Brasil or the executive board as a whole had ever formally authorized the Segurança Industrial to collaborate. The Volkswagen executives in Brazil were aware of German press reports about torture in Brazilian prisons and were probably too cautious to charge themselves with a written authorization to support the torturers.

The special investigator Guaracy Minguardi of the State Attorney of São Paulo recently published a document which seems to prove his position that the CEO of VW do Brasil officially approved the collaboration with the security agencies of the military dictatorship. A report by the SNI from 11 September 1975 indicates that VW do Brasil's CEO Wolfgang Sauer (1930–2013) authorized Rudge to collaborate with the intelligence agencies of the military dictatorship in the struggle against subversive activities.[45] This document, however, does not allow historians to conclude that this official authorization was already valid in 1972. Contrary to this assumption, the SNI report indicates that CEO Sauer was going to consult the head of VW do Brasil's legal department, Jacy Mendonça, in order to clarify the legal aspects of collaboration. This wording rather indicates a first-time authorization than a confirmation of a previous agreement.

Volkswagen drew heavy profits from its Brazilian operation during the military dictatorship. With a set of socially repressive policies like the suppression of strikes and free wage negotiations, the military rulers created favourable conditions for the increase of corporate revenues in the manufacturing industries. Volkswagen do Brasil acted in full compliance with the security policy of the regime and established an informal but dependable and durable cooperation with the Political Police. Volkswagen's proactive compliance with the Political Police was not the result of political pressure, but of a supportive attitude towards the military dictatorship.

Christopher Kopper is Professor of Economic and Social History at the University of Bielefeld, Germany. He studied History, Economics and Political Science, and earned his PhD degree at the Ruhr-Universität Bochum (Germany) with a dissertation about banking in Nazi Germany. He worked as Assistant Professor at the Universität Göttingen. After five years as DAAD Visiting Professor in the United States, he published his second book on the history of the Deutsche Bundesbahn. He has authored numerous books on the history of banking, transport and insurance. His most recent book about Volkswagen do Brasil during the military dictatorship was released in December 2017.

Notes

1. Only a few historical monographs about German foreign direct investments have been published so far. See, e.g., F.J. Nellißen, *Das Mannesmann-Engagement in Brasilien von 1892 bis 1995: Evolutionspfade internationaler Unternehmenstätigkeit aus wirtschaftshistorischer Sicht* (Munich: Oldenbourg, 1997); V. Kleedehn, *Die Rückkehr auf den Weltmarkt: Die Internationalisierung der Bayer AG Leverkusen nach dem Zweiten Weltkrieg bis zum Jahr 1961* (Stuttgart: Franz Steiner, 2007); J. Bähr, *Zwischen zwei Kontinenten: Hundert Jahre Dresdner Bank Lateinamerika vormals Deutsch-Südamerikanische Bank* (Frankfurt am Main: Eugen-Gutmann-Gesellschaft, 2007).
2. 'Überall Deutschland', *Der SPIEGEL* 51 (1969), 54–68.
3. On the establishment of VW do Brasil and the decision process for a full-fledged car factory in Brazil, see V. Wellhöner, *'Wirtschaftswunder', Weltmarkt, westdeutscher Fordismus: Der Fall Volkswagen* (Münster: Westfälisches Dampfboot, 1996), 295–96; and H. Shapiro, *Engines of Growth: The State and Transnational Auto Companies in Brazil* (Cambridge: Cambridge University Press, 1994).
4. Law 12528, 18 November 2011, retrieved from www.planalto.gov.br/ccivil_03/_Ato2011-2014/2011/Lei/L12528.htm.
5. On the legal aspects of coping with the dictatorial past in Brazil, see U. Neumann et al. (eds), *Transitional Justice: Das Problem gerechter strafrechtlicher Vergangenheitsbewältigung* (Frankfurt am Main: Lang, 2013).
6. The Brazilian amnesty law of 28 August 1979 (Law 6683, retrieved from www.planalto.gov.br/ccivil_03/leis/16683.htm) was based on a proposal by the military government and adopted by a two-party parliament that was not freely elected and acted under the potential threat of a relapse into political repression. See also N. Schneider, 'Das Schlusslicht Lateinamerikas? Neueste Auseinandersetzungen über Die Militärvergangenheit in Brasilien', *Zeitschrift für Geschichtswissenschaft* 59 (2011), 641–53.
7. E. Teles and V. Safatle (eds), *O que resta da ditadura: A exçecão Brasileira* (São Paulo: Biotempo, 2010).
8. E. Gaspari, *A ditadura envergonhada* (São Paulo: Editora Intrinseca, 2002; *A ditadura escancarada* (São Paulo: Editora Intrinseca, 2002); *A ditadura derrotada* (São Paulo: Editora Intrinseca, 2003); *A ditadura encurrelada* (São Paulo: Editora Intrinseca, 2004).
9. D. Arao Reis, Herbert S. Klein, Francisco Vidal Luna (ed.), *A ditadura que mudou o Brasil* (Rio de Janeiro: Zahar, 2014); D. Arao Reis, *Modernização, ditadura e democracia 1964–2010* (Rio de Janeiro: Objetiv2a, 2014).
10. See M.C. D'Araujo, 'Taking Stock (with Discomfort) of the Military Dictatorship Fifty Years after the 1964 Coup: A Bibliographical Essay',

Brazilian Political Science Review 3 (2015), 143–63 for the current state of research about the dictatorship.

11. Comissão Nacional de Verdade (CNV), *Relatório*, 3 vols (Brasília, 2014) (online: http://cnv.memoriasreveladas.gov.br).
12. Testimony of Lucio Bellentani to the truth commission of the city of São Paulo, 19 July 2012, printed in: Comissao Municipal de Verdade 'Vladimir Herzog', *Relatório Final* (São Paulo, 2013), 48–51 (German translation retrieved 10 January 2019 from https://lateinamerika-nachrichten.de/artikel/manchmal-wenn-du-in-einer-menschenmenge-bist-fuehlst-du-dich-allein/).
13. Comissão Nacional de Verdade, *Relatório*, Vol. 2, 66–67, 321–22, 330.
14. Comissão da Verdade do Estado de São Paulo 'Rubens Pavia', *Relatório*, 2 vols (São Paulo, 2015).
15. Report by *Reuters Brazil*, 26 February 2015.
16. Report by *Rede Brasil Atual* about the testimony of Rogerio Varga (VW do Brasil) at the State Truth Commission, 28 February 2015, retrieved 18 January 2018 from www.redebrasilatual.com.br.
17. J. Segador, 'Die umstrittene Rolle von VW während der Militärdiktatur', 21 March 2015, retrieved from https://www.deutschlandfunk.de/brasilien-die-umstrittene-rolle-von-vw-waehrend-der.799.de.html?dram:article_id=314919.
18. 'Reparação *requerendo* instauração da inquérito civil', *A Folha de São Paulo*, 22 September 2015.
19. C. Russau, 'Die langen Schatten der Folter', *Neues Deutschland*, 19 September 2015.
20. 'Zivilklage gegen VW in Brasilien eingereicht', *Süddeutsche Zeitung*, 23 September 2015; 'Klage gegen VW wegen Verhalten bei Diktatur in Brasilien', *Die Welt*, 23 September 2015.
21. S. Brünger, *Geschichte und Gewinn: Der Umgang deutscher Konzerne mit ihrer NS-Vergangenheit* (Göttingen: Wallstein, 2017), 272–79; H. Mommsen and M. Grieger, *Das Volkswagenwerk und seine Arbeiter im Dritten Reich* (Düsseldorf: Econ, 1996).
22. The author published his first book on banking in Nazi Germany and his second book on the history of the Deutsche Bundesbahn. In 2015, he co-authored a book on the history of the Munich Re, followed by the co-authorship of a book on prisoners' labour in communist East Germany in 2016.
23. Information by Christine Hohmann-Dennhardt, 1 December 2016.
24. 'Wissenschaftler attackieren Volkswagen', n-tv.de, 2 November 2016, retrieved from www.n-tv.de/wirtschaft/Wissenschaftler-attackieren-Volkswagen-article18982396.html. The successor of Grieger was hired in 2017.
25. 'Volkswagen nomeia especialista para apurar denuncias de tortura na ditadura brasileira', www.g1.globo.com, 3 November 2016; 'Volkswagen troca pesquisador que lidera estudo sobre ditadura brasileira', *A Folha de São Paulo*, 7 November 2016.

26. See the documentary available at: www.daserste.de/information/reportage-dokumentation/dokus/sendung/komplizen-vw-und-die-brasilianische-militaerdiktatur-100.html (24 July 2017).
27. VW kept only their annual reports, the corporate magazine *Familia* for employees and a collection of photos and advertising material.
28. See the short sketch about the history of Volkswagen do Brasil on the corporate website: http://vwbr.com.br/ImprensaVW/page/Historia.aspx.
29. For more details, see the complete report about Volkswagen do Brasil in C. Kopper, *VW do Brasil in the Brazilian Military Dictatorship 1964–1985: A Historical Study* (Wolfsburg: Volkswagen, 2017).
30. J.C.E. Silberfeld, *O Grupo Permamente de Mobilizaçao Industrial da FIESP 1964–1967* (Unpublished Master's thesis, PUC São Paulo, 1984).
31. Report by Schultz-Wenk to Nordhoff, 16 April 1964, Unternehmensarchiv der Volkswagen AG Wolfsburg (UVW) 174/559/1.
32. Letter from Nordhoff to Schultz-Wenk, 15 May 1964, UVW 174/559/1.
33. Letter from the VW AG (Novotny/Siebert) to the German Federal Minister for Economic Cooperation, 11 June 1964, UVW 174/479/1.
34. Kopper, *VW do Brasil*, 42.
35. See the long-term performance report in: UVW 587/6/229.
36. Interview by the CEO of VW do Brasil Werner P. Schmidt with *Süddeutsche Zeitung*, 16 February 1972.
37. Department of Information Operation – Centre for Internal Defence. See Gaspari, *A ditadura escancarada*, 62–64.
38. During his employment at Volkswagen, Rudge was promoted to the rank of reserve colonel.
39. Report by Rudge to DOPS, 11 December 1969, Arquivo do Estado de São Paulo (AESP), DOPS Inventory, 50-Z-030-0822.
40. The Security Department forwarded these newspapers to DOPS.
41. Confidential report by DOPS, 21 July 1971, AESP, DOPS, 50-D-7-1714.
42. See the minutes of DOPS with personal details of the detainees in: AESP, DOPS, 50-Z-009-26099, 50-Z-009-26092, 50-Z-009-26082 and 50-Z-009-26064.
43. Letter from the São Paulo military court to DOPS, 2 September 1974, AESP, DOPS, 50-Z-009-26099.
44. Letter from Schmidt to Leiding, 26 September 1972, UVW 174/575/1.
45. S. Roxo, 'Relatório do MPF mostra que Volks ajudou a ditadura militar no Brasil', *O Globo*, 13 January 2018; C. Russau, 'VW do Brasil-Chef, 1973: "Sicher foltern Polizei und Militär Gefangene"', *Taz blog latinorama*, 18 December 2017.

Bibliography

Arao Reis, Daniel, Herbert S. Klein, and Francisco Vidal Luna (eds). *A ditadura que mudou o Brasil*. Rio de Janeiro: Zahar, 2014.

Arao Reis, Daniel. *Modernização, ditadura e democracia 1964–2010*. Rio de Janeiro: Objetiv2a, 2014.

Bähr, Johannes. *Zwischen zwei Kontinenten: Hundert Jahre Dresdner Bank Lateinamerika vormals Deutsch-Südamerikanische Bank*. Frankfurt am Main: Eugen-Gutmann-Gesellschaft, 2007.

Brünger, S. *Geschichte und Gewinn: Der Umgang deutscher Konzerne mit ihrer NS-Vergangenheit*. Göttingen: Wallstein, 2017.

Comissão Municipal de Verdade 'Vladimir Herzog'. *Relatório Final*. São Paulo, 2013.

Comissão Nacional da Verdade (CNV). *Relatório*. 3 vols. Brasília, 2014.

Comissão da Verdade do Estado de São Paulo 'Rubens Pavia'. *Relatório*. 2 vols. São Paulo, 2015.

D'Araujo, M.C. 'Taking Stock (with Discomfort) of the Military Dictatorship Fifty Years after the 1964 Coup: A Bibliographical Essay'. *Brazilian Political Science Review* 3 (2015), 143–63.

Fico, C. 'Versões e controvérsias sobre 1964 e a ditadura militar'. *Revista Brasileira de Historia* 47 (2004), 29–60.

Gaspari, E. *A ditadura envergonhada*. São Paulo: Editora Intrinseca, 2002.

Gaspari, E. *A ditadura escancarada*. São Paulo: Editora Intrinseca, 2002.

Gaspari, E. *A ditadura derrotada*. São Paulo: Editora Intrinseca, 2003.

Gaspari, E. *A ditadura encurrelada*. São Paulo: Editora Intrinseca, 2004.

Gaspari, E. *A ditadura acabada*, São Paulo: Editora Intrinseca, 2016.

Kleedehn, V. *Die Rückkehr auf den Weltmarkt: Die Internationalisierung der Bayer AG Leverkusen nach dem Zweiten Weltkrieg bis zum Jahr 1961*. Stuttgart: Franz Steiner, 2007.

Kopper, C. *VW do Brasil in the Brazilian Military Dictatorship 1964–1985: A Historical Study*. Wolfsburg: Volkswagen, 2017.

Mommsen, H., and Gricger, M. *Das Volkswagenwerk und seine Arbeiter im Dritten Reich*. Düsseldorf: Econ, 1996.

Nellißen, F.J. *Das Mannesmann-Engagement in Brasilien von 1892 bis 1995: Evolutionspfade internationaler Unternehmenstätigkeit aus wirtschaftshistorischer Sicht*. Munich: Oldenbourg, 1997.

Neumann, U., et al. (eds). *Transitional Justice: Das Problem gerechter strafrechtlicher Vergangenheitsbewältigung*. Frankfurt am Main: Lang, 2013.

Roxo S. 'Relatório do MPF mostra que Volks ajudou a ditadura militar no Brasil'. *O Globo*, 13 January 2018.

Russeau, C. 'Die langen Schatten der Folter'. *Neues Deutschland*, 19 September 2015.

Russau C. 'VW do Brasil-Chef, 1973: "Sicher foltern Polizei und Militär Gefangene"'. *Taz blog latinorama*, 18 December 2017.

Schneider, N. 'Das Schlusslicht Lateinamerikas? Neueste Auseinandersetzungen über die Militärvergangenheit in Brasilien'. *Zeitschrift für Geschichtswissenschaft* 59 (2011), 641–53.

Segador, J. 'Die umstrittene Rolle von VW während der Militärdiktatur'. 21 March 2015. Retrieved 15 January 2018 from https://www.deutschlandfunk.de/brasilien-die-umstrittene-rolle-von-vw-waehrend-der.799.de.html?dram:article_id=314919.

Shapiro, H. *Engines of Growth: The State and Transnational Auto Companies in Brazil*. Cambridge: Cambridge University Press, 1994.
Silberfeld, J.C.E. *O Grupo Permamente de Mobilizaçao Industrial da FIESP 1964–1967*. Unpublished Master's thesis, PUC São Paulo, 1984.
Teles, E., and Safatle, V. (eds). *O que resta da ditadura: A exçecão Brasileira*. São Paulo: Biotempo, 2010.
Wellhöner, V. *'Wirtschaftswunder', Weltmarkt, westdeutscher Fordismus: Der Fall Volkswagen*. Münster: Westfälisches Dampfboot, 1996.

Section 3

First Assessments of Brazil's National Truth Commission

Chapter 10

The Outcomes of the Brazilian Truth Commission

Successes and Failures in a Lengthy Transitional Justice Process

Marlon Alberto Weichert

On 10 December 2014, after a thirty-one-month mandate, the Brazilian National Truth Commission – Comissão Nacional da Verdade (CNV) – issued its final report. This release marked an additional step in a slow transitional justice process concerning the legacy of human rights abuses during the military dictatorship that governed the country from 1964 until 1985, a process thus far characterized by a broad victims' reparation programme, perpetrator impunity, incipient initiatives of memory recovery, limited institutional reforms and, until 2011, a dearth of truth unveiling.[1] That year, two laws were enacted to expand truth-seeking efforts: one to establish a new legal framework concerning the right to access public information and another to create the truth commission.[2] Although civil society had been calling for both measures since at least 2007,[3] they only became law in 2011, after the Inter-American Court of Human Rights condemned Brazil in the case of *Gomes-Lund et al. (Guerrilha do Araguaia) v. Brazil*.[4]

Thus, on 18 November 2011, a federal law created the CNV, which was charged with elucidating and shedding light on the gross human rights violations that had occurred between 16 September 1946 and 5 October 1988.[5] That the Brazilian Truth Commission was established almost thirty years after the end of the repressive regime makes it an anomalous case, since most precedent commissions were established just after the end of a conflict or authoritarian era. Both strengths and shortcomings of the Commission may be attributed to this lengthy passage of time. Negative consequences included difficulties finding documents, taking testimonies and identifying remains of disappeared people. In addition, the restorative and reconciling impact that the Commission could bring to the victims' families was significantly affected, since many of these relatives – especially parents – had aged in the intervening years or had already passed away. However, there were also positive emanations from the passage of time. First, it enabled the Commission to analyse the facts at a distance from the ideological disputes surrounding the dictatorship era, and without fear of political turmoil. Second, the time lapse created conditions under which the remnants of authoritarianism in state structures could more easily be detected and the CNV could therefore recommend measures to overcome them.

This chapter's goals are multifold. First, it aims to describe the structure of the CNV report, the scope of the investigations, the most relevant decisions taken by the Commission during its mandate, the conclusions reached and the recommendations issued. Second, the chapter analyses some obstacles faced during the mandate and how these may have prejudiced the Commission's task. Finally, the article discusses the contributions the commission has made to the transitional justice process in Brazil and the challenges that remain after the conclusion of its mandate. Explaining some key aspects of the Brazilian Truth Commission's mandate, this chapter contributes to understanding of the transitional justice process in Brazil and sheds light on some of the reasons why dealing with the past is still a daunting task in this country.

Report Overview

The CNV's report comprises three volumes and has a total of 4,300 pages. Volume I was designed to meet the aims established by the Governing Law. It provides a 'description of the facts relating to serious human rights violations during the period investigated, with special attention to the military dictatorship that lasted from 1964 to 1985' and presents the Commission's findings and recommendations.[6]

The second volume incorporates texts that are not a result of the collective work of the commissioners, but research undertaken individually by some CNV members on nine different subjects: human rights violations perpetrated against military officers; human rights violations of workers; human rights violations of peasants; violations of human rights in Christian churches; violations of indigenous peoples' rights; human rights violations in universities; the dictatorship and homosexuality; civilians who collaborated with the dictatorship; and civil society's resistance to serious human rights violations. According to the introduction presented in Volume I, this second volume gathers 'thematic texts that are the personal responsibility of some commissioners, who prepared or supervised them with the support of consultants and advisors'.[7]

Finally, the third volume provides a detailed account of 434 cases of death or enforced disappearance. The report compiles and expands upon information from previous works developed by the Commission of Relatives of the Dead and Politically Disappeared and by the Special Commission on Dead and Disappeared Persons, adding, in some cases, new findings reached by the CNV itself or other public agencies.

Main Conclusion: Gross Human Rights Violations and Crimes against Humanity

The CNV fulfilled its legal mandate, according to the objectives established in Article 3 of Act No. 12,528. Although the major contribution was not the unveiling of human rights violations – on this subject the Commission mostly compiled previous materials – it is indisputable that the report made an expressive contribution through its analysis of the pattern of repression perpetrated in Brazil. The Commission investigated state structures and chains of command and asserted that the Brazilian military dictatorship systematically committed serious human rights violations and crimes against humanity.

The Commission concluded that between 1946 and 1988, but 'especially during the military dictatorship', a 'systematic practice of illegal and arbitrary imprisonment and torture, as well as … executions, enforced disappearances and concealments of corpses by Brazilian state agents' was perpetrated.[8] The Commission also gathered evidence establishing that these human rights violations were part of a policy adopted by the highest levels of the military: 'repression and elimination of political opponents became state policy, designed and implemented on the basis of decisions taken by the President of the Republic and military secretaries', and not 'a few isolated acts or excesses from the voluntarism of a few military officials', as usually asserted by the armed forces.[9] Finally, the report states that these practices 'by state agents during the military dictatorship characterized the committing of crimes against humanity'.[10]

The significance of these conclusions should not be understated. Because they were reached by the CNV, an official body established by federal statute, they amount to an official recognition that Brazilian state agents perpetrated crimes against humanity. The government can no longer ignore such findings and should guide its administrative and judicial action by the Commission's conclusions.

Although the CNV's conclusions do not legally bind either the courts (by virtue of their constitutional autonomy) or the government (the law did not establish this legal status), the report cannot be reduced to a mere collection of opinions. The legal system – like any system – demands consistency, forming an integrated and ordered whole, and it is obvious that the law instituted the Commission as an integral part of this system. The outcome of the Commission is therefore not a singularity disconnected from the legal universe. On the contrary, the report issued by the Commission is an official legal document produced to elucidate facts that had competing versions, and about which the state decided that an official version should be established. Inasmuch as the Commission states that human rights violations were perpetrated and that such acts constitute crimes against humanity, its conclusions indisputably carry legal authority and must be taken seriously by the entire public apparatus. At the very least, a refusal to accept its content would necessitate justification. If any public authority acts contrary to the conclusions of the report and its recommendations, for instance, it will be incumbent upon them to explain the decision, provide reasons for the divergence and seek approval at the highest levels of government. The truth revealed by the Commission is the official version of facts – the 'state truth' – and unless and until it is formally dismissed, it must be recognized by public authorities. In the same sense, officials should make efforts to implement those recommendations that are under their capacity.

Second Main Conclusion: Ongoing Gross Human Rights Violations

The CNV also concluded that Brazilian security forces continue to commit serious human rights violations, fuelled in part by impunity for past crimes. The report states that, although the abuses no longer occur in the context of political repression – as during the military dictatorship – 'the practice of illegal and arbitrary detentions, torture, executions, enforced disappearances and even concealment of corpses is no stranger to contemporary Brazilian reality'. Further, the Commission indicated that this pattern of violence is 'largely due to the fact that … serious human rights violations [were] not properly reported, nor were offenders held accountable'.[11]

It is important to note that the Commission was not granted the powers to investigate human rights abuses committed after 1985. Rather, commissioners presupposed that human rights violations are routinely perpetrated throughout the country, particularly by police forces and prison guards. Although the report does not detail how commissioners arrived at this conclusion – which would have been advisable – they probably relied on the reports of governmental, international and non-governmental organizations that have documented widespread torture, summary executions and enforced disappearances in Brazil. Indeed, evidence indicates that the country has soaring rates of violence involving state agents. Police officers often use lethal force unlawfully, and police and prison authorities systematically use torture to extract information or confessions, or as a form of punishment.[12]

The purpose of this second finding, therefore, was not to shed light on the nature of the abuses, but to connect impunity for past human rights violations with their recurrence in the present. In this sense, the commissioners endorsed the argument of many civil society leaders and scholars that ongoing authoritarian practices and human rights violations by security forces are linked to impunity for past crimes.[13] Indeed, criminal prosecutions reinforce the rule of law and give meaning to the principle of equality and are essential to prevent security force officials from believing that human rights abuses will be tolerated and that the government will grant them impunity.[14]

Key CNV Approaches

Investigation Conducted Abroad: Repression at the International Level

As seen above, the Commission focused its conclusions on two core topics. However, the report also contains other findings that reveal interesting lines of inquiry developed by the CNV, two of which will be highlighted here. The first concerns the participation of Brazilian authorities in human rights violations perpetrated abroad or in cooperation with foreign officials. Indeed, the Brazilian Truth Commission was probably the first of its kind to have extraterritorial jurisdiction, allowing its investigation to cover human rights violations perpetrated outside the country. A positive outcome of such power is the CNV's inclusion in the report of two chapters describing the participation of Brazilian authorities in serious human rights violations in foreign countries and the repressive alliance in the Southern Cone. While most of the report compiles information obtained from outside research, in this part new facts were unveiled. These are based on the CNV's analysis of Ministry of Foreign Affairs files, hitherto barely accessed, as well as information obtained abroad and through a set of testimonies.

The report reveals how the military government, through its diplomatic services, surveilled, spied on and persecuted Brazilians living in other countries. It also confirms that under 'Plan Condor', but even before, governments of Brazil, Chile, Argentina, Uruguay, Bolivia and Paraguay created a network, with the support of the United States, to track down, capture and interrogate dissidents outside their home countries, and deliver them to repressive agencies of the military governments from whom they had fled. In most cases, this would end in disappearance.

The report also depicts how the Brazilian government, through its armed forces and diplomatic channels, supported the military coup d'état in Chile in 1973 and refused protection for Brazilian people who had been arrested during the broad repression that followed the overthrow of President Salvador Allende.

Also worth mentioning are the report's references to cooperative efforts between the governments of the United Kingdom, France and the United States, which assisted and trained Brazilian military in repression techniques, including torture.[15]

Naming Offenders

The second notable feature to highlight is the report's naming of 377 offenders – a measure expressly requested by the Governing Law.[16] Given its lack of prosecutorial capacity, the Commission could not of course adjudicate the guilt of named offenders, nor did it sanction them. The CNV's task was to indicate suspects who were identified as a result of an inquisitorial investigation.

According to the report, 'the CNV proceeded with extreme caution' before pinpointing a perpetrator, 'always seeking support from documents, statements of victims and witnesses, including public officials who participated in repression'. All agents listed were 'mentioned elsewhere in the report – especially in Volume III, which is dedicated to the history of the dead and missing political dissidents …'. The Commission also notes that, although it was not bound by the rules of adversarial proceedings, where possible it collected the testimony of the identified individuals. But this process was impeded by difficulties in getting such individuals to testify, and the fact that many chose to remain silent before the CNV.[17]

The CNV established three sets of offenders. The first category contains those considered responsible, at the 'political and institutional level', for the 'general definition of the doctrine that allowed serious violations and the corresponding strategies, and the establishment of chains of measures that determined the practice of unlawful acts'.[18] In this group, the Commission included the five military presidents who governed during the dictatorship and the three members of the military junta who took power for four months in 1969. Another forty-five heads of agencies that provided direct assistance to the presidency were also pinpointed. The criterion was strict liability, that is, all officials who took up a post in one of the agencies that commanded the repression policy were listed.

The second group includes those considered responsible 'for monitoring and managing structures and procedures' directly linked to the committing of serious human rights violations, a list of eighty-three officials who managed the agencies and structures within which these acts were perpetrated. While the report asserts that the parameter for this category was strict liability, in most cases the Commission described which facts occurred under the command of the official named.[19]

Finally, the third set identifies 239 individuals who were directly involved in abuses. The report states that all named individuals took part in at least one case of murder or disappearance of persons and outlines the substantiating evidence. For this category of offences, a criterion of subjective responsibility was adopted.[20]

A final caveat is necessary. Since the CNV did not list – or even estimate – cases of illegal arrest and torture, and only included in the set of direct offenders those agents who were involved in cases of deaths or disappeared persons, or in 'emblematic cases' mentioned in the report, many other perpetrators may be missing, especially those who took part in cases of illegal detention or torture, but in which the victim did not die or disappear.[21]

Recommendations

The CNV made twenty-nine recommendations, divided into three groups: institutional arrangements, regulatory reformulations and follow-up measures. For analytical purposes, this chapter categorizes them differently, according to the five sets of transitional justice measures: promotion of *justice*; *institutional reforms*; *truth* seeking; victims' *reparation*; and recovery and protection of *memory*. We must note, however, that these categories are not watertight, since each of the transitional justice strategies serves more than one goal. Thus, the classification follows a prevalence criterion. For instance, the recommendation to promote criminal accountability, which is obviously the core measure of *justice*, is also relevant to the revelation of *truth* and *reparations* for victims and, to a lesser degree, to the production of *memory* and *institutional reforms* (a criminal conviction of an official implies in his or her vetting). In the same vein, when the Commission recommends the recognition by the military commanders that the army instituted a regime of human rights violations, it is not only demanding a symbolic *reparation* to victims and society, but it is also stimulating an act of recognizing facts (*truth*) and assumption of responsibility (*justice*). Therefore, every mechanism is able to contribute to more than one of the five immediate goals of transitional justice, and ultimately they all pursue the main aims of a transitional justice process: reconciliation, strengthening of democracy and guarantee of non-recurrence.

It is worth noting that the report alternates well-reasoned and detailed recommendations with some more generic ones, for which the Commission did not set forth clear explanations concerning the connection between them and the findings described throughout the report. It is more noticeable particularly in the field of institutional reform. However, they are all absolutely consistent with some of the most prioritized items on the Brazilian human rights agenda, which reveals that the Commission used its power as grounds to hear civil society and to boost many institutional reform measures considered by activists and organizations as essential to curb human rights violations in the country.

Promotion of Justice

The report presents two recommendations directly connected to perpetrators' accountability.[22] The first is that alleged perpetrators be criminally prosecuted for crimes against humanity. The recommendation is grounded in the jurisprudence of the Inter-American Court of Human Rights and, in particular, the ruling on the 2010 Gomes-Lund case, whereby Brazil was condemned to investigate, prosecute and punish serious human rights violations perpetrated during the Brazilian dictatorship, despite the provisions of the statute of limitations and the Amnesty Law.[23] Similarly, the Commission alludes to the *jus cogens* norms, which provide that domestic amnesty laws, statutes of limitation or any other substantive or procedural laws that grant impunity for crimes against humanity, genocide and war crimes are not valid.[24]

The Commission was under considerable pressure to avoid making such a statement, especially as the Brazilian Supreme Court has not decided whether the domestic courts are bound by the judgement of the Inter-American Court of Human Rights in the Gomes-Lund case. The Prosecutor General of the Republic as well as the Brazilian Bar Association and a leftist political party are demanding an affirmative decision, which is essential to overturn a previous Supreme Court ruling, in which the constitutionality of the Amnesty Law issued in 1979 was declared in favour of public agents.[25] Brazil is therefore experiencing a conflict between an internal decision of its Supreme Court and the judgement issued by the Inter-American Court of Human Rights. While theoretically there is no doubt that the Inter-American Court of Human Rights ruling is binding on any domestic agency or power, including the judiciary, there is still enormous opposition from politicians and judges to accepting that an international tribunal could supersede a decision of the highest domestic court. The CNV held a clear and coherent position on this issue, reinforcing the role of international human rights law and pressing for the accountability of perpetrators within the country.

In the second recommendation concerning accountability, the report calls for administrative and judicial measures against perpetrators compelling them to reimburse the National Treasury for the indemnification paid to victims of gross human rights violations. It should be noted that in Article 37 of the Brazilian Constitution, Paragraph 7 establishes that victims of injuries caused by officials are entitled to compensation by the state. In turn, the state must be refunded by employees who act wilfully, recklessly or negligently and, when necessary, should sue them for this purpose. Brazil's federal government has been developing a comprehensive reparation programme for victims of human rights violations during the dictatorship, comprising compensation for civil and economic damages.[26] However, the Solicitor General's Office has not yet adopted any initiative for suing offenders to reimburse the National Treasury for such expenses, mainly because it supports the idea that the statute of limitations blocks this possibility.[27]

Institutional Reform

The vast majority of recommendations made by the CNV refer to institutional reforms, the most relevant of which are briefly summarized below, according to the agency or branch to which they are related.

Armed forces – reformulation of admissions exams, curricula in military academies, and continuous assessment of members to strengthen appreciation of democratic principles and human rights.[28]

Police – dissolution of the military police, which has been responsible for ostensive patrolling in Brazil since the dictatorship.[29] This recommendation is based on compelling data connecting the high index of deaths by the police to its military structure, and the perception that it is inappropriate to use military forces to promote internal security in a democratic society.

Judiciary – removal of the military courts at the state level and exclusion of civilians from its jurisdiction on the federal level.[30]

Legislature – repeal of the National Security Law and its replacement with a law to defend democracy and the rule of law; provision of a legal definition of both crimes against humanity and enforced disappearance of persons in accordance with international human rights law; amendment of the criminal codes to repeal any discriminatory provisions against homosexuality; enactment of a legal provision to compel the investigation of any killing by policemen as potential murder rather than death after unlawful resistance by the suspect, which is the method still used to file these cases; introduction of a custody hearing with a judge for any arrested person within twenty-four hours of imprisonment.[31]

Truth-Seeking Initiatives

The CNV recommended the establishment of a permanent agency to continue the investigation it was unable to finish and to monitor compliance with the recommendations. It also requested the strengthening of procedures for searching, opening, organizing and disclosing archives, files and documents.[32]

Victim Reparation

There are five recommendations primarily related to non-pecuniary reparation for victims: recognition by the armed forces of its institutional responsibility for serious human rights violations during the military dictatorship; correction of the death certificates of those killed or disappeared to show their real cause of death, since, in certain situations, false information was entered to conceal the violence perpetrated; correction of the data inserted in public records whereby victims are still listed as criminals; provision of health care and permanent psychosocial assistance for victims; and continuation of search, identification and return to the families of the remains of disappeared people.[33]

Recovery and Protection of Memory

Finally, the Commission issued the following recommendations related to the recovery and protection of memory: prohibition of official events commemorating the 1964 military coup; recording and protection of places where human rights violations were perpetrated; establishment of a Museum of Memory in Brasília; revocation of honours granted to agents who were involved in serious human rights violations; and changing of the denomination of public parks, roads, buildings and public structures or institutions of any kind that still celebrate officials or private individuals who were involved in serious human rights violations.[34]

Unavoidable and Avoidable Difficulties

The institution of a truth commission generates great expectations and inevitably some frustrations. At the end of the mandate, it is likely that no social group will be fully satisfied. The supporters of the old regime will say that they were persecuted. The victims will claim that the work was less extensive than expected.

Many exogenous and endogenous factors influence the functioning of a truth commission. Some are avoidable, some not, as shown in Table 10.1. Among the inevitable arises, above all, the problem concerning the nature of the mandate, which deals with issues under political and ideological dispute that will obviously be opposed by the perpetrators of human rights violations and their supporters. Often created with very limited human and material resources, truth commissions also need to deal with bureaucratic requirements, which consume a significant portion of their limited terms of existence.

Besides these unavoidable contingencies, others may accrue, depending on the quality of the governing legislation, the selection process of commissioners, the political support that the commission receives during its work, and also the behaviour of the commissioners themselves.[35] A commission without sufficient legal powers to search for and produce information, made up of members nominated with no public consultation or without requisite skills, or without political support at the highest government levels, therefore tends to deliver unsatisfactory results.

In the Brazilian case, all these difficulties mentioned in Table 10.1 were present to a greater or lesser extent: the military and conservative

Table 10.1. Difficulties faced by truth commissions.

	Unavoidable	**Avoidable**
Exogenous factors	Ideological and political dispute Opposition of perpetrators and their supporters Bureaucracy	Sufficient powers Selection process (public consultation) Commissioners' skills Government support Administrative apparatus
Endogenous factors	Human idiosyncrasy – internal conflicts	Commitment of commissioners Definition of leadership Dialogue with civil society and other public institutions

Source: Author's elaboration taking some ideas from United Nations High Commissioner for Human Rights, *Rule of Law Tools for Post-Conflict States – Truth Commissions*, UN Doc. HR/PUB/06/1 (2006); P. Hayner, *Unspeakable Truths: Facing the Challenge of Truth Commissions*, 2nd ed. (New York and London: Routledge, 2010); D. Orentlicher, *Report of the Independent Expert to Update the Set of Principles to Combat Impunity*, UN Doc. E/CN.4/2005/102 (18 February 2005); and L. Joinet, *Question of the Impunity of Perpetrators of Human Rights Violations (Civil and Political)*, UN Doc. E/CB.4/Sub.2/1997/20 (26 June 1997).

sectors of society clearly opposed the Commission's work and tried to impede it; civil society was not involved in the members' selection process, which delegitimized the Commission before some victim groups; the military commanders repeatedly challenged the Commission's authority; the law provided weak administrative support, forcing the Commission to hire its work teams in precarious conditions and with several breaks in continuity; the Governing Law did not confer legal powers to access private archives; and most of the commissioners had little or no knowledge of the Commission's role, or experience in conducting investigations.

The confrontation with military commanders was undoubtedly one of the most significant episodes to prejudice the Commission's mandate. The report narrates two situations in which the Commission's authority was challenged by the armed forces. Initially, there was a lack of cooperation in providing documentation. Just one quarter of the eighty-four letters sent by the Commission to the Ministry of Defence and the armed forces were answered, and just a small proportion of these responses contributed to the Commission's research.[36] As the Commission highlighted, 'had the military made available to the CNV' the files of their intelligence services 'produced during the dictatorship, and also provided all required information', the 'history of executions, torture and concealment of corpses of political opponents to the military dictatorship could have been better elucidated'.[37]

Another issue that affected the mandate and could have been avoided by a better Governing Law, presidential regulation, or even an internal decision of the commissioners was a lack of full commitment to the Commission's work on the part of some of its members. Indeed, as the CNV had only seven members and a few clerks, one would expect that they would be completely dedicated to the mandate through their permanent and active participation. However, contrary to expectations, some had other professional commitments and were only partially engaged in the investigation. This situation was exacerbated when one commissioner left the CNV for medical reasons in the fifth month of its mandate and was never replaced.

In addition to these exogenous factors, certain internal Commission decisions may also have hindered its work, one being the isolation in which its activities took place during the first year. Although it was understandable that the Commission initially had to build on unity and institutional strength, and, for that reason, to work reclusively, it was expected that the commissioners would soon interact closely with civil society and other institutions committed to transitional justice initiatives. However, this only happened in the second half of the mandate, when the Commission's detachment from civil society and some regional and sectorial truth commissions had already jeopardized its relationship with them.

Furthermore, the Commission chose to prioritize the compilation of documents and the production of a report, instead of leading a national network of public and non-governmental stakeholders dedicated to promoting a broad discussion of the causes and legacies of the coup d'état, the military dictatorship and the gross human rights violation regime instituted within the country. The Commission could have catalysed a strategy in which all public bodies involved in the process of repression and violation of fundamental rights would be invited to analyse their institutional responsibilities with hindsight and to build tools to prevent repetition. This process never took place, either because the Commission did not consider it a priority, or because it was politically unfeasible, due to the dearth of governmental support.

Curiously, this lack of initiative at the federal level was minimized by the creation of more than one hundred commissions at the state and municipal levels, as well as in universities, trade unions, student organizations and Bar associations. This bottom-up dynamic started before the CNV's members were appointed by the government. Indeed, the institution of regional and sectorial commissions was initially a reaction to the delay in appointing commissioners and beginning the mandate at the federal level.[38] The outcome of establishing multiple truth commissions is yet to be seen. Given the *sui generis* nature of this truth commission model, it warrants close observation and analysis over the coming years.

A final remark should be added regarding the administrative decision to establish a rotating system with the head of the Commission changing every three months. While the democratic spirit underpinning this decision is laudable, the selection of a president or a permanent coordinator would probably have benefited the mandate, since it would have given the Commission a face, eased dialogue with society, and offered the administrative team leadership. Fortunately, this rotation ended in November 2013, when it was decided that the same coordinator should remain until delivery of the report.

Unresolved Issues

It is undeniable that the report has made a tremendous contribution to the Brazilian transitional justice process, especially because it compiled and reviewed previous investigations, added new information, and issued timely and relevant recommendations to overcome the legacy of authoritarianism and human rights violations that still jeopardize the strengthening of democracy. It is also clear that the CNV's mandate could not exhaust the entire set of facts to be investigated, even if it had worked under ideal conditions. In this section, the chapter addresses some questions that have remained unanswered by the CNV, although they were relevant and could (or should) be considered in the report.

Quantification of Unlawful Arrest, Torture, Executions and Enforced Disappearance

Although the CNV presented a list of victims of death and disappearance, the report did not provide data on the number of victims of illegal detention or torture. This is probably the foremost gap in the research, since it was essential to determine the impact of repression on Brazilian society. While such information is not easy to collect – especially since the armed forces did not contribute to the investigations – there was an expectation that at least an estimate would be given.

The Commission, however, did not submit any new information on this issue, instead adopting the number used by the Secretary of Human Rights, which found that around twenty thousand people were arrested by repressive means.[39] This information has never been confirmed, however, and is more guesswork than estimation, which requires more precise calculation.

The report only provides a figure indicating the number of dead and missing political prisoners, based on the compilation and updating of earlier research. Even these data are probably incomplete, as they are also the outcome of limited investigation, conducted by representatives of victims who were part of city resistance movements or involved in rural guerrilla activities. Although the reports produced by these victim representative groups were reliable on their own, they lacked the tools and resources to include other social segments that were not directly involved in resistance but nevertheless suffered repression. Many peasants and indigenous peoples were clearly victims of authoritarian policies of repression that may have caused thousands of deaths, yet these figures were not established by the Commission or included in the final report.

Questions concerning the number of victims of arbitrary detention and torture in general, and death and disappearance among indigenous peoples and peasants in particular, therefore remain unanswered.

Indigenous Peoples

As mentioned in the 'Report Overview' section above, certain investigation issues were addressed in separate texts prepared or supervised by individual commissioners, and their findings and conclusions were published in Volume II of the report. It is not clear why individual members' findings were not incorporated into the main text in Volume I, particularly when some of these themes (notably violations perpetrated against military, labourers and peasants) are also covered in that volume.

Regrettably, some subjects of paramount importance to the mandate were not developed by the Commission collectively, but only through these individual texts published in the second volume. The main missing subject concerns the rights of indigenous peoples, who were not involved in political activism or ideological disputes during the dictatorship, but nevertheless suffered severe consequences as a result of authoritarianism. Indeed, the military government considered the protection of indigenous reserves and cultural rights a major barrier to national development plans, such as the building of roads and large dams, and to the establishment of agricultural settlements. As a result, they were often fiercely persecuted to ensure they would not hinder authorities' projects. Text number five of Volume II asserts that at least 8,350 victims were murdered during the period examined as a result of such conflicts, and reports that official forces perpetrated many massacres against indigenous peoples, such as the Waimiri-Atroari in the Amazon, who opposed road construction on their land.[40] It is hard to comprehend why such serious human rights violations were left out of the main part of the report.

Exiles

The coup d'état of 1964 and the increase in violent repression after 1968 caused two waves of Brazilian people to seek refuge or exile in foreign countries for fear of imprisonment, torture or death. Quantifying these victims would also be an important source of information to gauge the effects of repression. Again, the Commission did not explore this subject.

Social and Economic Rights

The CNV differed from its foreign counterparts in the time gap between its institution and the end of the authoritarian period. This distance posed difficulties for the investigation but should also have enabled the Commission to assess the impact of the authoritarian regime on social and economic rights from a historical standpoint. Though not a formal objective of the Commission (since the violation of economic and social rights is not considered a gross human rights abuse under international law), the Commission's disclosure of the consequences of a dictatorial government on several areas of civil life could have been an important way of raising social awareness about the importance of democracy and the rule of law. Indeed, the lack of democracy is reflected in the quality and logic of public services and leaves a legacy for years or even generations. An undemocratic and authoritarian regime not only affects political dissidents and their families, but also jeopardizes civil, political, social, cultural and economic rights for the whole of society. Measuring the impact of the authoritarian regime on social or economic rights such as education, health, welfare, home and land distribution would strongly contribute to revealing the harmful effects of a dictatorship for most of the population. The Commission, however, touched on this subject only superficially within the individual texts in Volume II.

Vetting

As explained above, the Commission recommended civil and administrative sanctions for perpetrators, but failed to address measures in this respect, such as vetting procedures or the withdrawal of military ranks (the report only addressed the loss of awards).

Public agents involved in gross human rights violations, such as murder, torture and enforced disappearances, not only betrayed their duties but also showed that they lacked the moral standards required of a state representative. For these reasons, they should not remain in civil or military service. As the Office of the United Nations High Commissioner for Human Rights has pointed out, 'public employees who are personally responsible for gross violations of human rights or serious crimes under international law revealed a basic lack of integrity and breached the trust of the citizens they were meant to serve'.[41] And, for that reason, the citizens, and in particular the victims of abuses, 'are unlikely to trust and rely on a public institution that retains or hires' them.[42] Therefore, they should be screened and, if found responsible for serious human rights violation, removed.[43] It is worth mentioning that the Brazilian legislation dealing with civil and military public servants expressly requires the exclusion from public service of any agent who commits serious crimes while on duty, especially physical harm to individuals. Vetting procedures would therefore not be a novelty.

Vetting – or the forfeiture of retirement benefits and military ranks for those military or civil servants who retired – obviously has a punitive dimension for the person screened and can therefore only be decided through a formal procedure, where due process of law is fully guaranteed.[44] In this sense, no sanction, even administrative, can therefore be imposed solely on the basis of the report. However, this does not explain why the Commission did not recommend the adoption of administrative or judicial proceedings with these goals.

Executive Summary

One final but very important aspect of the report warrants discussion: the difficulty of reading it. The publication contains 4,300 pages and its key section, Volume I, has 975 pages. Such great length renders the report inaccessible to its most important recipients: civil society and the common citizen.

The magnitude of the Commission's mandate certainly justifies the report's size. Nonetheless, its perusal by society at large should be facilitated by an Executive Summary summing up its main content. The full text would stand as a reference book, while the Executive Summary would promote social awareness and outreach, especially as it could be more easily distributed in schools, universities, unions, associations and civil society organizations. Preparation of an even shorter version would also be advisable, using appropriate language to teach children and adolescents about the past human rights violations perpetrated in Brazil and the impact on their lives.

Since the Commission did not prepare an Executive Summary, perhaps because of time constraints, the onus should be on the government to do so.

Conclusion

Transitional justice comprises a set of measures for the promotion of justice, revelation of truth, protection and dissemination of memory, reparation of victims and institutional reforms. The goals of transitional justice – strengthening democracy, reconciliation and non-repetition guarantees – will materialize more effectively to the extent that such initiatives are executed simultaneously or at least sequentially.[45] They are strategies that articulate and complement each other, as parts of a whole.[46] While each strategy is relevant by itself as a concrete implementation of democratic values, it is the comprehensive application of the whole set that will more likely guarantee the achievement of transitional justice's aims. Against this background, while truth commissions are the main mechanism for seeking truth in the aftermath of gross human rights violations, they are just one measure in a whole series of recommended strategies. The issuing of a truth commission report obviously does not signal the end of the transitional justice process. In the Brazilian case, the report itself stresses the need to deepen this process through measures including: criminal, civil and administrative accountability of perpetrators of gross violations of human rights; institutional reforms in the security forces, army and judiciary; institution of memory spaces; non-pecuniary reparation of victims; and the search for remains of disappeared persons.

This chapter has aimed to demonstrate that the Commission did not establish certain facts in a sufficiently exhaustive manner, leaving many questions unanswered that now require new strategies to expand on truth revelation. Yet the criticisms raised here in no way diminish the enormous importance of the report; they are purely intended as contributions to stimulate broader discussion on the legal and political role played by the Truth Commission and as encouragement to reinforce the transitional justice process in Brazil.

The National Truth Commission was neither the beginning nor the end of the transitional justice process in Brazil. It was a strategy demanded by civil society and delivered – albeit belatedly – by the state. The Commission's main contribution is official acknowledgement that Brazilian dictators and repressors committed crimes against humanity during the military regime, and that two essential requirements remain pending to overcome this legacy: perpetrator accountability and institutional reform of the security forces.

Marlon Alberto Weichert has been a federal prosecutor in Brazil for twenty-three years, primarily dedicated to human rights litigation and advocacy. He is currently acting as Deputy Federal Ombudsman at the Office of the General Prosecutor. He has worked in a variety of transitional justice initiatives in Brazil in his capacity as federal prosecutor as well as during his mandate as a member of the Amnesty Commission (2013–17). He holds an MA in Constitutional Law and was a researcher at the New York University School of Law (Hauser Global Fellows Program) during 2014–15.

Notes

1. On victims' reparations programmes, which have already granted approximately a billion dollars for more than thirty-five thousand people, see Marcelo D. Torelly, *Justiça de Transição e Estado Constitucional de Direito: perspectiva teórico-comparativa e análise do caso brasileiro* (Belo Horizonte: Fórum, 2012). For justice initiatives by the Federal Prosecution Service, see Brasil, Ministério Público Federal, Câmara de Coordenação e Revisão, 2, *Grupo de trabalho justiça de transição: atividades de persecução penal desenvolvidas pelo Ministério Público Federal: 2011–2013* (Brasília: MPF, 2ª CCR, 2014). See also Marlon A. Weichert, 'Proteção penal contra violações aos direitos humanos', in Emilio Peluso Neder Meyer and Marcelo Andrade Cattoni de Oliveira (eds), *Justiça de Transição nos 25 anos da Constituição de 1988* (Belo Horizonte: Initia Via, 2014), 563-606. Brazil has no comprehensive policy on memory protection and recovery. Isolated initiatives, however, include memorials for the victims in São Paulo City and Belo Horizonte (currently under construction). Several other monuments around the country commemorate resistance and mourn the victims. Regarding institutional reforms, Brazil enacted a new Constitution soon after the end of the authoritarian era (1988). This led to institutional

reform of the political system, judiciary and Public Prosecution Service. The police and armed forces, however, did not undergo reform.

2. See Lei No. 12.527, adopted 18 November 2011, Diário Oficial da União [DOU] de 18 November 2011 and Lei No. 12.528, adopted 18 November 2011, DOU de 18 November 2011.
3. Recommended by the Eleventh Human Rights National Conference in 2008 and later inserted in the Third National Plan on Human Rights (2009).
4. *Gomes-Lund et al. (Guerrilha do Araguaia) v. Brazil*, Preliminary Objections, Merits, Reparations, and Costs Judgement, Inter-Am Ct. HR, (ser. C) No. 219 (24 November 2010). In this case, Brazil was declared in non-compliance with the American Convention on Human Rights regarding the legacy of human rights violations during the dictatorship.
5. The frame adopted was based on the last Brazilian Constitution before the military dictatorship (enacted on 18 September 1946) and the first constitution after it (promulgated on 5 October 1988). Human rights activists advocated that the CNV should be instituted to investigate only facts directly related to the military dictatorship (1964–85), and, despite the law provision, the CNV focused its work on this narrowed time period.
6. Comissão Nacional da Verdade, *Relatório*, Vol. I (2014), 15. All translations from the original report in Portuguese have been made by the author.
7. Ibid., 16.
8. Ibid., 962.
9. Ibid., 963.
10. Ibid., 964.
11. Ibid., 964.
12. In 2014, on-duty and off-duty policemen killed 3,009 people, an average of eight per day, or one every three hours, repeating a trend of the last few years. Between 2009 and 2013, Brazilian security forces killed a total of 11,197 people, surpassing the number of police killings in the United States in thirty years. See Fórum Brasileiro de Segurança Pública, *Anuário Brasileiro de Segurança Pública 2015*, 26–27, retrieved 27 October 2015 from http://www.forumseguranca.org.br/storage/download//anuario_2015-retificado.pdf; and Fórum Brasileiro de Segurança Pública, *Anuário Brasileiro de Segurança Pública 2014*, 40–42, retrieved 7 August 2015 from http://www.forumseguranca.org.br/produtos/anuario-brasileiro-de-seguranca-publica/8o-anuario-brasileiro-de-seguranca-publica. For torture data, see United Nations Subcommittee on Prevention of Torture and Other Cruel, Inhuman or Degrading Treatment or Punishment, *Report on the Visit to Brazil*, UN Doc. CAT/OP/BRA/1 (5 July 2012), retrieved 29 October 2015 from http://tbinternet.ohchr.org/_layouts/treatybodyexternal/Download.aspx?symbolno=CAT%2fOP%2fBRA%2f1&Lang=en.
13. See Kathryn Sikkink, *The Justice Cascade: How Human Rights Prosecutions Are Changing World Politics* (New York: W.W. Norton & Co., 2011).
14. See United Nations Human Rights Council, *Report of the Special Rapporteur on the Promotion of Truth, Justice, Reparation and Guarantees of Non-*

recurrence, Pablo de Greiff, Submitted Pursuant to Human Rights Council Resolution 18/7, UN Doc. A/HRC/27/56 (27 August 2014).
15. Comissão Nacional da Verdade, *Relatório*, Vol. I, 141, 189, 330, 334, 352.
16. Naming names in truth commission reports has always been a controversial issue. See Mark Freeman, *Truth Commissions and Procedural Fairness* (Cambridge: Cambridge University Press, 2006).
17. Comissão Nacional da Verdade, *Relatório*, Vol. I, 843.
18. Ibid., 844.
19. Ibid., 855.
20. Ibid., 845, 874.
21. This subject is further analysed in the section 'Unresolved Issues' later in this chapter.
22. See Comissão Nacional da Verdade, *Relatório*, Vol. I, 965 and 967.
23. *Gomes-Lund et al. (Guerrilha do Araguaia) v. Brazil*, Inter-Am Ct. HR.
24. These are the same arguments that have been developed by the Federal Prosecution Service in its initiatives of criminal and civil accountability since 2008.
25. This decision was taken in the trial of a constitutional claim called 'Noncompliance with a fundamental principle action', held in 2010. See ADPF No. 153, Supremo Tribunal Federal, Relator: Min. Eros Grau, 29 April 2010, R.T.J. 216/11 (Braz.). See Weichert, 'Proteção penal contra violações aos direitos humanos'.
26. For details, see Torelly, *Justiça de Transição*.
27. This agency, indeed, has opposed the Federal Prosecution Service, which has argued since 2008 that the recovery of expenses with indemnifications paid for crimes against humanity is not subject to limitation periods. The CNV's recommendation therefore reinforces the Prosecutors' arguments.
28. See Comissão Nacional da Verdade, *Relatório*, Vol. I, 967.
29. Ibid., 971.
30. Ibid., 972.
31. Ibid., 971–72.
32. Ibid., 973, 975.
33. Ibid., 964, 968, 970, 974.
34. Ibid., 967, 974.
35. See Priscilla Hayner, *Unspeakable Truths: Facing the Challenge of Truth Commissions*, 2nd ed. (New York and London: Routledge, 2010).
36. Comissão Nacional da Verdade, *Relatório*, Vol. I, 64.
37. Comissão Nacional da Verdade, *Relatório*, Vol. III (2014), 35–36.
38. Act 12,528 was passed in November 2011, but the Presidency of the Republic only appointed the commissioners in May 2012. See Lei No. 12.528, DOU de 18 November 2011.
39. Comissão Nacional da Verdade, *Relatório*, Vol. I, 350.
40. Comissão Nacional da Verdade, *Relatório*, Vol. II (2014), 199 and 228.
41. United Nations High Commissioner for Human Rights, *Rule of Law Tools for Post-Conflict States – Vetting: An Operational Framework* (2006),

4, retrieved 7 August 2015 from http://www.ohchr.org/Documents/Publications/RuleoflawVettingen.pdf.
42. Ibid.
43. United Nations Secretary-General, *The Rule of Law and Transitional Justice in Conflict and Post-Conflict Societies: Report of the Secretary-General*, UN Doc. S/2004/616 (23 August 2004).
44. See Alexander Mayer-Rieck, 'On Preventing Abuse: Vetting and Other Transitional Reforms', in Alexander Mayer-Rieck and Pablo de Greiff (eds), *Justice as Prevention: Vetting Public Employees in Transitional Societies* (New York: Social Science Research Council, 2007), 482–521.
45. See Marlon A. Weichert, *Justiça Transicional* (São Paulo: Estúdio editores.com, 2015), 38–40.
46. See Pablo de Greiff, 'Theorizing Transitional Justice', in Melissa Williams (ed.), *Transitional Justice* (New York: NYU Press, 2012), 34.

Bibliography

Ambos, Kai. 'O marco jurídico da Justiça de Transição', in Kai Ambos, Marcos Zilli, Maria Thereza R.A. Moura, and Fabíola G. Monteconrado (eds), *Anistia, Justiça e Impunidade: Reflexões sobre a Justiça de Transição no Brasil* (Belo Horizonte: Fórum, 2010), 21–132.

Amnesty International. *Amnesty International Report 2013: The State of the World's Human Rights* (2013). Retrieved from http://files.amnesty.org/air13/AmnestyInternational_AnnualReport2013_complete_en.pdf.

Arthur, Paige. 'How "Transitions" Reshaped Human Rights: A Conceptual History of Transitional Justice'. *Human Rights Quarterly* 31 (2009), 321–67.

Brasil. Constituição do Brasil, adopted 5 October 1988. Retrieved from http://www.planalto.gov.br/ccivil_03/Constituicao/ConstituicaoCompilado.htm.

Brasil, Ministério Público Federal, Câmara de Coordenação e Revisão, 2. *Grupo de trabalho justiça de transição: atividades de persecução penal desenvolvidas pelo Ministério Público Federal: 2011–2013*. Brasília: MPF, 2ª CCR, 2014.

Brasil, Secretaria Especial dos Direitos Humanos. Comissão Especial sobre Mortos e Desaparecidos Políticos. *Direito à verdade e à memória*. Brasília: Secretaria Especial de Direitos Humanos, 2007.

Comissão de Familiares de Mortos e Desaparecidos Políticos. *Dossiê Ditadura: Mortos e Desaparecidos Políticos no Brasil (1964–1985)*. São Paulo: Imprensa Oficial de São Paulo, 2009.

Comissão Nacional da Verdade. *Relatório*, Vol. I, 2014.

Comissão Nacional da Verdade. *Relatório*, Vol. II, 2014.

Comissão Nacional da Verdade. *Relatório*, Vol. III, 2014.

De Greiff, Pablo. 'Theorizing Transitional Justice', in Melissa Williams (ed.), *Transitional Justice* (New York: NYU Press, 2012), 31–77.

Fórum Brasileiro de Segurança Pública. *Anuário Brasileiro de Segurança Pública 2014*. Retrieved 7 August 2015 from http://www.forumseguranca.

org.br/produtos/anuario-brasileiro-de-seguranca-publica/8o-anuario-brasileiro-de-seguranca-publica.

Fórum Brasileiro de Segurança Pública. *Anuário Brasileiro de Segurança Pública 2015*. Retrieved 27 October 2015 from http://www.forumseguranca.org.br/storage/download//anuario_2015-retificado.pdf.

Freeman, Mark. *Truth Commissions and Procedural Fairness*. Cambridge: Cambridge University Press, 2006.

Hayner, Priscilla. *Unspeakable Truths: Facing the Challenge of Truth Commissions*. 2nd ed. New York and London: Routledge, 2010.

Henkin, Louis, Cleveland, Sarah H., Helfer, Laurence R., Neuman, Gerald L., and Orentlicher, Diane F. *Human Rights*. 2nd ed. New York: Thomson Reuters; Foundation Press, 2009.

Holston, James, and Caldeira, Teresa P.R. 'Democracy, Law, and Violence: Disjunction of Brazilian Citizenship', in Felipe Agüero and Jeffrey Stark (eds), *Fault Lines of Democracy in Post-Transition Latin America* (Miami: North South Center Press, 1998), 263–96.

Human Rights Watch. *Letter to Brazilian Authorities* (28 July 2014). Retrieved from http://www.hrw.org/sites/default/files/related_material/20140728_Brazil_Torture_EN.pdf.

Joinet, Louis. *Question of the Impunity of Perpetrators of Human Rights Violations (Civil and Political)*. UN Doc. E/CB.4/Sub.2/1997/20 (26 June 1997).

Ladisch, Virginie, and Ramirez-Barat, Clara. 'Between Protection and Participation: Involving Children and Youth in Transitional Justice Processes', in Clara Ramirez-Barat (ed.), *Transitional Justice, Culture, and Society: Beyond Outreach* (New York: Social Science Research Council, 2013), 173–210.

Mayer-Rieck, Alexander. 'On Preventing Abuse: Vetting and Other Transitional Reforms', in Alexander Mayer-Rieck and Pablo de Greiff (eds), *Justice as Prevention: Vetting Public Employees in Transitional Societies* (New York: Social Science Research Council, 2007), 482–521.

O'Donnell, Guillermo. 'Teoria democrática y política comparada'. *Desarollo Económico* 39 (2000), 519–70.

Orentlicher, Diane. *Report of the Independent Expert to Update the Set of Principles to Combat Impunity*. UN Doc. E/CN.4/2005/102 (18 February 2005).

Prado, Mariana, Trebilcock, Michael, and Hartford, Patrick. 'Police Reform in Violent Democracies in Latin America'. *Hague Journal on the Rule of Law* 4 (2012), 252–85.

Ramos, André de Carvalho. 'Crimes da ditadura militar: a ADPF 153 e a Corte Interamericana de Direitos Humanos', in Luis Flavio Gomes and Valerio de Oliveira Mazzuoli (eds), *Crimes da ditadura militar: uma análise à luz da jurisprudência atual da Corte Interamericana de Direitos Humanos: Argentina, Brasil, Chile, Uruguai* (São Paulo: Revista dos Tribunais, 2011), 174–225.

Sikkink, Kathryn. *The Justice Cascade: How Human Rights Prosecutions Are Changing World Politics*. New York: W.W. Norton & Co., 2011.

Teitel, Ruti G. 'Transitional Justice Genealogy'. *Harvard Human Rights Journal* 16 (2003), 69–94.

Torelly, Marcelo D. *Justiça de Transição e Estado Constitucional de Direito: perspectiva teórico-comparativa e análise do caso brasileiro*. Belo Horizonte: Fórum, 2012.

United Nations. *Guidance Note of the Secretary General: United Nations Approach to Transitional Justice (2010)*. Retrieved from https://www.un.org/ruleoflaw/files/TJ_Guidance_Note_March_2010FINAL.pdf.

United Nations Commission on Human Rights. *Report of the Special Rapporteur, Sir Nigel Rodley, Submitted Pursuant to Commission on Human Rights Resolution 2000/43: Addendum Visit to Brazil*. UN Doc. E/CN.4/2001/66/ADD.2 (30 March 2001). Retrieved from http://ap.ohchr.org/documents/dpage_e.aspx?si=E/CN.4/2001/66/Add.2.

United Nations High Commissioner for Human Rights. *Rule of Law Tools for Post-Conflict States – Vetting: An Operational Framework* (2006). Retrieved 7 August 2015 from http://www.ohchr.org/Documents/Publications/RuleoflawVettingen.pdf.

United Nations Human Rights Council. *Report of the Special Rapporteur on the Promotion of Truth, Justice, Reparation and Guarantees of Non-recurrence, Pablo de Greiff, Submitted Pursuant to Human Rights Council Resolution 18/7*. UN Doc. A/HRC/27/56 (27 August 2014).

United Nations Secretary-General. *The Rule of Law and Transitional Justice in Conflict and Post-Conflict Societies: Report of the Secretary-General*. UN Doc. S/2004/616 (23 August 2004).

United Nations Subcommittee on Prevention of Torture and Other Cruel, Inhuman or Degrading Treatment or Punishment. *Report on the Visit to Brazil*. UN Doc. CAT/OP/BRA/1 (5 July 2012). Retrieved 29 October 2015 from http://tbinternet.ohchr.org/_layouts/treatybodyexternal/Download.aspx?symbolno=CAT%2fOP%2fBRA%2f1&Lang=en.

United Nations High Commissioner for Human Rights. *Rule of Law Tools for Post-Conflict States: Truth Commissions*. UN Doc. HR/PUB/06/1 (2006).

Weichert, Marlon A. *Justiça Transicional*. São Paulo: Estúdio editores.com, 2015.

Weichert, Marlon A. 'Proteção penal contra violações aos direitos humanos', in Emilio Peluso Neder Meyer and Marcelo Andrade Cattoni de Oliveira (eds), *Justiça de Transição nos 25 anos da Constituição de 1988* (Belo Horizonte: Initia Via, 2014), 563–606.

Chapter 11

The Struggle for the Voice of the Victims in the National Truth Commission (Brazil)

Memories and Truth, Yesterday and Today

San Romanelli Assumpção

During the period between 2013 and 2014, a small team known as the 'Dictatorship and Gender' Working Group operated in the office of the National Truth Commission (NTC) in São Paulo, where it was supervised by the commissioner, Paulo Sérgio Pinheiro, and managed at an executive level by Glenda Mezarobba. This team was devoted to hearing the victims of serious infringements of human rights in Brazil between 1946 and 1985 and responsible for dealing with most of the testimonies gathered by the NTC: 194 out of the 332 victims were heard. The aim of this chapter is to describe and provide a narrative for the work carried out by this team. It explains its methodology and reveals the difficulties encountered and the results obtained. It also investigates the team and its work within the NTC and within the transitional judicial procedures in Brazil, in general. It will furthermore conduct an empirical political and normative analysis of the work carried out by this team and the work of the NTC, and thus suggest possible avenues for researchers interested in examining both the achievements and limitations of this commission.

Interpretive Axis: The 'Political Struggles for Memory'

Transitional justice in Brazil has been a long process and, in the opinion of most activists for memory, truth, justice and redress, an unsatisfactory process that remains inconclusive. It is noted for the fact that amnesty has been granted to the perpetrators of political crimes, and the fact that there are 209 people who have 'disappeared' and whose whereabouts are still unknown. Moreover, it is handled by a truth commission that was set up belatedly and whose findings have been the subject of widespread criticism, as well as a good deal of praise.

The disputes surrounding the assessment and interpretation of the work of the NTC and its achievements suggest that the memory of the NTC is contested just as much as the memories of political repression and the serious infringements of human rights by the dictatorship. There are thus two domains of 'political struggles for memory', the term employed by Elizabeth Jelin.[1] These two domains are intertwined and indissoluble, since both form part of the same scenario of transitional justice, of which the NTC only makes up one part.

The path followed by political activists that eventually led to the setting up of the NTC was long and arduous. Since the dictatorship, the politically persecuted, the families of both the prisoners and the dead and disappeared, and a number of supporters had continuously struggled in a variety of ways; they had written individual and collective letters of denunciations of arrests, torture, murder and disappearances; political prisoners had been on hunger strike; lawyers had tried to help the persecuted and political prisoners through legal actions; protest movements had been organized, such as the amnesty movement or the Brazil Nunca Mais project (1985); families had sought the bodies of their relatives and struggled for the right to bury them; ex-political prisoners and political persecuted had founded movements and forums; they had contributed to the Special Committee on the Political Dead and Disappeared (CEMDP) and truth committees; and called for the creation of a National Truth Commission. The NTC is the outcome of a long process of struggle for memory, truth, justice and redress (MTJR) and, consequently, survivors of dictatorial repression and relatives of surviving, murdered and disappeared activists had high expectations. The creation of the NTC, its functioning and political results are part of political struggles for memory and truth and intricately linked to disputes over what should be a legitimate commission of truth. These disputes have taken place at several levels: (a) among the different strands of the MTJR movements; (b) among the MTJR movements, the violators who remain alive and the defenders of the military regime; (c) among the MTJR movements and the Brazilian state institutions in general; (d) among the MTJR and NTC in particular; and (e) also within the NTC itself, where a wide range of concepts concerning the right to transitional justice coexisted. These political struggles for memory, disseminated among so many political actors, are constitutive of the NTC itself and the interpretation of its work within the Brazilian transitional justice system. This is the interpretative axis that guides this chapter and the reason for the chapter's title.

In the light of this interpretive axis, it is important to clarify the role I played when working for the NTC. I have worked for several NTC teams, especially for the 'Dictatorship and Gender' Working Group. I was one of the NTC's advisors in the period between 2013 and 2014. I worked for (a) the 'Dictatorship and Repression of Workers and Trade Unions' Working Group, supervised by the commissioner Rosa Cardoso; (b) the 'Dictatorship and Gender' Working Group, supervised by the commissioner Paulo Sérgio Pinheiro; and (c) the 'Political Deaths and Disappearances' Working Group, supervised by the commissioners José Carlos Dias and Rosa Cardoso. Much of what I am describing, interpreting and analysing in this chapter is based on my own working experiences and personal reflections. This means that this chapter is also an exercise of memory with regard to the NTC ('memory-work', in the words of J.R. Gillis, or 'the labors of memory', in the words of Jelin) and forms an individual part of this fight for memory and interpretation ('state repression and the struggle for memory', again using Jelin's expression).[2] Since the whole labour of memory is entrenched in social positions and experiences, it should be noted that in addition to having worked for the NTC, I am a trained political scientist and make use of academic tools and resources. To control the subjectivity of memory, I relied on a collection of documents to validate the information. The main documents I used were (a) 'memory meetings' (documents in which the team recorded their activities and which are available in the National Archives, together with the NTC file in the 'Memórias Reveladas – Centro de Referência das Lutas Políticas no Brasil [1964–1985]'); (b) the NTC website (in its different versions and not only in its current final online version); (c) the transcriptions of the testimonies of the victims; (d) the statute of the NTC; and (e) the final report of the NTC.

Institutional Context of the 'Dictatorship and Gender' Working Group

The 'Dictatorship and Gender' Working Group needs to be contextualized within a broader understanding of transitional justice in Brazil and the institutional design of the NTC. Its operational capacity, scope of work and its relationship with the most important rightsholders – the direct and indirect victims – cannot be analysed otherwise.

Institutions are always impacted by diverse political visions and plural political forces, even when they are relatively small, and this was the case with the National Truth Commission, too. The NTC was a federal body that was less powerful than other federal institutions in a number of respects: its political mandate was limited or it had a short existence, it was staffed by a small number of employees, and although it had a sizable budget, this was also relatively small. It was an organ in which various political conceptions about transitional justice and human rights coexisted, with different understandings about the weight and importance of the various activities usually carried out by a truth commission. This plurality existed within a hierarchical organization involving different positions and their respective institutional privileges:

- Seven commissioners were appointed by the president, who had to decide on the following aspects: what exactly was the role of the NTC; how are human rights and serious infringements defined; what was meant by transitional justice; what should be the political priorities; and how should the NTC's mandate best be fulfilled? The commissioners were ranked equally in the hierarchy and had to reach their decisions collectively. As an expression of this democratic equality, the committee elected a new chairman every three months. This rotating system and the equality between the commissioners were key factors in the operations of the NTC and heavily affected the way it carried out its mandate. Symbolically, this committee of equals was the sovereign decision-making power and this symbolism was institutionally strong. Each commissioner had his/her own department of assistants, consultants, employees and researchers, divided into Working Groups with different responsibilities. In addition, each Working Group had one or two commissioners who acted as supervisors. The truth commissioners included: José Carlos Dias, José Paulo Cavalcanti, Maria Rita Kehl, Paulo Sérgio Pinheiro, Pedro Dallari (who replaced Fontelles on 3 September 2013) and Rosa Cardoso. Claúdio Fontelles resigned on 2 September 2013. Gilson Dipp was a commissioner but requested to be relieved of his post for health reasons on 9 April 2013.
- The office of chairman of the NTC was always exercised by a commissioner, elected every three months by the body of seven commissioners, with the right to re-election. Symbolically, the existence of a chairman did not affect the equality of commissioners.
- The executive secretary of the NTC was appointed by the body of commissioners. The following persons acted as executive secretaries: Ricardo de Lins e Horta (from 12 July 2012 to 4 April 2013), Pedro Helena Pontual Machado (from 4 April 2013 to 20 June 2013) and André Saboia Martins (from 21 June 2013 to 16 December

2014). The executive secretary possessed most of the institutional prerogatives of the NTC. Decisions about recruiting staff and the allocation of funds were implemented only by the executive secretary, which gave this person immense institutional power. However, within the hierarchy, the executive secretary was below the board of commissioners. According to the statute that commissioners drafted to govern the NTC, his institutional prerogatives made his decision-making power strong and effective, affecting the ability of the board of commissioners to implement decisions, the decision-making capacity of each commissioner, and the capacity of commissioners, advisors and consultants to perform the tasks assigned to them.

- A report executive secretary role was created in 2014 and permanently occupied by Vivien Ishaq.
- The commissioners collectively set up thirteen Working Groups; areas of responsibility were given to different advisors who worked in an independent but collaborative way. Each Working Group operated in a way that was politically determined by one or more commissioners and its activities were carried out by its managers, advisors, consultants,[3] assistants and researchers.
- A team of twelve NTC advisors, two NTC consultants and six collaborators was formed. The advisory body was also highly rotating, with many layoffs and appointments. The institutional prerogatives of these positions were established by the NTC statute, but they varied enormously over time. They changed depending on the political conception that prevailed in the NTC, on the appointed chairman and executive secretary, and with new executive management for the final report.

The 'Dictatorship and Gender' Working Group and Its Mission

The small team that systematically listened to victims' testimonies was called the 'Dictatorship and Gender' Working Group. Paulo Sérgio Pinheiro was the commissioner who supervised its political work and research activities. Within the NTC, Pinheiro systematically supported the need to work on serious infringements of human rights in a way that was grounded on a gender perspective. Pinheiro was also the NTC's main advocate of the policy of listening to the victims, understanding this as one of the key features of a truth commission. He supported the team that listened to the victims of gross human rights violations throughout its whole existence. The team formally began its work in April 2013 and completed it in November 2014. The executive manager of the 'Dictatorship and Gender' Working Group was the consultant of the NTC, Glenda Mezarobba, a political scientist who has conducted pioneering studies into transitional justice in Brazil.

Prior to the installation of this Working Group, the NTC had failed to give priority to listening to testimonies, as demonstrated by the following facts: (1) the number of victims who were heard was very low (only 332, according to the list written on the NTC's website); (2) of these 332 victims, 194 were heard by the 'Dictatorship and Gender' Working Group; (3) only four researchers in this team were recruited to listen to the victims; (4) the researchers who listened to the victims worked as volunteers for several months before their contracts came into effect; (5) the NTC failed to recruit staff to transcribe the testimonies before writing the final report; (6) the institutional body created after the end of the NTC (with the aim of compiling a collection for the National Archives) dealt so carelessly with the testimonies that it failed to ensure the right to confidentiality that some of the victims had requested when making their testimonies.

This small team was comprised of Mezarobba and six researchers: Álvaro Okura, Ariana Bazzano, Camila Braga, Gustavo Macedo, Márcia Baratto and Raissa Wibhy. In February 2014, Monique Tiezzi den Hartog was selected to join the NTC as a UN volunteer. In March 2014, I also began to work with the team in my position as an advisor. In 2013, Luci Buff, a consultant of the NTC like Glenda Mezarobba, also worked for the group, although she mainly worked for another Working Group ('Dictatorship and Church Repression').

This team discussed its work at regular meetings and the topics have been recorded in so-called 'memory meetings'. Thirty-two of these meetings were documented between 5 April 2013 and 17 October 2014. The records list the team activities, goals and schedules and describe some of the difficulties encountered. The main problems the Working Group recorded include: (a) the difficulties of hiring researchers to listen to victims; (b) the researchers worked as volunteers most of the time rather than being paid for their work; (c) the NTC failed to hire professionals to make use of computer programs and statistics in order to standardize the quantitative information obtained from the testimonials; and (d) the NTC failed to hire a team to transcribe the testimonies. In my view, the difficulties of recruiting show that listening to the testimony of victims was never given priority by the NTC. Budgetary expenditures are perhaps the best indication of a commission's political priorities.

In the first 'memory meeting' from 5 April 2013, the six researchers are described as volunteers and priority is given to the fact that the consultants (Mezarobba and Buff) should seek their recruitment through the Foundation for Research Development (FUNDEP) or the United Nations Development Program (UNDP). Hence, the NTC was not providing funds to pay for the Working Group's researcher salaries. At that time, only one researcher from the team had been hired (Wibhy) and her appointment was funded through FUNDEP in December 2012. Out of the six researchers in the team mentioned above, only she has been paid a salary for almost all the time she has worked for the NTC, and she had signed two contracts, one with FUNDEP and one later with the UNDP. In 2013, the main method of recruiting researchers for the NTC was by means of contracts obtained through FUNDEP. Mezarobba and Buff were only able to persuade FUNDEP to employ one other volunteer researcher, Okura.

The epic struggle to hire the volunteer researchers lasted for the whole of 2013, but apart from the volunteers mentioned above, it was not possible to hire any other researchers. In the memory meeting of 2 August 2013, it was announced that the NTC would not recruit any more researchers through FUNDEP and that the commission would make an arrangement with the UNDP to start recruiting again. In the memory meeting of 23 August, Buff announced that the NTC was still examining hiring models in partnership with the UNDP. More than a month went by before the question of hiring was raised again. There was an announcement in the memory meeting of 4 October 2013 that a partnership had finally been formed between the NTC and the UNDP for hiring new researchers and overcoming the problem of the volunteers who had been in the service of the NTC since February 2013. The memory meeting of 22 November 2013 mentioned that the interviews for the selective procedure carried out by the UNDP would take place on 27 and 28 November. The memory meeting of 13 December 2013 included the following paragraph:

> The hiring process carried out by UNDP is in its final stage, according to Mezarobba. It is worth pointing out that two of the researchers have been working for three months without receiving any remuneration and the other five researchers have not been paid their salaries for nine months.

The issue returned to the memory meeting of 12 January 2014 in a note with the following information:

> Hiring process carried out by UNDP. Four researchers were hired: Ariana, Márcia, Camila and Raissa. This is the first paid employment for Ariana, Márcia and Camila, who have been working on a voluntary basis since April 2013. The researcher (Macedo) has been working as a volunteer since February 2013. Okura has stated that he will continue his activities without being paid.

The memory meeting of 24 February 2014 announced that Monique Tiezzi den Hartog had been selected as a UN volunteer and would begin work for the NTC as an assistant in the São Paulo office where the team carried out its activities. The memory meeting of 10 March 2014 announced that the question of whether or not Okura and Macedo would be employed remained unresolved and stressed that Macedo had been working for a year without any salary. It emerged from the memory meeting of 24 March 2014 that a new request had been issued to the commissioners and the executive secretary asking if the job situation of Okura and Macedo could be settled. It was announced in the memory meeting of 14 July 2014 that:

> The researcher, Álvaro Okura, who has been seeking a position through UNDP, since he ceased to obtain a grant from FUNDEP, has been appointed through the NTC selection process (in partnership with the Rubens Paiva State Truth Commission). Okura will no longer be involved in the Dictatorship and Gender Working Group .... Gustavo Macedo, who has been a volunteer since February 2013, officially announced his withdrawal from the Working Group.

What is shown by the information on the recruitment system in the memory meetings is that hardly any researchers were employed in this team – only five. The team consisted of six researchers, but one of them, Macedo, worked from February 2013 to July 2014 without ever having his contract officially signed. Moreover, Wibhy was the only one of the six researchers who was paid a salary for virtually the whole time (although there were two small periods when she was not paid anything). Four of the researchers – Okura, Bazzano, Braga and Baratto – worked for a longer time as volunteers than as paid employees. The tiny number of researchers who were hired and the fact that all of them, except for Wibhy, worked for several months without being paid a salary illustrates the extent of the institutional disregard for the activities they carried out. It also shows how far the members of this team were prepared to work in a selfless and intrepid way for the NTC. It is worth underlining this institutional disregard and the altruism of these six researchers, since their work is of an extremely stressful nature. It should be remembered that it involves hearing accounts of torture, kidnapping and arbitrary imprisonment told by the survivors and the families of those who have been murdered or disappeared for political reasons. As is well known from academic studies on truth commissions, this activity has an indelible effect on those who undertake it. However, despite all these difficulties, the small team managed to hear the testimonies of a total of 194 victims (115 women and 79 men).

In consideration of the emotional stress arising from the activity of hearing these reports, the team of the Hospital das Clínicas kindly volunteered to provide psychological support without compensation to the six researchers in the team. From August 2013 onwards, the psychiatrists Lucia Bagatella and Sonia Maria Duarte Sampaio performed this psychological support work.

When hearing the testimony of the victims, this small group of researchers employed a set of methods and rules established by the team consultant and manager, Glenda Mezarobba. The first part of the process involved finding out which people would be heard. The preliminary list of people chosen included the names of those persecuted for political reasons mentioned in books, theses, dissertations and documentaries about the dictatorship, as well as those referred to by activists who had survived the dictatorship and worked as collaborators for the NTC (in particular, José Luiz Del Roio, Anivaldo Padilha and Darci Myiaki, who followed and supported the work of the team throughout its existence). As the work of the team evolved, the members began to be known and trusted by the various surviving activists, who began to seek them out and tell their stories.

The testimonies were given in private, always heard by two researchers and, before starting, the witness was informed that the report would be recorded and that the name of the witness could be kept confidential or publicized, according to his or her personal decision. After annotating the general personal data of the witness (date and place of birth, schooling, profession, address), the witness was free to tell her/his story. This free narrative choice was designed to make the painful work of memory as convenient as possible and to allow the victim to tell his or her ideas in a rhythm in which he or she felt more comfortable. The researchers were given direct instructions to respect any period of silence or repetition, not to rush the reports, and to show empathy. They should only interrupt the witness when it was necessary to ask a question to clarify dates, locations and other information that could assist in discovering the whereabouts of the disappeared and the identity of the torturers. After hearing the report, the researchers filled in three standardized forms to record the information they had heard: (a) a general form about the kind of activism carried out and of repression suffered; (b) another about sexual torture; and (c) another for recording information about each torturer mentioned in the testimonial statement. The idea was to use the three forms to gather pieces of information and systematize them to be accessible to all researchers of the NTC. One of the main purposes of the forms was to efficiently use the information recorded by the victims, particularly regarding the methods of torture, the locations of human rights violations and the dates on which the crimes took place, the victims cited by the witness who had their rights violated in the same place and on the same date, the forms of political activism practised by the persecuted militants, and the political organizations in which the victims of political repression had taken part.

As documented in the memory meetings, the general administration and the executive secretary of the NTC did not authorize the hiring of computer programmers or statisticians to standardize the information contained in the forms. There were constant difficulties in completing and uploading the forms online. Owing to the need to write a draft of the chapter on gender and sexual violence for the final report of the NTC, in August 2014 it was decided that since there was a lack of statisticians and computer programmers, the advisor, San Romanelli Assumpção, and the UN volunteer, Monique Tiezzi den Hartog, should carry out the task of standardizing the information included in the forms.

It was announced in the memory meeting of 7 October 2014 that the 'Dictatorship and Gender' Working Group would complete the chapter on gender violence by 7 October 2014 and then bring its activities to an end. The last memory meeting of 17 October 2014 includes the following dispiriting paragraph:

> The difficulties faced by the 'Dictatorship and Gender' Working Group during the whole time of its existence were great and there was a growing atmosphere of tension that permeated the work in recent weeks. Among the main difficulties pointed out by Glenda are the lack of a data repository that allows the upload and correction of the forms in a single platform; the tiny team authorized by the executive secretary; the lack of a statistician; the slowness in hiring professionals specialized in transcription of audios; and the lack of standardization in bureaucratic procedures, especially those involving requests for transportation for those who listen to testimonies of victims.

Conclusions from the Activities of the 'Dictatorship and Gender' Working Group

The fact that the NTC team that heard the largest number of testimonies from victims was the 'Dictatorship and Gender' Working Group led to an atypical result: out of a total of 332 people who were heard, 147 were women and 185 men. The 'Dictatorship and Gender' Working Group itself heard testimonies from 115 women and 79 men. The other NTC teams heard testimonies from 32 women and 106 men. All of these statements were transcribed and are available on the NTC website (as calculated on the basis of information from this official site).[4]

Gender, as defined by Joan Scott, is the social organization of the relationship between the sexes.[5] Catharine MacKinnon characterized gender in terms of its ubiquity; gender permeates every relationship and social institution.[6] Combining the conceptual framework of these two authors, this ubiquitous organization constitutes relations of power that are publicly and privately constructed in the lives of men and women, transcending the traditional dichotomy between public and private, while at the same time generalizing the public as masculine and private as feminine. As Elizabeth Jelin shows, this has enormous repercussions for political memory. Politics is a space that has been traditionally established as public and masculine. Women have to battle against immense powers to gain entry into this masculine space and often achieve this in categories that are socially established as feminine. Thus, to quote from Jelin:

> If we close our eyes and attempt to envision the 'human' side of the dictatorships in the Southern Cone, one image dominates the scene: the Madres de Plaza de Mayo. Then, other women come into sight: the Familiares, Abuelas, Viudas, Comadres (Relatives, Grandmothers, Widows, and Other Kin) of the disappeared or of political prisoners, denouncing the arrests and searching for their children (which in the image are usually sons), their grandchildren, their husbands, or partners. On the other side, we see the military in full display of their masculinity. There is a second image that emerges, specific to the Argentine case: that of young pregnant female prisoners, giving birth in clandestine detention centers and then disappearing. This image is haunted by the uncertainty about the whereabouts of their children, kidnapped or stolen, who would later be given false identities. On the other side, once again, is the image of the hypermasculine military. The gender contrast in these images is clear and comes back time and again in a wide range of contexts. Personalized symbols of pain

> and suffering tend to become embodied in women, while institutional repressive mechanisms appear to 'belong' to men.[7]

In the list of testimonies heard by the NTC, the gendering in which women are predominantly female family figures (mothers, wives, widows and grandmothers) does not occur. In this kind of gender attribution, women enter into human rights activism to find out what happened to their male militant relatives or to claim justice for what happened to them. It is a gender attribution in which men enter politics for their own political projects and women to claim the human rights of men taken from them by repression. The memory built by the list of testimonies heard by the NTC subverts this type of gender attribution and women victims appear as subjects with their own political projects. This is not to say that gender attribution disappears, but it occurs differently, in a more feminist way.

Gender relations appear in the NTC final report[8] in a number of ways. In the memory of torture, gender constructions are revealed in many facts. First, acts of violence against men and women are different practices and the torture of women is more sexualized, with a higher incidence of rape and other forms of sexual violation. Second, the gendering and sexualization of torture occurs in different ways when practised against men than when practised against women, because the intersubjective relation among male torturers and female victims is distinct from the intersubjective relation among male torturers and male victims. In other words, the meanings of sadism are not the same, because there is social erotization of sexual violation of women by men and because female honour is in chastity and in a non-violated body while male honour is in strength and resistance to pain. Third, women interpret forced denudation and electric shocks in the genitals as sexual torture, while men are reluctant to characterize such violence as sexual. This difference of interpretation is likely related to gender hierarchies in which men are at the top and women are at the bottom and in which the violable bodies are the female bodies. Thus, when men perceive themselves as sexually violated, they feel the menace of feminization. Fourth, there is competition over masculinity between the male torturer and the male victim, which appears in three main forms: the rape of men as an emasculating or feminizing procedure; the sexual violation of the woman interpreted as the wife or girlfriend of a male victim as a mechanism of male humiliation; and the intersubjective understanding that resistance to pain is a masculine attribute and obligation. These four aspects appear in the testimonies given to the NTC and demonstrate that in the memory of political activism and political repression, gender constructions appear in the social roles reserved for men and women and in the gendered ways of framing reality in the narratives.

The reports of the survivors of torture show that the perpetrators of these crimes resort to (a) the sexualization and gendering of violence, and (b) the gendering of the social roles traditionally assigned to women and men. The attempts by the torturers to humiliate women and men are systematically determined by their social conceptions of gender: what women and men are like and how they should act. Women are systematically accused of the following:

1. straying from their gender roles (as wife, mother, carer) and devoting themselves to activism and political resistance;
2. playing gender roles that have no legitimate social status (they are regarded as indecent and impure and associated with prostitutes); and
3. threatening the concept of feminine decency (through being the victims of rape and other forms of sexual torture and the accusation that they 'like' to be sexually assaulted).

In contrast, men are systematically threatened and victimized through:

1. emasculation by rape and sexual violence against them; and
2. sexual violence against 'their women' (whether they are wives or girlfriends, or companions of activists), whom they will be unable to protect in their emasculated state.

These are just some of the examples found in the testimonies heard by the 'Dictatorship and Gender' Working Group in particular and by the NTC in general. They can be found in Chapters 9 and 10 of the first volume of the final report.

The Ethical and Political Importance of Victims' Voices

The political struggle for memory is of crucial importance in a democracy. This is a statement of considerable political significance. The value of democracy is that it always expresses some idea of collective self-government. Concepts such as democratic political representation, democratic responsiveness, electoral accountability, democratic participation and democratic deliberation are all among the wide-ranging theories and ideologies, expressions of collective self-government. The notion that the government must, to some degree, be responsive to its citizens also encompasses the idea that there is something deliberative that the government must address. In other words, it involves something that can be intellectually understood as belonging to the public sphere, public opinion and a public political culture.

If there is a public sphere, public political culture, public opinion and public debate – and these are the areas that a democratic government must take into account – *political memory* should render justice to every citizen. In view of this, political struggles to preserve the memory and truth of those whose rights have been infringed are essential to ensure that self-government means a self-government that embodies the collective will of equal citizens and not just the collective interests of elites. Moreover, nothing can be regarded as pertaining to the memory and truth of victims of serious violations of human rights that does not emerge from the voices of the victims themselves. Thus, it is a question of the memory and truth that is viewed from particular and situated perspectives. In the absence of victims' voices, there is no voice of all, and public opinion is therefore far from the ideal of equal and democratic collective self-government. Here we have a fundamental connection between struggles for political memory and the ideal of democracy.

One of the paramount responsibilities of truth commissions is to show the serious infringements of human rights that have taken place in the recent past and listen to the voices of victims. This entails hearing the voices of the victims and letting them tell the truth of these violations on the basis of their memory. It also involves showing public respect to the demands for truth, justice and redress. This respect for victims' voices is only complete when they are given a political and public resonance chamber; the two dimensions are linked.

The voices of victims of serious violations gain the first dimension of the resonance chamber when their stories are told and recognized as truth, and when their claims for truth, justice and reparation are publicly and officially recognized. This first dimension seeks to alleviate the pain and trauma arising from serious violations through state recognition and compliance with the right to the truth. These violations were a fact that was systematically denied during the dictatorship and which is still denied by some conservative groups. The survivors feel this fact minimized every time their narratives, memories and truths are delegitimized in the intolerant and authoritarian discourse of portions of the Brazilian population, and at every moment in which political disappearances and corpse concealment are perpetuated in continued violation. Publicizing their memories and recognizing their truth officially is a matter of political respect.

The second dimension of the resonance chamber that is due to the victims of the Brazilian dictatorship is a public debate on the serious human rights violations and unacceptability of the state's use of violence in arbitrary arrests, torture, murder and enforced disappearances and corpse concealment. These violations are still a Brazilian reality. A public discussion that incentivizes the rooting of democratic and liberal political values against the arbitrary use of violence is a basic aspect of a society that aims to be a democratic state.

The resonance chambers for the victims' voices help to consolidate a democratic public culture in a potentially very effective way. Here I follow Richard Rorty, for whom telling stories of people suffering human rights violations is one of the most effective forms of 'sentimental education'.[9] It shows people who have never suffered them that those who are victimized are equally human and worthy of respect. This 'sentimental education' cannot continue to be conducted only by empathetic people who are not survivors of serious violations, because they lack the perspective of those who suffered them. It needs to be done by incorporating the perspectives and voices of those who have been violated, so that these perspectives and voices become part of the prevailing public political culture and known to the public.

Because the NTC failed to prioritize listening to victims and publicizing their voices, this truth commission missed a golden opportunity to offer the politically persecuted these two dimensions of the resonance chamber. The NTC could have done a better job to incorporate the perspectives of the victims of the dictatorship into the political culture in Brazil.

San Romanelli Assumpção is a political scientist with a Master's and PhD degree from the University of São Paulo (USP) and a post-doctorate degree from the Institute of Social and Political Studies (ISPS) at the State University of Rio de Janeiro (IESP-UERJ). She was an advisor for the NTC during the period 2013–14 and is currently a lecturer at ISPS-UERJ.

Notes

1. E. Jelin, *State Repression and the Labors of Memory* (Minneapolis: University of Minnesota Press, 2003).
2. J.R. Gillis, 'Memory and Identity: The History of a Relationship', in J.R. Gillis (ed.), *Commemorations: The Politics of National Identity* (Princeton, NJ: Princeton University Press, 1994), 3–24; Jelin, *State Repression*.

3. Advisors (*assessores*) and consultants (*consultores*) had similar functions in regard to coordination and realization of political works and research. The different titles were related to distinct job contracts. Advisors were contracted directly by the Presidency of the Republic and consultants were contract by United Nations Development Programme (UNDP). The relative importance of each advisor and consultant was determined by their seniority in the area of human rights, transitional justice and experience in political work and public service.
4. http://cnv.memoriasreveladas.gov.br/ (http://cnv.memoriasreveladas.gov.br/).
5. J. Scott, 'Gender: A Useful Category of Historical Analysis', *American Historical Review* 91(5) (1986), 1053–75.
6. C. MacKinnon, *Feminism Unmodified: Discourses on Life and Law* (Cambridge, MA: Harvard University Press, 1987).
7. Jelin, *State Repression*, 76.
8. Comissão Nacional da Verdade (CNV). *Relatório*. Vol. 1. Brasília: CNV, 2014. NTC Report is available at http://cnv.memoriasreveladas.gov.br/.
9. R. Rorty, 'Human Rights, Rationality, and Sentimentality', in S. Shue and S. Hurley (eds), *On Human Rights: The Oxford Amnesty Lectures* (New York: Basic Books, 1993), 11–134.

Bibliography

Comissão Nacional da Verdade (CNV). *Relatório*. Vol. 1. Brasília: CNV, 2014.

Gillis, J.R. 'Memory and Identity: The History of a Relationship', in J.R. Gillis (ed.), *Commemorations: The Politics of National Identity* (Princeton, NJ: Princeton University Press, 1994), 3–24.

Jelin, E. *State Repression and the Labors of Memory*. Minneapolis: University of Minnesota Press, 2003.

MacKinnon, C. *Feminism Unmodified: Discourses on Life and Law*. Cambridge, MA: Harvard University Press, 1987.

Rorty, R. 'Human Rights, Rationality, and Sentimentality', in S. Shue and S. Hurley (eds), *On Human Rights: The Oxford Amnesty Lectures* (New York: Basic Books, 1993), 11–134.

Scott, J. 'Gender: A Useful Category of Historical Analysis'. *The American Historical Review* 91(5) (1986), 1053–75.

Chapter 12

'Nunca Mais'
Lessons from Brazil's Dictatorial Past

Gisele Iecker de Almeida

In 2011, the Brazilian Congress approved a temporary working group of seven commissioners 'of recognized competence and ethical conduct': the Brazilian National Truth Commission (BNTC).[1] Charged with the investigation of gross human rights violations that occurred between 1946 and 1988, the BNTC was an effort to fulfil the Brazilian state's responsibility, to enforce the right to memory and promote national reconciliation and historical truth. After two years, the BNTC was to deliver a comprehensive report, containing a description of the commission's activities, findings, conclusions and recommendations.

The recommendations should include public policies and measures to promote national reconciliation and prevent the repetition of human rights violations. Hence, the recommendations were to serve a double pedagogical function: they should comprise *lessons learned* from the past, and at the same time *instruct* present and future policymakers.

This chapter investigates the different types of 'learning from the past' included in the BNTC's recommendations. Specifically, it focuses on the question of how knowledge of the past was turned into instructions for policymakers to prevent the repetition of human rights violations. The chapter is structured as follows. The first part presents the BNTC's goal to prevent repetition. In the second part, the theoretical underpinnings of 'learning from the past' are examined, with particular attention to some of its more problematic tenets for historians and historical theorists. In the third part, the BNTC recommendations are critically analysed in light of the lessons from the past that they condense. The conclusion assesses the BNTC's efficacy in learning from the past, drawing on a critical use of history's lessons, which takes into consideration the fact that history rarely repeats itself *ipsis litteris*.

Prevention as a Goal of the BNTC

Academics defend the assertion that 'establishing a credible and authoritative record of events' is a central task of truth commissions, with such a record leading to 'a new national narrative of acknowledgement, accountability, and civic values'.[2] There is no doubt that truth commissions are established due to the conviction that 'telling the truth about past abuses leads or contributes to preventing similar abuses from occurring again',[3] but their recommendations display a different kind of hope. Based on knowledge obtained during their investigations, truth commissions around the globe[4] have proposed improvements to further the transition to a peaceful democratic society in the hope that, if enforced, recommended measures can prevent the repetition of negative past events. These recommendations tend to encompass legislative and structural change, new laws and offices (or doing away with old ones), and reforms in the political and security system.

The recommendations section of the report also gives truth commissioners the opportunity to formulate a strategy for the afterlife of the commission, outlining the continuity of efforts to obtain truth, peace and reconciliation after the report is made public. Such commission reports may discuss the enforcement of recommendations, how to progress towards accountability for past crimes, and further reparations to victims. There is a risk of recommendations not being enforced, which is dependent on how much power the old regime managed to retain. Although the lack of assurance that the recommended actions will be carried through is a problematic aspect of transitional justice, the 'wish list' approach to recommendations is still deemed an asset. Scholars have pointed out that recommendations underline areas that need further development and can provide social movements with leverage in future negotiations with government.[5]

Victims of dictatorial regimes have repeated the future-oriented formulation of *Nunca Mais* ('Never Again') throughout Latin America, echoing the categorical imperative of 'creating a better future' for humanity after the extreme violence and barbarism of the twentieth century.[6] 'Encouraging learning to emerge from the catastrophe' – to use the phrase coined by Habermas – 'never again' also denotes the tragic character of Brazil's most recent authoritarian regime.[7] The motto first emerged in the title of the unofficial report *Brasil: Nunca Mais*.[8] It appears in materials published by memorialization projects coordinated by the Brazilian state, including the Amnesty Commission, the Revealed Memories project, and the 2007 report 'Direito à Verdade e à Memória', which shows us that the goal of preventing repetition of negative past events is not unique to the BNTC.[9]

The BNTC was established twenty-seven years after the transition to democracy, and most of the content of its report was already available in history books.[10] Still, it performed an important role in the reformation of Brazil's national narratives as an official acknowledgement that propagates a past that had been hidden, denied and left out of the social memory of the dictatorial past.[11] The acts of remembering, and the offering of a new national historical narrative, are acts of deterrence.[12]

Like previous truth commissions, the BNTC reframes past events, delimiting society's red lines and setting out 'what was wrong and never justifiable'.[13] In its mandate, BNTC recommendations are described as 'measures and public policies to be adopted by the government with the purpose of preventing the violation of human rights, *ensuring their non-repetition* and promoting the effective national reconciliation'.[14] The wording suggests that the recommendations focus on measures to prevent the repetition of human rights violations *that occurred in the past*, namely those designated in the mandate as BNTC's research themes. Attention is drawn in particular to the right to (human) life, which makes the BNTC consistent with the human rights movement's 'principled resistance to moral relativism when it comes to the suffering of bodies'.[15]

The mention of 'national reconciliation' as a BNTC goal gave considerable leeway for broadening the scope of recommendations beyond the particular crimes against humanity perpetrated during Brazil's dictatorship. Commissioner Paulo Sérgio Pinheiro saw the potential to adopt a more holistic approach and extract wide-ranging lessons, making use of 'the process, dynamics and recommendations of the BNTC to contribute to overcoming the authoritarian legacy'.[16] Crimes akin to those the BNTC investigated in the past are still part of Brazil's present:

> This report exposes these methods and instruments in the conviction that the knowledge of these acts … can contribute to society's capacity to prevent such conduct *from persisting* or repeating itself, that is, so that they will never happen again.[17]

Theoretical Underpinnings

How to instruct policymakers to avoid the woes of the past? When putting forward recommendations, truth commissioners tend to look at the past, while remaining alert to traces of the continuity, circularity, successions, articulations, returns and repetitions of past crimes, institutions and traditions. At least a couple of different steps are involved in marking a clear boundary between the past and preventing its repetition, as the BNTC case illustrates. First there was making the past present and accessible in 'lessons'. This involved sifting through large amounts of evidence and transmitting the knowledge of the past amassed during the course of those investigations by drafting a report.

Then, BNTC commissioners were expected to turn those lessons into recommendations, instructing policymakers on how to avoid the repetition of past events. This was done through the report's demarcation of which acts were 'prohibited' or considered 'grossly unacceptable conduct'.[18] Those tasked with formulating the BNTC recommendations established a relationship between the past and an envisaged future by focusing on negative aspects of the past perceived as still present in society. When traces of the continuity, circularity, successions, articulations, returns and repetitions of past events, institutions and traditions are identified as still taking place in the historical present, the learning changes its temporal orientation and takes the form of considering how to eradicate it.

The double approach of looking to the past, towards society's 'space of experience' (past), while also considering its 'horizon of expectation' (future), is not a form of learning from the past exclusive to truth commissions' recommendations.[19] Historical analogies are ubiquitous in society. This is how the legal system can reach verdicts and medicine can give diagnoses, for example. Five different pedagogical uses of the past are discussed below, and will later inform an analysis of the learning from the past captured in the BNTC recommendations.

Historia magistra vitae is a traditional type of learning from the past in which history is seen as 'a storehouse of exemplary models for the betterment of later generations'[20] that has been exploited since ancient Greece. In the case of negative events, one would learn by avoiding reproducing certain characteristics of the past by applying the formula: (a) terrible actions were performed in the past; (b) we can observe where things went wrong; and (c) refrain from engaging in those same actions; and thus (d) avoid making the same mistakes.[21] Hegel was a critic of this method and only saw value in *historia magistra vitae* for the moral education of children, not for politics: 'In the crush of world events, there is no help to be had from general principles, nor from the memory of similar conditions in former times'.[22]

A multifaceted and more intricate understanding of the relation between past, present and future superseded the cyclical view enshrined in the ancient process of learning from the past. In the modern understanding of time, the arrow of history is pointed towards an ever-new future. Events are seen as *unique* because conditions change with the passing of time; clear-cut, straightforward discontinuity became a distinctive feature of the horizon of expectation. Society found itself in a status of perpetual modernizing, 'in evolution'.[23]

Even as academics questioned determinism, the objectivity of the historical object and the metaphysical reality of the past, public debates continued to draw on previous experience, thinking over past events and using that knowledge for self-improvement. Learning from past mistakes (at least in theory) is something human beings do all the time. However, there is no limit to the examples, anecdotes and imageries of the past. Consider, in its vastness, Charles Beard's definition of it as 'all that has been said, done, felt and thought by human beings on this planet'.[24] The claim that if 'properly studied' it could yield unambiguous recipes for dealing with similar situations in the future is problematic for many historians in part for this reason. They are conscious that a selection of which past or which lesson occurs, because the past is so immense that alternative lessons, or even contrary 'teachings', are easy to find. Each historical episode can be the source of a plurality of lessons, and the choice of which will be taken up depends on the historical observer.

The past depends on the purpose it serves in the present. It is not a neutral recipient that exists 'out there', independent of a specific cultural frame and political constellation from which individuals create, reconstruct, receive and propagate *representations of past events.*[25] Heterogeneous memories of the regime coexist in Brazilian society, think of how different groups (victims, non-victims, perpetrators and beneficiaries) have experienced the regime, and now hold and propagate radically different views of what occurred between the 1960s and 1980s. Something to be wary of when dealing with state-sponsored historical projects is the political agenda of those 'mobilising their power and resources to create particular histories and memory regimes'.[26]

The contingency of the past in light of its selection, interpretation and use in the present prompted historian Tzvetan Todorov to make a plea for the return of an 'exemplary' form of learning. In his view, we need to 'use the past in light of the present'.[27] The key is to apply the lessons against the injustices, inequality and violence occurring in the present, using awareness of terrible deeds committed in the past to positively affect conditions for the most vulnerable groups today.[28] Todorov presents Nazi concentration camp survivor David Rousset as an example. After the war, he campaigned to raise awareness among his fellow survivors of the (then still existing) Soviet camps. A parallel in Brazil would be former victims of the regime embracing the *Mães de Maio* movement.[29] Todorov contrasts the 'exemplary' learning with a 'literal' learning, in which a representation of the past is 'singularized', that is, considered so unique that any instruction to the present is lost. In this sterile reading, the past can only be mourned and compulsively memorialized, at the risk of exonerating the present from both dealing with past injustices and remaining alert to present injustice.

Yet another possible use is to think of the past as a source of information on the likelihood of certain things to happen, a probability estimation based on prior experience of causality. This 'scientific use of the past' is based on the fact that 'if one has extensive past knowledge of processes one can predict that in the same circumstances the same conjunctions will occur in the same way in the future'.[30] It is applied for example in business investment and the military, where the past is used 'to know what their chances of success are … [get] lessons about how to proceed and some warning about what is … likely to happen'.[31] This logical learning from the past helped BNTC commissioners to estimate the likelihood of success when drafting their recommendations to avoid the ills of the past. This *temporal scaling* produces a knowledge of the past that goes beyond facts and figures, and can be regarded as a step forward. However, applying this approach exclusively means overlooking any potentially transformative analysis.

A reflexive attitude sits at the core of Adorno's *working through* a difficult past. This critical acknowledgement entails an interpretation of what the lessons from the past might be, and the identification of similarities and differences between present and past. The objective in his view must be to enlighten society about the broader causes, context and circumstances that enabled violent acts to occur, so the 'causes of what happened' can be dealt with.[32] The lesson is only over once an alteration is produced in the existing state of affairs, diverting the present to a course fundamentally different from what has gone before. The learning leads to a reconsideration of how the national identity is held together, in this case a rethink of what it means to be part of Brazilian society.

BNTC Recommendations

The BNTC was designed to serve a double pedagogical function: to investigate Brazil's recent past and, based on the lessons learned, instruct policymakers. Firstly, it was expected to learn by scrutinizing aspects of the recent past that had for years been hidden, denied or questioned. It was then expected to transmit the knowledge of the past amassed, including the events it investigated, into an authoritative official report. There is potential for a societal recognition that what is described in the report *really happened*, and if the report's truth is perceived as more credible than the lies it challenged, a new framework of reference is produced.[33] The report and recommendations can be understood as part of an educational campaign that raises awareness of past injustice and challenges conventional understandings of the past.[34] Such reports and their recommendations also have the potential to act as an inflexion point, the moment when violence becomes unacceptable, and awareness of present abuses is enhanced and notions of due process are disseminated.[35] At this level, the learning of the BNTC can increase the odds of a future in which the promise of non-repetition/*nunca mais* is fulfilled.

The final BNTC report comprises three volumes. The last section of the first volume consists of eleven pages that offer twenty-nine recommendations. They were formulated based on research findings and suggestions from civil society, and truth commissioners' observations of Brazil's failures and advances, in relation to the challenge of establishing a human rights culture.[36] Each recommendation emphasizes the importance of establishing a human rights culture and a *status quo* in which the state no longer violates the human rights of its citizens. The recommendations reflect the range of factors required for this change: institutional reforms (seventeen recommendations), new legal measures (eight recommendations) and follow-up measures (four recommendations) are included. Fifteen recommendations relate to security (with eight recommendations for the judiciary and seven for the armed forces); four to accountability for historic crimes; seven to the right to memory and truth; and three to promoting a human rights culture. No reference is made to a timeframe for implementing the measures, or the steps policymakers should follow to ensure their execution.

The opening recommendations consist of the institutional acknowledgement of wrongdoing by the armed forces [1] and the repeal of the 1979 amnesty law in cases of crimes against humanity [2].[37] Both recommendations send a clear message that a consensus on what the errors of the past were must be reached and shared across different groups in society. Without a clear 'red line', disputes over the legitimacy of past crimes and exculpatory discourses will continue to exist. Furthermore, as long as past criminals continue to be institutionally shielded from prosecution, security officials committing similar crimes in present-day Brazil are given no reason to believe they will be held accountable for their acts in the future – in what is the clearest failure to mitigate the risk of a repetition of human rights abuses.

The connection between past and present human rights violations appears most clearly in the BNTC's fourth conclusion:

> In examining the spectrum of serious human rights violations that occurred during the period it investigated, the BNTC has been able to verify that this situation persists in the present. Although ... no longer in a context of political repression ... the practice of illegal and arbitrary detention, torture, executions, enforced disappearances and even concealment of human remains is not alien to contemporary Brazilian reality. ... this situation results largely from the fact that the serious human rights violations committed in the past have not been adequately denounced or their perpetrators made accountable.[38]

In its ruling of the *Gomes-Lund* case, the Inter-American Court of Human Rights (henceforth 'the Court') held Brazil accountable for the forced disappearance of sixty-two militants between 1972 and 1974 in the Araguaia region. The Court invalidated Brazil's amnesty law, deeming it 'incompatible with the American Convention'.[39] The BNTC reinforced this interpretation. However, there was no unanimity among BNTC commissioners over the issue.[40] Pedro Dallari declared being extra careful when formulating the recommendation that perpetrators be prosecuted: 'each word in there was carefully considered'.[41] It remains to be seen whether the Court ruling will lead to a change in policy. A second revision of the validity of the amnesty law is due to be heard by the Supreme Court.[42]

The BNTC report's findings were the starting point in a comparison between present and past injustice. In a learning from the past that resembles the age-old *historia magistra vitae*, past crimes were held up as examples of misconduct, and information about perpetrators' *modus operandi* was used to raise awareness of the continuation of the past in the present, traces of the authoritarian regime thought to have persisted. The truth commissioners identified separate and specific instances of past behaviours continuing into the present, and denounced them in their recommendations, calling for these behaviours to be modified or suppressed. For example, the report suggests that the institute of forensic medicine be detached from the security services [recommendation 10]; reform of the prison system [12]; the de-militarization of state police forces [19]; revocation of the National Security Law [18]; and elimination of the classification of 'resistance followed by death' (*autos de resistência*) from police forms [24].

The method of eliminating similarities to rid the present of the unwanted past is reversed in the case of positive actions BNTC commissioners thought should be emulated. For example, they recommend strengthening the public defence services [11], community counsels for custodial facilities [14], and expanding the lexicon of Brazilian legislation to include making forced disappearances a criminal offence [19]. In some cases, the object of the recommendation did not yet exist – this was the case with preventive action against torture [9], the induction of ombudspersons at correction facilities [13] and the introduction of custodial hearings within twenty-four hours of imprisonment [25].

According to the former Human Rights Secretary General, Minister Ideli Salvatti, a total of twelve recommendations were already public policy as the report's recommendations were being drafted, which indicates an interest in demonstrating expediency in dealing with Brazil's recent military past. After all, *partially addressed* measures allow the country to present itself internationally as 'making improvement'.[43] How else to understand recommendations such as the prohibition of official celebrations of the 1964 coup three years *after* the date was abolished from the official calendar of the armed forces? Another example is the recommendation that a 'Memory Museum' be established in Brasilia [28] – a bewildering suggestion, as details of the 'Amnesty Memorial' have been in the public domain since before the establishment of the BNTC.[44] In addition, there is a recommendation that the state 'ensures permanent medical and psychosocial care for victims of gross human rights violations' [15].[45] The proposal makes no reference to the Testimonial Clinics, a sub-project of the Amnesty Commission offering psychological treatment to victims of the military regime since 2012.

In the report, the criminal system through which the Brazilian state oversaw the gross violation of the human rights of its citizens is recognized as 'the catastrophe' that should never again be repeated. However, commissioners were reluctant to launch a wider investigation or provide explanations of the causes that enabled the violent regime to come into being. According to Dallari, BNTC commissioners made a deliberate choice to strive for an 'objective description' of past events, rather than give a 'historical explanation' for the authoritarian regime. They sought to present the 'raw facts' of Brazil's recent past, devoid of any contextual historical analysis: 'there is no flab in the report. It is all muscle and bone'.[46] The option not to use the term 'civil-military dictatorship', for example, is a consequence of the truth commission's decision *not* to try to explain the past.[47]

We should take heed of the critical thinking proposed by Adorno and Todorov. Both claim that it is only through probing what has gone before that a transformative learning from the past can emerge. If following Adorno's process of working through the past, the BNTC's line of inquiry would have encompassed an analysis of how the armed forces obtained and maintained power for over two decades, looked for explanations for the support the regime garnered among conservative sectors of society, as well as the socio-political developments that made a prolonged obstruction of democracy possible.

Todorov's 'exemplary learning' would involve a holistic understanding of peace and justice that goes beyond the framing of physical violence and human rights violations of transitional justice. In this form of learning from the past, the focus is no longer on how to address historic crimes and their reoccurrence in the present time, but on the structural changes necessary to address present grievances, inequality, and how to create an inclusive political community as part of a stable and peaceful democratic society. This is the underlying logic of the unfulfilled suggestion made by Bohoslavsky and Torelly that the BNTC investigate the national public debt and that an official audit is conducted.[48]

The absence of recommendations for significant change in civil-military relations is an indication of the commission's constraints. Under the ruling of Gen. Figueiredo (1979–85), a pact was negotiated between the incoming political elite and leaders of the outgoing regime. The political subordination of the military and return to an open democratic political system was exchanged for privileges enjoyed to this day by armed forces personnel, including the amnesty for perpetrators of gross human rights violations, corporate independence, and control over the defence budget.[49]

The unhealthy relationship between the armed forces, civil society and the state was barely denounced by the CNV; the controversial Article 142 of the Brazilian Constitution was not raised as a cause for concern, and there was no mention of lustration or direct compensation payments to victims.[50] However, it was recommended that perpetrators be made to contribute financially to the state reparations programme [3], and distinctions and civic honours bestowed upon perpetrators be withdrawn [28]. Other recommendations related to the armed forces include the already mentioned prohibition of official commemorations of the coup [4]; the reformulation of the selection process [5] and curriculum of military academies to include the values of human rights and democracy [6]; restricting the military legal system to the federal level [21]; and the exclusion of civilians from the mandate of its courts [22].

The BNTC's focus was on human rights violations and specifically on particular types of physical violence that restricted the potential for lessons that could be extracted from Brazil's recent past. This limitation became apparent during the official ceremony marking the release of the report, when President Rousseff stressed the *nunca mais* motto as an ambition to prevent the return of the violent and authoritarian past: 'With the creation of this commission, Brazil has expressed the importance of knowing *the period* in order to prevent *its* repetition'.[51]

The BNTC report, on the other hand, claims to have pursued 'knowledge of all *the acts* that the Brazilian state had the capacity to carry out ..., so *they* never happen again'.[52] This seemingly innocuous mismatch between Rousseff's expectation and the BNTC's outcome puts in evidence the fact that the lessons the BNTC extracted from the past are conducive to a very specific *nunca mais*: never again *certain types* of human rights violations – *not* never again an authoritarian regime. If carried through, the BNTC recommendations would enhance the Brazilian state's capacity to mitigate the risks of repetition[53] of arbitrary imprisonments, torture, unlawful killings and enforced disappearances in the country. Advancing towards a more meaningful democracy and strengthening Brazil's democratic culture requires a different toolkit. It would involve, for example, building the spaces of respectful debate from which emerges a society that can deal democratically with difference and express conflict through recognition, civic trust and social solidarity.

Truth commissioners applied knowledge of the past to estimate the chances of success of their recommendations, identify the most adequate wording and define the most valuable measures to propose. For example, recommendation 1 calls for an institutional *acknowledgement* of the crimes of the past committed by the armed forces, not for an *apology* from the institution. Despite the BNTC's efforts, an unambiguous acknowledgement by the armed forces was not achieved: 'in this area we had great difficulty', explained Pedro Dallari.[54]

The physical violence and human rights violations committed by agents of the state against Brazilian citizens during the country's most recent military regime were singled out as that which should not happen again – yet they *never ceased to repeat*. In this sense, the BNTC's lessons from the past preserve the past as occurs in Todorov's 'literal' use; the past was not a springboard to understanding *new situations* with *different agents*, past human rights violations 'remained an intransitive fact, leading nowhere beyond themselves'[55] – because they never ceased to occur. That being said, BNTC commissioners had some leeway to broaden the scope of investigations and set their own priorities, and played an active role in establishing the remit of both the investigations that would be carried out and the recommendations it would present for policymakers. It was the decision of BNTC commissioners to include illegal and arbitrary imprisonment as a category of crime against humanity to be examined;[56] announce that only crimes perpetrated 'by public agents, persons at their service, with the support or in the interest of the state' would be examined;[57] and declare that 'special attention' would be given to the 1964–85 period commonly associated with the military dictatorship.[58]

All of these choices further delimited the BNTC's remit and meant that, for the most part, the commission failed to emphasize the importance of other political, civil, social, economic and cultural rights violations endured by Brazilian populations during the military regime – issues that have not yet been officially investigated. These include censorship and the mass surveillance that characterized the undemocratic regime, the establishment of a democratic façade, genocide against the indigenous populations (only partially acknowledged in the second volume of the BNTC report; the term 'genocide' is not employed), and corporate and institutional complicity in the formation of a media monopoly. Because of its failure to denounce all articulations, returns and repetitions of events, institutions and traditions connected to the dictatorial past, to propose measures that would significantly alter the impact of the afterlives of the military regime, and to eradicate all traces of its continued occurrence in the present, the BNTC may come to be seen as a missed opportunity.

Conclusion

It is a known fact that Brazil became *less stable* after the transition to democracy. Years before his stint as BNTC commissioner, Paulo Sérgio Pinheiro had already noted that the 'authoritarian practices have survived democracy'.[59] The BNTC investigations were driven by this legacy. As discussed above, BNTC commissioners identified institutional or structural aspects of the past violence that persisted, allowing the perpetuation of human rights violations. It was their task to propose measures to *stop their reoccurrence*. The moral imperative of preserving human life may explain the BNTC's choice of focusing almost exclusively on physical violence, but the decision has come at the expense of limiting the scope of lessons extracted from the past, narrowing the past to a binary opposition between victims and perpetrators, and excluding from their investigations other types of injustice.

A more thorough investigation of the array of crimes committed against the Brazilian population would have led to a different set of questions, amassing other types of information, which would have allowed for the extraction of other possible lessons from the past. This means the BNTC report is an unfinished attempt to work through the Brazilian recent past. According to Adorno, 'the past will have been worked through only when the causes of what happened have been eliminated'.[60] The problem then becomes one of identifying the causes, and identifying what it is that we would not like to see repeated.

The BNTC recommendations offer some insight into what needs doing in order that state agents do not torture, unlawfully kill or make citizens disappear, but they fail to address the systemic aspect of these crimes against the civilian population. The crimes were committed by the security forces of an authoritarian militarized state that bent the law as and when required. The 'socially rooted authoritarianism' that characterizes Brazilian society is an issue that needs to be addressed head-on, from the conservatism of the political and economic elites to the lenient attitude towards police violence by the silent majority.

The responsibility to educate future generations involves the understanding that a constant re-reading of past issues in light of new questions is necessary, the answers to which, in their turn, will lead to new representations of the past. It is only through facing what has happened before now that the ability to deal with new occurrences can be strengthened. Enhancing the sense of belonging of all Brazilians and engaging the existing plurality of historical cultures in a democratic debate, strengthening their capacity to forge the social ties that are needed to live together, should be the way forward. The legitimate right of citizens to collectively choose and change their rulers by peaceful means has to be the ultimate goal of all people across the nation. Clearly, Brazil still has much to reflect upon and learn from its past.

Gisele Iecker de Almeida is a PhD researcher in the History Department of Ghent University and a Fellow of the Brazilian Federal Agency CAPES (BEX 177213-9). She has been a visiting researcher at King's College Brazil Institute (2016) and the School of Law and Politics of Cardiff University (2017). Her area of research is the interconnection between the changing nature of our relation with the past and its effects in the present. She is part of the International Network for Theory of History team and a founding member of the Latin American Network Historia Pensada.

Notes

1. Brazil, Law no. 12.528/2011 that Creates the National Truth Commission within the Office of the Chief of Staff of the Presidency of the Republic, *Federal Official Gazette of Brazil* (2011).
2. M.U. Walker, 'Nunca Más: Truth Commissions, Prevention, and Human Rights Culture', in L. May and E. Edenberg (eds), *Jus Post Bellum and Transitional Justice* (Cambridge: Cambridge University Press, 2013), 284; M. Minow, *Between Vengeance and Forgiveness: Facing History after Genocide and Mass Violence* (Boston, MA: Beacon Press, 1998), 78.
3. Walker, 'Nunca Más', 263.
4. P. Hayner, *Unspeakable Truths: Transitional Justice and the Challenge of Truth Commissions* (New York: Routledge, 2010), 320–27.
5. On truth commissions' lack of enforcement, see Hayner, *Unspeakable Truths*, 169; T.D. Olsen et al., 'When Truth Commissions Improve Human Rights', *International Journal of Transitional Justice*, 4 (3) (2010), 461; O. Bakiner, 'Truth Commission Impact', *International Journal of Transitional Justice*, 8 (1) (2014), 15. On the positives of having the recommendations, see M.A. Weichert, 'O Relatório da Comissão Nacional da Verdade: Conquistas e Desafios?', *Projeto História*, 50 (2014), 86–137; E. Wiebelhaus-Brahm, 'Truth Commissions and the Construction of History', in B. Bevernage and N. Wouters (eds), *The Palgrave Handbook of State-Sponsored History after 1945* (London: Palgrave Macmillan, 2018).
6. S. Clift, *Committing the Future to Memory: History, Experience, Trauma* (New York: Fordham University Press, 2014), 3.
7. J. Habermas, 'Learning from Catastrophe? A Look Back at the Short Twentieth Century', in J. Habermas, *The Postnational Constellation: Political Essays* (Cambridge, MA: MIT Press, 2001), 38–57.
8. Arquidiocese de São Paulo, *Brasil: Nunca Mais* (Petropolis: Vozes, 1985).
9. Brazil, Special Office for Human Rights, CEMDP. *Direito à Verdade e à Memória: comissão especial sobre mortos e desaparecidos*. Brasilia: CEMDP, 2007.
10. M. Napolitano, 'Recordar é Viver: as Dinâmicas e Vicissitudes da Construção da Memória sobre o Regime Militar Brasileiro', *Antíteses* 8(15) (2015), 38.
11. Brazil's process of reconfiguring the official memory of the dictatorship can be traced back to 1995 with the work of the Comissão Especial sobre Mortos e Desaparecidos Políticos (CEMDP; Special Commission on Political Deaths and Disappearances).
12. R. Meister, *After Evil: A Politics of Human Rights* (New York: Columbia University Press, 2011).
13. Minow, *Between Vengeance and Forgiveness*, 78.

14. Brazil, Law no. 12.528/2011, Art. VI, my italics.
15. Meister, *After Evil*, 142. The mandate refers to the crimes of torture, summon executions, forced disappearances and concealment of bodies. The commissioners also investigated cases of illegal and arbitrary imprisonment. Brazil, CNV, *Relatório/Comissão Nacional Da Verdade/Vol. I* (Brasília: CNV, 2014), 279.
16. Pinheiro, in B. Barbosa, 'Na ditadura, o Presidente, os generais e os executores dos crimes estavam inteirados dos excessos', IPEA, Desafios do Desenvolvimento (23 November 2012).
17. Brazil, CNV, *Relatório/Vol. I*, 365, my italics.
18. The report focuses on gross human rights violations, in particular torture, illegal imprisonment, forced disappearances and extrajudicial executions conducted by agents of the authoritarian regime. Walker, 'Nunca Más', 267.
19. R. Koselleck, *Futures Past: On the Semantics of Historical Time* (New York: Columbia University Press, 2004).
20. Clift, *Committing the Future to Memory*, 143.
21. B. Forchtner, 'Historia Magistra Vitae: The Topos of History as a Teacher in Public Struggles over Self and Other Representation', in C. Hart and P. Cap (eds), *Contemporary Critical Discourse Studies* (London: Bloomsbury Academic, 2014), 19–44.
22. Hegel, in Clift, *Committing the Future to Memory*, 142.
23. K. Popper, in P. Gardiner, *Teorias da História* (Lisbon: Fundação Calouste Gulbekian, 2004), 339.
24. C. Beard cited by A.C. Danto, *Narration and Knowledge* (New York: Columbia University Press, 1985), 88.
25. A. Assmann and L. Short, 'Memory and Political Change: Introduction', in *Memory and Political Change* (New York: Palgrave Macmillan, 2012), 3.
26. B. Bevernage and N. Wouters, 'State-Sponsored History after 1945: An Introduction', in Bevernage and Wouters, *The Palgrave Handbook of State-Sponsored History*.
27. T. Todorov, 'The Abuses of Memory', *Common Knowledge* 5(1) (1996), 14.
28. T. Todorov, *Los Abusos de la memoria* (Barcelona: Paidós, 2000), 43–44.
29. The Brazilian movement *Mães de Maio* ('Mothers of May') seeks justice for the massacre of 564 alleged suspects of criminal activities over ten days by law enforcement personnel in 2006.
30. B. Adam and C. Groves, *Future Matters: Action, Knowledge, Ethics* (Leiden: Brill, 2007), 25.
31. M. MacMillan, *Dangerous Games* (New York: The Modern Library, 2008), 150–53.
32. T.W. Adorno, 'The Meaning of Working through the Past', in T.W. Adorno, *Critical Models: Interventions and Catchwords*, translated by Henry Pickford (New York: Columbia University Press, 1998), 103.
33. Walker, 'Nunca Más', 272.
34. B.A. Leebaw, 'The Irreconcilable Goals of Transitional Justice', *Human Rights Quarterly* 30(1) (2008), 109.

35. Walker, 'Nunca Más', 273; Wiebelhaus-Brahm, 'Truth Commissions and the Construction of History'.
36. Pinheiro, in Barbosa, 'Na ditadura'. A two-month consultation process was carried out towards the end of the writing process of the BNTC report; civil society proposed 399 recommendations to be considered for inclusion in the report. See Brazil, CNV, *Relatório/Vol. I*, 964.
37. Numbers in square brackets correspond to recommendations from the first volume of the BNTC: Brazil, CNV, *Relatório/Vol. I*, 964–75.
38. Ibid., 964.
39. *Gomes-Lund et al. (Guerrilha do Araguaia) v. Brazil*, Inter-American Court of Human Rights, 24 November 2010.
40. Truth commissioner José Paulo Cavalcanti diverged, being of the opinion that the prosecution of perpetrators lay beyond the scope of the BNTC and that the amnesty law must be upheld, as it is the result of a political agreement.
41. Dallari, in C.B. Hollanda, 'Entrevista Com Pedro Dallari', *Revista Estudos Políticos* VI(2) (2015), 309.
42. The amnesty law was upheld by the Supreme Court in April 2010, just months before the Court ruling was published. See Brazil, MPF (Federal Prosecutions Office), *Grupo de trabalho justiça de transição: atividades de persecução penal desenvolvidas pelo Ministério Público Federal: 2011–2013* (Brasília: MPF/2 CCR, 2014), 90.
43. Salvatti, in R. Arruda, 'Governo já segue recomendações da Comissão da Verdade, afirma ministra', blog, 4 February 2015. The Court's ruling against Brazil in the *Gomes-Lund* case in 2010 ordered the investigation of human rights violations and prosecution of those responsible, acting as a catalyst for the establishment of the BNTC. It is important not to lose this dimension when analysing the BNTC report.
44. Memorial da Anistia is a research centre and museum that has been under construction in Belo Horizonte since 2008. Another museum, Memorial da Resistência ('Resistance Memorial'), was established by the São Paulo state administration in 2009.
45. Brazil, CNV, *Relatório/Vol. I*, 970.
46. Dallari, in Hollanda, 'Entrevista Com Pedro Dallari', 314.
47. In the first volume of the BNTC report, the terminology employed to describe the regime is 'military dictatorship'; in Volume 2, the expressions 'civil-military regime' or 'civil-military coup' appear a few times.
48. J.P. Bohoslavsky and M. Torelly, 'Financial Complicity: The Brazilian Dictatorship under the "Macroscope"', in D.N. Sharp (ed.), *Justice and Economic Violence in Transition* (New York: Springer, 2014), 255–61.
49. A. Codato, 'A Political History of the Brazilian Transition from Military Dictatorship to Democracy', *Revista de Sociologia e Política* 25(2005), 27; M.C. D'Araújo, 'O Estável Poder de Veto Forças Armadas Sobre o Tema da Anistia Política no Brasil', *Varia Historia* 28(2012), 596.
50. Some argue that Article 142 of the 1988 Constitution should be abolished as it could be used as a shortcut to military intervention, as it

establishes the armed forces' role as 'the ultimate arbiter of unrest', arguably above the three constitutional powers. See T. Power, *The Political Right in Postauthoritarian Brazil: Elites, Institutions, and Democratization* (University Park, PA: Pennsylvania State University Press, 2000), 214.

51. D. Rousseff, 'Speech by Dilma Rousseff during the Presentation of the Final Report of the CNV' (Brasília, 2014).
52. Brazil, CNV, *Relatório/Vol. I*, 365.
53. I have avoided the problematic formulation of 'ensuring the *nunca mais*' used in the mandate – after all, it is impossible to ascertain whether something will happen (or not). At most, governments can shape public policy and institutions to increase the odds of a given future.
54. Dallari, in F. Betim, 'Provamos que a tortura foi uma política de Estado durante a ditadura', *El Pais Brasil*, 10 October 2014. When asked by the BNTC for clarifications, the armed forces responded with a double negative, declaring that they could 'neither deny nor confirm' the occurrence of human rights violations in their facilities during the regime. Brazil, CNV, *Relatório/Vol. I*, 65.
55. Todorov, 'The Abuses of Memory', 14.
56. Brazil, CNV, *Relatório/Vol. I*, 279.
57. Brazil, CNV, 'Resolução No. 2', *Federal Official Gazette of Brazil* (2012); Brazil, Law no. 12.528/2011.
58. Brazil, CNV, *Relatório/Vol. I*, 15.
59. P.S. Pinheiro, 'O Passado Não Está Morto: Nem é Passado Ainda', in G. Dimenstein (ed.), *Democracia Em Pedaços: Direitos Humanos no Brasil* (São Paulo: Cia. das Letras, 2006), 43. See also K. Sikkink and C.B. Walling, 'The Impact of Human Rights Trials in Latin America', *Journal of Peace Research* 44(4) (2007), 437.
60. Adorno, 'The Meaning of Working through the Past', 103.

Bibliography

Adam, B., and Groves, C. *Future Matters: Action, Knowledge, Ethics*. Leiden: Brill, 2007.

Adorno, T.W. 'The Meaning of Working through the Past', in T.W. Adorno, *Critical Models: Interventions and Catchwords*, translated by Henry Pickford (New York: Columbia University Press, 1998), 89–103.

Arquidiocese de São Paulo. *Brasil: Nunca Mais*. Petropolis: Vozes, 1985.

Arruda, R. 'Governo já segue recomendações da Comissão da Verdade, afirma ministra'. Blog, 4 February 2015. Retrieved 28 January 2018 from http://politica.estadao.com.br/blogs/roldao-arruda/governo-ja-segue-recomendacoes-da-comissao-da-verdade-afirma-ministra/.

Assmann, A., and Short, L. 'Memory and Political Change: Introduction', in *Memory and Political Change* (New York: Palgrave Macmillan, 2012), 1–14.

Bakiner, O. 'Truth Commission Impact'. *International Journal of Transitional Justice* 8(1) (2014), 6–30.

Barbosa, B. 'Na ditadura, o Presidente, os generais e os executores dos crimes estavam inteirados dos excessos'. IPEA, Desafios do Desenvolvimento, 23 November 2012. Retrieved 31 January 2018 from http://www.ipea.gov.br/portal/index.php?option=com_content&view=article&id=16148&catid=88&Itemid=2.

Betim, F. 'Provamos que a tortura foi uma política de Estado durante a ditadura'. *El Pais Brasil*, 10 October 2014. Retrieved 10 December 2014 from http://brasil.elpais.com/brasil/2014/10/09/politica/1412885347_047042.html.

Bevernage, B., and Wouters, N. 'State-Sponsored History after 1945: An Introduction', in B. Bevernage and N. Wouters (eds), *The Palgrave Handbook of State-Sponsored History after 1945* (London: Palgrave, 2018).

Bohoslavsky, J.P., and Torelly, M. 'Financial Complicity: The Brazilian Dictatorship under the "Macroscope"', in D.N. Sharp (ed.), *Justice and Economic Violence in Transition* (New York: Springer, 2014), 233–62.

Brazil, Special Office for Human Rights, CEMDP. *Direito à Verdade e à Memória: comissão especial sobre mortos e desaparecidos*. Brasilia: CEMDP, 2007.

Brazil. Law no. 12.528/2011 that Creates the National Truth Commission within the Office of the Chief of Staff of the Presidency of the Republic. *Federal Official Gazette of Brazil*, 2011.

Brazil, CNV. 'Resolução No. 2'. *Federal Official Gazette of Brazil*, 2012.

Brazil, CNV. *Relatório/Comissão Nacional Da Verdade/Vol. I*. Brasília: CNV, 2014.

Brazil, CNV. *Relatório/Comissão Nacional da Verdade/Vol. II*. Brasília: CNV, 2014.

Brazil, MPF (Federal Prosecutions Office). *Grupo de trabalho justiça de transição: atividades de persecução penal desenvolvidas pelo Ministério Público Federal: 2011–2013*. Brasília: MPF/2 CCR, 2014.

Clift, S. *Committing the Future to Memory: History, Experience, Trauma*. New York: Fordham University Press, 2014.

Codato, A. 'A Political History of the Brazilian Transition from Military Dictatorship to Democracy'. *Revista de Sociologia e Política* 25(2005), 1–33.

'O golpe de 1964 e o regime de 1968: aspectos conjunturais e variáveis históricas'. *História Questões & Debates* 40(1) (2005), 11–36.

D'Araújo, M.C. 'O Estável Poder de Veto Forças Armadas Sobre o Tema da Anistia Política no Brasil'. *Varia Historia* 28 (2012), 573–97.

D'Araújo, M.C. 'Taking Stock (with Discomfort) of the Military Dictatorship Fifty Years after the 1964 Coup: A Bibliographical Essay'. *Brazilian Political Science Review* 9(3) (2015), 143–63.

Danto, A.C. *Narration and Knowledge*. New York: Columbia University Press, 1985.

Forchtner, B. 'Historia Magistra Vitae: The Topos of History as a Teacher in Public Struggles over Self and Other Representation', in C. Hart and P. Cap (eds), *Contemporary Critical Discourse Studies* (London: Bloomsbury Academic, 2014), 19–44.

Gardiner, P. *Teorias da História*. Lisbon: Fundação Calouste Gulbekian, 2004.

Gomes-Lund et al. (Guerrilha do Araguaia) v. Brazil. Inter-American Court of Human Rights, 24 November 2010. Retrieved 13 January 2018 from http://www.corteidh.or.cr/docs/casos/articulos/seriec_219_ing.pdf.

Habermas, J. 'Learning from Catastrophe? A Look Back at the Short Twentieth Century', in J. Habermas, *The Postnational Constellation: Political Essays* (Cambridge, MA: MIT Press, 2001), 38–57.

Hayner, P. *Unspeakable Truths: Transitional Justice and the Challenge of Truth Commissions*. New York: Routledge, 2010.

Hollanda, C.B. 'Entrevista Com Pedro Dallari'. *Revista Estudos Políticos* VI(2) (2015), 298–316.

Koselleck, R. *Futures Past: On the Semantics of Historical Time*. New York: Columbia University Press, 2004.

Leebaw, B.A. 'The Irreconcilable Goals of Transitional Justice'. *Human Rights Quarterly* 30(1) (2008), 95–118.

MacMillan, M. *Dangerous Games*. New York: The Modern Library, 2008.

Meister, R. *After Evil: A Politics of Human Rights*. New York: Columbia University Press, 2011.

Minow, M. *Between Vengeance and Forgiveness: Facing History after Genocide and Mass Violence*. Boston, MA: Beacon Press, 1998.

Napolitano, M. 'Recordar é Viver: as Dinâmicas e Vicissitudes da Construção da Memória sobre o Regime Militar Brasileiro'. *Antíteses* 8(15) (2015), 9–44.

Olsen, T.D., et al. 'When Truth Commissions Improve Human Rights'. *International Journal of Transitional Justice* 4(3) (2010), 457–476.

Pinheiro, P.S. 'O Passado Não Está Morto: Nem é Passado Ainda', in G. Dimenstein (ed.), *Democracia em Pedaços: Direitos Humanos no Brasil* (São Paulo: Cia. das Letras, 2006), 7–45.

Power, T. *The Political Right in Postauthoritarian Brazil. Elites, Institutions, and Democratization*. University Park, PA: Pennsylvania State University Press, 2000.

Rousseff, D. 'Speech by Dilma Rousseff during the Presentation of the Final Report of the CNV', Brasília, 10 December 2014. Retrieved 17 December 2018 from http://www.biblioteca.presidencia.gov.br/discursos/discursos-da-presidenta/discurso-da-presidenta-da-republica-dilma-rousseff-durante-entrega-do-relatorio-final-da-comissao-nacional-da-verdade-brasilia-df.

Sikkink, K., and Walling, C.B. 'The Impact of Human Rights Trials in Latin America'. *Journal of Peace Research* 44(4) (2007), 427–45.

Southgate, B. *Why Bother with History? Ancient, Modern and Postmodern Motivations*. London: Routledge, 2000.

Todorov, T. 'The Abuses of Memory'. *Common Knowledge* 5(1) (1996), 6–26.

Todorov, T. *Los Abusos de la memoria*. Barcelona: Paidós, 2000.

UN Human Rights Council. 'Report of the Working Group on the Universal Periodic Review. Brazil'. A/HRC/WG.6/27/BRA/2 (2017).

Walker, M.U. 'Nunca Más: Truth Commissions, Prevention, and Human Rights Culture', in L. May and E. Edenberg (eds), *Jus Post Bellum and Transitional Justice* (Cambridge: Cambridge University Press, 2013), 262–84.

Weichert, M.A. 'O Relatório da Comissão Nacional da Verdade: Conquistas e Desafios?' *Projeto História* 50 (2014), 86–137.

Wiebelhaus-Brahm, E. 'Truth Commissions and the Construction of History', in B. Bevernage and N. Wouters (eds), *The Palgrave Handbook of State-Sponsored History after 1945* (London: Palgrave Macmillan, 2018).

Part II

Truth Commissions in Context: Comparing Latin America

Section 1

Comparing Specific Truth Commissions

Chapter 13

Truth Commissions and Their Archives in El Salvador, Peru and Brazil

Ann M. Schneider

The human rights histories of Brazil, Peru and El Salvador are seldom considered together. Brazil is a giant of the Atlantic world; its 1964–85 dictatorship was an early one among the Cold War-era conflicts in Latin America. The regime – intent on destroying subversion and the 'internal enemy' – tortured, killed and disappeared, though in numbers that would be dwarfed by the staggering death tolls in both Peru and El Salvador. In Peru, an insurgency animated by unmitigated violence emerged just as the country was moving towards democracy in 1980. Twenty years of terror during a counter-insurgency war followed, leaving an estimated seventy thousand people dead. El Salvador, a tiny oligarchic nation facing the Pacific, stood in the heart of the long shadow of the United States, which funded and trained the Salvadoran military during the 1980–92 Civil War. The war, characterized at the time as a front line against the spread of communism in the western hemisphere, resulted in seventy-five thousand deaths.

This chapter considers those histories side by side vis-à-vis aspects of their truth commissions. It does so on three fronts: (1) by discussing how and why each commission identified alleged perpetrators of human rights violations; (2) by describing the plans established for an archive of the materials created and collected by the national truth commissions; and finally (3) by analysing how each commission approached dilemmas in connecting their investigative work to criminal accountability for human rights violations. While acknowledging setbacks and failures, the chapter highlights specific achievements of the commissions as each operated within its particular context.

The truth commission reports published by each country spanned a twenty-year period, beginning with El Salvador in 1993, followed by Peru in 2003, and then Brazil in 2014. Those same years witnessed transformations within Latin America in terms of accountability. By the time the Salvadoran truth commission conducted its investigations in the early 1990s, a consensus had already formed around the idea that pursuing trials for human rights abuses committed by former regimes could jeopardize delicate democratic transitions. To this point, Samuel Huntington famously synthesized what he called a 'guideline for democratizers' dealing with a legacy of authoritarian abuses: 'do not prosecute, do not punish, do not forgive, and, above all, do not forget'.[1] In the face of the prevailing advice against pursuing matters in courts, truth-telling promised an ostensibly victim-centric mechanism that could shine much needed light on some of the darkest periods of national history. The earliest commissions did the critical work of acknowledging events and victims, but did not expose the victimizers. In a noted departure from this practice, the commissioners on the Salvadoran truth commission identified and made public the names of individuals deemed responsible for atrocities. For reasons related to judicial capacity, however, they did not recommend trials.

By the early 2000s, when the commissioners in Peru were preparing their country's report, the possibility of prosecution had taken hold across the region. The decade-plus of distance from the earliest political transitions, coupled with the dramatic events related to the arrest of Chilean dictator Augusto Pinochet in London in 1998, made trials – even of the most powerful – seem possible.[2] In fact, the Peruvian truth commission worked quite deliberately towards criminal accountability, preparing dossiers that were turned over to prosecutors. In 2009, Peru became the first country in Latin America to convict its former head of state for human rights abuses when a national court sentenced Alberto Fujimori to twenty-five years in prison.[3]

The evolving tenor of the moments spanning the Salvadoran and Peruvian truth commissions captures the upward trajectory in demands for accountability for human rights violations since the end of the Cold War. By 2012, the year the Brazilian truth commission began its work, Kathryn Sikkink argued that trials, or at least efforts for trials, had become normative.[4] Scholars and university research centres tracking cases at that time, though acknowledging persistent obstacles to arriving at meaningful convictions, had tallied more than 2,600 individuals under active investigation for past human rights violations in Peru, Argentina and Chile. By 2012 in Peru, sixty-six former state agents had already been convicted, including Fujimori.[5]

There were no convictions, however, in Brazil. In 2010, the Brazilian Supreme Court reified the long-standing interpretation that the 1979 amnesty applied to human rights violations committed by state agents.

(An amnesty in El Salvador passed immediately after the release of its truth commission report likewise protected perpetrators.) Yet Brazil was not just a holdout on trials; it was doubly delayed. The truth commission itself came nearly a generation after nations throughout Latin America had opted for truth-telling and more than forty years after the darkest period of repression in Brazil. In El Salvador and Peru, with commissions conducting investigations in the immediate aftermath of armed conflicts, the work was both imagined and expected to be an engine for further mechanisms of transitional justice. In contrast, though perpetrators were identified in Brazil, the enterprise seemed more formally historical. Indeed, the commission's project can rightly be understood as more deliberately archival in its aim than in either El Salvador or Peru.

El Salvador

From Madness to Hope: Report on the Truth for El Salvador (1993)

El Salvador, a deeply oligarchic society, had been under a military dictatorship since a 1932 rebellion threatened elites, who turned to the military to maintain control. By the late 1970s, staggering human rights abuses were rampant. A reformist coup in 1979 set in motion modicums of land and other reforms. In response, hard-liners resisted. The notorious March 1980 assassination of Archbishop Oscar Romero by a death squad while he celebrated mass in a hospital chapel signalled the waging of a war that would know no bounds. The United Nations' brokered peace accords that brought the war to an end in 1992 mandated two commissions. One was a truth commission that would investigate and publish a report on egregious violations of human rights. The other would vet commissioned military officers on their record with regard to human rights and corruption. The latter was chaired by three Salvadoran officials who determined that more than a hundred officers had to be purged.[6] The truth commission, in contrast, was chaired by three international figures appointed by the Secretary-General of the United Nations. They were: Belisario Betancur, the former president of Colombia; Reinaldo Figueredo, the former Venezuelan Foreign Minister; and Thomas Buergenthal, a US-based law professor and former judge on both the Inter-American Court and the International Court of Justice. The peace accords mandated the truth commission to investigate 'serious acts of violence … whose impact on society urgently demands that the public should know the truth' and, notably, to clarify and put an end to 'any indication of impunity on the part of officers of the armed forces'.[7]

Buergenthal, in particular, brought gravitas to the truth commission. In 1944, at the age of ten, he arrived at Auschwitz after surviving two ghettos and one labour camp. In January 1945, he then survived a three-day death march out of Auschwitz in advance of the Soviet army, which would ultimately liberate him at Sachsenhausen in April 1945.[8] In a memoir written decades later, Buergenthal explained that until tasked with investigating the crimes in El Salvador, he had always thought that his experiences during the Holocaust had prepared him to deal with even the most egregious violations of human rights. Among a number of scenes that shook him, he recalls entering the hallway of the Jesuit residence where, in November 1989, six priests, together with their housekeeper and her daughter, had been pulled from their beds and executed on the lawn. In that hallway, he was shown a portrait of Archbishop Romero that had been pierced by a bullet. The soldiers, 'before marching the priests outside ... paused long enough to put a bullet through the painting – in the heart, where the real assassin had put his' nearly a decade earlier.[9]

All told, the truth commission investigated thirty-two cases, including the assassinations of Archbishop Romero and of the six Jesuit priests. The commissioners maintained that their mandate required them to name perpetrators 'when there is reliable testimony available, especially when the persons identified occupy senior positions and perform official functions directly related to violations or the cover-up of violations'. They established three levels of evidence for their findings that named individuals: (1) overwhelming (conclusive or highly convincing); (2) substantial (very solid); and (3) sufficient (more evidence to support than contradict). As part of their methodology, they were firm that no single source was considered sufficient and that at least two were required before naming an individual as complicit. Aiming to shift entrenched power dynamics, the 250-page final report, entitled *From Madness to Hope: The 12-Year War in El Salvador*, included the names of most of the high command of the armed forces, as well as some guerrilla leaders and civilians, especially judges.[10]

At that time, the decision to name names was both novel and controversial. The truth commission reports in both Argentina (1984) and Chile (1990) – the only two in the Americas that preceded the Salvadoran truth commission – identified the victims by name, but not the state agents responsible for the crimes. José Zalaquett, one of the commissioners for Chile, insisted on and later defended a strict prohibition to disclose names of alleged perpetrators as a matter of due process. He added to internal pressure within El Salvador when he met with the Salvadoran commissioners to advocate against publicly identifying those deemed responsible.[11]

Buergenthal and the other commissioners, however, were undeterred. In interviews and statements in the years following the publication of the report, Buergenthal explained that naming names mattered to the victims and was critical to confronting perpetrators. He noted that 'victims don't always want the people to be punished' and that the act of identifying perpetrators plays an important role in vindicating the victims.[12] He also spoke about the significance of confronting perpetrators with the truth. Within weeks of the publication of the report, he commented that the 'point of laying bare the past is not to feel shock or outrage or pity', but rather 'to say: this is what happened … and to say it to those who did it'.[13] He reported, with some pride, that the response of the military high command to the report was not to say that the commission was wrong. Rather, they called them 'insolent'. For Buergenthal, there was 'something wonderful in that word … because [it meant] we dared to tell them what they had done'.[14] The truth, however, was all that would confront them. Just days after the publication of the report, the Salvadoran Congress passed an amnesty law that would effectively insulate all those named as perpetrators from the possibility of prosecution.

Reflecting on the matter later, Margaret Popkin argued that the Salvadoran truth commission must be seen as an 'early model' in raising 'important issues about the relationship of a commission to the justice system … [and] subsequent efforts to address impunity'. In naming names, she explained, the Salvadoran truth commission acknowledged their contribution as an incremental one.[15] The commissioners would have likely agreed. In fact, they did not recommend trials, at least not immediately. Calling for those identified to be tried in Salvadoran courts only made sense, as Buergenthal later explained, if the commissioners thought the courts were 'capable of doing justice', but they did not. Instead, they called for lustration of military, civilian and judicial figures; public memorials and reparations; a forum to monitor compliance with recommendations; and a 'Foundation for the Truth' to house the papers of the commission and support further research and thus greater knowledge about the atrocities committed in El Salvador.[16]

A Foundation for the Truth

The mandate for the truth commission contained no provisions regarding the ultimate disposition of the records it would receive and create. The commission recognized, however, the significance of what it held, calling it 'a part of El Salvador's heritage' and a resource for 'those who wish to study this painful reality in order to reinforce the effort to spread the message "never again"'. The commission had received, by their own description, a 'mass of reports, testimony, newspaper and magazine articles and books' in such volume that they comprised a 'centre for documentation on the different forms of violence in El Salvador'.[17] The impulse to make materials accessible more broadly was tempered by serious restraints. Foremost among them, the commission had operated 'on a confidential basis' and held some materials that could most certainly put witnesses and informants at grave risk. Furthermore, they had no capacity or mechanism at the time to separate out sensitive materials from the larger collection.[18]

The final report announced a plan that would reconcile the need for preservation of materials and protection of sensitive information. The idea was that, within ninety days of the publication of the report, a permanent 'not-for-profit academic body' would be established to serve as the repository. This 'Foundation for the Truth' would at once protect the confidentiality of witnesses and provide for the possibility of consultation. Housed in Washington, DC at the International Rule of Law Center of George Washington University, where Buergenthal served on the law school faculty, it would operate under his direction and be managed by an international Board of Directors. They envisioned that the foundation would work with 'leaders and researchers' around the globe and expand access in El Salvador.[19] It would not, however, come to pass. Jesuit leaders at the Central American University in San Salvador, the very site of the Jesuit massacre of 1989, wanted the records and therefore opposed the proposal made in the truth commission report. Although arguably an ideal situation to have the records in the home country, doubts lingered over whether sensitive information could be secure in El Salvador. As a result, the records ended up neither with the Jesuits nor in a foundation. Instead, they were transferred to the United Nations where they were placed 'in the custody of the Secretary-General, but under the control of the UN Archives and Records Management Section'. To date, they are closed to researchers.[20]

The inaccessibility of the information, coupled with the blanket amnesty, arguably blunted efforts and stymied momentum within

El Salvador to seek accountability following the publication of the truth commission report. Though the commissioners notably withstood pressure not to identify individuals found complicit in crimes, they were unable to make their vision for a more dynamic, living legacy of the truth commission a reality. Nonetheless, in the long view, the report stands as a singular and enduring achievement. Courts in the United States – a generation after the US funded the Salvadoran military – have recently relied on the report as evidence in cases proceeding against former members of the Salvadoran high command. Two former Ministers of Defence, Generals José Guillermo Garcia and Carlos Eugenio Vides Casanova, were found liable in civil proceedings and ultimately deported from the United States on grounds that they were responsible for torture and extrajudicial killing in El Salvador. Similarly, Colonel Inocente Montano served a sentence in US federal prison before being extradited from the United States to Spain, where he is wanted in connection with the 1989 assassinations of the Jesuit priests.[21] Furthermore, recent steps in emblematic cases within El Salvador have been a cause for cautious optimism that some of the individuals identified by the commission, including those linked to the murder of Archbishop Romero, will be held to account.[22]

Peru

Truth and Reconciliation Report (2003)

Unlike in El Salvador, there were no peace negotiations between the government of Peru and the Shining Path or other insurgencies. In fact, neither the insurgency nor the state existed as it had during the conflict once a truth commission was considered. The force and capacity of the Shining Path had diminished since the capture of its leader, Abimael Gúzman, in 1992. Eight years later, in 2000, the authoritarian regime of President Alberto Fujimori collapsed as he faced corruption charges, resigned, and fled the country.[23] The truth commission was instituted by executive decree under the administration of Valentin Paniagua Corazao, who had been elected by the Peruvian Congress to serve as interim president in the wake of Fujimori's abdication. The decree empowered the commission to 'clarify the process, the events and the responsibility for the terrorist violence and the violations of human rights … attributable to both terrorist organizations and state agents' from May 1980 to November 2000. The tasks of the commission were to promote national reconciliation, the rule of law and the strengthening of constitutional democracy.[24]

The violence that the commission would investigate began in a paradox, with the emergence of an insurgency precisely at a moment of political liberalization. The Shining Path, in fact, announced itself with a fundamentally anti-democrat act: burning ballot boxes at the first national election in more than a decade. The terror and devastation that followed disproportionally impacted the poor, largely indigenous highlands, and heightened the centuries-old tension and mistrust between coastal Lima and the Andean region. John Drabinski described the conflict as 'exhibit[ing] a dynamic that without question reached into the founding violence of Peru itself', that is, 'with complete indifference to the meaning and significance of indigenous voices and lives'.[25] Indeed, the truth commission found that no less than 75 per cent of the victims spoke Quechua or another indigenous language as their first language and were rural, poor and illiterate. Nearly 40 per cent of the total victims were from the department of Ayacucho alone. In a notable divergence from the apportioning of responsibility for atrocities committed elsewhere in the region, the perpetrators of more than half such crimes in Peru were non-state actors. The truth commission found, in fact, that the Shining Path was responsible for 54 per cent of the violations while the state was responsible for 37 per cent.[26] The Salvadoran truth commission, in comparison, concluded that government forces bore responsibility for 85 per cent while 5 per cent were attributable to the guerrillas.[27]

Although here the Salvadoran and Peruvian truth commissions have been placed side by side, the Peruvians did not follow the lead of the Salvadoran commission. Rather, they more deliberately applied best practices from the Guatemala truth commission and the South African Truth and Reconciliation Commission. As in Guatemala and South Africa, the Peruvian commission was undeniably ambitious, involving five hundred professionals and taking more than seventeen thousand testimonies of victims.[28] The president of the commission, Salomón Lerner Febres, was a philosopher and the well-respected rector of the Catholic University in Peru.[29] In efforts to bridge the gap between Lima and the highlands, the commission opened several regional offices.[30]

Priscilla Hayner included the Peruvian truth commission among her list of the five strongest in her book, *Unspeakable Truths*, that analyses truth commissions around the globe. The category also included the commissions of South Africa, Guatemala, Timor-Leste and Morocco. She noted that the Peruvian commission was the first in Latin America to hold public hearings, which proved to be especially powerful for those living in Lima, a comfortable distance from the areas most affected by the terror. The final report, moreover, comprised nine volumes of a staggering eight thousand pages, plus an annex of an additional twelve volumes.[31] It also included a confidential report, discussed in more detail below, recommending criminal investigations in relation to dozens of accused perpetrators. The commission reported on the existence of 4,600 clandestine burial sites and an estimated 69,280 individuals killed or disappeared.[32]

Eduardo González, an expert on transitional justice who worked on the commission, commented on how the laudable ambition of the commission also raised expectations that proved difficult to satisfy. Among them were uncovering information about the disappeared, including the exhumation of mass graves, administering a comprehensive reparations programme, and prosecuting perpetrators. The last on that list was an innovation. Indeed, unlike other commissions that had preceded it, the Peruvian truth commission kept a keen eye on possible prosecutions. As such, González described the emergence during the work of the commission of 'competing positions regarding the pre-eminence of either an interpretative "historical" focus or a fact-finding "juridical" focus; … [that is] between explaining what happened and finding legal evidence'.[33] Ultimately, a balance was struck. The commissioners turned over dossiers on forty-three cases they had investigated to the Office of the Prosecutor General.[34] The final report included reports on the investigation of those cases plus thirty more, which were less ripe for prosecution but no less important to clarify. As was the case in the Salvadoran commission, the inclusion of those cases in the report served as 'symbolic acknowledgement to the victims' in the absence of criminal prosecution.[35]

The commission's investigations resulted in the identification of nearly two hundred alleged perpetrators.[36] Unlike the commissioners for the Salvadoran report, however, the Peruvian commissions decided not to make them public. An administrative court had advised them against doing so, which compounded their own concerns about due process and potential libel liabilities.[37] Names were nonetheless included in narratives and quotes from testimony of specific events, but the commission did not 'publish an accusation of specific crimes … [and] avoid[ed] language that would sound like an indictment'.[38] They left the possibility for resulting indictments to the Office of the Prosecutor General.[39] Their efforts, however, to thread the needle between a full public accounting and the demands of due process got muddled. The press seized upon the information in the report and generated lists of perpetrators. An official list submitted confidentially to the president was then leaked to the press.[40]

Centre of Information for the Collective Memory of Human Rights

Unlike El Salvador, the decree establishing the truth commission in Peru included provisions for an archive. The decree specified that the 'testimonies and documents' that the commission received would be retained and, upon conclusion of its work, 'delivered, with an inventory, to the Ombudsman's Office'. The same article stipulated that access to the materials may be subject to review and that the 'Executive Branch will comply with the recommendations of the Commission provided that they are compatible with the law'. The Ombudsman's Office, an autonomous government office, was chosen for its 'role of supervision in any matters related to human rights'. The sum of the archive accumulated during the course of the work of the commission reached an estimated two hundred cubic metres of materials, including paper, databases, videotapes, audiotapes, photographs and some material objects.[41]

The problem was that the decree instructing that the archives of the truth commission be deposited with the Ombudsman's Office ran counter to existing archival law in Peru requiring the transfer of official records to the National Archive.[42] Beyond the legal issue, logistics posed a further problem. The decree did not provide the Ombudsman's Office with additional space or resources to manage the archive, including processing documents to make them accessible to researchers. Ultimately, the Ombudsman's Office established a 'Centre of Information for the Collective Memory of Human Rights' that houses the truth commission archive and related materials.[43] It also established a three-person committee charged with reviewing records to determine what information could be made public.[44]

In spite of these early challenges, the Peruvian commission accomplished what the Salvadoran one could not. In addition to having a functioning archive with documentation available to researchers, the centre has expanded and continues to play a role in educating about the violence and in efforts for forms of justice. There has been a special emphasis placed on visual materials. A selection from an image bank of 1,700 photographs collected from a variety of sources became a travelling exhibition under the title *Yuyanapaq: para recorder*, the Quechua and Spanish terms, respectively, for remembering. An introduction to the exhibit underscores its transformative aim: 'the images don't change, but the eyes that see them do'.[45] More recently, in 2014, the archive hosted a different travelling exhibit whose aims were both education of the public at large and identification of specific victims.

The exhibit consisted of garments – shirts, jackets, trousers, shoes, socks, underwear and personal items like pocket combs – arranged with solemn care on tables that lined an anteroom to the archive. The items had been found on skeletal remains exhumed from clandestine graves on the Los Cabitos military base. Not only had government forces used the base as a clandestine torture centre where an estimated one thousand individuals lost their lives, but they had built four ovens where the bodies of some of those who had been tortured to death or executed were incinerated.[46] Within a week, relatives of six victims identified clothing on display as having belonged to their loved ones. One garment recognized was actually two – a pair of green trousers inside of a pair of blue ones. The woman who recognized them remembered that it was cold on the day her husband disappeared so he had worn two pairs.[47]

Justice for some of those victims would follow. In 2017, a court in Peru sentenced two former officers, Edgar Paz and Humberto Bari, to more than twenty years in prison for crimes that occurred at Los Cabitos. Two other officers were likewise found guilty but did not appear for sentencing and are now fugitives.[48] Though one cannot draw a direct line between the convictions back to the truth commission, its archive and the travelling exhibit of exhumed clothing, they are nonetheless connected. If in El Salvador the work of the commission ended with the report, in Peru the commission was in many ways institutionalized through its archive. The archive, in turn, endeavours to respond to evolving issues concerning truth, memory and justice. The events related to the Los Cabitos case underscore a parallel phenomenon at work in Peru and in other societies dealing with a legacy of state violence. On one hand, they bring to the fore the formidable and unending challenges in accounting for mass atrocities. On the other hand, they reveal the significance of seeing and responding to a single case.

Brazil

Preliminary and Final Reports (2014)

In February 2014, Brazil's National Truth Commission released the second in a series of eight preliminary reports. The report, 'The Rubens Paiva Case', presented documentary evidence and witness testimony about the torture and forced disappearance of a former federal deputy. Though, as the commission pointed out, Paiva was 'neither the first nor the last political prisoner executed by state agents ...', his case stood out for the long-standing and deeply cynical responses from the military as to his whereabouts since his arrest at his home in January 1971. The report read like an indictment, including the names of some of the agents and commanders complicit in the crimes, including Major José Antônio Nogueira Belham, the chief of the Operations and Information Detachment (DOI) in Rio de Janeiro at that time. Belham claimed, when interviewed by the commission in 2013, that he had been on leave during the period when Paiva was detained and disappeared. The commission, however, located documentation and obtained testimony showing that he was indeed on duty at the time in question, had been made aware of the torture of Paiva, and was warned that it would lead to his death. The commission noted further that Belham was also in charge when the military concocted a false story to explain his disappearance, namely that Paiva had been 'rescued by terrorists' while being transported, and thus was no longer in military custody.[49] The commission, in fact, published compendiums outlining the chain of command responsible for the disappearance as well as summaries of the cases of nine additional individuals disappeared under Belham's command.[50]

As was the case in El Salvador and Peru, the mandate of the commission took no explicit position on identifying perpetrators. Rather, it tasked the commission to 'examine and clarify grave violations of human rights, ... to effectuate the right to memory and historical truth and to promote national reconciliation'. That work included 'identifying and making public the structures, locations, institutions and circumstances related to the practice of violations of human rights', but not necessarily the individuals.[51] Nonetheless, the commission's final report, published in December 2014, named 377 perpetrators. When possible, their identification included the year of their birth (and death, if confirmed), details about their positions in the military, and specific victims linked to them. The names were organized in three categories: (1) those with political/institutional responsibility who instituted or maintained the structures and procedures in which human rights violations were committed; (2) those with structural/procedural responsibility who managed said structures and procedures; and (3) those with direct authorship responsibility who personally participated in human rights violations. The first category included fifty-three officers among the highest levels of the military government who had conceived and implemented policies that gave the green light to the commission of human rights abuses. At the time of the report, forty-one of the fifty-three were confirmed deceased. The second category included eighty-four names of officers who through their actions and omissions allowed, tolerated or encouraged human rights abuses, often in installations under their command (Belham is named in this category). A total of forty of the eighty-four named here were confirmed as deceased when the report was published. The third category included the names of 240 agents and officers who personally committed human rights violations. Of those, fifty-seven were confirmed deceased.[52]

Compounding the Brazilian judiciary's unbending position on the applicability of the amnesty, the fact that more than a third of identified perpetrators were deceased at the time of the publication of its report meant that the Brazilian commission faced challenges that neither the Salvadoran nor the Peruvian commissions had. The reactions to both its preliminary and final reports nonetheless reinforced the notion of the power of truth-telling expressed a generation earlier by Buergenthal in relation to the naming of military officers in El Salvador. They also reflected the emerging expectation for accountability. Yet, rather than preserving the evidence to allow the courts to act as in Peru, the Brazilian commissioners released information at press conferences and made it available online in real time. Thus, in the absence of criminal accountability, the Brazilian commission focused on collecting and preserving information that would establish an undeniable historical record about human rights abuses.

Reference Centre of Political Struggles in Brazil (1964–85): Revealed Memories

On 15 December 2014, five days after the submission of the final report, a presidential decree established a temporary administrative office responsible for organizing the archive obtained and produced by the commission during its thirty-one months of activities. The collection holds millions of documents, including testimonies of victims and family members of victims; depositions of agents of repression; forty-seven thousand photographs; videos of public hearings; and administrative documents. The commission also received documentation from state, municipal and sectoral commissions, family archival materials, and materials from cooperating foreign countries including Argentina, Germany, Chile, the United States and Uruguay. The materials were turned over to the custodial care of the National Archive in July 2015 and are accessible to the public.[53]

As in Peru, the plan for an archive had been part of the law establishing the truth commission itself.[54] Specifically, the law stipulated that all materials be sent to the National Archive for integration to the

Revealed Memories project.[55] Unlike in Peru, however, a formal and institutionalized archival structure predated the commission. Indeed, the commission relied on the archive for its investigation and was invested in its expansion, both in terms of the scope of the collection and access to it. A decade earlier, in 2005, the Special Secretary of Human Rights had designated a working group to develop a project 'for the implantation of a reference centre' that would 'protect information, documents, archives, and artistic objects with symbolic value about the violations of human rights during the period of military dictatorship in Brazil'. Later that year, documents produced and received by a number of former intelligence agencies were transferred to the National Archive. In 2007, files of special police forces were added. In 2009, the 'Reference Centre of Political Struggles in Brazil (1964–85): Revealed Memories', coordinated by the National Archive, was created with the following mission: 'So that it's not forgotten, so that it never again happens'.[56] It focuses primarily on the possibilities for academic work and other research to effectuate transformative knowledge about the past.

It is no small thing to have an archive that can continue to provide information about violations and thereby to confront perpetrators. Indeed, events during the weeks following the publication of the Rubens Paiva preliminary report emphasized the threat that truth-telling may hold and the stakes in repressing it. In testimony to the commission in March 2014, a retired Lieutenant Colonel, Paulo Malhães, admitted that he had committed torture and that bodies of individuals killed under torture had been mutilated to prevent their possible identification, should they be found. He had provided the information in relation to questioning about the so-called 'House of Death' in Petropolis, the former imperial city of Brazil in the mountains about an hour's drive from Rio de Janeiro.[57] Though his matter-of-fact tone and unapologetic manner disturbed the listening public, what would happen soon after redoubled the shock. Just weeks after his admissions, Malhães was murdered in a purported robbery of his home. The episode, widely described as an effort to destroy evidence – which in Portuguese is convened through the phrase 'burning of the archive' (*queima de arquivo*) – understandably had a chilling effect on the ongoing work of the truth commission.[58]

Though Malhães's death was a gross form of 'burning the archive', he had obfuscated and dissembled in his own statements in ways that damaged efforts to get to the bottom of cases, including that of Rubens Paiva. In what was reportedly the first time that a military official acknowledged participation, Malhães stated in an interview that he had been ordered to disinter the body, which he said had been moved previously from the Alto da Boa Vista to the sand in the Recreio dos Bandeirantes beach. He ominously described the operation as a 'final solution'. He would not say, however, what ultimately happened, stating that the body could have 'ended up in the sea or in a river'.[59] In a retraction a few days later, he said that the previous interview had been misunderstood and claimed that he had said he had been part of the operation 'because he thought that it was a very sad story … that for 38 years [the family] has been wanting to know the location of the body'. Clarifying that he is not sentimental, he stated that he said it 'so that there would not be a war to know where the body was'.[60]

There has been thoughtful criticism of the Brazilian commission, as there had been of the Salvadoran and Peruvian commissions too. It remains to be seen, however, what its lasting legacy and crowning achievements will be. The Salvadoran and Peruvian commissions faced unexpected challenges and part of what they had imagined ultimately was overcome by events. Yet some of the seeds that they had planted bore fruit. The Brazilian commission, much more so than the Salvadoran and Peruvian commissions, faced limits wrought by the passage of time and the long-standing impunity guaranteed by amnesty. As a result, its archival project to collect and preserve information arguably offered the best avenue through which to acknowledge violations and victims in a meaningful way.

Ann M. Schneider is a historian of Latin America and human rights. She is working on a book about amnesty in Brazil, but also researches and writes about accountability and impunity throughout Latin America. She earned her doctorate from the University of Chicago and works as a researcher in support of human rights-related investigations and prosecutions.

Notes

1. S. Huntington, *The Third Wave: Democratization in the Late Twentieth Century* (Norman: University of Oklahoma Press, 1991), 231.
2. N. Roht-Arriaza, *The Pinochet Effect: Transnational Justice in the Age of Human Rights* (Philadelphia: University of Pennsylvania Press, 2005).
3. J. Burt, 'Guilty as Charged: The Trial of Former Peruvian President Alberto Fujimori for Human Rights Violations', *The International Journal of Transitional Justice* (3) (2009), 384–405.
4. K. Sikkink, *The Justice Cascade: How Human Rights Prosecutions Are Changing World Politics* (New York: Norton, 2011).

5. C. Collins, L. Balardini, and J. Burt, 'Mapping Perpetrator Prosecutions in Latin America', *The International Journal of Transitional Justice* 7(1) (March 2013), 8–9.
6. R. Zamora with D. Holiday, 'The Struggle for Lasting Reform: Vetting Processes in El Salvador', in A. Mayer-Rieckh and P. de Greiff (eds), *Justice as Prevention: Vetting Public Employees in Transitional Societies* (New York: Social Science Research Council, 2007), 80–118.
7. Commission on the Truth for El Salvador, *From Madness to Hope: The 12-Year War in El Salvador*, United Nations S.25500 (April 1993), retrieved from http://www.derechos.org/nizkor/salvador/informes/truth.html.
8. United States Holocaust Memorial Museum, 'Thomas Buergenthal', in *Holocaust Encyclopedia*, retrieved from https://www.ushmm.org/wlc/en/idcard.php?ModuleId=10006193.
9. T. Buergenthal, *A Lucky Child: A Memoir of Surviving Auschwitz as a Young Boy* (New York: Little, Brown & Company, 2009), xvii and 215–16; and J. Trescott, 'Not the President's Men: Holocaust Council Dismissals Explained', *The Washington Post*, 7 April 1993.
10. El Salvador, *From Madness to Hope*. The commission also produced two annexes. One contained forensic reports on the notorious 1981 El Mozote massacre and the other comprised statistical information about the complaints and information received by the commission. See T. Buergenthal, 'The United Nations Truth Commission for El Salvador', in N. Kritz (ed.), *Transitional Justice: How Emerging Democracies Reckon with Former Regimes I, General Considerations* (Washington, DC: US Institute of Peace Press, 1995), 310–11.
11. M. Ensalaco, *Chile under Pinochet: Recovering the Truth* (Philadelphia: University of Pennsylvania Press, 2000), 189–95.
12. D. Cloud and N. Bendavid, 'Calls for Punishing Genocide Get Louder: Permanent Tribunal on War Crimes Faces Enormous Obstacles', *The Chicago Tribune*, 30 June 1997.
13. T. Thompson, 'The Painful Truth', *The Pittsburgh Post-Gazette*, 25 April 1993.
14. Ibid.
15. M. Popkin, 'The Salvadoran Truth Commission and the Search for Justice,' *Criminal Law Forum* 15 (2004), 105.
16. Buergenthal, 'The United Nations Truth Commission for El Salvador', 318; and El Salvador, *From Madness to Hope*, 16 and 176–87.
17. El Salvador, *From Madness to Hope*, 15.
18. T. Huskamp Peterson, *Final Acts: A Guide to Preserving the Records of Truth Commissions* (Washington, DC: Woodrow Wilson Center Press, 2005), 26.
19. El Salvador, *From Madness to Hope*, 16.
20. Huskamp Peterson, *Final Acts*, 66; Popkin, 'The Salvadoran Truth Commission', 112.
21. For information on the US cases, see Center for Justice & Accountability, 'Human Rights Crimes under Salvadoran Defense Ministers', retrieved

from http://cja.org/what-we-do/litigation/romagoza-arce-v-garcia-and-vides-casanova/; and 'Murder of Jesuit Priests and Civilians in El Salvador: The Jesuit Massacre Case', retrieved from http://cja.org/what-we-do/litigation/the-jesuits-massacre-case/.

22. B. Jones, 'Fresh Hope for Justice in 1980 Slaying of Archbishop Oscar Romero', *Newsday*, 17 August 2017, retrieved from https://www.newsday.com/long-island/fresh-hope-for-justice-in-1980-slaying-of-archbishop-oscar-romero-1.14070880.
23. J. Drabinski, '"That Gesture of Recognition": An Interview with Salomón Lerner Febres', *Humanity: An International Journal of Human Rights, Humanitarianism and Development*, 4(1) (Spring 2013), 171.
24. Decreto Supremo No. 065-2001-PCM, retrieved from http://www.cverdad.org.pe/lacomision/nlabor/decsup01.php.
25. Drabinski, '"That Gesture of Recognition"', 172.
26. P. Hayner, *Unspeakable Truths: Transitional Justice and the Challenge of Truth Commissions*, 2nd ed. (New York: Routledge, 2011), 37.
27. El Salvador, *From Madness to Hope*, 43.
28. E. González Cueva, 'The Peruvian Truth and Reconciliation Commission and the Challenge of Impunity', in N. Roht-Arriaza and J. Mariezcurrena (eds), *Transitional Justice in the Twenty-First Century: Beyond Truth versus Justice* (Cambridge: Cambridge University Press, 2006), 70.
29. Drabinski, '"That Gesture of Recognition"', 173.
30. Hayner, *Unspeakable Truths*, 36.
31. Ibid., 37; and Comisión de la Verdad y Reconciliación, *Informe Final* (August 2003), retrieved from http://www.cverdad.org.pe/ifinal/index.php.
32. Hayner, *Unspeakable Truths*, 37.
33. González, 'Challenge of Impunity', 79.
34. Ibid., 70.
35. Ibid., 87.
36. Hayner, *Unspeakable Truths*, 137–38.
37. González, 'Challenge of Impunity', 88; Hayner, *Unspeakable Truths*, 137–38.
38. González, 'Challenge of Impunity', 88.
39. Ibid., 70.
40. Hayner, *Unspeakable Truths*, 138.
41. Huskamp Peterson, *Final Acts*, 74.
42. Ibid., 74.
43. Defensoría del Pueblo Centro de Información para la Memoria Colectiva y los DD.HH., retrieved from http://www.defensoria.gob.pe/cinfo.php.
44. Huskamp Peterson, *Final Acts*, 74.
45. Comisión de la Verdad y Reconciliación, 'The Visual Legacy', retrieved from http://www.cverdad.org.pe/ingles/apublicas/p-fotografico/.
46. J. Burt, 'The Bones Tell the Story: The Search for Peru's Missing', *Al Jazerra*, 30 March 2013, retrieved from https://www.aljazeera.com/indepth/opinion/2013/03/201333014192699858 2.html.

47. O. Guerrero, 'Los Cabitos: La ropa que habla por los desaparecidos en Ayacucho', *Peru.com*, 17 September 2014, retrieved from https://peru.com/actualidad/cronicas-y-entrevistas/cabitos-ropa-que-sirve-identificar-desaparecidos-noticia-285088.
48. 'Peru Court Convicts Two of Human-Rights Abuses at Military Base', *Reuters*, 18 August 2017, retrieved from https://www.reuters.com/article/us-peru-human-rights/peru-court-convicts-two-of-human-rights-abuses-at-military-base-idUSKCN1AY238.
49. Comissão Nacional da Verdade (CNV), 'Relatório Preliminar de Pesquisa: Caso Rubens Paiva' (February 2014), retrieved from http://cnv.memoriasreveladas.gov.br/images/pdf/relatorio_preliminar_26-02.pdf.
50. CNV, 'Cadeia de Comando Caso Rubens Paiva' (24 February 2014), retrieved from http://cnv.memoriasreveladas.gov.br/images/pdf/cadeia-de-comando.pdf; and CNV, 'Mortos e Desaparecidos por Agentes do DOI do Rio de Janeiro sob o Comando de Antônio Belham' (24 February 2014), retrieved from http://cnv.memoriasreveladas.gov.br/images/pdf/mortos_agentes_doi.pdf.
51. Presidência da República, Lei No. 12.528, 'Cria a Comissão de Verdade no âmbito da Casa Civil da Presidência da República' (18 November 2011), retrieved from http://www.planalto.gov.br/ccivil_03/_Ato2011-2014/2011/Lei/L12528.htm.
52. CNV, *Relatório*, Vol. 1 (December 2014), 841–931.
53. CNV, 'Acervo da Comissão Nacional da Verdade' (5 August 2015), retrieved from http://www.cnv.gov.br/institucional-acesso-informacao/acervo.html.
54. Lei No. 12.528.
55. Ibid.
56. Memorias Reveladas, retrieved from http://www.memoriasreveladas.gov.br/.
57. CNV, 'Depoimento do coronel Paulo Malhães, ex-agente do CIE' (30 March 2014), retrieved from https://www.youtube.com/watch?v=e2Sns-SYG7O0.
58. K. Mello, 'Morte de coronel pode ser "queima de arquivo" ou "vingança", diz polícia', *O Globo*, 25 April 2014, retrieved from http://g1.globo.com/rio-de-janeiro/noticia/2014/04/morte-de-coronel-pode-ser-queima-de-arquivo-ou-vinganca-diz-policia.html.
59. 'Coronel reformado diz ter ocultado restos mortais de Rubens Paiva', *Folha de S. Paulo*, 20 March 2014, retrieved from https://www1.folha.uol.com.br/poder/2014/03/1428424-coronel-reformado-diz-ter-ocultado-restos-mortais-de-rubens-paiva.shtml.
60. C. Thomé, 'Coronel diz não ter dado fim a corpo de deputado: Malhães recua em caso Rubens Paiva, mas admite torturas em "centro de conveniências"', *O Estadão*, 25 March 2014, retrieved from https://politica.estadao.com.br/noticias/geral,coronel-diz-nao-ter-dado-fim-a-corpo-de-deputado,1145016.

Bibliography

Buergenthal, T. *A Lucky Child: A Memoir of Surviving Auschwitz as a Young Boy*. New York: Little, Brown & Company, 2009.

Buergenthal, T. 'The United Nations Truth Commission for El Salvador', in N. Kritz (ed.), *Transitional Justice: How Emerging Democracies Reckon with Former Regimes I, General Considerations* (Washington, DC: US Institute of Peace Press, 1995), 292–325.

Burt, J. 'The Bones Tell the Story: The Search for Peru's Missing'. *Al Jazeera*, 30 March 2013. Retrieved from https://www.aljazeera.com/indepth/opinion/2013/03/2013330141926998582.html.

Burt, J. 'Guilty as Charged: The Trial of Former Peruvian President Alberto Fujimori for Human Rights Violations'. *The International Journal of Transitional Justice* 3 (2009), 384–405.

Center for Justice & Accountability. 'Human Rights Crimes under Salvadoran Defense Ministers'. Retrieved from http://cja.org/what-we-do/litigation/romagoza-arce-v-garcia-and-vides-casanova/.

Center for Justice & Accountability. 'Murder of Jesuit Priests and Civilians in El Salvador: The Jesuit Massacre Case'. Retrieved from http://cja.org/what-we-do/litigation/the-jesuits-massacre-case/.

Cloud, D., and Bendavid, N. 'Calls for Punishing Genocide Get Louder: Permanent Tribunal on War Crimes Faces Enormous Obstacles'. *The Chicago Tribune*, 30 June 1997.

Collins, C., Balardini, L., and Burt, J. 'Mapping Perpetrator Prosecutions in Latin America'. *The International Journal of Transitional Justice* 7(1) (March 2013), 8–28.

Comisión de la Verdad y Reconciliación. *Informe Final.* August 2003. Retrieved from http://www.cverdad.org.pe/ifinal/index.php.

Comisión de la Verdad y Reconciliación. 'The Visual Legacy'. Retrieved from http://www.cverdad.org.pe/ingles/apublicas/p-fotografico/.

Comissão Nacional da Verdade. *Relatório*. Vol. 1. December 2010. Retrieved from http://cnv.memoriasreveladas.gov.br/.

Comissão Nacional da Verdade. 'Acervo da Comissão Nacional da Verdade'. 5 August 2015. Retrieved from http://www.cnv.gov.br/institucional-acesso-informacao/acervo.html.

Comissão Nacional da Verdade. 'Cadeia de Comando Caso Rubens Paiva'. 24 February 2014. http://cnv.memoriasreveladas.gov.br/images/pdf/cadeia-de-comando.pdf.

Comissão Nacional da Verdade. 'Depoimento do coronel Paulo Malhães, ex-agente do CIE'. 30 March 2014. Retrieved from https://www.youtube.com/watch?v=e2SnsSYG7O0.

Comissão Nacional da Verdade. 'Mortos e Desaparecidos por Agentes do DOI do Rio de Janeiro sob o Comando de Antônio Belham'. 24 February 2014. Retrieved from http://cnv.memoriasreveladas.gov.br/images/pdf/mortos_agentes_doi.pdf.

Comissão Nacional da Verdade. 'Relatório Preliminar de Pesquisa: Caso Rubens Paiva'. February 2014. Retrieved from http://cnv.memoriasreveladas.gov.br/images/pdf/relatorio_preliminar_26-02.pdf.

Commission on the Truth for El Salvador. *From Madness to Hope: The 12-Year War in El Salvador: Report of the Commission on the Truth for El Salvador*. United Nations S.25500. April 1993. Retrieved from http://www.derechos.org/nizkor/salvador/informes/truth.html.

'Coronel reformado diz ter ocultado restos mortais de Rubens Paiva'. *Folha de S. Paulo*, 20 March 2014. Retrieved from https://www1.folha.uol.com.br/poder/2014/03/1428424-coronel-reformado-diz-ter-ocultado-restos-mortais-de-rubens-paiva.shtml.

Decreto Supremo No. 065-2001-PCM. Retrieved from http://www.cverdad.org.pe/lacomision/nlabor/decsup01.php.

Defensoría del Pueblo Centro de Información para la Memoria Colectiva y los DD.HH. Retrieved from http://www.defensoria.gob.pe/cinfo.php.com.

Drabinski, J. '"That Gesture of Recognition": An Interview with Salomón Lerner Febres'. *Humanity: An International Journal of Human Rights, Humanitarianism and Development* 4(1) (Spring 2013), 171–80.

Ensalaco, M. *Chile under Pinochet: Recovering the Truth*. Philadelphia: University of Pennsylvania Press, 2000.

González Cueva, E. 'The Peruvian Truth and Reconciliation Commission and the Challenge of Impunity', in N. Roht-Arriaza and J. Mariezcurrena (eds), *Transitional Justice in the Twenty-First Century: Beyond Truth versus Justice* (Cambridge: Cambridge University Press, 2006), 70–93.

Guerrero, O. 'Los Cabitos: La ropa que habla por los desaparecidos en Ayacucho'. *Peru.com*, 17 September 2014. Retrieved from https://peru.com/actualidad/cronicas-y-entrevistas/cabitos-ropa-que-sirve-identificar-desaparecidos-noticia-285088.

Hayner, P. *Unspeakable Truths: Transitional Justice and the Challenge of Truth Commissions*. 2nd ed. New York: Routledge, 2011.

Huntington, S. *The Third Wave: Democratization in the Late Twentieth Century*. Norman: University of Oklahoma Press, 1991.

Huskamp Peterson, T. *Final Acts: A Guide to Preserving the Records of Truth Commissions*. Washington, DC: Woodrow Wilson Center Press, 2005.

Jones, B. 'Fresh Hope for Justice in 1980 Slaying of Archbishop Oscar Romero'. *Newsday*, 17 August 2017. Retrieved from https://www.newsday.com/long-island/fresh-hope-for-justice-in-1980-slaying-of-archbishop-oscar-romero-1.14070880.

Laplante, L., and Theidon, K. 'Truth with Consequences: Justice and Reparations in Post Truth Commission Peru'. *Human Rights Quarterly* 29(1) (February 2007), 228–50.

Mello, K. 'Morte de coronel pode ser "queima de arquivo" ou "vingança", diz polícia'. *O Globo*, 25 April 2014. Retrieved from http://g1.globo.com/rio-de-janeiro/noticia/2014/04/morte-de-coronel-pode-ser-queima-de-arquivo-ou-vinganca-diz-policia.html.

Memorias Revaladas. Retrieved from http://www.memoriasreveladas.gov.br/.

'Peru Court Convicts Two of Human-Rights Abuses at Military Base'. *Reuters*, 18 August 2017. Retrieved from https://www.reuters.com/article/us-peru-human-rights/peru-court-convicts-two-of-human-rights-abuses-at-military-base-idUSKCN1AY238.

Popkin, M. 'The Salvadoran Truth Commission and the Search for Justice'. *Criminal Law Forum* 15 (2004), 105–24.

Presidência da República. Lei No. 12.528. 'Cria a Comissão de Verdade no âmbito da Casa Civil da Presidência da República'. 18 November 2011. Retrieved from http://www.planalto.gov.br/ccivil_03/_Ato2011-2014/2011/Lei/L12528.htm.

Roht-Arriaza, N. *The Pinochet Effect: Transnational Justice in the Age of Human Rights*. Philadelphia: University of Pennsylvania Press, 2005.

Sikkink, K. *The Justice Cascade: How Human Rights Prosecutions Are Changing World Politics*. New York: Norton, 2011.

Thomé, C. 'Coronel diz não ter dado fim a corpo de deputado: Malhães recua em caso Rubens Paiva, mas admite torturas em "centro de conveniências"'. *O Estadão*, 25 March 2014. Retrieved from https://politica.estadao.com.br/noticias/geral,coronel-diz-nao-ter-dado-fim-a-corpo-de-deputado,1145016.

Thompson, T. 'The Painful Truth'. *The Pittsburgh Post-Gazette*, 25 April 1993.

Trescott, J. 'Not the President's Men: Holocaust Council Dismissals Explained'. *The Washington Post*, 7 April 1993.

United States Holocaust Memorial Museum. 'Thomas Buergenthal', in *Holocaust Encyclopedia*. Retrieved from https://www.ushmm.org/wlc/en/idcard.php?ModuleId=10006193.

Zamora, R., with Holiday, D. 'The Struggle for Lasting Reform: Vetting Processes in El Salvador', in A. Mayer-Rieckh and P. de Greiff (eds), *Justice as Prevention: Vetting Public Employees in Transitional Societies* (New York: Social Science Research Council, 2007), 80–118.

Chapter 14

Memory, Truth and Auto-Fiction in the Recent Latin American Novel

Jobst Welge

Transgenerational Memory and the Search for Truth

How does literary fiction engage with the problem of historical truth? And how does contemporary fiction's concern with private memories relate to, complement or contradict larger, collective forms of remembering? The strand of Latin American fiction to be discussed here forms part of a wider tendency of recent life writing, a hybrid constellation of biography, autobiography and fiction, in which the narrating subjects explore their own identity by way of relation to their (grand-)parents or siblings under conditions of the legacies of twentieth-century dictatorships.

The category of memory has been an important component for what I have called the 'genealogical novel' of the twentieth century.[1] Yet arguably the more recent, subject-centred literature of the twenty-first century, insofar as it is concerned with familial and historical relations, tends to foreground a memorial practice that informs the relationships between different generations of a family or a given community. More specifically, the concept of transgenerational memory refers to the idea of *post-memory*, as it has been developed by Marianne Hirsch: 'Postmemory describes the relationship that the generation after those who witnessed cultural or collective trauma bears to the experiences of those who came before, experiences that they "remember" only by means of the stories, images, and behaviours among which they grew up'.[2] In this perspective, the family is the central institution for the intergenerational transmission of, in this case, the Shoah as a specifically Jewish experience. Although Hirsch relates her concept not only to a vertical-generational transmission but also to horizontal, 'affiliative' structures, memory is clearly understood here within the horizon of a collective memory, which, in the understanding of Maurice Halbwachs or Jan Assmann, is seen in the context of the communicative system of a specific social group.[3] As we will see, the texts to be discussed here are all distinguished by the assumption that a group identity with its transmission of memories is no longer a natural given. Therefore, familial memories are shown here as inherently contradictory, they are surrounded by silences and ambiguity; the narrative voice compensates for the aporia of testimony by way of imagination and virtuality, yet it never abandons the ultimate grounding in reality.[4]

In this recent, transgenerational literature the question of temporal and generational discontinuity comes itself to the fore, and hence also the very process of relating to these more remote events as well as the problem of historical justice by the means of literary narration.[5] In many cases, this sort of literature is at least in part conceived as auto-fictional, that is, the subject position of the narrator is close to the experiential position of the author, which means in turn that the literary text to varying degrees hybridizes fictional, documentary and autobiographical elements – and thus gives voice to a specifically generational consciousness.[6]

In the following, I want to discuss these issues with regard to two different, symptomatic constellations of time and space, first using two examples from a somewhat older generation of Brazilian writers and their memorial relation to the time of dictatorship in Brazil, and secondly with respect to two younger writers of the Cono Sur and their transgenerational exploration of the chronologically more recent dictatorship in that region.

The Older Generation: Brazil

In the case of Bernardo Kucinski's novel *K*, there is a narrator-son (auto-fictionally, to be equated with the author) who engages in an imaginary projection, in order to get into the head and feelings of his father ('K'). Instead of memorial immediacy ('I remember'), we are confronted with the imaginary (and thereby transgenerational) relation to the memory of the father. For the father's investigations into the fate of his disappeared daughter are said to have triggered other memories, namely of his own resistance activities in 1930s Poland, as well as those of his sister, who had died there in prison. While ascending the stairs of the neoclassical military club in São Paulo, 'K' is said to recall the more distant past: 'He suddenly remembered other stairs in other times, in Warsaw, likewise in marble and also in a neoclassical style'.[7] This scene, as well as other passages of the novel, constructs a parallel between the anti-Semitic persecutions in wartime Poland and the disappearance of revolutionary activists during the Brazilian dictatorship of the 1970s.

Kucinski's novel, then, engages with this complex constellation of an already mediated and therefore partly imaginary memory on the part of the narrator-son, whose own existence and feelings may only discretely be surmised by this indirect form of narration, whereby the subject position is alternately marked by the first and by the third person singular.[8] The contested nature of memory politics becomes most evident in a chapter in which the father debates with a severe rabbi the question of whether his daughter may be honoured by an empty tomb in the Jewish cemetery of Butantã, São Paolo. While such a tomb is erected there to the victims of the Holocaust – and while the father concurs with the rabbi about the historical uniqueness of the Holocaust – 'for him [the father] the tragedy was a continuation of the Holocaust'.[9] One chapter of the novel reconstructs the meeting of the Institute for Chemistry at the University of São Paolo (USP) during which the daughter of 'K' is expelled by the hypocritical, self-satisfied professors because of her political activities. The narrator harps on the historical irony that the chemistry institute was originally founded by German immigrants who were fleeing from Nazism.[10]

By way of this bitter background of personal family history, the novel exemplifies what Michael Rothberg has called *multidirectional memory*, that is, the extension of the memory of the Holocaust into other areas of traumatic experience in different (trans-)national contexts; or, as in this case, the Holocaust as an 'ironic' background for the dictatorship's politics of disappearance.[11] Moreover, the moral pathos of the scene in Kucinski's novel is foregrounded through the claim that it is based in reality: 'This account was imagined based on the acts of the meeting'.[12] The auto-, or rather bio-fictional discourse on reality acknowledges its artificial nature, yet it refuses to be reduced to, or to be confounded with fiction.[13]

Such devices of the imaginary projection into the psyche of an older relative and the multidirectional 'continuity' of memorial legacies may also be observed in a novel that approaches the period of the Brazilian dictatorship more indirectly. Chico Buarque's novel *O irmão alemão* (*The German Brother*, 2014) is an equally sophisticated instance of an auto-fictional novel as the one by Kucinski.[14] The specificity of the genre of auto-fiction (according to the definition by the French critic Serge Doubrovsky) is above all centred in the essentially undecidable distinction between autobiography and fiction, and it is qualified, of course, by the reader's possible knowledge of external facts that may be able to (in)validate the assertions and details of the narrative.[15] The paratext is often crucial in establishing a pact of credibility with the reader: in this case, it is an epilogue in which the author thanks researchers, historians, friends and relatives of the book's protagonist (i.e. the narrator's brother). The title of the novel refers to a brother of the Brazilian author, who came to understand (first at the age of twenty-two) that his father, while living in Berlin during the early 1930s, engendered a son out of wedlock, whose adoption by foster parents was complicated by the 'Arian' requirements of the Nazi regime, and who later grew up in the GDR, where he became a TV host for a music programme. The auto-fictional premise of the novel is this real-life search for a lost brother on the part of the author. Moreover, the auto-fictional truth reflects back on the biography of the author, one of the foremost stars in the area of Brazilian popular music, as well as the biography of his father, Sérgio Buarque de Holanda, a social historian and one of the most famous Brazilian intellectuals from the first half of the twentieth century.

The book reproduces a series of historical documents, namely the correspondence between the father and his German lover Anne Ernst, as well as his correspondence with the Nazi authorities during the 1930s, regarding the 'Arian' genealogy of his unofficial son (as required for the possibility of adoption). Yet there are also numerous signals that alert the reader to the book's distance from regular autobiography. For instance, the narrator-protagonist is called Ciccio, signalling a likeness to, but also a distance from the author's name 'Chico'. Buarque's biographical research about the mystery of the lost brother was reignited when his Brazilian publisher helped to establish a contact with Brazilian and German publishers, who then unearthed further facts and documents that finally led to the identification of the brother. In 2013, the author himself conducted interviews with the descendants of Sergio Günther.[16] Despite these clarifications, for the auto-fictional narrator of the novel the ultimate 'truth' about the brother continues to be an open question.

This autobiographical inspiration gives way to a series of imaginations of what the lost brother would have been like, such as fantasies about the brother Sergio's attempt to interrogate his mother about the identity of his father, or the lost son's hypothetical voyage to Brazil, where he would have been embraced as a legitimate son by his stepmother. Some of these passages are explicitly introduced as imaginary extensions of reality (by being said to be dreams, speculations or novelistic fantasies),[17] which has the obvious effect to qualify the other, more straightforwardly related passages as all the truer to reality. To cite just one example, regarding the lost brother's mother, Anne Ernst:

> Here is a hypothesis that came to me only during my worst dreams, namely that Anne Ernst possessed a quantum of Jewish blood. And thus, I can understand, with premonitory instinct, that in May 1932 she had consigned Sérgio Ernst to the tutelage of the state, requesting that the natural father of the child, Sergio de Hollander, would be informed about this.[18]

Similarly, the narrator-son imagines how his father, namely Sérgio Buarque de Holanda, would have reacted if he could have been reading the novel we are reading,[19] or how he might have visited his German lover for a second time in Berlin during the 1930s.[20] Yet this emphasis on the hypothetical, the imaginary projection of the lives of others, is always spurred on by material objects or documents, such as a sepia photograph of the father together with Anne Ernst, leading the narrator to speculations and inquiries.

Finally, and most importantly for our concerns here, the history of the search for the secret brother is paralleled with the relationship to a second brother, Domingos, called Mimmo, who is sequestered during the dictatorship. The narrator has a highly ambivalent relation to this brother, from whom he 'inherits' a series of girlfriends and who comes across as rather frivolous. He keeps a photo of this ill-loved brother, who is a 'desaparecido' and therefore remains 'eternally young, like the person of a novel'.[21] The novel even creates scenes where the two brothers are confused, thus further reinforcing the parallels between the two 'disappeared' brothers, as well as the peculiar conditions pertaining to Nazi Germany during the 1930s and the Brazilian dictatorship during the 1970s. The fate of the disappeared Brazilian brother thus serves for the narrator as an incitement to track down the history of his German brother: 'And I, who never have died out of love for that brother, I who would have exchanged him for a German brother without batting an eyelid, came to be confronted with the threat of having no brother at all'.[22]

Long after the disappearance of the brother, the members of the police force, surviving from the dictatorship, have an interest to foster with 'futile hopes' the belief that the lost brother Mimmo might still be alive. This aspect of unlikely and maddening hopes regarding the disappeared, as fictions deliberately engineered by the secret police, is used with great psychological acumen also in Kucinski's novel. Chico Buarque's novel, on the other hand, lays greater emphasis on the ways in which the absence of the lost brother engenders fictional projections on the part of the narrating auto-fictional subject. In the culminating scene of the novel, when the narrator finally sits in the UFA (Universal Film AG) studios of Babelsberg and is presented with a black and white film of his German brother, his first thought is that this man named Sergio Günther may in fact be his lost Brazilian brother, Mimmo – although, in reality, the identity of this other Sergio as his father's hidden son is actually confirmed:

> There even went an idea through my head that Sergio Günther was the actual Mimmo, with thirty years of age, exiled in East Berlin with a nebulous past and a false name. But as the camera zoomed in closer on Sergio, the more I saw in him the oblong face, the potato-like nose, and even the eyes of my father. ... And if I'm not mistaken, his beak was like mine, when he set out to whistle a sad melody, with a potent and precise hiss of which few are capable as I am.[23]

Towards the end of the novel, we find the narrator spending some days in the Adlon Hotel in Berlin, now coming close to the discovery of the fate of his German brother. Incidentally he spends the evening reading a book ('with never-ending paragraphs') which he would have liked his father to have been able to read, something that is impossible since we come to understand that this must be a novel by W.G. Sebald (paratextual evidence confirms it is *Austerlitz*, 2001). This at first appears to be an arbitrary detail, yet it is possible to recognize here the implicit poetics of the novel: similar to Sebald, Chico Buarque has incorporated in this novel facsimiles of documents and photos that appear to validate the historical truth of the narrative, in conjunction with the auto-fictional set-up. Similar to the poetics of Sebald, the inclusion of documentary elements coexists with signals of the text's deliberate fictionality.

The novels by Kucinski and Buarque, then, work with a transnational dimension that foregrounds an underlying parallel between the anti-Semitic persecutions of the Nazi regime and the experience of 'disappeared' and tortured relatives during the Brazilian dictatorship (1964–85). Both Kucinski (born 1937) and Chico Buarque (born 1944) belong to a generation that experienced the Brazilian dictatorship and that went for some time into European exile. As a consequence, their auto-fictional involvement focuses on the psychic investment, and perhaps the survivor guilt with respect to their siblings.

The Younger Generation: Cono Sur

The generational perspective is important also with regard to other Latin American countries, where recent works by younger authors have explored the distinct forms of Latin American dictatorship and political violence from a transgenerational perspective. In this scenario, typically, the current generation's relation to the past is necessarily fragmentary, full of lacunae, and often prompted by the death of, or alienation from, the parent figure, and can only be imagined as a process of intergenerational interrogation and mediation of witnesses and sources. Moreover, given the present generation's distance from the past, there is often the wish to overcome this past, to no longer be determined by it – even as the narrator ultimately insists on the continued relevance of the past and the transgenerational legacy for the life-world of the younger generation. This means not only that the reader's perception of family history is filtered through the subjective, perspectival focus of a narrating 'I', but that the narrative play with fiction and reality is mediated dialectically by way of a deliberate engagement with the real, which is in turn seen as relevant for the nation's or the subject's coming to terms with its own past.[24] In the following, I will briefly illustrate these points with reference to two recent novels by writers from Chile and Argentina. Both writers were born in the year 1973, and the two novels happen to have been published in the same year, 2011.

The novel *Formas de volver a casa* (*Ways of Going Home*, 2011), by the Chilean author Alejandro Zambra (1973), is distinguished by a focalization through the auto-fictional perspective of a child, who grows up in Chile during the military dictatorship of the 1980s, and hence by a retrospective position of innocence and ignorance vis-à-vis the goings-on of the dictatorship, in this case the regime of Augusto Pinochet. The narrative is framed by the occurrence of two earthquakes in Chile, in March 1985 and February 2010.

The first-person narration is evidently centred in the child's perspective, yet it is filtered through a retrospective reflection on memory and temporal difference, which reads the past via the insight that 'during those times we were just that, secondary characters', *personajes secundarios*, which is also the title of the first part of the novel.[25] Although the members of this younger generation have not been the protagonists of the epoch of dictatorship, the novel vindicates the right and the necessity to tell their own version of the story, more than twenty years after the events. The conversation between the generations thus becomes an attempt to retrieve and expose the silences and secrets of history, which constitute a sort of haunting absence/presence:[26]

> The decade of the nineties was the time of questions .... Hours of talking with my parents, I asked them about details, I obliged them

> to remember, and then repeated these memories as if they had been my own; in a terrible, secret manner, I searched for their place in this history .... We asked questions in order to fill a void.[27]

Zambra's novel is noticeable for its sustained meta-fictional exploration of memory: different chapters alternate between the account of the auto-fictional narrator-novelist's youth (and the relation to his love interest Eme) and a fictionalized version of the young boy's experience (and his relation to a girl named Claudia, whom he first meets during the events of the earthquake). Claudia asks the protagonist to watch over her mysterious uncle Raúl, since she cannot see him regularly. Attracted by Claudia, the protagonist carries out this task and reports his observations to Claudia every week. As it turns out, the 'uncle' is really her father, living with a different name and undercover, since he was working clandestinely for the resistance movement. The narrative puts the reader into the innocent and ignorant perspective of the child, yet this perspective is repeatedly shot through with the refracted posterior knowledge of hindsight, often marked by the contrasting adverbs 'entonces' ('back in those times') and 'después' ('afterwards'), or 'ahora' ('now').[28] For instance, the young boy disliked Pinochet as a 'boring character on television', yet 'later' he hated him for being an 'assassin'.[29] Take another example. The protagonist remembers a conversation with a sympathetic school teacher about the possible crime of being a communist. While the school teacher's answer is rendered in the immediate present of dialogue, its content proleptically points towards a moment in the future, which coincides with the conception of the novel we are reading:

> It is not good that you talk about these things, he said to me after having looked at me for quite a while. The only thing that I can say to you is, that we live in a moment in which it is not good to talk about these things. Yet one day we will be able to talk about this and everything.[30]

This co-presence of two different temporal perspectives is complemented with the essential difference of generational experience:

> While the adults killed or were killed, we drew pictures in the corner. While the country was falling to pieces, we were learning to talk, to walk, to fold napkins in the shape of boats, of airplanes. While the novel was happening, we played hide-and-seek, we played at disappearing.[31]

This sort of double confrontation between different realms of experience, both on a personal-biographical and a generational level, is also evident in the novel *El espíritu de mis padres sigue subiendo en la lluvia* (*My Father's Ghost Is Climbing in the Rain*, 2011), by the Argentine writer Patricio Pron, where, in contrast to Zambra, the parent generation exemplifies political resistance.[32] The young auto-fictional protagonist returns from a sojourn in Germany to Argentina in order to confront his dying father, and thus also the relation to his own country, the memories of which he had for a long time subdued with medication and drugs. The filial relation to the father hinges on a feeling of personal, political and generational disconnect, pointing to a 'silent war that had been his and his entire generation's'.[33] The protagonist's deceased father has left behind piles of newspaper clippings and documents, referring to the mysterious murder of one Alberto Burdisso, who, like his sister Alicia, a former friend of the father, had 'disappeared' during the military dictatorship of the 1970s.

The son's quest to make sense of the documentary material becomes simultaneously a quest to make sense of the life of his father. As it turns out, both of his parents had been members of the non-militant, oppositional organization Guardia de Hierro.[34] The quest-structure, which is reflected and reiterated by the reader's confrontation, in the second part of the novel, with the largely 'unfiltered' exposure of journalistic material from the region of Treból in which the disappearance had occurred (including quotations, statistics and interviews), amounts to the opening up of the 'folder' ('carpeta'),[35] the dossier on Burdisso assembled by the father. The idea of the quest is explicitly formulated by a sentence from the first chapter of the novel that may be said to be emblematic for this specific genre of transgenerational literature: 'One day, I suppose, at a certain moment, the children feel the necessity to know who their parents were, and they throw themselves into finding out the truth. The children are the detectives of their parents, ...'.[36] Moreover, the novel creates a transgenerational echo or parallel, insofar as the detective work of the son repeats and complements the original search of the father, which thus becomes part of his own mystery: '...there was a symmetry, namely one according to which I was searching for my father and my father was witnessing the search for another person, of a person that he might have known and who had disappeared'.[37] The novel harps on the idea of symmetry by also applying this to the fact that the two disappeared were siblings and that the narrator's father knew both.[38]

Similar to Zambra's novel, Pron's work is composed of a large number of sometimes extremely short fragments, the unresolved juxtaposition of different textual formats and voices, which has the effect of halting the narrative flow and instead focuses on discrete, almost autonomous scenes that circle around a central enigma and approach it from different angles. Characteristically, the fragmentary form of the text echoes the fragmentary, flash-like nature of memory itself.[39] A central, self-conscious image for the novel's poetics is the idea of photography, as when the narrator encounters an old photograph of his father, showing him at an age before his son knew him, an image that amplified the physical traits of the father into abstract dots.[40] Photography, specifically the technique of 'blow-up', thus becomes a metaphor for a (literary) reality-bound representation of the truth, which is at the same time surrounded by an enigmatic mystery, in this case the unknowability of one's own father.

If the narrator repeatedly comes back to the point that the children are the detectives of their parents, this leads also to a meta-literary observation which precisely seeks to guard against the temptation to write the novel with the generic conventions of a detective novel, and instead invokes the idea of an unfinished puzzle ('un puzzle inacabado')[41] that needs to be completed by the reader. In a later passage, the narrator again invokes the genre of detective fiction, yet explicitly rejects it as a literary model, for this recourse to convention would 'betray' the anti-conventional intentions of his father.[42] The rhetorical defiance of such generic stereotypes is precisely what creates a sort of reality effect, since it points to something that is incommensurable with the machinery of generic plotting.[43] The novel proposes itself as a search for truth, yet for this truth to be open towards the life-world of the reader, it cannot simply be solved and laid to rest, and thus betray the struggle of the father:

> … For to narrate his history in the manner of a detective tale would merely contribute to ratify the existence of a system of genres, that is, of a convention, and this would mean to betray his struggles, which aimed at putting these conventions into question, the social ones, as its pale reflection in literature.[44]

In other words, the very form of Pron's novel aims to avoid the trivialization of turning the socio-political struggles of the past into 'literature'. The son's investigation is paralleled with our experience of reading the novel, a novel true to the legacy of his father, structured like 'a minimal theme repeated a number of times as in a symphony'.[45] The meta-fictional conceit of the novel is motivated by a desire for, as well as an impossibility of, generational continuity, leading the narrator to the realization of an essentially political and explicitly national legacy, namely the 'sensation to stand united in defeat, parents and children',[46] thus transcending the fundamental generational differences.

As in Zambra, this memorial investigation accords a fundamental role to the imagination in its pursuit to complement the nation's representation of history and thus to propose an alternative, more open-ended approach to historical truth in the context of a wider discursive constellation and of conflictive memories. As Geoffrey Maguire has argued, 'the works of many of this generation emphasize the breakdown of family narratives through the rupture of a generational heritage and thus problematize the "already resolved" issues of testimonial coherence'.[47] The 'performative index of post-memory',[48] shaped by affects and desires, points to 'the continual tension between memory and history', as well as the creative potential and continued meaning for the protagonist's present sense of identity. The central paradox and propulsion resides in the narrator's question of 'what would my father think of my telling this story – the story of all of us – without really knowing the facts, with dozens of loose ends?'[49] This paradox, then, is forcing the narrator (and, by implication, the reader) to be both 'author and reader' of the story,[50] assuming the position of a child who impossibly speaks for its father. The doubts about one's own authority to speak from a position of half-ignorance and hearsay are vindicated by the assertion that the story's 'right to exist is guaranteed by the fact that it is also my story'.[51]

I want to end these reflections by pointing out that Zambra and Pron, as representatives of a younger generation, focus on an inter-generational and hence more present-oriented perspective, while the somewhat older Brazilian writers discussed above tend to privilege the representation of a multidirectional memory, which here amounts to a largely past-oriented resonance of the Brazilian dictatorship with the German history of 1930s Nazism. Aside from the different temporal frameworks and perspectives, what seems relevant from a broader perspective is the fact that all the novels I have discussed here can be said to be symptomatic of a self-consciously 'post-postmodern literature', characterized by an auto- and often also meta-fictional transformation of social, biographical and historical realities.[52] These texts are concerned with the traces and traumas of the real and of the past in the present, but also with the reconstructive efforts of a subject or implicit narrator; they are distinguished by a common interest in the hypothetical, that is, an imaginative extension of the real, grounded in the notion of the self as the locus of lived experience and reflexivity. Especially in the case of the younger authors, the narrators insist on the representative quality of their subject-centred accounts: 'Es la historia de mi generación'.[53]

Jobst Welge is a professor in the Department of Romance Studies at Universität Leipzig. His most recent book publication is *Genealogical Fictions: Cultural Periphery and Historical Change in the Modern Novel* (Baltimore, 2015). He has authored related articles on Latin American memory politics, as well as on modernist and postmodern literature from Argentina and Brazil, in particular.

Notes

1. J. Welge, *Genealogical Fictions: Cultural Periphery and Historical Change in the Modern Novel* (Baltimore, MD: Johns Hopkins University Press, 2014).
2. M. Hirsch, *Family Frames: Photography, Narrative and Postmemory* (Cambridge, MA: Harvard University Press, 1997), 106. Cf. Hirsch, 'The Generation of Postmemory', *Poetics Today* 29(1) (2008), 103–28.
3. J. Assmann, *Das kulturelle Gedächtnis: Schrift, Erinnerung und kulturelle Identität in frühen Hochkulturen* (Munich: C.H. Beck, 2007).
4. On imagination and the crisis of testimony, see M. Seligmann-Silva, 'Narrar o trauma: Escrituras híbridas das catástrofes', *Niterói* 24 (2008), 102–4. For the theoretical discussions surrounding the representation of the Holocaust, see A. Huyssen, *Twilight Memories: Marking Time in a Culture of Amnesia* (New York, 1995); E. Bouju, *La Transcription de l'histoire: Essai sur le roman européen de la fin du XXe siècle* (Rennes, 2006).
5. S. Carter, 'Next Generation Latin American Fiction: What Happens when the Dictators Are Gone?', *The New Republic*, 27 May 2012.
6. M. Alberca, '¿Existe la autoficción hispanoamericana?', *CUADERNOS DEL CILHA* 7/8 (2005–06). Retrieved 20 December 2018 from http://bdigital.uncu.edu.ar/objetos_digitales/1095/albercacilha78.pdf.
7. B. Kucinski, *K. Relato de uma busca* (São Paolo: Cosac Naify, 2014 [2011]), 36. All translations, unless otherwise noted, are my own.
8. Ibid., 35. On the mediated nature of memory in contemporary fiction, see A. Erll, 'Narratology and Cultural Memory Studies', in S. Heinen and R. Sommer (eds), *Narratology in the Age of Cross-Disciplinary Narrative Research* (Berlin: Walter de Gruyter, 2009).
9. Kucinski, *K. Relato de uma busca*, 79.
10. Ibid., 151.
11. M. Rothberg, *Multidirectional Memory in the Age of Decolonization* (Stanford, CA: Stanford University Press, 2009). On the post-national significance of the Holocaust and its 'metaphorical' deployments, see A.S. Gross and S. Rohr (eds), *Comedy-Avantgarde-Scandal: Remembering the Holocaust after the End of History* (Heidelberg: Winter, 2010).
12. Kucinski, *K. Relato de uma busca*, 15.

13. For a discussion of this relation to reality as a general feature of contemporary literature, see R. Donnarumma, *Ipermodernità: Dove va la narrativa contemporanea* (Bologna: il Mulino, 2014), 175–77.
14. C. Buarque, *O irmão alemão* (São Paolo: Companhia das Letras, 2014).
15. See E. Achermann, 'Von Fakten und Pakten: Referieren in fiktionalen und autobiografischen Texten', in M. Wagner-Egelhaaf (ed.), *Auto(r) fiktion: Literarische Verfahren der Selbstkonstruktion* (Bielefeld: Aisthesis, 2013), 23–54; C. Gronemann, 'L'autofiction ou le moi dans la chaîne des signifiants: de la constitution littéraire du sujet autobiographique chez Serge Doubrovsky', in A. de Toro and C. Gronemann (eds), *Autobiographie Revisited: Theorie und Praxis neuer autobiographischer Diskurse in der französischen, spanischen und lateinamerikanischen Literatur* (Hildesheim: Georg Olms, 2004), 153–76.
16. A. del Vecchio de Lima, 'Aspectos da Escrita contemporânea em *O Irmão alemão*, de Chico Buarque', *Inventário* 17 (2015), 1–12 (3).
17. Buarque, *O irmão alemão*, 148.
18. Ibid., 149.
19. Ibid., 150.
20. Ibid., 207.
21. Ibid., 197.
22. Ibid., 160.
23. Ibid., 226.
24. For this dialectic between meta-literary self-reflection and 'the will to talk about the world', as representative for the best in contemporary fiction, see Donnarumma, *Ipermodernità*, 62.
25. A. Zambra, *Formas de volver a casa* (Barcelona: Anagrama, 2011), 58.
26. Cf. G. Schwab, *Haunting Legacies: Violent Histories and Transgenerational Trauma* (New York: Columbia University Press, 2010), 13: 'The processing of trauma and transgenerational haunting, even after collective histories of war or genocide, is always mediated through intensely private individual histories. Family legacies of transgenerational haunting often operate through family secrets and other forms of silencing. Such silences and secrets inevitably affect artistic forms and modes of production and representation in second-generation narratives about the legacies of violent histories'.
27. Zambra, *Formas de volver a casa*, 115.
28. Ibid., 23.
29. Ibid., 20–21.
30. Ibid., 40.
31. Ibid., 57.
32. P. Pron, *El espíritu de mis padres sigue subiendo en la lluvia* (Barcelona: Mondadori, 2011).
33. Ibid., 23.
34. Ibid., 166.
35. Ibid., 57.

36. Ibid., 12. For another novelistic example of the trope of the detective in this type of quest fiction, see also F. Bruzzone, *Los topos* (Buenos Aires: Mondadori, 2008).
37. Pron, *El espíritu de mis padres*, 60.
38. Ibid., 96.
39. B. Sarlo, *Tiempo pasado: Cultura de la memoria y giro subjetivo. Una discusión* (Buenos Aires: Siglo Veintiuno Editores, 2005), 136.
40. Pron, *El espíritu de mis padres*, 52, 93.
41. Ibid., 143.
42. Ibid., 142–43.
43. I follow here F. Jameson, *The Antinomies of Realism* (London: Verso, 2013), 7.
44. Pron, *El espíritu de mis padres*, 143.
45. Ibid., 136.
46. Ibid., 39; cf. 184.
47. See G. Maguire, 'Bringing Memory Home: Historical (Post)Memory and Patricio Pron's *El espíritu de mis padres sigue subiendo en la lluvia*', *Journal of Latin American Cultural Studies* 23(2) (2014), 211–28.
48. Cf. Hirsch, *Family Frames*, 124.
49. Pron, *El espíritu de mis padres*, 145.
50. Ibid., 144.
51. Ibid., 190.
52. On this 'return of the real' in Latin American literature, see J. Welge, 'Reality, Fiction, and the Limits of Postmodernity in the Contemporary Novel: The Case of Bernardo Carvalho', in I. Hron (ed.), *Einheitsdenken: Figuren von Ganzheit, Präsenz und Transzendenz nach der Postmoderne* (Nordhausen: Traugott Bautz, 2015), 105–22.
53. Zambra, *Formas de volver a casa*, 96. Cf. Pron, *El espíritu de mis padres*, 168, 184.

Bibliography

Achermann, E. 'Von Fakten und Pakten: Referieren in fiktionalen und autobiografischen Texten', in M. Wagner-Egelhaaf (ed.), *Auto(r)fiktion: Literarische Verfahren der Selbstkonstruktion* (Bielefeld: Aisthesis, 2013), 23–54.

Alberca, M. '¿Existe la autoficción hispanoamericana?', *CUADERNOS DEL CILHA* 7/8 (2005–06). Retrieved 20 December 2018 from http://bdigital.uncu.edu.ar/objetos_digitales/1095/albercacilha78.pdf.

Assmann, J. *Das kulturelle Gedächtnis: Schrift, Erinnerung und kulturelle Identität in frühen Hochkulturen*. Munich: C.H. Beck, 2007.

Bouju, E. *La Transcription de l'histoire: Essai sur le roman européen de la fin du XXe siècle*. Rennes, 2006.

Bruzzone, F. *Los topos*. Buenos Aires: Mondadori, 2008.

Buarque, C. *O irmão alemão*. São Paolo: Companhia das Letras, 2014.

Carter, S. 'Next Generation Latin American Fiction: What Happens when the Dictators Are Gone?' *The New Republic*, 27 May 2013.

Donnarumma, R. *Ipermodernità: Dove va la narrativa contemporanea*. Bologna: il Mulino, 2014.

Erll, A. 'Narratology and Cultural Memory Studies', in S. Heinen and R. Sommer (eds), *Narratology in the Age of Cross-Disciplinary Narrative Research* (Berlin: Walter de Gruyter, 2009).

Gronemann, C. 'L'autofiction ou le moi dans la chaîne des signifiants: de la constitution littéraire du sujet autobiographique chez Serge Doubrovsky', in A. de Toro and C. Gronemann (eds), *Autobiographie Revisited: Theorie und Praxis neuer autobiographischer Diskurse in der französischen, spanischen und lateinamerikanischen Literatur* (Hildesheim: Georg Olms, 2004), 153–76.

Gross, A.S., and Rohr, S. (eds). *Comedy-Avantgarde-Scandal: Remembering the Holocaust after the End of History*. Heidelberg: Winter, 2010.

Hirsch, M. *Family Frames: Photography, Narrative and Postmemory*. Cambridge, MA: Harvard University Press, 1997.

Hirsch, M. 'The Generation of Postmemory'. *Poetics Today* 29(1) (2008), 103–28.

Huyssen, A. *Twilight Memories: Marking Time in a Culture of Amnesia*. New York, 1995.

Jameson, F. *The Antinomies of Realism*. London: Verso, 2013.

Kucinski, B. *K. Relato de uma busca*. São Paolo: Cosac Naify, 2014 [2011].

Maguire, G. 'Bringing Memory Home: Historical (Post)Memory and Patricio Pron's *El espíritu de mis padres sigue subiendo en la lluvia*'. *Journal of Latin American Cultural Studies* 23(2) (2014), 211–28.

Pron, P. *El espíritu de mis padres sigue subiendo en la lluvia*. Barcelona: Mondadori, 2011.

Rothberg, M. *Multidirectional Memory in the Age of Decolonization*. Stanford, CA: Stanford University Press, 2009.

Sarlo, B. *Tiempo pasado: Cultura de la memoria y giro subjetivo. Una discusión*. Buenos Aires: Siglo Veintiuno Editores, 2005.

Schwab, G. *Haunting Legacies: Violent Histories and Transgenerational Trauma*. New York: Columbia University Press, 2010.

Seligmann-Silva, M. 'Narrar o trauma: Escrituras híbridas das catástrofes'. *Niterói* 24 (2008), 101–17.

Vásquez, J.G. *El ruido de las cosas al caer*. México: Alfaguara, 2011.

Vecchio de Lima, A. d. 'Aspectos da escrita contemporânea em *O Irmão alemão*, de Chico Buarque'. *Inventário* 17 (2015), 1–12.

Welge, J. *Genealogical Fictions: Cultural Periphery and Historical Change in the Modern Novel*. Baltimore, MD: Johns Hopkins University Press, 2014.

Welge, J. 'Reality, Fiction, and the Limits of Postmodernity in the Contemporary Novel: The Case of Bernardo Carvalho', in I. Hron (ed.), *Einheitsdenken: Figuren von Ganzheit, Präsenz und Transzendenz nach der Postmoderne* (Nordhausen: Traugott Bautz, 2015), 105–22.

Welge, J. 'Transgenerationelle Erinnerung in der argentinischen und brasilianischen Gegenwartsliteratur (Sergio Chejfec, Michel Laub)', in E. Kilchmann (ed.), *Artefrakte: Holocaust und Zweiter Weltkrieg in experimentellen Darstellungsverfahren in Literatur und Kunst* (Cologne and Vienna: Böhlau, 2016), 269–82.

Zambra, A. *Formas de volver a casa*. Barcelona: Anagrama, 2011.

Part III

Truth Commissions between the Global and the Local

Section 1

Truth Commissions' Worldwide Dispersion and Function

Chapter 15

Reconfigurations of Transitional Justice in the Wake of the Arab Uprisings

Global, Regional and Local Developments

Fatima Kastner

When the Tunisian street vendor Mohamed Bouazizi set himself on fire on 17 December 2010, he may not have intended to trigger a social-political tsunami that swept across North Africa and the Middle East (MENA), leaving behind fallen authoritarian regimes and former dictators dethroned, imprisoned or even lynched. However, among the reasons that might have forced him into such an act of despair was his bitter hunger for justice and a better life. His dramatic self-immolation was a hopeless call for humanity that was shared by a multitude of protesters throughout the Arab world, who then generated that revolutionary wave that is referred to as the 'Arab Spring'. Although each individual protester represents a unique human being with specific personal experiences of injustice, what is common to all demonstrators across the region are the grave human rights violations committed by the former regimes during their hold on power. Facing these dramatic popular uprisings and the following delicate transitional phase, in which the old order did indeed fall but has not yet completely vanished, socio-legal scholars from Arab and Western countries have emphasized the need to initiate processes of political transitions in accordance with the global transitional justice model in order to help post-revolution societies overcome their precarious situation of passage from authoritarianism and dictatorship to a new order of society. By this means, according to the general reasoning, they can determine how best to address systematic abuses of human rights committed in the past and during the time of transition in order to reconcile divided societies, strengthen democratic institution-building and to realize a new and just social order, which is above all worth living.[1]

However, by general definition, classical judicial transitional justice instruments such as ad-hoc, special and hybrid international criminal tribunals, or non-judicial restorative and restitutive mechanisms, such as commissions of inquiry, truth and reconciliation commissions, lustration policies and reparation programmes, can be set up only when severe injustice and systematic human rights abuses, as typically practised during periods of dictatorship, autocratic suppression and civil war, have come to an end.[2] This means that transitional justice can only be put to work after a certain regime change and a political process of consolidation have already taken place, or at least after a somehow pacified and stabilized social environment has been realized.[3] This includes, for example, the replacement of governments and the renewal of important state bodies and institutions such as the security services and the judicial system in order to provide grounds for processes of reconciliation, democratization and the establishment of the rule of law.[4] In the case of the post-'Arab Spring' societies, some former government leaders did indeed fall and new executive powers took their place, but overall, the hopes and dreams of most of the protesters did not come true. In fact, some turned into true nightmares, as documented by the exodus of hundreds of thousands of Syrians and other refugees from the MENA region to Northern Europe, fleeing the deadly threats of civil war, systematic terrorism and inhuman living conditions in their own countries.

However, the transitions being experienced in the aftermath of the Arab uprisings are not finished yet, and the future of most of these fragile state entities that have seen some kind of regime change appears to be more than just uncertain.[5] Even though some political reforms and transitional justice strategies have already been launched in countries like Tunisia, Bahrain, Yemen and Egypt, observers are quite sceptical about the short-term results, since transitional justice instruments are highly time-consuming measures.[6] One illustrative example of this is certainly Argentina and the decades-long fight of its civil society against painful silence and imposed impunity concerning the perpetrators and those responsible for the mass crimes committed during the former military regime in the years 1976–83. It clearly shows that post-conflict justice sometimes can only be achieved, if at all, after decades of efforts to combat politics of repression and systematic human rights abuses by means of domestic as well as international criminal tribunals, including regional human rights courts.[7] Thus, given this function of time in regard to the possible effectiveness of transitional justice mechanisms, it might be simply too early to evaluate the outcomes of transitional justice policies in post-'Arab Spring' societies, at least from today's perspective. However, how would it be the other way around? Have the Arab uprisings altered the discourse of socio-legal studies on transitional justice? Have any lessons been learned from the extraordinary revolutionary transitions in the MENA region? Could they potentially even have an effect on future attempts at justice in transition?

In the following, I will try to give a tentative answer to these questions. Given the embryonic status of most of the social transitions in the region, it is of no surprise that I have to highlight the speculative nature of my statements. However, after a short historical overview of the emergence of the normative concept of transitional justice as a global model of dealing with systematic human rights abuses, I will first outline the crucial steps in developments that have shaped today's understanding of transitional justice as a certain set of legal and non-legal means that count as tools with which to foster post-conflict justice and enable democratic institution-building as well as processes of reconciliation in any specific transitional society in the world. In a second step, I then ask whether and to what extent the processes of transitions experienced so far in the aftermath of the Arab uprisings have challenged or modified this general liberal understanding of the present global transitional justice model. Lastly, in a third step, I will reflect on some possible learning effects from the ongoing dynamic processes in the MENA region that might enlarge the existing toolbox of transitional justice and thereby expand or eventually even transform socio-legal discourse on transitional justice.

Lex Transitus: On the Global Diffusion of Transitional Justice in World Society

The normative concept of transitional justice emerged historically in the period after the geopolitical caesura of 1945. Its first appearance resulted from the exceptional context of the institutionalization of the international criminal tribunals at Nuremberg and Tokyo after the Second World War. Although some legal scholars have criticized the ambiguous legality of these trials, which contradicted fundamental moral principles in international criminal law such as 'nullum crimen sine lege', the lasting influence of this first attempt to implement transitional justice cannot be questioned today.[8] Indeed, in the following years international criminal courts were established to conduct transitional justice trials that relied strongly on the legal principles that had been created by the international tribunals of Nuremberg and Tokyo.

Both tribunals dealt with war crimes committed before and during the war by the former leaders of the warring parties, Germany and Japan. From the very beginning, the trials were tainted by the desire to punish and replace former members of the Nazi regime and the Japanese empire who were considered most responsible for systematic or widespread human rights violations, and to establish international law as a new tool in determining the accountability of individual actions as well as international aggression.[9] Notably, the latter, with the invention of a new legal principle called 'crimes against humanity', set a novel precedent that had never been used before in international human and humanitarian law and therewith initiated an extraordinarily dynamic chain of legal and institutional developments in the post-war era that radically changed the very nature of the international legal system.[10] Since that time, numerous international criminal courts have been created on a global level to deal with large-scale human rights violations, including, for example, the international extraordinary tribunals for the former Yugoslavia, Rwanda, Cambodia, East Timor, Liberia and Sierra Leone. Following the massive waves of societal and political transitions that occurred in Latin America, Central and Eastern Europe, and Africa in the early 1980s, these bodies were institutionalized with the goal of achieving recognition for victims and bringing the perpetrators of abuses to justice, with the broader additional aims of promoting peace, the development of democratic institutions, and the rule of law. Other post-conflict, post-authoritarian and post-dictatorial countries, such as Argentina after the end of the military dictatorship, South Africa after the end of the apartheid regime, and Morocco after the end of the so-called 'Years of Lead', used truth and reconciliation commissions to deal with their violent pasts. Such commissions have also been established in other states in transition with a history of repressive rule, including South Korea, the Solomon Islands, El Salvador, Ghana and the Fiji Islands. The general goal of transitional justice tools, be these ad-hoc international criminal tribunals or truth and reconciliation commissions, is to overcome the former repressive suppressive state system by contributing to politics of human rights, democratization and national reconciliation.[11]

Since the end of the Cold War, international organizations such as the United Nations, the European Union and the World Bank have increasingly acknowledged these politics of dealing with past human rights violations by, for example, granting public sector loans and supporting economic development dependent on specific transitional justice policies. Not least due to these redefined lending conditions and standards of development aid from international donors, dealing with past human rights violations has become a global model for action in world society that has taken the transitional justice model from its beginnings as a normative exception to its present status as a global political rule.[12]

While international organizations have played a key role in the global proliferation of the transitional justice model, the International Center for Transitional Justice (ICTJ), a transnationally operating NGO, has served as a further very influential creator and disseminator of this normative concept. This NGO has its headquarters in New York, but also maintains regional offices in Europe, Latin America, Asia, Africa, the Maghreb region and the Near East. In establishing the ICTJ in March 2001, its creators laid the foundations for a global culture of post-conflict justice.[13] The ICTJ has monitored political transitions with the aim of promoting peace, bolstering rule of law reforms, and supporting democratic governance in more than fifty countries worldwide. It has collaborated in creating and implementing international criminal tribunals, truth and reconciliation commissions, and other alternative instruments of transitional justice in post-conflict societies around the globe.[14] ICTJ staff members make their expertise in dealing with past systematic human rights abuses and state-rebuilding after political transitions available not only to local protest groups, but also to national and international institutions such as national human rights organizations, the European Union and the United Nations.[15] They advise diplomats and legal scholars in matters related to the judicialization of transition issues, and help social interest groups, research organizations and governments with the work of reconstructing and documenting human rights violations, as well as preparing and using databases and archives. They provide information on survey methods and techniques for interviewing victims, train people to work with witnesses, and help establish witness protection programmes. ICTJ members also offer advice on conducting public hearings and contribute to the development of programmes providing restitution and compensation for victims. Their work now also includes consultation on the creation of memorial and commemorative sites, and on formulating and implementing recommendations for political and structural reforms after the respective transitional justice instruments have completed their work. The accumulation and global dissemination of this special expertise in dealing with past state-aided human rights violations has also been reflected in a series of notable international conferences, guidelines and resolutions of the United Nations on the normative concept of transitional justice, which even led the United Nations to declare 2009 the International Year of Reconciliation.[16] As a matter of fact, transitional justice is now viewed as a key element of the United Nations' toolbox for dealing with post-conflict issues, with the United Nations Department of Peacekeeping even having established a new Security Sector Reform and Transitional Justice Unit.[17] This has further promoted and solidified the process of transnational networking, professionalization and standardization in the realm of activities related to dealing with past human rights violations. In sum, the enlarged normative concept of transitional justice has become a conventional instrument for dealing with the past, which has spread globally thanks to the consultation and training programmes of the ICTJ and the launching of countless academic journals and books, new research institutes at universities, and other highly specialized international, transnational and local NGOs in the field of post-conflict justice.[18]

As a result of the formation of this increasingly dense context of know-how transmission, a world political arena has emerged in which various actors involved in the politics of dealing with the past appear as protagonists and disseminators of specific norms, standards and institutions of transitional justice. Within this multidimensional, constantly self-reinforcing transnational social field, a functionally specified global legal regime of transitional justice has emerged to advocate the following: firstly, institutionalized international normative expectations, such as the obligation of the international legal system to investigate past state-aided human rights violations and the victim's right to truth; secondly, behavioural routines and post-conflict measures, such as victim-oriented processes of truth-seeking, and reparation and reconciliation programmes; and, thirdly, standardized non-judicial institutions, such as historical commissions of inquiry, truth commissions, and truth and reconciliation commissions, as well as judicial institutions such as ad-hoc international and hybrid criminal tribunals.[19]

The creation of the International Criminal Court (ICC) in 2002, a permanent and independent supranational judicial body that prosecutes the perpetrators of war crimes, genocide and crimes against humanity – when national courts of the contracting state parties are either unwilling or unable to deal with these crimes – so far represents the ultimate culmination of this ongoing process of evolution of the normative concept of transitional justice into a global legal regime, which I have called 'Lex Transitus' in reference to scholarly works that address in critical and analytical fashion the changing frames of normative orders under the structural conditions of globalization.[20]

Moreover, in the course of this process, we can observe the world cultural institutionalization of a form of cosmopolitan ethics that resembles what was described in connection with the Holocaust and the moral outcomes of the Nuremberg and Tokyo tribunals as the increasing consolidation of a global morality and the associated moral imperative of memory, atonement and commemoration.[21] States' approaches to past state-aided atrocities, war and genocide are now directed by global institutional models that dictate extremely ritualized procedures for confronting past human rights violations. In the context of this global diffusion of discourses and practices of remembering and dealing with violent pasts, the actors involved – individuals as well as collective actors – are constantly observed and evaluated by a transnational civil society network. Even if they merely stage a superficial show of compliance with world cultural norms, standards and institutions of transitional justice, as is the case in many post-conflict states, they are nevertheless confirming them even against their own political will.[22] As part of a general process of the dissemination of global cultural patterns of behaviour and normative patterns of expectations, which simultaneously overlays the dominant functional structures of global society and the international political system of nation states, transitional justice tools can be described, at least from a macro-sociological point of view, as transcultural transformers. One should take care not to overestimate the evolutionary potential of their broad sociocultural effects, but we should also not make the mistake of underestimating them.[23] Only then will we also gain an explanation for the exceedingly remarkable phenomenon that – despite the empirical fact of the global diffusion of the normative concept of transitional justice and with it the worldwide proliferation of specific norms, standards and institutions of post-conflict justice – to date there has not been a single case in which, quite literally, the work of dealing with past systematic crimes has been 'successful'.[24]

Reconfigurations of Transitional Justice Emerging from the 'Arab Spring' Experiences

Transitional justice has become a conventional global model for action in dealing with past systematic human rights violations. As a result of the different manifestations of local contextualization that have occurred worldwide so far, the normative concept has massively changed since its invention after the Second World War from an originally pure, criminal, legal, that is to say, retributive normative concept to a hybrid, that is to say, a restorative cross-societal-oriented post-conflict justice model. This in turn has changed the significant actors working in the field of transitional justice. Initially dominated by professional international lawyers, it is now primarily influenced by human rights activists, diplomats, scholars, policymakers, donors, international organizations and transnational non-governmental organizations, such as the ICTJ. These new and diverse actors in the field of post-conflict justice conceive the aims and mechanisms of transitional justice not primarily in retributive terms, that is to say, from a strictly criminal law and perpetrator-oriented perspective, but also within more holistic cross-societal categories. This hybridization of the concept of transitional justice in the form of an increasing amalgamation of legal and social norms also explains the newly achieved recognition of victims' perspectives within the international criminal law system, as well as the redefined central role of victims within the framework of transitional justice policies.[25] Indeed, one of the decisive new institutional elements of the transitional justice concept are truth and reconciliation commissions, where the central procedural focus of investigation no longer lies on the crimes committed by former perpetrators, but on the testimonials provided by the victims and the harm they endured. The severe and controversial socio-legal debates that accompanied the implementation of these victim-oriented commissions as a non-judicial means of confronting the needs of post-conflict societies in transitional contexts have mirrored the dynamic, adaptive and hybrid nature of the normative concept of transitional justice in a very demonstrative manner. This is also one of the reasons why the enlarged normative concept is frequently criticized as having a corrosive effect on the international legal system's values rather than fostering universal principles.[26] In particular, the controversial discussion on accountability as one of the key aspects of the international criminal legal justice system, which notably ensures that those responsible for massive crimes committed in the past are held accountable for their wrongdoings, as well as the continuing debate on non-Western notions of finding justice for past abuses that accompanied the installation of the South African Truth and Reconciliation Commission especially, strongly unsettled and rearranged the field of transitional justice studies. To take a case in point, during the suspense-packed course of the South African transition process, leading figures such as Archbishop Desmond Tutu and Nelson Mandela emphasized the need for a genuinely African approach to transitional justice, primarily by focusing on social forgiveness and collective healing guided by a local justice concept called *Ubuntu*.[27] They argued that a localized manifestation of transitional justice was very much needed in this context, since purely individual prosecutions along the lines of the Western conception of liberal legality would not generate the desired outcome for the entire society. The concept of *Ubuntu* ultimately did indeed have great influence on the societal, political and moral justification for the transitional justice process in post-apartheid South Africa, and was explicitly legally laid down in the first post-apartheid South African constitution of 1993, though the term itself does not appear in today's valid constitution.[28] Quite similar strategies of combining particular local notions of justice with the globally enacted strategies of the international criminal legal system, in the sense of combining locally legitimate rituals of justice and reconciliation with standardized elements of the global transitional justice model, were also carried out in other post-conflict African societies such as Kenya, Uganda and Rwanda.[29] Have any similar genuinely regional approaches to transitional justice emerged from the post-revolution transitions in Arab countries?

Given the short period of time since the outbreak of the popular upheavals in the year 2011, it is surely too early to give any satisfactory answer regarding possible effects that these transitions might have on the normative concept of transitional justice. However, what can be said to date is that current endeavours in the MENA region to initiate politics of transitional justice have been largely shaped by the objective of establishing classical national retributive judicial institutions rather than by mechanisms derived from the global transitional justice model. Aside from some exceptions like the recently established truth commissions in Tunisia and the Kingdom of Morocco, most attempts, such as the trials against former President Mubarak in Egypt and other efforts made in Libya and Yemen, were in fact purely national retributive proceedings.[30]

Following the so-called 'Jasmine Revolution' or the 'Sidi Bouzid Revolt', as it is referred to in the Arab world, the Truth and Dignity Commission in Tunisia was established by law in 2013 and formally launched in 2014 in order to investigate the systematic nature of human rights violations committed by the Tunisian state since 1955. The Commission was given a four-year mandate (2014 to 2018) with the possibility of a one-year extension. Its purpose is to use both judicial and non-judicial mechanisms. The Commission held its first public hearing in Tunis on 17 November 2016. Therefore, possible outcomes are as yet quite uncertain. The other exception is the Kingdom of Morocco with the implementation of the Equity and Reconciliation Commission on behalf of the present monarch Mohammed VI. Its aim was to address gross human rights violations committed during the so-called 'Years of Lead' (1956–99). However, this first attempt at transitional justice in the Arab-Islamic world, which was launched without the country having experienced a regime change or a revolution, was indeed initiated and realized as early as 2004, long before the outbreak of the Arab uprisings.[31]

Given the economic and financial distress and social instability of most of the post-revolution societies, the preference for classical national criminal trials rather than for alternative approaches according to the global transitional justice model might be simply the consequence of the persistence of the old regime's institutions (army, police, judiciary, etc.), or might be due to other particular reasons, like the need to correspond to international obligations.[32]

A vital factor that is shaping current socio-legal debates on transitional justice is the unique feature of the political, cultural and religious aspects of the MENA region. Compared, for example, to the transitions in Latin American societies starting in the early 1980s, in which authoritarian regimes and bloody dictatorships were replaced by a political culture of liberal democracy, post-revolution Arab societies do not seem to share such a political consensus about the best way forward. In fact, the concept of liberal democracy seems to have lost its brilliance, and is no longer seen by a majority of the population as the only solution, but is rather regarded as part of a larger 'neocolonial' problem.[33] This is paired with another unique pattern in the post-revolution Arab societies, notably the rise of so-called political Islam, a long and strongly suppressed religious political movement that is currently disrupting all societies in the Arab world. With the lack of a consensus about a common political strategy, it might also be difficult to define the specific goals of potential processes of transitional justice in post-'Arab Spring' countries. Therefore, possible alterations to the global transitional justice model emerging from the experiences in the aftermath of the Arab uprisings may not be based on liberal Western notions of justice but rather on genuine regional, cultural conditions, such as Islamic morality, Islamic ethics and Islamic law.[34] The resultant challenge for our present understanding of the global transitional justice model is then the question of how and to what extent a combination of these contradicting value systems would indeed be socially applicable. That is to say, how can a generally secular and democratically oriented notion of a genuine liberal transitional justice model indeed engage with some illiberal elements of so-called political Islam, for instance with regard to the rights of religious minorities and gender equality? Though at this point one should also recall that neither religion in general nor the contested category of *Sharia* in particular was originally behind the motives of the protest movements at the outbreak of the Arab uprisings, where there was, on the contrary, an urgent call for universal values and human rights. However, the unexpected collapse of a multitude of totalitarian Arab regimes only allowed the advent of what had been massively oppressed for decades by the former regimes of repression. This could also be an explanation for why there are so many references to *Sharia* in almost all the recently reformed and newly adopted constitutions in post-revolution Arab societies.[35] They show an increasing process of delegitimization of secular concepts of justice and re-legitimization of illiberal elements and religion both as an instrument and as a central goal of politics, which is in fact criticized by local lawyers and human rights activists as well as socio-legal scholars from abroad.[36]

A further peculiarity of the transitions in the MENA region, which is regarded as a centric element that has to be taken into account for future attempts at transitional justice, is the attention being given to the issues of poverty and unemployment as well as corruption and other economic and financial wrongdoings committed during the former authoritarian and dictatorial regimes that drove the revolutions of the 'Arab Spring'.[37] This newly developed access point, which highlights economic injustice and economic problems as important challenges to transitional justice's aims of social peace and reconciliation, could serve as a source for innovative approaches to future attempts at transitional justice, since the conventional global model does indeed prioritize civil and political rights over other rights.[38] Therefore, both legal academia and scholars from the social sciences are increasingly debating the need to expand the current liberal model of transitional justice in the direction of economic crimes, and therewith economic accountability, in order to be able to address the systematic nature of economic abuses and financial criminality. Though at this point one has to admit that current debates about the inclusion of economic and financial wrongdoings in the current international criminal legal system are nascent and are still to be elaborated.[39]

Conclusion and Outlook

In this chapter, I have argued that transitional justice has become a global model for action in dealing with past systematic human rights violations. As a result of the differing social foundations and local contextualization of transitional justice that occurred in a multitude of countries in Latin America, Central and Eastern Europe, Africa,

Asia and Oceania since the early 1980s, the normative concept of transitional justice has undergone continuous change since its invention following the Second World War, evolving from an originally purely perpetrator-oriented retributive legal instrument into a victim-oriented restorative post-conflict justice model. The intense socio-legal debates that accompanied this transformation from an originally pure criminal law model into a more holistic tool that connects legal with social norms mirrored the very dynamic, adaptive and hybrid nature of the normative concept of transitional justice, which has evolved into a functionally specified global legal regime that I call Lex Transitus.

Legal academia and scholars from the social sciences are currently discussing two possible alterations to the present global model of transitional justice emerging from the 'Arab Spring' experiences. One of these changes may be based on regional cultural factors, such as Islamic morality, Islamic ethics and Islamic law. This poses a potential challenge for the present liberal, secular and democracy-oriented conception, insofar as it remains unclear how and to what extent a combination of these contradictory value systems, that is, combining locally legitimate notions of justice with standardized elements of the global transitional justice model, would be socially, politically and legally applicable. A second alteration emerging from the post-uprising transition policies already realized in some Arab countries could be the demand to include economic and financial crimes within the present normative concept of transitional justice. However, it remains to be seen whether these local solutions can or will in fact reconcile divided post-revolution societies in the MENA region and thus have any ability to inspire future attempts at transitional justice.

Fatima Kastner is Professor for Theories of Globalization and Digital Transformation at the Academy of Media Arts Cologne, Germany. Having studied law, philosophy and social sciences at the London School of Economics and Political Science (LSE), UK and the Collège International de Philosophie (CIPh), Paris, France, she holds a Master's and a Doctoral degree from the Goethe-University of Frankfurt am Main, Germany as well as a Habilitation from Bielefeld University, Germany. Before joining the Academy of Media Arts Cologne, Fatima Kastner held the position of a research fellow at the Hamburg Institute for Social Research and worked as Associate Professor at the Universities of Hamburg, Bielefeld and Bonn. Fatima Kastner received several prizes, research grants and scholarships from the Hessian Academic Scholarship Foundation, the German Research Organization (DFG) and the German Federal Ministry of

Education and Research (BMBF). Recently she was awarded the Adam Podgorecki Prize by the Research Committee on Sociology of Law (RCSL) of the International Sociological Association (ISA) in the category 'outstanding achievements in socio-legal research'. Her current research interests include Theories of Globalization, Sociology of Law and Global Constitutionalism, Theory of World Society and World Culture, Transitional Justice and Human Rights, Digital Society and Robot Law. Her publications include: *Academia in Transformation* (Nomos, 2018), *Transitional Justice in der Weltgesellschaft* (Hamburger Edition, 2015), *From Globalization to World Society: Neo-Institutional and Systems-Theoretical Perspectives* (Routledge, 2015) and *Law as a Social System* (Oxford University Press, 2008).

Notes

1. K.J. Fisher and R. Stewart (eds), *Transitional Justice and the Arab Spring* (New York: Routledge, 2014).
2. Compare W.A. Schabas and D. Shane (eds), *Truth Commissions and Courts: The Tension between Criminal Justice and the Search for Truth* (Dordrecht: Kluwer Academic Publishers, 2004). See also R.G. Teitel, *Globalizing Transitional Justice: Contemporary Essays* (Oxford: Oxford University Press, 2015); A. Mihr, 'Regime Consolidation through Transitional Justice in Europe: The Cases of Germany, Spain and Turkey', *The International Journal of Transitional Justice* 11(1) (2017), 113–31.
3. Compare T.D. Olsen, L.A. Payne, and A.G. Reiter (eds), *Transitional Justice in Balance: Comparing Processes, Weighing Efficacy* (Washington, DC: United States Institute of Peace Press, 2010). See also A. Eser, J. Arnold, and H. Kreicker (eds), *Strafrecht in Reaktion auf Systemunrecht: Vergleichende Einblicke in Transitionsprozesse*, Vols 1–14 (Max-Planck-Institut für ausländisches und internationales Strafrecht in Freiburg, 1999–2012).
4. A. Hinton (ed.), *Transitional Justice: Global Mechanisms and Local Realities after Genocide and Mass Violence* (New Brunswick, NJ: Rutgers University Press, 2010). See also S. Engert and A. Jetschke (eds), 'Transitional Justice 2.0', *Journal of International Peace and Organization* 86(1–2) (2011); P. Hazan, 'Beyond Borders: The New Architecture of Transitional Justice?', *The International Journal of Transitional Justice* 11(1) (2017), 1–8.
5. W. Gephart, R. Sakrani, and J. Hellmann (eds), *Legal Cultures in Transition – Rechtskulturen im Übergang: Von Südafrika bis Spanien, von Nachkriegsdeutschland bis zum Aufbruch der arabischen Welt* (Frankfurt am Main: Vittorio Klostermann, 2015).
6. I. Fraihat, *Unfinished Revolutions: Yemen, Libya, and Tunisia after the Arab Spring* (New Haven, CT: Yale University Press, 2016).
7. R.G. Teitel, 'Transitional Justice Genealogy', *Harvard Human Rights Journal* 16 (2003), 69–94. Compare also K. Sikkink, *The Justice Cascade:*

How Human Rights Prosecutions Are Changing World Politics (New York: W.W. Norton and Company, 2011).
8. See Schabas and Shane, *Truth Commissions and Courts*.
9. C. Safferling, *Internationales Strafrecht: Strafanwendungsrecht – Völkerstrafrecht – Europäisches Strafrecht* (Heidelberg and Wiesbaden: Springer, 2011).
10. T. Bonacker and C. Safferling (eds), *Victims of International Crimes: An Interdisciplinary Discourse* (Den Haag: Springer/T.M.C. Asser Press, 2013).
11. Teitel, *Globalizing Transitional Justice*.
12. See F. Kastner, 'Transitional Justice: Von der normativen Ausnahme zur weltpolitischen Regel', in I.-J. Werkner and K. Ebeling (eds), *Handbuch Friedensethik* (Wiesbaden: Springer VS, 2016), 893–902.
13. A. Boraine, 'Transitional Justice: A Holistic Interpretation', *Journal of International Affairs* 60(1) (2006), 19–25. Compare also F. Kastner, 'Retributive versus restaurative Gerechtigkeit: Zur transnationalen Diffusion von Wahrheits- und Versöhnungskommissionen in der Weltgesellschaft', in R. Kreide and A. Niederberger (eds), *Staatliche Souveränität und transnationales Recht* (Munich: Hampp, 2010), 194–211.
14. Transitional justice processes have been initiated to date in: Argentina, Bolivia, Burundi, Brazil, Central African Republic, Chad, Chile, Côte D'Ivoire, Democratic Republic of Congo, Ecuador, El Salvador, Ethiopia, Federal Republic of Yugoslavia, Germany, Ghana, Grenada, Guatemala, Haiti, Indonesia, Liberia, Mexico, Morocco, Nepal, Nigeria, Panama, Paraguay, Peru, Philippines, Tunisia, Sierra Leone, South Africa, South Korea, Sri Lanka, Timor-Leste, Uganda, Uruguay and Zimbabwe. Compare the list provided by the ICTJ, retrieved 5 May 2017 from http://ictj.org/. See also the list provided by the website of the United States Institute of Peace, retrieved 5 May 2017 from http://www.usip.org/library/tc.
15. See F. Kastner, 'Soziologie der Menschenrechte: Zur Universalisierung von Unrechtserfahrungen in der Weltgesellschaft', *Österreichische Zeitschrift für Soziologie* 42(3) (2017), 217–36.
16. Compare the UN resolution A/RES/61/17, adopted by the General Assembly at its 61st session, 23 January 2007, retrieved 5 May 2017 from http://www.un.org/en/ga/search/view_doc.asp?symbol=A/RES/61/17&Lang=E.
17. Retrieved 5 April 2017 from http://www.un.org/en/events/peacekeepersday/pdf/securityreform.pdf.
18. Compare F. Kastner, *Transitional Justice in der Weltgesellschaft* (Hamburg: Hamburger Edition, 2015).
19. Compare Chapter 7 of the United Nations Charter, retrieved 5 May 2017 from http://www.un.org/documents/charter/chapter7.shtml.
20. See G. Teubner, *Verfassungsfragmente: Gesellschaftlicher Konstitutionalismus in der Globalisierung* (Berlin: Suhrkamp Verlag, 2012). See also M. Neves, *Transconstitutionalism* (Oxford and Portland, OR: Hart Publishing, 2013); G.-P. Calliess (ed.), *Transnationales Recht* (Tübingen: Mohr Siebeck, 2014); P.F. Kjaer, *Constitutionalism in the Global Realm: A Sociological Approach* (London and New York: Routledge, 2014);

F. Kastner, 'Lex Transitus: Zur Emergenz eines globalen Rechtsregimes von Transitional Justice in der Weltgesellschaft', *Zeitschrift für Rechtssoziologie* 35(1) (2015), 29–47; C. Thornhill, *A Sociology of Transnational Constitutions: Social Foundations of the Post-National Legal Structure* (Cambridge: Cambridge University Press, 2016).
21. Compare D. Levy and N. Sznaider, 'Cosmopolitan Memory and Human Rights', in M. Rovisco and M. Nowicka (eds), *The Ashgate Research Companion to Cosmopolitanism* (Farnham, Surrey: Ashgate Publishing, 2011), 95–210.
22. Compare the contributions to the volume B. Holzer, F. Kastner, and T. Werron (eds), *From Globalization to World Society: Neo-Institutional and Systems-Theoretical Perspectives* (London and New York: Routledge, 2015).
23. Compare Kastner, *Transitional Justice in der Weltgesellschaft*, 347 ff.
24. On this rather paradoxical effect, see F. Kastner, 'Auf dem Weg zu einer Weltkultur der Versöhnung? Transitional Justice und die Versöhnungspolitik der Vereinten Nationen', in I. Dingel and U. Pekala (eds), *Ringen um Versöhnung: Versöhnungsprozesse zwischen Religion, Politik und Gesellschaft. Veröffentlichungen des Instituts für Europäische Geschichte* (Göttingen: Vandenhoeck & Ruprecht, 2017), 125–50.
25. Bonacker and Safferling, *Victims of International Crimes*.
26. See Hazan, 'Beyond Borders'.
27. Compare A.A. An-Na'im, 'From the Neocolonial Transitional to Indigenous Formation of Justice', *International Journal of Transitional Justice* 7(2) (2013), 197–204.
28. See D. Cornell and N. Muvangua (eds), *Ubuntu and the Law: Indigenous Ideals and Postapartheid Jurisprudence* (New York: Fordham University Press, 2012).
29. G. Lugano, 'Counter-Shaming the International Criminal Court's Intervention as Neocolonial: Lessons from Kenya', *The International Journal of Transitional Justice* 11(1) (2017), 9–29.
30. Gephart, Sakrani, and Hellmann, *Legal Cultures in Transition – Rechtskulturen im Übergang*.
31. See Kastner, *Transitional Justice in der Weltgesellschaft*, 277–359.
32. Compare Fraihat, *Unfinished Revolutions*.
33. See Lugano, 'Counter-Shaming the International Criminal Court's Intervention'.
34. U. Baxi, 'The Sharia and the Contexts of Justice: Marginal Notes toward Understanding the Human Rights Debate amidst the Arab Spring', in Gephart, Sakrani, and Hellmann, *Legal Cultures in Transition – Rechtskulturen im Übergang*, 261–69.
35. R. Sakrani, 'From the Revolutionary Sacred to Transitional Justice: How is Sharia Referenced?', in Gephart, Sakrani, and Hellmann, *Legal Cultures in Transition – Rechtskulturen im Übergang*, 185–99.
36. Compare the contributions to the volume Gephart, Sakrani, and Hellmann, *Legal Cultures in Transition – Rechtskulturen im Übergang*.
37. See Fisher and Stewart, *Transitional Justice and the Arab Spring*.

38. Compare R.G. Teitel, *Humanity's Law* (Oxford: Oxford University Press, 2011).
39. See F. Jeßberger, 'Transnationales Strafrecht, Internationales Strafrecht, Transnationale Strafrechtsgeltung – eine Orientierung', in Calliess, *Transnationales Recht*, 527–37.

Bibliography

Al-Azm, S.J. 'The Sharia from a Secular Perspective', in W. Gephart, R. Sakrani, and J. Hellmann (eds), *Legal Cultures in Transition – Rechtskulturen im Übergang: Von Südafrika bis Spanien, von Nachkriegsdeutschland bis zum Aufbruch der arabischen Welt* (Frankfurt am Main: Vittorio Klostermann, 2015), 177–83.

An-Na'im, A.A. 'From the Neocolonial Transitional to Indigenous Formation of Justice'. *The International Journal of Transitional Justice* 7(2) (2013), 197–204.

Baxi, U. 'The Sharia and the Contexts of Justice: Marginal Notes toward Understanding the Human Rights Debate amidst the Arab Spring', in W. Gephart, R. Sakrani, and J. Hellmann (eds), *Legal Cultures in Transition – Rechtskulturen im Übergang: Von Südafrika bis Spanien, von Nachkriegsdeutschland bis zum Aufbruch der arabischen Welt* (Frankfurt am Main: Vittorio Klostermann, 2015), 261–69.

Bonacker, T., and Safferling, C. (eds). *Victims of International Crimes: An Interdisciplinary Discourse*. Den Haag: Springer/T.M.C. Asser Press, 2013.

Boraine, A. 'Transitional Justice: A Holistic Interpretation'. *Journal of International Affairs* 60(1) (2006), 19–25.

Calliess, G.-P. (ed.). *Transnationales Recht*. Tübingen: Mohr Siebeck, 2014.

Cornell, D., and Muvangua, N. (eds). *Ubuntu and the Law: Indigenous Ideals and Postapartheid Jurisprudence*. New York: Fordham University Press, 2012.

Engert, S., and Jetschke, A. (eds). 'Transitional Justice 2.0'. *Journal of International Peace and Organization* 86(1–2) 2011.

Eser, A., Arnold, J., and Kreicker, H. (eds). *Strafrecht in Reaktion auf Systemunrecht: Vergleichende Einblicke in Transitionsprozesse*. Vols 1–14. Max-Planck-Institut für ausländisches und internationales Strafrecht in Freiburg, 1999–2012.

Fisher, K.J., and Stewart, R. (eds). *Transitional Justice and the Arab Spring*. New York: Routledge, 2014.

Fraihat, I. *Unfinished Revolutions: Yemen, Libya, and Tunisia after the Arab Spring*. New Haven, CT: Yale University Press, 2016.

Gephart, W., Sakrani, R., and Hellmann, J. (eds). *Legal Cultures in Transition – Rechtskulturen im Übergang: Von Südafrika bis Spanien, von Nachkriegsdeutschland bis zum Aufbruch der arabischen Welt*. Frankfurt am Main: Vittorio Klostermann, 2015.

Hazan, P. 'Beyond Borders: The New Architecture of Transitional Justice?' *The International Journal of Transitional Justice* 11(1) (2017), 1–8.

Hinton, A. (ed.). *Transitional Justice: Global Mechanisms and Local Realities after Genocide and Mass Violence*. New Brunswick, NJ: Rutgers University Press, 2010.

Holzer, B., Kastner, F., and Werron, T. (eds). *From Globalization to World Society: Neo-Institutional and Systems-Theoretical Perspectives*. London and New York: Routledge, 2015.

Jeßberger, F. 'Transnationales Strafrecht, Internationales Strafrecht, Transnationale Strafrechtsgeltung – eine Orientierung', in G.-P. Calliess (ed.), *Transnationales Recht* (Tübingen: Mohr Siebeck, 2014), 527–37.

Karstedt, S. 'The End of Impunity? Global Law-Making and Atrocity Crimes'. *Zeitschrift für Rechtssoziologie* 34(1–2) (2014), 125–48.

Kastner, F. 'Auf dem Weg zu einer Weltkultur der Versöhnung? Transitional Justice und die Versöhnungspolitik der Vereinten Nationen', in I. Dingel and U. Pekala (eds), *Ringen um Versöhnung: Versöhnungsprozesse zwischen Religion, Politik und Gesellschaft*. Veröffentlichungen des Instituts für Europäische Geschichte (Göttingen: Vandenhoeck & Ruprecht, 2017), 125–50.

Kastner, F. 'Lex Transitus: Zur Emergenz eines globalen Rechtsregimes von Transitional Justice in der Weltgesellschaft'. *Zeitschrift für Rechtssoziologie* 35(1) (2015), 29–47.

Kastner, F. 'Retributive versus restaurative Gerechtigkeit: Zur transnationalen Diffusion von Wahrheits- und Versöhnungskommissionen in der Weltgesellschaft', in R. Kreide and A. Niederberger (eds), *Staatliche Souveränität und transnationales Recht* (Munich: Hampp, 2010), 194–211.

Kastner, F. 'Soziologie der Menschenrechte: Zur Universalisierung von Unrechtserfahrungen in der Weltgesellschaft'. *Österreichische Zeitschrift für Soziologie* 42(3) (2017), 217–36.

Kastner, F. *Transitional Justice in der Weltgesellschaft*. Hamburg: Hamburger Edition, 2015.

Kastner, F. 'Transitional Justice: Von der normativen Ausnahme zur weltpolitischen Regel', in I.-J. Werkner and K. Ebeling (eds), *Handbuch Friedensethik* (Wiesbaden: Springer VS, 2016), 893–902.

Kastner, F., Nobles, R., Schiff, D., and Ziegert, R. (eds). *Law as a Social System*. Oxford: Oxford University Press, 2008.

Kjaer, P.F. *Constitutionalism in the Global Realm: A Sociological Approach*. London and New York: Routledge, 2014.

Levy, D., and Sznaider, N. 'Cosmopolitan Memory and Human Rights', in M. Rovisco and M. Nowicka (eds), *The Ashgate Research Companion to Cosmopolitanism* (Farnham, Surrey: Ashgate Publishing, 2011), 95–210.

Lugano, G. 'Counter-Shaming the International Criminal Court's Intervention as Neocolonial: Lessons from Kenya'. *The International Journal of Transitional Justice* 11(1) (2017), 9–29.

Mihr, A. 'Regime Consolidation through Transitional Justice in Europe: The Cases of Germany, Spain and Turkey'. *The International Journal of Transitional Justice* 11(1) (2017), 113–31.

Neves, M. *Transconstitutionalism*. Oxford and Portland, OR: Hart Publishing, 2013.

Olsen, T.D., Payne, L.A., and Reiter, A.G. (eds). *Transitional Justice in Balance: Comparing Processes, Weighing Efficacy*. Washington, DC: United States Institute of Peace Press, 2010.

Safferling, C. *Internationales Strafrecht: Strafanwendungsrecht – Völkerstrafrecht – Europäisches Strafrecht*. Heidelberg and Wiesbaden: Springer, 2011.

Sakrani, R. 'From the Revolutionary Sacred to Transitional Justice: How Is Sharia Referenced?', in W. Gephart, R. Sakrani, and J. Hellmann (eds), *Legal Cultures in Transition – Rechtskulturen im Übergang: Von Südafrika bis Spanien, von Nachkriegsdeutschland bis zum Aufbruch der arabischen Welt* (Frankfurt am Main: Vittorio Klostermann, 2015), 185–99.

Schabas, W.A., and Shane, D. (eds). *Truth Commissions and Courts: The Tension between Criminal Justice and the Search for Truth*. Dordrecht: Kluwer Academic Publishers, 2004.

Sikkink, K. *The Justice Cascade: How Human Rights Prosecutions Are Changing World Politics*. New York: W.W. Norton and Company, 2011.

Teitel, R.G. *Globalizing Transitional Justice: Contemporary Essays*. Oxford: Oxford University Press, 2015.

Teitel, R.G. *Humanity's Law*. Oxford: Oxford University Press, 2011.

Teitel, R.G. 'Transitional Justice Genealogy'. *Harvard Human Rights Journal* 16 (2003), 69–94.

Teubner, G. *Verfassungsfragmente: Gesellschaftlicher Konstitutionalismus in der Globalisierung*. Berlin: Suhrkamp Verlag, 2012.

Thornhill, C. *A Sociology of Transnational Constitutions: Social Foundations of the Post-National Legal Structure*. Cambridge: Cambridge University Press, 2016.

Chapter 16

Truth Commissions

A Bottom-Up Approach to Institution-Building

Anja Mihr

Truth commissions (TCs) may employ a lower burden of proof since their findings are non-judicial and do not directly result in criminal prosecution or fines. In consequence, they may also allow easier access for victims and perpetrators alike to 'tell their story' and provide information that otherwise would not be provided to clarify past wrongdoings, crimes and human rights violations. On the other hand, the fact that those presenting at TCs provide information that is not based on criminal investigation or forensic evidence allows for almost anyone to tell his or her version of the past without legal or criminal investigation or historical evidence. The fact that TCs have a low entry point means that they represent a pivotal bottom-up approach for citizens and society to be included in the wider context of Transitional Justice (TJ). To atone or reconcile, to bring the truth to light, or even to seek justice, can be possible outcomes of TCs. They do depend, however, on the specific mandates that these commissions have.

TCs are non-judicial bodies and thus may also prohibit direct challenges to victim testimony by the accused and will generally examine cases as both individual instances of abuse and as evidence of overarching patterns of abuse. This can result in finding responsibilities in a case or story where the testimony alone would not sustain a criminal conviction but where the evidence meets a pattern suggesting the truthfulness of the individual violation.

Hence, TCs have a number of objectives and outcomes. They can bring together opponents from various factions of society that have been violently divided and who would otherwise never meet in the aftermath of a conflict. TCs serve as intermediators when addressing individual or even corporate accountability in a state where – due to amnesty laws or lack of an independent judiciary – paramilitaries, mafia, warlords or businesses cannot be prosecuted. In conflict-torn societies, where state institutions no longer work or are dysfunctional and weak, TCs may be the only means to account for the role of these perpetrators or corporations. There are other reasons that might justify using a TC to pursue personal or corporate accountability at the local level when institutions fail to do so, where judges are biased or corrupt, or where the courts simply are no longer functional. TCs can engage with non-legal or so-called traditional forms of complicity, which would be inappropriate if addressed through a criminal trial. Additionally, the use of a TC could allow for the state to focus prosecutions on natural persons, that is to say, individuals, but the state might still need to address other potential victimizers involved in the conflict. Last but not least, in post-conflict societies people ask for some way in which to seek justice or truth, and thus policy-makers have to choose quickly from among a variety of TJ measures and tools to determine which one is most applicable to the situation in the country. Where mistrust prevails among opponents and state institutions collapse or are corrupt, TCs are sometimes a compromise needed to move forward.

According to McAdams, political calls for trials, TCs, reparations and even amnesties ought to be negotiated with elites and the society at large, and not imposed without warning or explanation of the consequences.[1] Trials in particular can be a dangerous intervention and spoil peaceful transitions. Although trials have a particular relevance to regime change because they aim to (re-)establish the rule of law, they can also be perceived as a tool in the hands of new political elites engaging in 'crusades to root out the dictator'.[2] The best prevention against vengeance in such situations, in which courts no longer work and judges cannot be independent, is to allow for an open and even competitive discourse on different narratives within TCs. They can, as much as other TJ measures, shape, change and contribute public and general narratives that are constructed either in the family or in public media and political discourse.

Numerous TCs have addressed corporate and individual responsibilities, too, which otherwise would not have been addressed at all. Argentina's TC, for example, identified eleven companies involved in the military's crimes during the junta regime. Businesses were invited to participate in the South African Truth and Reconciliation Commission (TRC) process, but few did. The TRC did, however, reach conclusions about the responsibility of businesses and commented on the credibility of business testimony. Additionally, TCs for Timor-Leste, Brazil, Sierra Leone, Colombia, Tunisia and Liberia addressed the responsibility of corporations, either generally or by identifying specific companies. Thus, TCs are not only a low entry point for victims and individual victimizers, they also allow for a bottom-up approach to hold corporate or organizational actors accountable, such as companies, who have not previously been addressed as responsible entities in post-conflict societies.

The Effect of Truth Commissions

When Ruti Teitel and Priscilla Hayner analysed transitional processes in Africa and Latin America in the 1980s and 1990s, they came to the conclusion that TJ measures are somewhat crucial for social and political stability and thus form the foundation of a stable democracy and peaceful society.[3] Both argue that none of the concepts of rule of law, constitution-building and institution-making can be understood without drawing at least some links to TJ. They emphasize that TCs during periods of transition and transformation are essential for justice and accountability in young democracies – and fragile states in particular – and are thus prerequisites for democratic institution-building.[4] In the same vain, Martha Minow observed that after mass atrocities and human rights violations in the second half of the twentieth century, historical memory, narratives, memorials, recognition and the role of TCs were somewhat interlinked when re-establishing societal trust, which in return is essential for stable democratic institutions.[5] There is more to the role that TCs play in the early stage of regime change, namely that they can rebuild trust within the society and among citizens and their political institutions that otherwise might not be (re-) established if other forms of accountability were applied. When James Gibson reviewed the TRC in South Africa, he emphasized that truth – or rather facts – about the past contributes positively to reconciliation, which in and of itself impacts somewhat on the creation of trust and a democratic culture and even consolidation of new political regimes.[6] But in any 'fact and truth finding' processes, he argues, it is important that blame and responsibilities for past atrocities are placed on all members in societies who violated the law of human rights, otherwise a TC has no positive impact and recurrence to injustice might occur.[7] Thus, any TJ process ought to be conducted as inclusively as possible, and in cases where neither trials nor blanket amnesties are suitable options, TCs might be a compromise after all. However, the direct impact of trials, reparations or TCs remains difficult to prove. The idea that TCs alone contribute to a 'justice cascade', as Kathryn Sikkink has argued, is therefore much disputed.[8] It is rather a combination of various TJ measures and the way they are sequenced.

Thus, TCs either compete or correlate with other TJ measures, such as trials (when society and institutions are ready for them), reparations, memorials or partial amnesties. But they are effective if they support the democratic institution-building process by building trust and trustworthy relationships among institutions and citizens at large, for example by making stories public and defining responsibilities on all sides, and consequently winning trust back through going public. TCs should also respect international human rights norms, that is to say providing fair and equal hearings to everyone, and protect witnesses' privacy and safety, regardless of their stories and roles during the conflict. By telling people's story, these commissions' hearings demystify and delegitimize the past and its narratives. Yet their first main purpose is backward-looking, because they aim to delegitimize past regimes. By shedding light on the wrongdoings and responsibilities of all actors involved in a conflict, they provide a chance to (re-) establish trust and confidence by bringing to light some facts that otherwise would never be revealed.

Nonetheless, TCs should be set up through national or local parliamentarian vote and debate, with the support or monitoring of international organizations, if necessary. They should neither be imposed nor run entirely by international or local NGOs or aid organizations, despite their best intentions. Most importantly, there should be a national or local catharsis among those affected by the conflict, that triggers bottom-up citizen-based initiatives in favour of setting up a TC. Only if those who suffered are ready to seek and bear the (often unpleasant) truth is the establishment of a commission a useful tool. The successful implementation of TCs therefore depends on a number of circumstances, such as: (1) state peace or a ceasefire agreement and thus a suitable level of personal and individual security and safety for people to testify; and (2) a guarantee of freedom to speak without being threatened and thus freedom from want and freedom to assemble. Usually, these freedoms are also safeguarded by international community actors, such as the UN, the Organization for Security and Cooperation in Europe (OSCE), the Organization for American States (OAS), or the African Union (AU) and other monitoring mechanisms, but they are also difficult to uphold. Furthermore, the implementation of a TC depends (3) on those running and heading these commissions, distinguished and well-recognized people accepted by all sides; and (4) on the nature and severity of the conflict, the dimension of violence and human rights abuses to be investigated. The set-up is also influenced by the nature of the political transition, that is, whether the post-conflict era comes after a lost war, genocide, a violent revolution or a negotiated and negotiated peaceful transition. TCs also depend on (5) the mix of old and new elites that support or boycott these commissions and the extent of the dominance and power of perpetrators or combatants and victims after the transition.

Such circumstances will determine whether the focus of any such TC will be, firstly, on the truth, historical facts and justice, or, secondly, on atonement, personal healing and reconciliation, or, thirdly – in the best-case scenario – on both. TCs shape narratives of the past based on the level and inclusiveness of participation of all parties, particularly the victims and victimizers and the civil society at large. The outcomes and the quality of TCs depend on their inclusiveness. A commission can fill 'niches of knowledge', facts and figures on all levels. Their reports usually trigger some political and legal actions, even if the consequence is to deny the commission's final reports, recommendations or conclusions. Those who chair TCs have to be ready to compromise on the level of accountability to perpetrators, bystanders and victims alike, because no perpetrator will report to any TC if the next day he or she is likely to be extradited to a police station and a courtroom for trial. There needs to be a clear understanding that trials (legal justice) will not interfere with commissions' reporting (their truth and fact-finding mission).

Hence, most TCs state the objectives of 'hearing and healing' in a societal context, ensuring that both statutory and administrative measures are put in place to achieve the goals set. They also aim to be non-discriminatory to all sides and instead encourage and empower – in an ideal world – a diverse and inclusive range of civilians to testify and report. Only if the blame is placed on all sides do TCs have a significant impact on lasting peace and institution-building.

TC should nevertheless have linkages to other TJ measures, such as memorials and reparations, which can only be set up or granted if the past wrongdoings are truthfully reported on. Finally, their main purpose is to contribute to building a culture of respect for human rights, democracy and the rule of law.

Building Up Trust and Institutions

TCs can be effective if they build trust among adversary parties, former enemies and those who for a long time harmed and mistrusted each other. Democratic institutions are built and strengthened through the adherence to constitutional norms, by complying with free and fair elections and an independent judiciary. Hence, TCs provide the first steps – shortly after a conflict has ended – and a shared window of opportunity to make a written constitution a living one; and secondly, to provide the ground for further acts and laws regarding reparations, compensations, punishment, investigations, reintegration and even reconciliation among perpetrators and victims alike.[9] In this way they legitimize the present and future of newly established political institutions.

Similar to this assessment, Gurr et al.'s Polity IV democracy and autocracy scale shows the importance of cumulative causal effect between trust and democratic performance and its institutions. The level of citizen participation, the recruitment of technocrats and political elites, and the constitutional limits on executive powers correlate with TJ measures, when these are used as a catalyst or tool to purge or lustrate technocrats of the former state bureaucracy or when creating public memorials.[10] For example, TCs increase victims' and victimizers' participation in and engagement with new state institutions; vetting and lustration measures determine who can and will be part of the future political or bureaucratic elite. Gurr et al.'s political indicators implicitly reveal when TJ measures will help to increase participation or limit the return of corrupt and criminal elites to political power. Regime change towards autocracy or the return to dictatorship is more likely if TJ measures are used in a biased and non-transparent way, for example if commissions of inquiry such as TCs allow only a specific victim group to testify in front of the commission but do not allow any other groups or the adversary party to do so.

Seymour M. Lipset highlighted regime legitimacy as 'the capacity of a political system to engender and maintain the belief that existing political institutions are the most appropriate ones for society'.[11] A regime is legitimized if citizens support its rules and behaviour over a longer period, regardless of what type of regime the citizens would actually prefer if they had the choice. Others have added a nuance to this description by emphasizing that a regime is legitimized if a large majority of citizens support it, despite the fact that they know alternative regime types exist.[12] It is imperative to win citizen support and have public opinion on the side of the regime during the first decade of transition, during which time political elites have to make tactical concessions and compromises to (re-)stabilize society and the new regime, regardless of whether it turns out to become authoritarian or democratic. Since vetting procedures, amnesty laws or TCs with former political elites help to change people's perception of the past regime, they do not automatically legitimize the new regime.

However, one must not be too idealistic about the early years of regime change in any political context, and less so about the miracles that TCs can perform. During the first ten years of transition after a conflict, most TJ measures are employed as tactical concessions to international and external pressure, in order to gain financial benefits, international recognition and party support, as outlined earlier. Any sense of a moral obligation to atone for the past is usually absent among the elites. TCs are often set up as a rational compromise between not having trials, because people fear revenge of the former elites, or blanket amnesties, which would leave those responsible without any accountability.

It is in this first decade after the end of a conflict that TJ measures are most often misused as a way to purge political opponents, to place blame only on former enemies, and to increase prejudice and resentment. Juan Linz and Alfred Stepan referred to this first phase of political and institutional transition as a period of 'about eight years of breathing space' for new democracies, during which the first two election terms (each four years) and subsequent legislative periods take place. For them, it is this period and the choices made therein that determine whether the regime will follow a path towards democracy or authoritarianism.[13]

A sense of moral or ethical obligation to use TJ measures is usually experienced later, when the next generation comes into power, a generation that has no personal responsibility for the past. TCs can fill this gap, because of their low and bottom-up entry point, to shed light on past injustice.

These situations lend great support to Dankwart Rustow's assumption that regime consolidation and the full embrace of new values and norms only take place twenty to twenty-five years after the initial regime change. Interestingly, this 20+ generation shows up on the political horizon after regime consolidation is on the way, but not much earlier.[14] It reflects Wolfgang Merkel's fourth level of democratic institution-building and consolidation by civil society. This is a period or decade during which the demos is the most pivotal actor, and it is the last and most important level in order to complete the consolidation process.[15] Whether the 20+ generation emerges in the public arena as a voice in favour of TJ depends on whether fundamental participatory and freedom rights are guaranteed (at least formally) and whether people had positive experiences of these rights in earlier times, such as provided by TCs. In other words, the 20+ generation is able to emerge and push for further TJ measures or reconciliation and thus increase democratic performance based on the level of freedom rights that are guaranteed, a sense of moral and ethical obligation, and whether an independent judiciary (at least in theory) exists. The first generation of post-conflict civil society and victims usually opt for TCs as 'in-between' measures between trials and amnesties, measures that imply neither harsh punishment nor impunity.

Hence, institution-building and the legitimacy of a new political regime depend on citizens accepting the regime's new values and rules, whether they are democratic or autocratic.[16] Leslie Holmes and Richard Rose have analysed the processes of (de-)legitimation that occurred after the communist regimes of Eastern Europe declined. They discovered that in these countries, regime change was significantly driven by external pressures from old elites but not necessarily revolution by new elites, such as the desire to become respected members of international organizations, the desire to gain support from external NGOs or the desire to compare well against other 'successful and prosperous' regimes in the West.[17] Despite the fact that strong Civil Society Organizations (CSOs) existed in Poland, Czechoslovakia, Hungary and East Germany, the transitions have mainly been pushed by former elites and by external – often European or US – political forces. TCs did not play a pivotal role, because legal and political institutions already existed in these countries. Their elites were replaced, but the institutions continued to work.

Often, dealing with past injustices – or at least showing the willingness to do so – increased these countries' chances of gaining membership of international organizations and of becoming respected members of the international community. Thus, commissions of inquiry (including TCs) are also used for tactical reasons to achieve these goals. One fortunate by-product of using TCs and other measures in this tactical way is that the previous regime and its leadership were brought to public attention, but there was little popular consent to put them on trial.

Ideally, after a regime change has taken place, democratically elected leaders will distance themselves from the autocratic political practices of the previous regime and promise to hold accountable those responsible for the crimes of the past; a TC is one way of doing this. In doing so, the new policy-makers send the message that the new regime adheres to new values and rules, under which such crimes have no place. Based on a comparison of several Southern European and Latin American transition and regime change processes, Leonardo Morlino argued that democratic institution-building practices must have one eye on the country's past authoritarian legacy and one eye on the country's future after transition.[18] Governments that do not want to or cannot come to terms with the past will sooner or later have to deal with problems such as the culture of impunity.

A government's level of responsiveness to TCs' recommendations and their achievement of the allotted objectives indicates whether the government aims to demystify and delegitimize the past, or whether old loyalties prevent a distancing from the previous regime.

If the new elite distances itself from the old regime, it confirms its intention to take a different political direction in the future. If the executive and legislative branches pass laws and regulations to exclude people from amnesty and instead grant reparations and allow for testifying in front of a TC, this indicates a higher level of political legitimacy. In contrast, if governments refuse or restrict claims without providing reasons, then unrest, civil disobedience and even turmoil may occur.

In order to call for trials that may have a delegitimizing effect on the past and a legitimizing effect on the new political and democratic institutions, citizens must enjoy the human right to free expression and assembly, which requires a minimum level of constitutionalism and rule of law (at least on paper). Once citizens start feeling free to speak without fear, they will push for more TJ measures and governments will need to respond by making tactical concessions. Governments may introduce a partial TC (with specific mandates) that deals with a limited number of the past injustices, as applied in many transitional societies in Latin America. After some time has passed and it becomes apparent that it is possible to demand more measures, such as reparations or memorials, without fear of repercussions, victim groups begin to call for more.

Amnesty laws and lack of transparency within any trial or any TC will intimidate and demotivate civil society to engage with political institutions. Therefore, egalitarian distribution of power is an important ideal that must be espoused in citizens' collective decision-making processes, if effectiveness and legitimacy are to increase. The fear of opening 'old wounds' and triggering acts of revenge is a valid argument against using TCs, but more so against using trials as a strong pervasive way to achieve justice, during the first decade post regime change.[19]

It follows from the arguments mentioned above that the full spectrum of TJ measures is applied more often in regimes with a clear and determined commitment to democracy – the above-mentioned 'constitutional' and 'represented' consolidated regime[20] – rather than in those that pretend to be democratic but in fact are headed towards a new authoritarian regime. TJ measures are much appreciated accomplices for truly democratic policy-makers, but they are merely tactical tools for those who try to re-establish authoritarian regimes.

Nevertheless, what all political regime types have in common is that in the early transition period they may focus on only one or two measures and omit others due to the fear that a comprehensive and inclusive TJ process will threaten security and public safety by eliciting acts of revenge, because too many potential spoilers of the democratic shift are still in power.

There is a general assumption that the likelihood of TJ measures being used increases with the level of democracy a society knows, and vice versa. However, the frequency of using TCs often has little to do with the level of democracy in a society, as they do not provide full and legal accountability, punishment or justice. In post-war Rwanda, for example, almost all TJ measures, including commissions of inquiry, were applied top-down, leading to a new authoritarian regime. Thus, the difference is whether TJ measures are used bottom-up with top-down support. If they are only used top-down, they have less of a legitimizing effect than when applied bottom-up.

Challenges and Conclusion

The effectiveness of a bottom-up approach to TCs and the impact on democratic institution-building depends on (1) the willingness and level of catharsis of civil society; and (2) the inclusiveness and the level of safety and security of those victims and victimizers (as well as bystanders) who are willing to testify, report and talk in front of a TC. If there is no such support and willingness, there will be no effective outcome that could influence the rebuilding of trust in any conflict-torn society. Neither will commissions' reports impact institution-building in these societies.

Yet TCs can address the underlying causes of a conflict even when not addressing institutional reforms in order not to interfere in political decisions. They can reduce the lack of recognition of victims and victimhood, which may otherwise cause further trauma and lead to a sense of re-victimization, and minimize the feeling of deep betrayal at the behaviour of the political elites who have benefited from the transition. In order to establish a rule of law and a human rights-based political regime, TCs can thus contribute to overcoming the persistence of inequalities, because there is little or no outreach to victims and victimizers alike. TCs can also protect a society from a culture of impunity, when trials are not the first option after a violent conflict has ended.

A public catharsis and claim for political responsiveness are pivotal to achieve successful consolidation of a new (democratic) political regime. Despite its many weaknesses in terms of legal accountability, a TC can incentivize the much-needed first steps towards more accountability and rule of law, both of which are fundamental for democracy. TCs mirror in positive and negative ways the efforts by which governments balance public versus constitutional interests and respond to citizens' claims. The balancing of legal imperatives, public safety and pragmatic considerations is crucial in any regime consolidation and TJ process.[21] Therefore, it is (1) helpful to examine when and how political and civil societies formally acknowledge or respond to past wrongdoings through parliamentarian or public debates. Possible responses include issuing and/or supporting TCs and implementing their recommendations, publicly apologizing, establishing memorials, introducing memorial days, initiating or reacting to public debates, and opening archives for investigations.[22] Furthermore, (2) political society and elites, particularly governments and parliaments, can establish restitution or reparation funds, and initiate rehabilitation or compensation for expropriations, imprisonment and loss of family members.

TCs can also set quotas for working relationships among former enemies or combatants in public institutions or issue amnesties to political prisoners of the former regime, as well as to old elites. Parliaments can enact laws creating funds to restore and maintain memorials and publicly exhume mass graves. To a large extent, these measures are also seen when restoring buildings and converting them into memorials or in maintaining historical or religious sites with donations or public money. Reports by TCs are not binding and, if this is their weakness, it is also their strength, because they go beyond state obligations of a restitution-based nature as set out in the 1949 Geneva Conventions. They do refer to international standards, but their advice is neither political nor legally binding with reference, for example, to the 2006 UN Basic Principles and Guidelines on the Right to a Remedy and Reparation for Victims of Gross Violations of International Human Rights Law and Serious Violations of International Humanitarian Law as a foundation for setting up TCs.

The same elites and political society can set up a framework for criminal justice by passing necessary legal reforms to support international tribunals and court procedures against perpetrators and victimizers. They can apply international human rights and humanitarian law in order to confront past injustices and perpetrators, to reform national legislation, criminal codes and criminal justice in general, and to introduce the vetting of civil servants. These mechanisms not only help to establish a new national court system, but also help to improve the judiciary in consolidated democracies. Such measures combat impunity and reform the security system. Governments and parliaments can introduce amnesty laws according to agreements between old and new political elites and the government. These measures can be issued through pacts, informal agreements, laws or national legislation. However, the culture of impunity that emerges in many post-conflict countries for a non-determined period is counterproductive to the rule of law and, therefore, democracy. Blanket amnesties allow former perpetrators to remain unchallenged and unaccountable for their wrongdoings, leaving them untouched in their professional and personal capacities.

Many of these procedures and policies are labelled as TJ measures, even though they lead to the opposite of what TJ often claims to achieve, namely societal peace and institutional stability. By increasing levels of accountability and improving the responsiveness of executive and legislative powers, an end can be brought to unfair vetting and lustration processes.[23] Studies compiled by Olson, Payne, and Reiter, as well as an earlier one by Neil Kritz, conclude that executives that deal with past injustices can provide rationale and momentum for the new government to reform its institutions and ideologies.[24]

The way in which executive powers, that is to say, governments, establish TCs, support them and respect their outcomes is essential to whether they contribute to the effective functioning of democracy or are counterproductive and perpetuate divisions in society. If, however, TCs do not result in actions, acts, laws or degrees to reintegrate and deal with crimes in the past and future, they do not offer any tools for demystifying the past and legitimizing democratic institutions. Through free and unrevengeful engagement by civilians (victims and victimizers alike), and the delivery and response of institutions (parliaments, courts, governments) to perpetrators and victims alike, the necessary trust and change in behaviour are established. This is much easier said than done, but TCs can offer a low entry point to get these changes started.

If all these measures aim to strengthen new political regimes, that do not allow for a return to violence or war, democratic regime consolidation goes hand in hand with a high level of transparency and institutional independence. The functioning of an independent judiciary and the capability to bring perpetrators to justice within one's own country are indicators of the level of the rule of law and thus reflect the levels of 'representative' and 'behavioural' consolidation.[25]

The stories, the narratives, the facts and even the 'truth' and thus the transparency that is provided by TCs is pivotal for change, consolidation and thus the quality of any democracy, too. Commissions of inquiry, truth or historical commissions and even traditional, local and customary justice mechanisms can trigger other political actions and claims for more accountability and transparency. The independence of the judiciary and the rule of law is one of the most, if not the most difficult hurdle for young democracies to clear, and upholding these principles remains a struggle for consolidated democracies.[26]

It takes a great deal of effort to restore trust where denial and impunity once reigned. Hence, these processes are frequently attacked as destabilizing and vindictive.[27] Executive and legislative powers have to decide whether to confront the dilemma through the hard and legal prosecution of the former regime's leaders, or to leave the past behind them with pacts of silence and blanket amnesty laws. TCs are often plan B and an effective alternative to both these options.

Anja Mihr is a social scientist, the founder of the Center on Governance through Human Rights at the HUMBOLDT-VIADRINA Governance Platform in Berlin. and is currently holding a DAAD Professorship for Human Rights, Governance and Transitional Justice at OSCE Academy in Bishkek, Kyrgyzstan.

Notes

1. J.A. McAdams, 'Preface', in J.A. McAdams (ed.), *Transitional Justice and the Rule of Law in New Democracies* (Notre Dame: University of Notre Dame Press, 1997), xii.
2. Ibid., x.
3. R. Teitel, 'Transitional Justice Globalised', *International Journal of Transitional Justice* 2 (2008), 1–4; P.B. Hayner, *Unspeakable Truths: Facing the Challenges of Truth Commissions* (New York and London: Routledge, 2002).
4. A. Mihr and C.L. Sriram, 'Rule of Law, Security, and Transitional Justice in Fragile and Conflict-Affected Societies', in W. Durch, J. Larik, and R. Ponzio (eds), *Just Security in an Undergoverned World* (Oxford: Oxford University Press, 2018), 118–40.
5. M. Minow, *Between Vengeance and Forgiveness: Facing History after Genocide and Mass Violence* (Boston, MA: Beacon Press, 1998).
6. J.L. Gibson, *Overcoming Apartheid: Can Truth Reconcile a Divided Nation?* (New York: HSPC Press, 2004).
7. J.L. Gibson 'The Contribution of Truth to Reconciliation: Lessons from South Africa', *Journal of Conflict Resolution* 50 (2006), 409–32.

8. K. Sikkink, *The Justice Cascade: How Human Rights Prosecutions Are Changing World Politics* (New York: W.W. Norton & Company, 2011).
9. A. Mihr, *Regime Consolidation and Transitional Justice: A Comparative Study of Germany, Spain and Turkey* (Cambridge: Cambridge University Press, 2018), 79–82.
10. T.R. Gurr, K. Jagger, and W. Moore, 'The Transformation of the Western State: The Growth of Democracy, Autocracy, and State Power since 1800', *Studies in Comparative International Development* 25(1) (1990), 73–108.
11. S.M. Lipset, *Political Man* (Baltimore, MD: Johns Hopkins University Press, 1980), 460.
12. W. Merkel and H. Puhle, *Von der Diktatur zur Demokratie: Transformationen, Erfolgsbedingungen, Entwicklungspfade* (Opladen: Westdeutscher Verlag, 1999), 176.
13. J. Linz and A. Stepan, *Problems of Democratic Transition and Consolidation: Southern Europe, South America, and Post-Communist Europe* (Baltimore, MD: Johns Hopkins University Press, 1996), 79.
14. D.A. Rustow, 'Transition to Democracy: Toward a Dynamic Model', *Comparative Politics* 2(3) (1970), 337–63.
15. W. Merkel, *Systemtransformation: Eine Einführung in die Theorie und Empirie der Transformationsforschung* (Wiesbaden: VS Verlag, 2010), 124.
16. D. Lambach, 'Legitimität', in R. Kollmorgen, W. Merkel, and H.-J. Wagener (eds), *Handbuch Transformationsforschung* (Wiesbaden: Springer VS, 2014), 599–604.
17. L. Holmes, *Post Communism: An Introduction* (Durham, NC: Duke University Press, 1997); R. Rose, *Understanding Post-Communist Transformation: A Bottom-Up Approach* (London: Routledge, 2009).
18. L. Morlino, 'Authoritarian Legacies, Politics of the Past and the Quality of Democracy in Southern Europe: Open Conclusions', in A. Costa Pino and L. Morlino (eds), *Dealing with the Legacy of Authoritarianism: The 'Politics of the Past' in Southern European Democracies* (New York: Routledge, 2011), 166.
19. In the South African TRC Report introduction of Report 1.
20. Merkel, *Systemtransformation*, 112.
21. T.D. Olson, L.A. Payne, and A.G. Reiter, *Transitional Justice in Balance: Comparing Processes, Weighing Efficacy* (Washington, DC: US Institute of Peace, 2010), 154–55.
22. N.J. Kritz, 'Policy Implications of Empirical Research on Transitional Justice', in H. Van der Merwe, V. Baxter, and A.R. Chapman (eds), *Assessing the Impact of Transitional Justice: Challenges for Empirical Research* (Washington, DC: USIP Press, 2009), 17.
23. O.N.T. Thoms, J. Ron, and R. Paris, 'State-Level Effects of Transitional Justice: What Do We Know?', *International Journal of Transitional Justice* 4 (2010), 329–42.
24. Olson, Payne, and Reiter, *Transitional Justice in Balance*; Kritz, 'Policy Implications of Empirical Research'.
25. Merkel, *Systemtransformation*, 118–24.

26. B. Weiffen, 'Der vergessene Faktor: Zum Einfluss von Transitional Justice auf die Entwicklung von Rechtsstaatlichkeit in Demokratisierungsprozessen', *Zeitschrift für Vergleichende Politikwissenschaft (Comparative Governance and Politics)* 5 (2011), 51–74.
27. J.E. Mendez, 'In Defence of Transitional Justice', in McAdams, *Transitional Justice and the Rule of Law*, 1–26.

Bibliography

Gibson, J.L. 'The Contribution of Truth to Reconciliation: Lessons from South Africa'. *Journal of Conflict Resolution* 50 (2006), 409–32.

Gibson, J.L. *Overcoming Apartheid: Can Truth Reconcile a Divided Nation?* New York: HSPC Press, 2004.

Gurr, T.R., Jagger, K., and Moore, W. 'The Transformation of the Western State: The Growth of Democracy, Autocracy, and State Power since 1800'. *Studies in Comparative International Development* 25(1) (1990), 73–108.

Hayner, P.B. *Unspeakable Truths: Facing the Challenges of Truth Commissions*. New York and London: Routledge, 2002.

Holmes, L. *Post Communism: An Introduction*. Durham, NC: Duke University Press, 1997.

Kritz, N.J. 'Policy Implications of Empirical Research on Transitional Justice', in H. Van der Merwe, V. Baxter, and A.R. Chapman (eds), *Assessing the Impact of Transitional Justice: Challenges for Empirical Research* (Washington, DC: USIP Press, 2009), 13–22.

Lambach, D. 'Legitimität', in R. Kollmorgen, W. Merkel, and H.-J. Wagener (eds), *Handbuch Transformationsforschung* (Wiesbaden: Springer VS, 2014), 599–604.

Linz, J., and Stepan, A. *Problems of Democratic Transition and Consolidation: Southern Europe, South America, and Post-Communist Europe*. Baltimore, MD: Johns Hopkins University Press, 1996.

Lipset, S.M. *Political Man*. Baltimore, MD: Johns Hopkins University Press, 1980.

McAdams, J.A. 'Preface', in J.A. McAdams (ed.), *Transitional Justice and the Rule of Law in New Democracies* (Notre Dame: University of Notre Dame Press, 1997), ix–xviii.

Mendez, J.E. 'In Defence of Transitional Justice', in J.A. McAdams (ed.), *Transitional Justice and the Rule of Law in New Democracies* (Notre Dame: University of Notre Dame Press, 1997), 1–26.

Merkel, W. *Systemtransformation: Eine Einführung in die Theorie und Empirie der Transformationsforschung*. Wiesbaden: VS Verlag, 2010.

Merkel, W., and H. Puhle. *Von der Diktatur zur Demokratie: Transformationen, Erfolgsbedingungen, Entwicklungspfade*. Opladen: Westdeutscher Verlag, 1999.

Mihr, A. *Regime Consolidation and Transitional Justice: A Comparative Study of Germany, Spain and Turkey*. Cambridge: Cambridge University Press, 2018.

Mihr, A., and C.L. Sriram. 'Rule of Law, Security, and Transitional Justice in Fragile and Conflict-Affected Societies', in W. Durch, J. Larik, and R. Ponzio (eds), *Just Security in an Undergoverned World* (Oxford: Oxford University Press, 2018), 118–40.

Minow, M. *Between Vengeance and Forgiveness: Facing History after Genocide and Mass Violence*. Boston, MA: Beacon Press, 1998.

Morlino, L. 'Authoritarian Legacies, Politics of the Past and the Quality of Democracy in Southern Europe: Open Conclusions', in A. Costa Pino and L. Morlino (eds), *Dealing with the Legacy of Authoritarianism: The 'Politics of the Past' in Southern European Democracies* (New York: Routledge, 2011), 165–88.

Olson, T.D., Payne, L.A., and Reiter, A.G. *Transitional Justice in Balance: Comparing Processes, Weighing Efficacy*. Washington, DC: US Institute of Peace, 2010.

Rose, R. *Understanding Post-Communist Transformation: A Bottom-Up Approach*. London: Routledge, 2009.

Rustow, D.A. 'Transition to Democracy: Toward a Dynamic Model'. *Comparative Politics* 2(3) (1970), 337–63.

Sikkink, K. *The Justice Cascade: How Human Rights Prosecutions Are Changing World Politics*. New York: W.W. Norton & Company, 2011.

Teitel, R. 'Transitional Justice Globalised'. *International Journal of Transitional Justice* 2 (2008), 1–4.

Thoms, O.N.T., Ron, J., and Paris, R. 'State-Level Effects of Transitional Justice: What Do We Know?' *International Journal of Transitional Justice* 4 (2010), 329–54.

Weiffen, B. 'Der vergessene Faktor: Zum Einfluss von Transitional Justice auf die Entwicklung von Rechtsstaatlichkeit in Demokratisierungsprozessen'. *Zeitschrift für Vergleichende Politikwissenschaft (Comparative Governance and Politics)* 5 (2011), 51–74.

Afterword

Nina Schneider

This volume has set out to critically explore local, national and global approaches to truth commissions empirically, methodologically and epistemically. While these chapters may have only provided preliminary answers to some of the unresolved questions raised in the introduction, they have shown that truth commissions may be best regarded as the product of a variety of interest groups engaging in a complex process of political negotiation. Truth commissions (and similar human rights institutions) may be conceived of as a process involving different actors that can be studied empirically (at least in hindsight) and contextualized in terms of power constellations ranging from the local to the global. Each of the chapters in this volume has contributed to this puzzle, offering a collaborative research output whose multi-scalar and interdisciplinary approach could be called a holistic study of truth commissions. Any serious scholarship of the functioning, meaning and impact of a truth commission will have to untangle the dynamic interrelations among a variety of actors. Thus, truth commissions may be read as a performative rather than fixed phenomenon.

All chapters in this volume have shown that writing about truth commissions involves raising larger questions about the relation between past and present. An important question remains: how do we write about truth commissions – as scholars, historians and engaged intellectuals? This question seems to be ever more urgent in a period of rising human rights adversaries, populist nationalists, and xenophobia in the Americas, Europe and elsewhere. While this volume has asked how to approach truth commissions as a larger, interdisciplinary topic, it is worthwhile to narrow in on this question by adopting a historical perspective. What may historians add to truth commission research and to what extent can truth commissions, in turn, stimulate historians to 'reflect on their craft'?[1]

In an inspiring chapter published in 2000, Charles S. Maier ponders the parallels between historians and truth commissioners. He suggests that historians must critically interpret truth commission operations and outcomes like any other subject and dare to raise questions that commissioners may not ask.[2] Maier emphasizes that both commissioners and historians ultimately need to '[render] a historical verdict' which demands 'drawing a moral bottom line, much as the trial does', even though historians feel 'uncomfortable with the idea of serving as judges and seeking to establish guilt or innocence'.[3] Historians, too, try to 'do justice', whether by giving voice to dissidents or by crafting their synthetic argument in a specific way.[4] After all, Maier contends, every historical narrative is a political act, too.[5] In other words, the historian's account also makes justice choices and represents a political act of some kind, especially in such contentious cases as in the aftermath of violence, when highly polarized histories compete with one another.

Another historian who addresses the role of historians and truth commissioners is Elazar Barkan, though he does so in a very different way. In his 2009 article in the *American Historical Review*, Barkan directly appeals to historians to leave their ivory towers, engage in conflict resolution, and help 'delegitimize the nationalist (and often hateful) historical myths that feed ethnic and national xenophobia and conflict'.[6] In their capacities as both scholars and historical activists, historians can, like a 'midwife', help give birth to 'a narrative on which the [antagonistic] stakeholders can agree', what Barkan calls a 'shared narrative'.[7] Although the exact meaning of the term remains vague – some kind of agreed-upon set of narratives – Barkan does clarify what is *not* implied by the term: the necessity of forging a *single* 'compromise' narrative.

Dialoguing with both Maier's endorsement of historical judgement and Barkan's call for proactive measures, I have myself discussed the role of historians as engaged intellectuals and their possible contribution to *true* rather than *rhetorically proclaimed* human rights enforcement.[8] While I acknowledged Barkan's ideas as visionary, noble and sophisticated, I cautioned that the concrete steps needed to put catalysing 'shared narratives' into practice remain vague and theoretical. My argument drew on my personal dilemma as to how to write about the empirical example of the Brazilian Truth Commission. I called this the act of 'choosing a narrative in a minefield' and concluded that there is no clear answer as to what kind of historical narrative actually best serves the purpose of human rights. The difficult part for most historians is the ultimate question of judgement or political action as problematized by Maier, because historians do not receive professional training in this domain. Yet historians write in a non-neutral discursive field, not a power vacuum, and they need to decide what kinds of narratives they use and which ones they seek to dismantle. Collaborative research – like this volume – may be one way of resolving that dilemma. Bringing multiple viewpoints and historical judgements together has been precisely the goal of this book.

While this volume has collectively explored ways to study truth commissions and give meaning to these initiatives, it has also served as an intellectual response to recent events in Brazil. I therefore close by teasing out the relevance of the Brazilian National Truth Commission at this specific political juncture.

The NTC's key output was a massive final report including twenty-nine recommendations, most of which condemn the persistence of human rights violations in Brazil.[9] The first two recommendations are that the armed forces recognize their responsibility for mass human rights crimes between 1964 and 1985, and that the blanket immunity for crimes against humanity under the 1977 Amnesty Law be revoked.[10] The 2014 final report further proposes to reform and re-educate the armed forces, restructure the criminal justice system, and decouple the military and state police.[11] As of this writing, none of these recommendations has been translated into direct policy. On the contrary, with the rise of Bolsonaro we witness a new militarization of the country (a third of his cabinet are active or former military staff including the president and vice-president) and a revived nostalgia for the dictatorship. Had the recommendations been enforced, would Marielle Franco (1979–2018) still be alive?

Still, the story is more complex than this. On 10 December 2014, when the Brazilian Truth Commission officially presented its final report, President Dilma Rousseff gave a speech. Many reporters highlighted the fact that she, a former guerrilla fighter brutally tortured under military rule, had to pause as tears rolled from her eyes. Yet those who listened carefully also heard something more. Rousseff made it unmistakably clear that she was not willing to lift the blanket amnesty and punish the perpetrators – the number one recommendation of the NTC's final report. If the current human rights backlashes in Brazil first under the unelected and unpopular President Michel Temer and now under Bolsonaro are alarming and demand careful attention, the Workers' Party, too, failed to enforce the NTC's recommendations while still in power from 2014 to 2016. Rousseff herself had ruled out the end of impunity from the start; during the inaugural ceremony of the Truth Commission, she had publicly declared that she would not punish former torturers.[12] No post-1985 Brazilian government has ever shown the political will to tackle the punishment of offenders, military and police reform, a new criminal justice system, or any of the other delicate tasks recommended by the NTC. This window of opportunity has now closed with Bolsonaro's victory and the current political climate in Brazil. Zooming up from the Brazilian to the international level reveals that many governments have happily ignored the recommendations of truth commissions, Guatemala being another fine example.

Even though truth commissions have varied greatly as to their scope and quality, they have the potential to denounce gross and systematic human rights transgressions and to inspire a policy shift towards greater human rights enforcement. Unlike the many politicians today who justify both former and current human rights violations, truth commissions have been able to denounce violence of the past and present. Still, this should not free us from scrutinizing each truth commission's work, and remaining vigilant in identifying the often-striking mismatches between human rights rhetoric and lived experience.

Nina Schneider is Senior Research Fellow at the Käte Hamburger Kolleg/Centre for Global Cooperation Research (KHK/GCR21) at the University of Duisburg-Essen, Germany. She was Visiting Scholar at Columbia University's Institute for the Study of Human Rights (ISHR, 2012), Marie-Curie Fellow at the Zukunftskolleg, at the University of Konstanz (2013–15), Visiting Scholar at the National University of Brasília (UNB, 2015), and Senior Research Fellow of the Global South Studies Center (GSSC) at the University of Cologne (2015–18). She is the author of *Brazilian Propaganda: Legitimizing an Authoritarian Regime* (University Press of Florida, 2014); 'Between Promise and Skepticism: The "Global South" and Our Role as Engaged Intellectuals', *The Global South* 11(2) (2017), 18–38; and (with M. Esparza), eds. *Legacies of State Violence and Transitional Justice in Latin America: A Janus-faced Paradigm?* (Lexington/Rowman & Littlefield, 2015).

Notes

1. C.S. Maier, 'Doing History, Doing Justice: The Narrative of the Historian and the Narrative of the Truth Commission', in R. Rothberg and D. Thomson (eds), *Truth v. Justice: The Morality of Truth Commissions* (Princeton, NJ: Princeton University Press, 2000), 261.
2. Ibid., 264–66.
3. Ibid., 267 (quote 1), 269 (quote 2).
4. Ibid., 270.
5. Ibid., 272.

6. E. Barkan, 'AHR Forum: Truth and Reconciliation in History. Introduction: Historians and Historical Reconciliation', *American Historical Review* 114(4) (2009), 900.
7. Ibid., 903. Barkan defines a shared narrative as 'a historical narrative that intertwines and brings closer the perspectives of two or more national histories that are in direct conflict. It is unlikely to be linear or monovocal and will most likely have distinct registers. There may be meta-agreement and a variety of interpretations about the local and the specifics, or the other way around. The aim of a shared narrative is to erase the dichotomies along national lines'. Barkan, 'AHR Forum', 908.
8. N. Schneider, 'Professional Historical Writing and Human Rights Engagement in the Twenty-First Century: Innovative Approaches and Their Dilemmas', in S. Berger (ed.), *The Engaged Historian: Perspectives on the Intersections of Politics, Activism and the Historical Profession* (New York: Berghahn, forthcoming in 2019), 5, 9–11 [numbered consecutively].
9. The recommendations include three parts: institutional reform (seventeen recommendations), constitutional and legal provisions (eight suggestions), and follow-up actions (four recommendations). Comissão Nacional da Verdade (CNV), 'The Final Report of the Brazilian Truth Commission', retrieved 20 December 2014 from http://www.cnv.gov.br/index.php/outros-destaques/574-conheca-e-acesse-o-relatorio-final-da-cnv, 964.
10. CNV, 'Final Report', 964, 965.
11. Ibid., 967, 968, 971.
12. For a more detailed analysis of the Workers' Party's paradoxical human rights agenda in German, see N. Schneider, 'Ambivalenzen der brasilianischen Vergangenheitspolitik und Erinnerungskultur', in J. Burghart and S. Peters (eds), *Geschichte wird gemacht: Tagungsband Weingartner Lateinamerikatage* (Baden B.: Nomos, 2015), 71–86.

Bibliography

Barkan, E. 'AHR Forum: Truth and Reconciliation in History. Introduction: Historians and Historical Reconciliation'. *American Historical Review* 114(4) (2009), 899–913.

Comissão Nacional da Verdade (CNV). 'The Final Report of the Brazilian Truth Commission'. Retrieved 20 December 2014 from http://www.cnv.gov.br/index.php/outros-destaques/574-conheca-e-acesse-o-relatorio-final-da-cnv.

Maier, C.S. 'Doing History, Doing Justice: The Narrative of the Historian and the Narrative of the Truth Commission', in R. Rothberg and D. Thomson (eds), *Truth v. Justice: The Morality of Truth Commissions* (Princeton, NJ: Princeton University Press, 2000), 261–78.

Schneider, N. 'Ambivalenzen der brasilianischen Vergangenheitspolitik und Erinnerungskultur', in J. Burghart and S. Peters (eds), *Geschichte wird gemacht: Tagungsband Weingartner Lateinamerikatage* (Baden B.: Nomos, 2015), 71–86.

Schneider, N. 'Professional Historical Writing and Human Rights Engagement in the Twenty-First Century: Innovative Approaches and Their Dilemmas', in S. Berger (ed.), *The Engaged Historian: Perspectives on the Intersections of Politics, Activism and the Historical Profession* (New York: Berghahn, forthcoming in 2019).

Appendix 1
List of Selected Local Truth Commissions in Brazil by Region and State

This list is compiled on the basis of information found online, in press releases and on the official webpage of the National Truth Commission. It presents research findings up to 7 February 2014.[1]

Centre-Eastern Region (Centro-Oeste)

Federal District (Distrito Federal)

1. Comitê pela Verdade, Memória e Justiça

Goias

2. Comitê Goiano da Verdade, Memória e Justiça

Mato Grosso

3. Comitê Estadual da Verdade do Mato Grosso

Mato Grosso do do Sul

4. Comitê pela Verdade, Memória e Justiça do Mato Grosso do Sul

South-Eastern Region (Sudeste)

Espírito Santo

5. Fórum Direito à Memória e à Verdade do Estado do Espírito Santo
6. Comissão Estadual da Verdade do Espírito Santo

São Paulo

7. Comissão da Verdade do Estado de São Paulo Rubens Paiva
8. Comissão da Verdade da PUC-SP
9. Comissão da Verdade da USP
10. Comissão Municipal da Verdade Vladimir Herzog – Comissão da Verdade do Município de São Paulo
11. Comitê Paulista Pela Memória, Verdade e Justiça

12. Comitê Pró-Comissão da Verdade, Memória e Justiça Campinas SP
13. Coletivo de Mulheres pela Verdade e Justiça
14. Núcleo de Preservação da Memória Política
15. Comitê Pró-Comissão da Verdade, Memória e Justiça Sorocaba SP

Rio de Janeiro

16. Coletivo RJ pela Memória, Verdade e Justiça
17. Niterói pela Memória, Verdade e Justiça
18. Comitê pela Verdade, Memória e Justiça de Niterói
19. Comissão da Verdade do Rio

Minas Gerais

20. Comitê pela Verdade, Memória e Justiça de Minas Gerais
21. Associação Amigos do Memorial da Anistia Política do Brasil
22. Comitê Pró-Comissão da Verdade, Memória e Justiça Universidade Newton Paiva
23. Comitê da Verdade e do Memorial da Anistia Política da OAB/MG
24. Associação dos Trabalhadores Anistiados de Ipating/Centro de Documentação e Memória Operário Popular da Região Metropolitana do Vale do Aço
25. Comitê pela Verdade, Memória e Justiça
26. Comissão da Verdade em Minas Gerais

Southern Region (Sul)

Parana

27. Fórum paranaense de Resgate da Memória, Verdade e Justiça
28. Comitê Paranaense pela Verdade, Memória e Justiça
29. Comitê Memória, Justiça e Verdade do Oeste do Paraná
30. Comissão Estadual da Verdade do Estado do Paraná

Rio Grande do Sul

31. Comitê Popular da Memória, Verdade e Justiça
32. Comitê Gaúcho da Verdade, Memória e Justiça
33. Comitê à Memória, Verdade e Justiça do Rio Grande do Sul
34. Comitê Santa Mariense de Direito à Memória e à Verdade
35. Comitê pela Verdade Memória e Justiça Pelotas e Região
36. Comissão Estadual da Verdade do Rio Grande do Sul

Santa Catarina

37. Comitê pela Verdade, Memória e Justiça de Santa Catarina
38. Coletivo Catarinense Memória, Verdade e Justiça
39. Coletivo Verdade, Memória e Justiça João Batista Rita – Criciúma
40. Comitê pro-Memoria Catari nense – Blumenau
41. Comissão Estadual da Verdade Paulo Stuart Wright (CEV)

Northeastern Region (Nordeste)

Alagoas

42. Comitê Pró-Comissão da Verdade, Memória e Justiça
43. Comissão Estadual da Memória e Verdade Jayme Miranda

Bahia

44. Comissão Especial da Verdade
45. Comitê Baiano pela Verdade
46. Comitê Baiano pela Verdade, Memória e Justiça
47. Comissão Estadual da Verdade na Bahia

Ceará

48. Comitê pela Verdade, Memória e Justiça CE
49. Comissão da Verdade das Universidades do Ceará
50. Comissão da Verdade dos Jornalistas do Ceará

Maranhão

51. Comitê Maranhense da Verdade
52. Comissão Parlamentar da Verdade

Paraíba

53. Comitê pela Verdade, Memória e Justiça da Paraíba
54. Comissão Estadual da Verdade e da Preservação da Memória

Pernambuco

55. Comitê pela Verdade, Memória e Justiça de Pernambuco

Piauí

56. Comitê pela Verdade, Memória e Justiça do Piauí

Rio Grande do Norte

57. Comitê Estadual pela Verdade, Memória e Justiça RN

58. Comissão pela Verdade OAB/RN
59. Comissão da Verdade UFRN

Sergipe

60. Comitê pela Verdade, Memória e Justiça de Sergipe

Northern Region (Norte)

Acre

61. Comitê Estadual pela Verdade, Memória e Justiça do Acre

Amapá

62. Comitê Estadual pela Verdade, Memória e Justiça do Amapá
63. Comissão Estadual da Verdade Francisco das Chagas Bezerra "Chaguinha"

Amazonas

64. Comitê pró-Comissão da Verdade, Memória e Justiça

Pará

65. Comitê Paraense em Defesa da Comissão da Verdade Paulo Fonteles

Rondônia

66. Comitê Estadual da Verdade de Rondônia

Roraima

67. Comissão Estadual da Verdade de Roraima

Note

1. While the Nucleus for the Preservation of Political Memory (Núcleo de Preservação da Memória Política) may not qualify as a local truth commission proper, it is included here, because it supported and interacted with both the Brazilian National Truth Commission and local commissions.

Appendix 2

Selected List of Brazilian Online Resources (in alphabetical order)

Institute of Religious Studies, ISER (Instituto de Estudos da Religião, ISER). A civil society organization founded during the 1970s and dedicated to the promotion of human rights and democracy, ISER received funding from the Ford Foundation to monitor the work of the National Truth Commission. It published several reports which provide details about the NTC's activities, the NTC's coverage in the press and its relation to civil society. Retrieved 20 January 2017 from http://www.iser.org.br/site/?portfolio=redes.

Latin American Transitional Justice Network (Rede Latino-Americana de Justiça de Transição, RLAJT). Established in 2011 by the Brazilian Amnesty Commission (a subsection of the Ministry of Justice), the Brazilian Foreign Ministry, and the United Nations Development Program (UNDP), the RLAJT webpage offers a wealth of information on transitional justice initiatives in Latin America, including yearly reports. Retrieved 20 January 2017 from http://rlajt.web2403.uni5.net/.

National Truth Commission, NTC (Comissão Nacional da Verdade, CNV). Besides the Final Report, this official website contains information on the emergence and functioning of the NTC, on public testimony events, and photographs. Retrieved 20 December 2014 from http://www.cnv.gov.br.

Nucleus for the Preservation of Political Memory (Núcleo de Preservação da Memória Política), São Paulo. Retrieved 20 December 2014 from https://www.nucleomemoria.com.br/.

Truth Commission of the State of São Paulo Rubens Paiva (Comissão da Verdade do Estado de São Paulo Rubens Paiva). Retrieved 20 January 2015 from http://www.al.sp.gov.br/comissoes/comissao-da-verdade/.

Appendix 3
Photos from the Brazilian Truth Commission

Figure A 3.1. President Dilma gives a speech on the occasion of the presentation of the Brazilian National Truth Commission's final report on 10 December 2014. Palácio do Planalto, Brasília. Photo: Nina Schneider.

Figure A 3.2. President Dilma Rousseff receives the Brazilian National Truth Commission's final report from Coordinator Pedro Dallari. 10 December 2014, Palácio do Planalto, Brasília. Photo: Nina Schneider.

Figure A 3.3. Press meeting with truth commissioners after the handover of the final report. From the left: Commissioner Rosa Cardoso and Coordinator Pedro Dallari. 10 December 2014, Palácio do Planalto, Brasília. Photo: Nina Schneider.

Figure A 3.4. A protest banner of the organization Levante Popular (Popular Uprising) demanding the punishment of perpetrators of the military regime. The banner was shown at the end of the official ceremony handing over the final report to the president on 10 December 2014 in the Palácio do Planalto, Brasília. Photo: Nina Schneider.

Figure A 3.5. Public hearing on violence against women. When Amelinha Teles recounts her experience of sexual violence in prison, Eleonore Menicucci shows her solidarity. For decades, Amelinha Teles has been engaged in the struggle for clarification of the political disappeared. She is also a leading protagonist of the Brazilian feminist movement and has published on Brazilian women's history. In the local truth commission of the state of São Paulo (Rubens Paiva Commission), she was one of the key coordinators. Photo: official photo by the National Truth Commission in Brazil. Retrieved 10 May 2017 from http://www.cnv.gov.br/fotos.html.

Index

Aarão Reis, Daniel, 185
accountability, 64–65
adaptive industrialists, 171–72
Adorno, Theodor, 248–55
de Albuquerque Bello, José María, 79n11
Alencar, Joaquim Eduardo de, 132–33
Allende, Salvador, 208
Almedia Filho, Hermógenes da Silva, 77
de Almeida, Gisele Iecker, 19
American Historical Review (Barkan), 340
Amnesty Laws, 7, 65, 75, 258n40, 258n42, 341
  Amnesty Commission, 126–27, 132
  Araguaia massacre and, 210–11
  for censorship, 184–85, 267–68
  against human rights, 184
  impunity and, 26n66
  military for, 195n6
  partial amnesty, 94–97
  for regimes, 118
  for victims, 61–62, 101
Anderson, Benedict, 12
Angel Jones, Stuart, 66n2, 90
Angel Jones, Zuleika, 66n2, 94–95
Anísio Teixeira Truth and Memory Commission (CATMV), 5–6, 127–28, 133–35
approaches, 16–17, 339–42. *See also* bottom-up approaches; global approaches
  local approaches, 13, 18, 21n12, 95, 307, 345–48
  national approaches, 11–14, 18, 118–19, 129–30, 245
April Package, 95
Arab uprisings, 305–7, 311–15
Araguaia massacre, 97–100, 105n56, 118, 210–11, 250, 258n43
Argentina, 9, 60, 268–69
Arraes, Miguel, 91
assassinations, 1–3, 21n5
Assmann, Jan, 286–87
Ato Institucional no. 5, 191
authoritarian regimes. *See* regimes
auto-fiction, 287–97
Ayres Filho, Paulo, 160, 162
Azevedo, José Carlos, 130
Azevedo, Reinaldo, 148

Bagatella, Lucia, 235
Bakiner, Onur, 15
Baratto, Márcia, 232
Bari, Humberto, 275
Barkan, Elazar, 13, 340, 343n7
Basílio Rossi, Luiz, 72–73
Bazzano, Ariana, 232
Beard, Charles, 247
Bellentani, Lucio, 186, 193
Benário, Olga, 193
Benetazzo, Antonio, 72
Betancur, Belisario, 267–68
BNM. *See* Brasil Nunca Mais Report
Boilesen, Henning, 157–58, 168, 173
Bolivia, 9
Bolsonaro, Jair Messias, 2, 18, 21n11, 48–49, 73–74, 341–42

bottom-up approaches, 328–31
for institution-building, 323–25, 332–35
for TJ, 325–27
Bouazizi, Mohamed, 305
Braga, Camila, 232
Branco, Castello, 166–67
Brasil Nunca Mais Report (BNM), 8, 75, 100
Brazil. *See also* Amnesty Laws; Latin America; National Truth Commission
Ato Institucional no. 5, 191
auto-fiction in, 287–97
censorship in, 150
civil police for, 116
Cold War for, 58, 111
communism in, 88–89, 162
culture of, 206–7
democracy in, 6, 54n7, 254–55
DOPS, 183–86, 189
education in, 128–29
elections in, 21n10
El Salvador compared to, 279
exiles from, 218
feminism in, 352
Final Report, 10, 21n13, 275–79, 350–52
Germany and, 183
global approaches for, 113
history of, 17–18, 22n14, 74–77, 256n11
Honestino Guimarães Bridge, 133–35
human rights in, 5, 20, 38, 62–66, 106n68, 222n4
IACHR in, 61, 203
industrialists in, 159–62
IPES, 159–63, 165–66, 176n24, 176n28, 176n33
local approaches in, 13
media in, 48, 139–40
military in, 18
Museum of Memory, 213
Peru compared to, 277–78
politics in, 18
poverty in, 41
Raízes do Brasil (Buarque de Holanda), 71
revolução brasileira (Prado Jr.), 71
state violence in, 157
Testimony Clinics in, 50, 53
TJ in, 42–43, 143, 341
TRCs in, 18–19, 345–48
US and, 161, 165, 190, 222n12
violence in, 56n28
Brilhante Ustra, Carlos A., 2, 74
Brizola, Leonel, 176n35
Buarque, Chico, 288–91
Buarque de Holanda, Sérgio, 71, 289–90
Buergenthal, Thomas, 267–69
Buff, Luci, 232–33
bureaucratic-authoritarian state, 171–72. *See also* regimes
business-military dictatorships. *See* corporations; military; regimes

Camargo, Ivan, 128
Capanema, Gustavo, 129
Cardoso, Ciro, 72
Cardoso, Fernando Henrique, 38
Cardoso, Rosa, 158, 229, 351
catharsis, 333
Catholic Church. *See* religion
CATMV. *See* Anísio Teixeira Truth and Memory Commission
Cavalcanti, José Paulo, 258n40
CDDPH. *See* Council for the Defence of Human Rights
CEMDP. *See* Special Commission of The Political Dead and Disappeared
censorship
Amnesty Laws for, 184–85, 267–68
in Brazil, 150
in history, 68–74, 77–78
IPES for, 176n24
LAI, 127
in media, 89

national approaches and, 129–30
NTC and, 208–9
OBAN, 167–68
by police, 90
in politics, 212
regimes and, 79n11, 106n64, 306–7
by Rousseff, 120
in TRCs, 74–77, 207–8
for UN, 270–71
for UnB, 128–31
of victims, 114–15
by Volkswagen do Brasil, 197n27
Chile, 70–71, 266, 268–69
civil accountability, 97–100
civil police, 116
classified information, 50–53
Cold War, 48, 58, 111, 265
for Latin America, 7, 10, 22n22
for US, 91
Collor de Mello, Fernando, 38
Comisión Nacional sobre la Desaparición de Personas (CONADEP), 9, 22n22
Comissão Nacional da Verdade. *See* National Truth Commission
communism, 88–89, 160–61, 162, 167, 176n35, 192–93
Comparato, Fábio K., 102
CONADEP. *See* Comisión Nacional sobre la Desaparición de Personas
Copersucar, 167–68
corporations
adaptive industrialists and, 171–72
coups and, 159–62
economics of, 191
Petrobras, 47
politics and, 18, 165–71
psychology of, 162–65, 182
for regimes, 157–59, 172–74, 174n6
Correia, Camargo, 167–68
corruption
by IPES, 176n28, 176n33
in law, 323–24
in politics, 21n11, 76–77
psychology of, 314
by Rousseff, 38–46
da Costa, Maria Emília Viotti, 71
Council for the Defence of Human Rights (CDDPH), 89–90
coups, 6, 20n1, 47, 157, 215, 267
coup (1964), 86–89, 159–62, 164, 213, 218
politics of, 162–65
for regimes, 68–69
US for, 66n1
do Couto e Silva, Golbery, 92, 161
CPI. *See* Parliamentary Committee of Investigation
culture, 46, 206–7, 259n53, 332–33

Dallari, Pedro, 230, 251–52, 351
Delgado, Ieda, 130
Del Rio, José Luiz, 235
democracy, 10–11, 59–60, 90–96, 147–48, 172
in Brazil, 6, 54n7, 254–55
civil accountability for, 97–100
economics of, 168–69
NTC for, 42, 44–46
psychology of, 329–30
for regimes, 100–102, 330–32
state violence and, 86–89
theory of, 328, 332
Departamento de Operações de Informações (DOI), 42, 50, 72, 86–88
O Dia que Durou 21 Anos (Taváras), 46
Dias, José Carlos, 229–30
Dias da Silva, Santo, 90
'Dictatorship and Gender' Working Group, 229–39
dictatorships. *See* regimes
Dipp, Gilson, 230
disappearances, 86–89, 97–98
Dodge, Raquel, 106n68, 119
DOI. *See* Departamento de Operações de Informações

DOPS. *See* Political Police
Doubrovsky, Serge, 288–89
Drabinski, John, 272

East Timor, 16
economics, 157, 168–69, 182–83, 191, 218
    IPES, 159–63, 165–66, 176n24, 176n28, 176n33
    of regimes, 158, 175n8
    of victims, 221n1, 223n27
education, 128–29, 130–31
elections, 21n10, 60–61, 100
El Salvador, 267–71, 273, 279. *See also* Latin America
endogenous factors, in TRCs, 214
Erasmo Dias, Antônio, 43
Esparza, Marcia, 16
El Espíritu de mis padres sigue subiendo en la lluvia (Pron), 294–97
Evaristo Arns, Dom Paulo, 90, 92
exiles, 218
exogenous factors, in TRCs, 214
extraterritorial responsibility, 120–21

Facebook, 18, 142–50
fact-finding commissions. *See* truth and reconciliation commissions
family, 44–45, 61, 66n3, 131
Federal Police, 133
feminism, 352
Fico, Carlos, 75–76
Figueiredo, João, 96–98, 252
Figueredo, Reinaldo, 267–68
Final Report, Brazil (2014), 10, 21n13, 275–79, 350–52. *See also* National Truth Commission
Fonteles, Hecilda, 132
Fonteles, Paulo, 133
Fonteles Filho, Paulo, 132
Formas de volver a casa (Zambra), 292–97
Foundation for Research Development (FUNDEP), 233–34
Franco, Marielle, 1–3, 21n5, 341
Freedom of Information Law (LAI), 127
Freyre, Gilberto, 79n11
From Madness to Hope: The 12-Year War in El Salvador (Final Report), 268
Fujimori, Alberto, 271
FUNDEP. *See* Foundation for Research Development
Furtado, Celso, 70

Gandin, Greg, 12–14
Garcia, José Guillermo, 271
Gaspari, Elio, 185
Geisel, Ernesto, 88, 92–94
gender. *See* 'Dictatorship and Gender' Working Group
Germany, 182–83, 186–88, 192, 196n22, 296–97
Gibson, James, 325
Gillis, J. R., 229
global approaches
    for Brazil, 113
    for Cold War, 265
    extraterritorial responsibility, 120–21
    for Facebook, 142
    for human rights, 6–7, 12, 43, 326–27
    Latin America in, 8–9
    to law, 270
    to memory, 277–79
    national approaches compared to, 14
    to NTC, 207–8, 341–42
    to oppression, 37
    for regimes, 123n12
    to scholarship, 19–20
    for TJ, 25n52, 158–59, 307–11, 315–16
    for TRCs, 3, 9, 19–20, 152n12
Gomes, Ângela de Castro, 72
Gomes-Lund v. Brazil. *See* Araguaia massacre
González, Eduardo, 273
Gorender, Jacob, 72

Goulart, João, 47, 73, 89, 159–65, 172, 176n36
Grabois, Maurício, 59
Greiger, Manfred, 187
Guatemala, 272
Guedes Miranda, Reinaldo, 77
Guimarães, Honestino, 128, 130, 133–35
Günther, Sergio, 289–91
Gúzman, Abimael, 271

Haddad, Fernando, 73–74
Halbwachs, Maurice, 286–87
den Hartog, Monique Tiezzi, 232–36
Hayner, Priscilla, 8, 9, 272–73, 325
Hegel, Georg Willhelm, 246
Herzog, Vladimir, 90
Hirsch, Marianne, 286–87
História combatente (Honório Rodrigues), 71
História nova do Brasil (textbook), 69–70
historians. *See also* censorship; *specific historians*
- Cold War for, 48
- impunity for, 77
- politics for, 68
- regimes for, 185
- scholarship for, 340–41
- state violence for, 328
- in TJ, 339–40
- in TRCs, 14–15, 248–54
- violence for, 325

history
- of Brazil, 17–18, 22n14, 74–77, 256n11
- censorship in, 68–74, 77–78
- education and, 130–31
- of El Salvador, 270–71
- of Germany, 296–97
- *História combatente* (Honório Rodrigues), 71
- *História nova do Brasil* (textbook), 69–70
- of human rights, 311–12
- of impunity, 121–22
- of local approaches, 307
- NTC and, 2–3, 63, 121–22
- politics of, 247–48
- psychology of, 245–46
- of regimes, 58–66, 117–18, 134, 329
- scholarship and, 13
- *Sociedade e história do Brasil* (Antonio Villa), 73
- of TJ, 24n40, 307–8
- of TRCs, 7–11, 19–20, 126–35
- of victims, 315–16
- of violence, 54n5
- of Volkswagen do Brasil, 189–94

Hohmann-Dennhardt, Christine, 187–88
de Holanda, Buarque, 79n11
Holocaust. *See* Germany
Honestino Guimarães Bridge, 133–35
Honório Rodrigues, José, 70–71
human rights, 27n76, 92, 100, 131, 204, 310–12. *See also* Inter-American Court of Human Rights
- Amnesty Laws against, 184
- for Araguaia massacre, 250
- in Brazil, 5, 20, 38, 62–66, 106n68, 222n4
- CDDPH, 89–90
- global approaches for, 6–7, 12, 43, 326–27
- IACHR, 7, 61–64, 76, 90–91, 99–100, 123n6, 203
- institutional responsibility for, 276–77
- in Latin America, 208, 217–18, 265–67
- memory and, 274–75
- in MENA, 305–7
- national approaches for, 245
- NTC for, 111–15, 158, 205–7, 257n18, 259n54
- politics of, 17, 308–9
- state violence and, 14, 49–50
- for UN, 113–14, 120–21, 333
- for victims, 8, 41, 53, 341–42

Huntington, Samuel, 266

IACHR. *See* Inter-American Court of Human Rights
ICC. *See* International Criminal Court
ICTJ. *See* International Center for Transitional Justice
impeachment, 20n1, 102, 123n6
impunity, 26n66, 77, 105n58, 121–22, 332–33
indigenous peoples, 217–18, 272
industrialists, 159–62, 171–72
Institute for Economic and Social Research (IPES), 159–63, 165–66, 176n24, 176n28, 176n33
Institute of Religious Studies (ISER), 349
institutional measures, 116–19, 229–31, 248–54, 258n36
institutional responsibility, 122, 211–12, 276–77
institution-building. *See* bottom-up approaches
Inter-American Court of Human Rights (IACHR), 7, 61–64, 76, 90–91, 99–100, 123n6, 203
intergenerational perspectives, 131–33, 138–39
International Center for Transitional Justice (ICTJ), 309–10
International Criminal Court (ICC), 310–11
IPES. *See* Institute for Economic and Social Research
O irmão alemão (Buarque), 288–91
irreconcilable analysis, 11–14
ISER. *See* Institute of Religious Studies
Ishaq, Vivien, 231

Jelin, Elizabeth, 11–12, 237
journalism. *See* media
juntas. *See* coups
justice. *See* transitional justice

K (Kucinski), 287–91
Kastner, Fatima, 12
Kehl, Maria Rita, 230
Kent, Lia, 16
Klein, Herbert S., 185
Klubock, Thomas, 12
Kritz, Neil, 334
Krüger, Anne, 12
Kubitschek de Oliveira, Juscelino, 166–67, 189
Kucinski, Bernardo, 287–91

LAI. *See* Freedom of Information Law
LAJT. *See* Latin America Transitional Justice Network
Lamarca, Carlos, 59
Latin America, 8–9, 19, 59–60, 162–63, 182–83, 352
  Cold War for, 7, 10, 22n22
  human rights in, 208, 217–18, 265–67
  MENA compared to, 314–15
  postmemory in, 286–87
Latin America Transitional Justice Network (RLAJT), 349
law. *See also* Amnesty Laws
  April Package, 95
  Ato Institucional no. 5, 191
  corruption in, 323–24
  for disappearances, 97–98
  global approaches to, 270
  ICC, 310–11
  LAI, 127
  military law, 98–99, 211, 250–51, 258n50
  NTC for, 120–21, 173
  for partial amnesty, 94–97
  for police, 212
  politics and, 92
  for reciprocity, 104n43
  in South Africa, 312–13
  for state violence, 106n65, 252–53
  for TJ, 331
  for torture, 102n7
  for victims, 327–28, 333–34
Law of National Security (LSN), 97

Leiding, Rudolf, 193–94
Leme, Egle Vannucchi, 95
Lerner Febres, Salomón, 272
Lex Transitus, 307–11, 316
de Lima Rocha, João Augusto, 131
Lindenberg, Adolpho, 168
Linhares, Maria Yedda, 68–69
de Lins e Horta, Ricardo, 230–31
Linz, Juan, 329
Lipset, Seymour M., 328
literary fiction, 286–97
Lobo, Eulália Lahmeyer, 69
local approaches, 13, 18, 21n12, 95, 307, 345–48
LSN. *See* Law of National Security
Lula da Silva, Luiz Inácio, 2, 21n11, 38
Luta Operaria, 192–93

Macedo, Gustavo, 232–35
Maciel, Lysâneas, 92–93
Maguire, Geoffrey, 296
Maier, Charles S., 339–40
Malhães, Paulo, 50, 278
Maluf, Paulo, 167–68
Mandela, Nelson, 312–13
Marighella, Carlos, 59
Marinho, Djalma, 96
Martins Saldanha, Afonso Henrique, 72
Marxism, 69–70
Maurício, Manoel, 69
McKinnon, Catharine, 237
media, 39–40, 49, 76, 89, 91. *See also* social media
  in Brazil, 48, 139–40
  in Germany, 187–88, 192
  human rights in, 92
  Luta Operaria, 192–93
  politics in, 45–46, 143–44
  propaganda in, 135
  regimes in, 73–74
  Rousseff in, 47–48, 51–53
  TJ in, 44, 55n19, 148–49, 329–30
  TRCs and, 140–41
  violence against, 58–59
Melo, Carolina de Campos, 5
memory, 148–49, 213, 231–36, 274–79
  Nucleus for the Preservation of Political Memory, 348n1, 349
  politics and, 227–29, 245–48
  transgenerational memory, 286–87, 291–92, 298n26
MENA (North Africa snd the Middle East), 305–7, 313–15
Mendonça, Jacy, 194
Menicucci, Eleonore, 352
Merkel, Angela, 47
Merkel, Wolfgang, 329
methodology, 4, 15, 27n74, 146, 153n13
Mezarobba, Glenda, 227, 232–35
Middle East. *See* MENA
military, 18, 97, 105n58, 195n6, 208. *See also* regimes
  coups for, 6, 215
  institutional responsibility for, 122
  military law, 98–99, 211, 250–51, 258n50
  NTC for, 39
  as police, 55n14, 75, 88, 96, 105n63, 116–17, 193
  politics of, 4, 132–33
  for regimes, 105n61, 191, 222n5
  scholarship on, 22n14, 170–71
  torture by, 113–14, 208
  TRCs for, 278–79
  victims of, 20, 37
  violence from, 54n6, 59–60
  Volkswagen do Brasil for, 18
Minguardi, Guaracy, 194
minority rights, 13
Minow, Martha, 325
Molinas Dias, Júlio Miguel, 50
Mommsen, Hans, 187
Montano, Inocente, 271
de Moraes, Márcio José, 98
Morlino, Leonardo, 330–31
el Mozote massacre, 280n10
MTJR. *See* memory

Mubarak, Hosni, 313
Museum of Memory, 213
Museum of Resistance, 42, 258n44
Myiaki, Darci, 235

national approaches, 11–14, 18, 118–19, 129–30, 245
National Integration Network of Public Safety Information, 116
National Truth Commission (NTC), 349
  censorship and, 208–9
  for democracy, 42, 44–46
  'Dictatorship and Gender' Working Group for, 229–39
  for economics, 218
  on Facebook, 143–50
  Final Report for, 10, 21n13, 275–79, 350–52
  global approaches to, 207–8, 341–42
  history and, 2–3, 63, 121–22
  for human rights, 111–15, 158, 205–7, 257n18, 259n54
  IACHR and, 63–64
  indigenous peoples, 217–18
  institutional measures by, 116–19, 248–54, 258n36
  for institutional responsibility, 211–12
  for law, 120–21, 173
  local approaches for, 21n12
  for military, 39
  for political vetting, 219
  politics of, 275–79
  psychology of, 213–16, 219–21
  against regimes, 119–20, 243–45
  Rousseff for, 153n15, 183–84, 341
  on state violence, 216–17
  studies on, 4–7, 16–17
  for TJ, 203–4, 209–11, 227–29, 239–41, 254–55
  torture for, 185–86
  for victims, 212, 227–29
Nazis. *See* Germany
neoliberalism, 12
NGOs. *See* non-governmental organizations
Nogueira Belham, José Antônio, 276
Nogueira de Carvalho, Francisco Gilson, 77
non-governmental organizations (NGOs), 9–10, 99–100
Nordoff, Heinrich, 190
North Africa. *See* MENA
NTC. *See* National Truth Commission
Nucleus for the Preservation of Political Memory, 348n1, 349
Nunca Mais. *See* National Truth Commission; truth and reconciliation commissions

OAS. *See* Organization of American States
Obama, Barack, 47, 50–53
OBAN. *See* Operation Bandeirantes
Oettler, Anika, 12–13
Okura, Álvaro, 232–34
Olga (film), 193
Operation Bandeirantes (OBAN), 167–68
oppression, 37, 39–40
Organization of American States (OAS), 7
Otávio Guimarães, José, 6

Padhila, Anivaldo, 235
Paiva, Eunice, 42
Paiva, João Francisco, 44
Paiva, João Henrique, 38–43
Paiva, Rubens, 17, 49–53, 90, 106n68, 275–77
Paixão, Cristiano, 6
Pandolfi, Dulce, 72
Paniagua Corazao, Valentin, 271
Parliamentary Committee of Investigation (CPI), 92–93, 95–96
partial amnesty, 94–97

Passarinho, Jarbas, 93, 100–101, 105n61
Paulo Cavalcanti, José, 230
Paz, Edgar, 275
Peru, 271–75, 277–78. *See also* Latin America
Petrobras, 47
Pinheiro, Paulo Sérgio, 227, 229–32, 245, 254–55
Pinochet, Augusto, 266
police, 64, 90, 116, 133, 212
 military as, 55n14, 75, 88, 96, 105n63, 116–17, 193
 state violence by, 207, 222n12
Political Police (DOPS), 183–86, 189, 192–94
politics. *See also* Special Commission of The Political Dead and Disappeared
 of accountability, 64–65
 of Amnesty Laws, 75
 April Package, 95
 of Araguaia massacre, 258n43
 in Brazil, 18
 censorship in, 212
 corporations and, 18, 165–71
 corruption in, 21n11, 76–77
 of coups, 162–65
 culture of, 259n53
 of democracy, 92–94
 disappearances in, 86–89, 97–98
 of elections, 60–61
 of Goulart, 159–65
 for historians, 68
 of history, 247–48
 of human rights, 17, 308–9
 of institutional measures, 229–31
 in Latin America, 162–63
 law and, 92
 of literary fiction, 287–97
 local approaches for, 13
 of Marxism, 69–70
 in media, 45–46, 143–44
 memory and, 227–29, 245–48
 in MENA, 313–14
 of military, 4, 132–33
 NGOs in, 9–10
 of NTC, 275–79
 Nucleus for the Preservation of Political Memory, 348n1, 349
 political prisoners, 38, 40–42, 50, 71, 96, 228, 275–77, 333
 propaganda in, 144–45
 psychology of, 149–50, 175n14
 of regimes, 7–8, 103n10, 330, 334–35
 of religion, 314–15
 religion and, 168
 scholarship on, 11
 on social media, 44–45, 54n4
 of TJ, 324–25
 of torture, 74
 of TRCs, 28n82, 126–27, 151n2, 249–54
 in US, 47–48, 58
 vetting in, 219
 of victims, 239–41
 of violence, 49
Pontual Machado, Pedro Helena, 230–31
Popkin, Margaret, 269
Portugal, 70
poverty, 41
Prestes, Anita Leocádia, 193
Prestes, Luís Carlos, 193
Pron, Patricio, 294–97
propaganda, 135, 144–45, 160–61, 167
protests, 176n35, 352
psychology
 of catharsis, 333
 of corporations, 162–65, 182
 of corruption, 314
 of coup (1964), 164
 of democracy, 329–30
 of history, 245–46
 of human rights, 204–5
 of memory, 148–49, 231–36
 of NTC, 213–16, 219–21
 of politics, 149–50, 175n14
 of reconciliation, 25n45

psychology (*cont.*)
of regimes, 165–71, 240–41
of state violence, 5–6
statistical bias in, 16
of transgenerational memory, 298n26
of TRCs, 326
of victims, 43, 217, 274–75, 327
of violence, 237–39

Quadros, Caio Prado, Jr., 70–71, 79n11
Quadros, Jânio, 70

Raízes do Brasil (Buarque de Holanda), 71
reciprocity, 104n43
reconciliation, 25n45
redress. *See* National Truth Commission
regimes
Amnesty Laws for, 118
bottom-up approaches for, 327–32
censorship and, 79n11, 106n64, 306–7
in Chile, 266
corporations for, 157–59, 172–74, 174n6
coups for, 68–69
democracy for, 100–102, 330–32
economics of, 158, 175n8
global approaches for, 123n12
for historians, 185
history of, 58–66, 117–18, 134, 329
for IACHR, 76
IACHR against, 63, 90–91
in Latin America, 352
in media, 73–74
military for, 105n61, 194, 222n5
NTC against, 119–20, 243–45
oppression by, 39–40
politics of, 7–8, 103n10, 330, 334–35
psychology of, 165–71, 240–41
TRCs against, 119–20
victims of, 49
violence from, 45
religion, 8, 111–1112, 168, 314–15
repression. *See* censorship
revolução brasileira (Prado Jr.), 71
Ribeiro, Darcy, 129
Ricardo, Sérgio, 90
RLAJT. *See* Latin America Transitional Justice Network
Romero, Óscar (archbishop), 268, 271
Rorty, Richard, 241
do Rosário, Maria, 2, 21n10, 39–43
Rose, Richard, 330
Rothberg, Michael, 288
Rousseff, Dilma, 1–2, 4, 253, 350–51
censorship by, 120
corruption by, 38–46
impeachment of, 102, 123n6
in media, 47–48, 51–53
for NTC, 153n15, 183–84, 341
Rousset, David, 247–48
Rubens Paiva Commission (São Paulo), 352
Rustow, Dankwart, 329
Rwanda, 308, 313, 332

Saboia Martins, André, 5, 230–31
Salgado, Solange, 99
Salvatti, Ideli, 251
Sampaio, Sonia Maria Duarte, 235
Santa Cruz, Rosalina, 95–96
Sarney, José, 38, 93
Schmidt, Werner P., 193–94
scholarship
global approaches to, 19–20
for historians, 340–41
history and, 13
on human rights, 27n76
irreconcilable analysis in, 11–14
methodology for, 153n13
on military, 22n14, 170–71
on politics, 11
on TJ, 151n1, 334
on TRCs, 3–4, 10, 15, 244

in US, 24n40
on victims, 25n45
Schultz-Wenk, Friedrich, 190
Scott, Joan, 237
Sebald, W. G., 291
Sese, Salvatore, 91
The Shining Path, 271–72
Sikkink, Kathryn, 266, 325
Silva, Héloio, 70
Soares, Manoel R., 105n47
social media
democracy and, 147–48
Facebook, 18, 142–50
intergenerational perspectives on, 138–39
politics on, 44–45, 54n4
studies from, 18
for TJ, 140–41
for TRCs, 138–40, 142–43
Twitter, 144
for victims, 142
YouTube, 144
*Sociedade e história do Brasil (*Antonio Villa), 73
de Sousa, José Geraldo, Jr., 127
South Africa, 9, 16, 138, 140, 183–84, 312–13
de Souza, Amarildo, 53
Special Commission of The Political Dead and Disappeared (CEMDP), 1, 6–7, 64–65, 228, 256n11
for family, 61
TRCs for, 76
for victims, 126
state violence
Araguaia massacre, 97–100, 105n56
in Bolivia, 9
in Brazil, 157
CONADEP, 22n22
democracy and, 86–89
in Germany, 186, 196n22
for historians, 328
human rights and, 14, 49–50
against indigenous peoples, 272
law for, 106n65, 252–53
in media, 91
El Mozote massacre, 280n10
NTC on, 216–17
OBAN, 167–68
by police, 207, 222n12
psychology of, 5–6
religion against, 111–1112
as terrorism, 149
torture, 61–62, 100–102, 257n15
Ustra in, 2
victims of, 17–18, 184–85
statistical bias, 16
Stepan, Alfred, 329
da Sulva Telles, Gofredo, Jr., 94
system-theoretical approach, 12

Tarquínio de Sousa, Octávio, 79n11
de Tarso Celestino, Paulo, 130
Taváres, Flavio, 46
TC. *See* truth and reconciliation commissions
Teitel, Ruti, 325
Teixeira, Anísio, 5–6, 127–28
Teles, Janaína de Almeida, 73–74
Teles, Maria Amélia de Almeida (Amelinha), 73–74, 352
Temer, Michel, 1, 76–77, 341
terrorism, 149
testimonies, 5, 8, 50, 53
Tito, Frei, 41–42
TJ. *See* transitional justice
Todorov, Tzvetan, 247–48, 251–54
torture
law for, 102n7
in media, 76
by military, 113–14, 208
for NTC, 185–86
politics of, 74
state violence, 61–62, 100–102, 257n15
UN against, 73
victims of, 97, 147
transgenerational memory, 286–87, 291–92, 298n26

transitional justice (TJ), 10–11, 126–27, 151n2. *See also* democracy
Arab uprisings and, 305–7, 311–15
bottom-up approaches for, 325–27
in Brazil, 42–43, 143, 341
global approaches for, 25n52, 158–59, 307–11, 315–16
historians in, 339–40
history of, 24n40, 307–8
intergenerational perspectives for, 131–33
law for, 331
local approaches to, 345–48
in media, 44, 55n19, 148–49, 329–30
NTC for, 203–4, 209–11, 227–29, 239–41, 254–55
politics of, 324–25
scholarship on, 151n1, 334
social media for, 140–41
theory of, 323
victims of, 16
TRCs. *See* truth and reconciliation commissions
Trump, Donald, 138
truth and reconciliation commissions (TRCs). *See also* transitional justice
approaches for, 16–17, 339–42
assessments for, 14–17
in Brazil, 18–19, 345–48
CATMV (Brasilia), 5–6, 127–28, 133–35
for CEMDP, 76
censorship in, 74–77, 207–8
CPI, 92–93, 95–96
in El Salvador, 267–71
endogenous factors in, 214
exogenous factors in, 214
global approaches for, 3, 9, 19–20, 152n12
historians in, 14–15, 248–54
history of, 7–11, 19–20, 126–35
for institution-building, 327–32
in Latin America, 9, 19
media and, 140–41
methodology for, 27n74
for military, 278–79
national approaches for, 11–12
Nucleus for the Preservation of Political Memory, 348n1, 349
in Peru, 271–75
politics of, 28n82, 126–27, 151n2, 249–54
psychology of, 326
against regimes, 119–20
Rubens Paiva Commission (São Paulo), 352
scholarship on, 3–4, 10, 15, 244
social media for, 138–40, 142–43
in South Africa, 183–84
system-theoretical approach for, 12
theory of, 245–48
transgenerational memory in, 286–87
Truth Commission of the State of São Paulo Rubens Paiva, 349
UN and, 233–36, 242n3, 267–68, 280n10
US for, 142
for victims, 323–25
violence for, 111
by Volkswagen do Brasil, 187–89
Tutu, Desmond (Archbishop), 312–13
Twitter, 144

Ubuntu, 312–13
Ultragas, 157
UN. *See* United Nations
UnB. *See* University of Brasília
United Nations (UN), 309–11
censorship for, 270–71
human rights for, 113–14, 120–21, 333
IACHR and, 123n6
against torture, 73
TRCs and, 233–36, 242n3, 267–68, 280n10

United States (US)
- Brazil and, 161, 165, 190, 222n12
- classified information in, 50–53
- Cold War for, 91
- corporations in, 167
- for coups, 66n1
- Holocaust Museum in, 147–48
- minority rights in, 13
- politics in, 47–48, 58
- scholarship in, 24n40
- for TRCs, 142

University of Brasília (UnB), 128–31
Unspeakable Truths (Hayner), 272–73
US. *See* United States

Vannucchi Leme, Alexandre, 42–43, 90, 95
Vargas, Getúlio, 189
vetting, in politics, 219
Viana, Eremildo Luiz, 68–69
victims
- Amnesty Laws for, 61–62, 101
- CEMDP for, 126
- censorship of, 114–15
- economics of, 221n1, 223n27
- family of, 44–45
- history of, 315–16
- human rights for, 8, 41, 53, 341–42
- law for, 327–28, 333–34
- in media, 39–40
- of military, 20, 37
- national approaches for, 118–19
- NTC for, 212, 227–29
- politics of, 239–41
- psychology of, 43, 217, 274–75, 327
- of regimes, 49
- scholarship on, 25n45
- social media for, 142
- of state violence, 17–18, 184–85
- testimonies of, 5, 8
- of TJ, 16
- of torture, 97, 147
- TRCs for, 323–25

Vides Casanova, Carlos Eugenio, 271
Villa, Marco Antonio, 73
Villas Bôas, Eduardo, 1
violence. *See also* state violence; torture
- in Brazil, 56n28
- against family, 66n3
- for historians, 325
- history of, 54n5
- against media, 58–59
- from military, 54n6, 59–60
- politics of, 49
- psychology of, 237–39
- from regimes, 45
- for TRCs, 111
- against women, 352

Volkswagen do Brasil, 18, 159, 197n27
- DOPS and, 183–86, 189, 192–94
- history of, 189–94
- TRCs by, 187–89

war crimes, 307–8
Weichert, Marlon Alberto, 6, 18–19, 61–62
Weiss, Hugo, 68–69
Whitman, Walt, 135
Wibhy, Raissa, 232–33
Wiebelhaus-Brahm, 15–16
women, 352

YouTube, 144
Yuyanapaq: para recorder (art exhibit), 274–75

Zalaquett, José, 268–69
Zambra, Alejandro, 292–97

CPSIA information can be obtained
at www.ICGtesting.com
Printed in the USA
BVHW011049060322
630761BV00002B/20

9 781789 20003